W9-DEA-317

The Catholic
Theological Union
LIBRARY
Chicago, Ill.

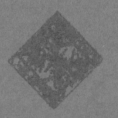

# FIGURE DRAWING

*The Structure, Anatomy, and Expressive
Design of Human Form*

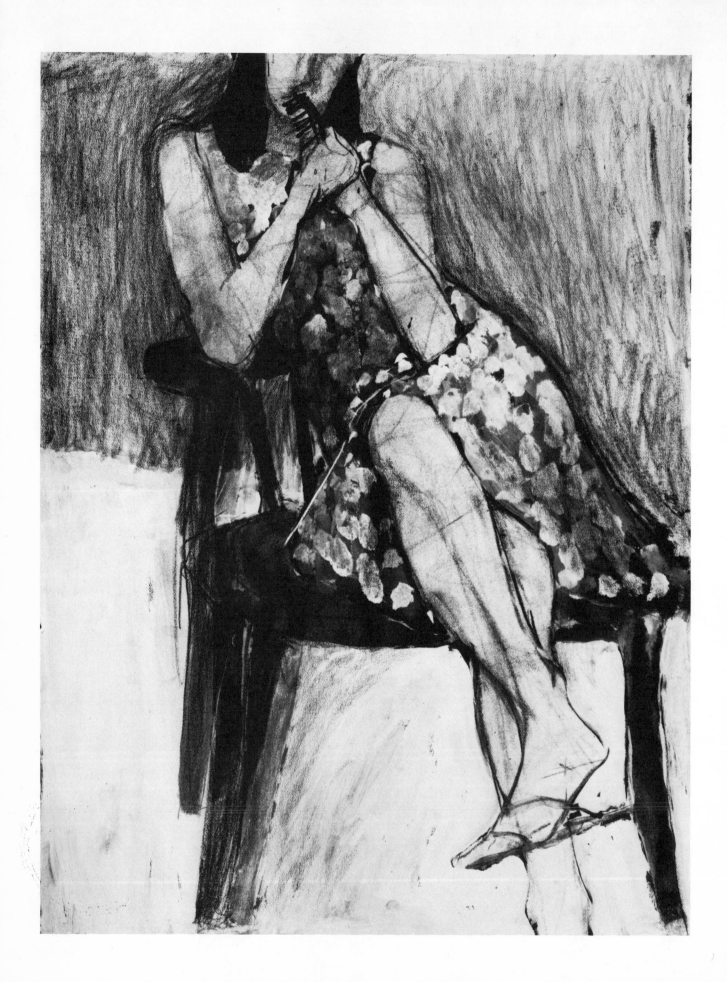

*Second Edition*

# FIGURE DRAWING

*The Structure, Anatomy, and Expressive*
*Design of Human Form*

# NATHAN GOLDSTEIN

The Catholic
Theological Union
LIBRARY
Chicago, Ill.

WITHDRAWN

Prentice-Hall, Inc., Englewood Cliffs, New Jersey 07632

*Library of Congress Cataloging in Publication Data*

GOLDSTEIN, NATHAN.
  Figure drawing.

  Bibliography: p.
  Includes index.
  1. Figure drawing.  I. Title.
NC765.G64  1981      743′.4        80-23895
ISBN 0-13-314518-2
ISBN 0-13-314435-6 (pbk.)

© 1981 and 1976 by Prentice-Hall, Inc., Englewood Cliffs, N.J. 07632

All rights reserved. No part of this book
may be reproduced in any form or
by any means without permission in writing
from the publisher.

Printed in the United States of America

10  9  8  7  6  5  4  3  2

Editorial/production supervision by Virginia Rubens
Cover design by Lorraine Mullaney and Judy Matz
Manufacturing buyer: Harry P. Baisley

PRENTICE-HALL INTERNATIONAL, INC., *London*
PRENTICE-HALL OF AUSTRALIA PTY. LIMITED, *Sydney*
PRENTICE-HALL OF CANADA, LTD., *Toronto*
PRENTICE-HALL OF INDIA PRIVATE LIMITED, *New Delhi*
PRENTICE-HALL OF JAPAN, INC., *Tokyo*
PRENTICE-HALL OF SOUTHEAST ASIA PTE. LTD., *Singapore*
WHITEHALL BOOKS LIMITED, *Wellington, New Zealand*

FRONTISPIECE:
**RICHARD DIEBENKORN** (1922–   )
*Seated Woman No. 44* (1966)
Watercolor, gouache, crayon. 30 1/4 x 23 1/2 in.
*Gift to the University at Albany Student Art Council
by President Evan Collins.*

# CONTENTS

TWO

# THE

# STRUCTURAL FACTOR
*The Figure as a Constructional System*
35

THREE

# THE

# ANATOMICAL FACTOR
*Part One: The Skeleton*
79

FOUR

# THE

# ANATOMICAL FACTOR
*Part Two: The Muscles*
125

FIVE

# THE

# DESIGN FACTOR
*The Relational Content of Figure Drawing*
197

SIX

# THE
# EXPRESSIVE FACTOR

*The Emotive Content of Figure Drawing*

255

SEVEN

# THE
# FACTORS INTERACTING

*Some Examples*

283

# BIBLIOGRAPHY

# INDEX

*For my father, who first noticed and cared*

# PREFACE

The first edition of *Figure Drawing,* in its departure from the more traditional approaches to the study of the figure, attempted to bring together vital, interacting considerations concerning the figure's inner and outer forms and its dynamic forces. It seemed necessary to me to provide the art student, the professional, and the interested general public with a probing discussion of how these factors affect each other, our perceptions, our visual judgments, and our imagery. That the first edition met with wide interest and favor indicates that it answered an existing need for just this kind of *integrated* presentation.

It was, then, with much gratitude and enthusiasm that I turned to the present revision; for in the intervening years, I had the opportunity of examining the book's effect on countless readers, had the good counsel of colleagues and students alike, and, of course, had the benefit of the insights and adjustments in thought that time provides. As a result, some chapters (such as Chapter Two, "The Structural Factor" and Chapter Five, "The Design Factor") have been considerably expanded to better meet the reader's needs, and additional drawings,

many by contemporary artists, have been included to further strengthen the points being made. Those familiar with the first edition will notice changes, large and small, throughout the present volume; each change is an effort to embrace new considerations or further clarify various themes in the text. Finally, where necessary, new photographs and illustrations have been added.

As before, this book is designed to assist the art student, the amateur, the art teacher, and the practicing artist in developing a more extensive understanding of the figurative and abstract considerations of drawing observed or envisioned human forms.

I continue to hold the single assumption that the artist-reader's interest in expanding his or her understanding is motivated by a wish to comprehend those universal elements present in the best examples of figure drawing by old and contemporary masters alike, rather than by a wish for ready-made formulas and techniques. Although five of the seven chapters provide suggested exercises, these exercises are intended to clarify and reinforce the particulars and potentialities of the chapter's subject, not to suggest canons of figure drawing. The exercises may be simplified, embellished, or otherwise varied, or may be bypassed without interrupting the flow of the text.

The term *figure drawing* as used here refers to drawings of the draped as well as nude figure, and drawings of parts of the figure or, where the figure represents only a small segment, of the configuration. Very often the beginner is too much in awe of the figure to utilize those skills he or she does possess, and which are more readily applied to still life and landscape subjects. This broader view, in regarding the figure in its context among the multitude of things that make up our physical world, helps us to recognize that many of the concepts and skills we call on in responding to the objects and organisms that surround us apply just as much to the figure's spirit and form.

For the same reason I have abandoned the traditional approach to anatomy, which is isolated from the figure's dynamic and humanistic qualities and often seems clinical and remote from the living individuals around us. Instead, I have tried to integrate with master drawings creative applications of the various parts of anatomy under discussion, and to show anatomy's role as both servant and source of structural and dynamic inventions.

In this volume, anatomy is regarded as only one of the four basic factors of figure drawing. The best figure drawings always reveal a congenial interaction among the factors of structure, anatomy, design, and expression. The best teachers, sensitive to this interplay, try to show students the mutually reinforcing behavior of these factors, both in their teaching and in their own creative work.

To my knowledge, no one has previously written a comprehensive discussion of the ways in which the four factors assist and govern each other. If this formulation of the concepts at work (and at play) in the figure helps the reader to better focus on the options and obstacles of figure drawing, or even if in contesting aspects of this presentation the reader is aided in forming a pattern of issues more suited to his or her views, I will have achieved my goal.

I would like to acknowledge my debt to the writings of Rudolf Arnheim, whose important contributions to the psychology of perception frequently clarified and occasionally confirmed my views on various aspects of perception as they apply to figure drawing.

I wish to express my gratitude and thanks to the many students, artists, and friends whose needs, advice, and interest helped to shape and test the views presented in the first edition of this book and in its present revised form. I wish also to thank the many, many museums and individuals who granted permission to reproduce works from their collections; Charles D. Wise of Medical Plastics Laboratory, Gatesville, Texas, for his cooperation in providing the skeleton replica reproduced in Chapter Three; David Yawnick and Gabrielle Keller for their excellent photographic skills; Walter R. Welch and Bud Therien of Prentice-Hall, whose cooperation and generosity in numerous ways have made this a better book; and Joe DiDomenico, Lorraine Mullaney, and Virginia Rubens for their gifted efforts in helping to give the book its present form.

And, as before, my deepest gratitude to my family for their practical assistance and understanding.

NATHAN GOLDSTEIN

# FIGURE DRAWING

*The Structure, Anatomy, and Expressive*
*Design of Human Form*

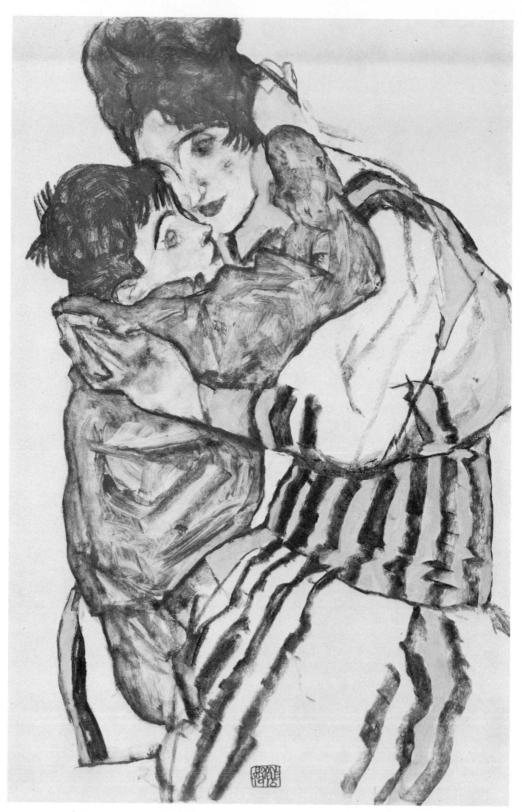

**Figure 1.1**
**EGON SCHIELE** (1890–1918)
*Mother and Child*
Black crayon, watercolor, gouache. 7 x 9 1/4 in.
*Courtesy Museum of Fine Arts, Boston.*
*Edwin E. Jack Fund.*

ONE

# THE
# EVOLUTION
# OF INTENT

*Major Factors and Concepts of Figure Drawing*

## SOME COMMON DENOMINATORS

Drawings of the human figure have always held a special fascination for artists and viewers alike. Indeed, to most artists and connoisseurs, the skill with which the figure is drawn is a telling standard for evaluating not only an artist's essential drawing ability, but his or her spirit and sensitivity as a human being. The psychological and philosophical implications embodied in human subjects, and the manner used to establish these implications through the act of drawing, can evince powerful expressive meanings. By losing ourselves in the intensity of a visual encounter with another's living nature we emerge with gain to *ourselves*—the satisfaction of better apprehending our own essential creative and human nature, as well as of achieving important insights about the people around us.

Nor is an ability to draw the figure well of importance only to the representationally oriented student or professional artist. Something of the figure's spirit and form can be sensed as underlying many of the finest examples of abstract art, pottery, ornament, and architecture. As the noted art historian

Kenneth Clark has observed, "The nude does not simply represent the body, but relates it, by analogy, to all structures that have become part of our imaginative experience." * It is no coincidence that so many of the best abstract artists of the twentieth century—for example, Picasso, Klee, de Kooning, and Diebenkorn—are all highly gifted exponents of figure drawing. Perhaps it is the visual analogies to human form and character—some inflections of shape, line, and color that set off human associations in our mind—that give their later subjective works a special dimension of meaning for us.

But mere facility in figure drawing is not enough to attract the interest of the gifted artist *or* the sensitive viewer. Something else is necessary. Some figure drawings have the power to affect and involve us deeply. The reasons why this is so have little to do with the artist's facility, objective accuracy, or choice of subject. Nor is time a factor, for some of these drawings have been with us for centuries, while others are very recent. What all compelling

* Kenneth Clark, *The Nude: A Study in Ideal Form* (New York: Pantheon Books, Bollingen Foundation, 1953), p. 370.

3

figure drawings seem to possess are certain extra-ordinary though hard to define energies and meanings that make them important creative statements for many people—connoisseurs and laymen alike. Naturally, not every one of these drawings appeals in the same way to every viewer, but each has its admirers, and many enjoy universal esteem.

Other figure drawings, though deftly stated, ana-tomically correct, and fascinating in subject matter, do not have these special qualities. They lack any interest beyond their descriptive content. Indeed, drawings preoccupied merely with facility, accuracy, or "story-telling" usually go no further than these creatively dubious goals. They lack the vitality and the lasting power found in master drawings.

What is there about the figure drawings of Michelangelo, Rembrandt, Matisse, and other old and contemporary masters that makes them alive

and enduring, that attracts and engages us so? It is not their success as faithful documents of observed individuals or situations, for many are wholly invented images. Nor are they the most thoroughly precise or objectively detailed accounts. Sometimes, as in Schiele's drawing *Mother and Child* (Figure 1.1), such works are strikingly subjective interpretations. Often they are boldly concise, as is Kollwitz's *Woman Weeping* (Figure 1.2). It is not that the best figure drawings exemplify some cultural standard of beauty, for many do not meet even minimal standards of attractive human proportion. Still, no matter how plain or misshapen the forms, the best figure drawings always impart some degree of psychological or spiritual attraction, as in Grünewald's study *An Old Woman with Closed Eyes* (Figure 1.3). Finally, the appeal of master drawings doesn't depend on their compositional inventiveness. Many

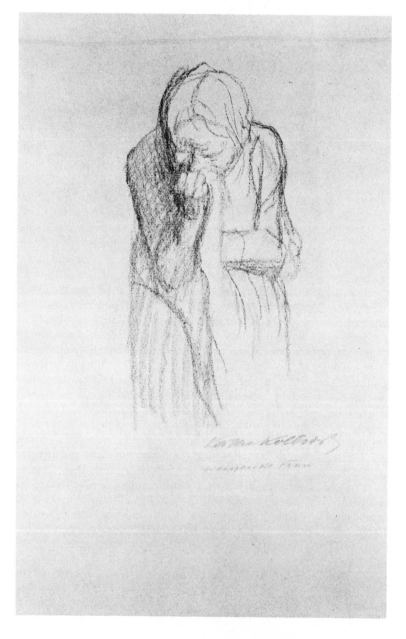

FIGURE 1.2
KÄTHE KOLLWITZ (1867–1945)
*Woman Weeping*
Charcoal on blue paper. 24 x 19 in.
*National Gallery of Art, Washington, D.C.*

FIGURE 1.3
MATTHIAS GRÜNEWALD (1470?–1528)
*An Old Woman with Closed Eyes*
Black Chalk. 22.8 x 28.9 cm.
*Cabinet des Dessins. Musée du Louvre, Paris.*

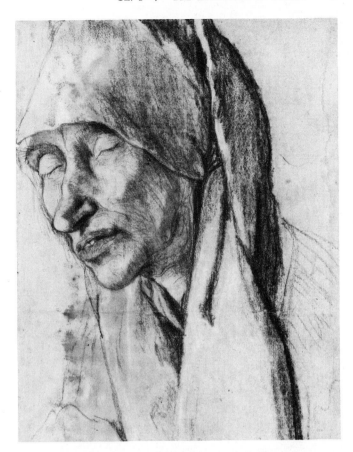

FIGURE 1.4
ANDREA DEL SARTO (1486–1530)
*Red Chalk Drawing*
Red chalk. 14 7/8 x 8 in.
*Trustees of the British Museum, London.*

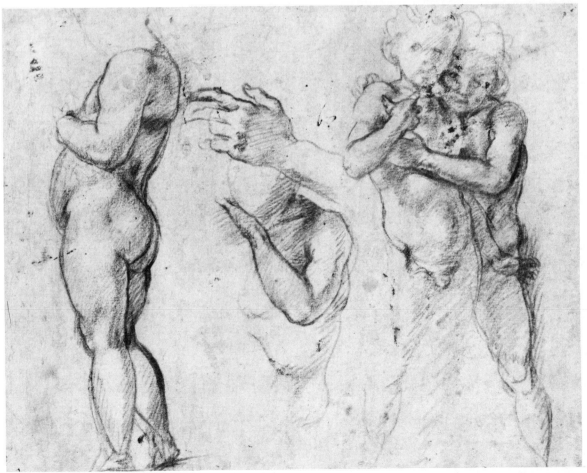

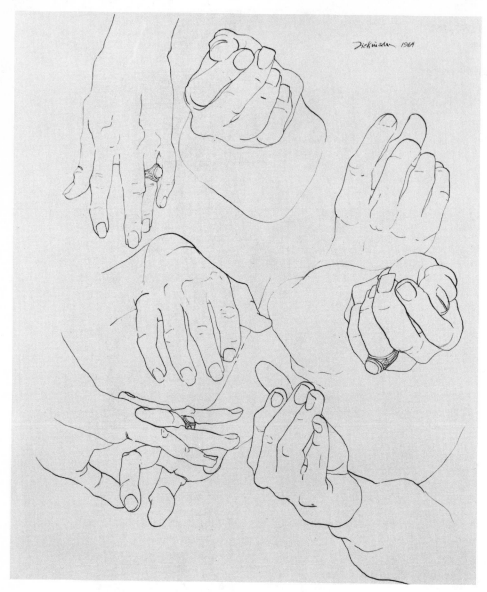

**FIGURE 1.5**
**ELEANOR DICKINSON** (1931–  )
*Study of Hands* (1964)
Pen and ink. 13 1/4 x 10 1/4 in.
*Stanford University Museum of Art*
*Gift of Dr. and Mrs. Louis J. Rattner*

are private preparatory studies, as are del Sarto's and Dickinson's sketches (Figures 1.4 and 1.5). Yet even such preparatory works by masters show a sensitivity to the balance and order among the drawing's parts.

It would seem, then, that the impact of master drawings cannot be explained solely in terms of facility, cultural ideals, accuracy, design, or depictive theme. To understand why certain works have the power to hold our attention, to please, provoke, and inform us, we must begin with the recognition that we respond to far more than their representational or *figurative* content. All such works possess a "plastic life"—a network of visual relationships and energies between the marks employed and the forms they create. This network of activities—of movements, rhythms, and tensions, of similarities and con-

trasts—generates forces and feelings that the visually sensitive viewer apprehends. Those activities which issue from the interactions of the lines and tones themselves we should understand to be a drawing's *abstract* character; those inherent in a drawing's recognizable forms, its *figurative* character. In master drawings these two graphic considerations are inseparable and mutually supportive aspects of the drawing's *design*.

Additionally, these interacting design themes, by the nature of their activities, convey expressive meanings. Hence, in the best figure drawings expressive meanings exist at both the figurative and abstract levels. To illustrate this point let us again turn to Figure 1.2. Both the woman *and* the lines and tones that shape her reveal similar expressive qualities. Notice that the downward flow of the lines, like the lines of a weeping willow tree, complement and intensify the figure's expressive mood. Such lines do not flow from conscious choice alone. Rather, their emotive character reflects the artist's intuitive as well as empathic response to the subject's state. Kollwitz feels her subject at both the conscious and subconscious level. The best figure drawings are never merely descriptions of people, places, and things. They form out of the negotiations between the subject's *measurable,* figurative actualities and the artist's relational and empathic interests in those actualities—his or her interpretation of the subject's abstract activities and expression, that is, its *dynamics.*

The figure's measurable properties—its differing masses and their various shapes, planes, values, textures, sizes, and locations in space—like the figure's dynamic qualities, can also be reduced to two fundamental considerations: its general architectural, structural nature and its specific anatomical one. We will refer to these as the *structural factor* and the *anatomical factor.* Although these factors are always interdependent aspects of a figure's draped or undraped forms, in the next three chapters we will consider them separately so as to better examine the nature of each and see how they interact. Similarly, for purposes of discussion, we will divide the figure's dynamic properties—its potential for order and impact—into the *design factor* and the *expressive factor.* These two factors are also interdependent, but by separating them (in Chapters Five and Six) we can explore each more fully. Because we make these arbitrary divisions, it is important to bear in mind that a drawing's design and expression are really understood by artists as aspects of the same phenomenon in the subject: its allusions to emotive order. Furthermore, in practice, all four factors are interrelated. One of the major themes of this book is to call attention to the high degree of interdependence of the measurable and dynamic factors.

In the best figure drawings, then, representational content not only coexists but interacts with a system of abstract relational and expressive content. A drawing's figurative and abstract content issues from the behavior of the *visual elements*—the six basic visual tools of graphic communication. These elements are: line, shape, value, volume, space, and texture. The element of color, because it is incidental to drawing, is not discussed here. Chapters Five and Six examine these visual tools and the energies they release. Here it is important to recognize that this first universal common denominator of creative figure drawing—*the interacting of abstract and figurative meaning*—is a fundamental, given responsibility of the artist. All marks relate in *some* way. Left unregarded, the abstract behavior of a

drawing's elements will produce confusing discords and inconsistencies—a kind of visual noise that obscures representational meanings. The best exponents of figure drawing have always understood that the organizational and emotive powers of the visual elements affect the clarity and meaning of the figurative forms they denote; that the dynamic nature of the marks and of the recognizable forms they produce *are interdependent considerations.*

In creative figure drawings, then, the marks not only define, they enact and evoke the character of the subject, bringing the image to life. And master drawings are always "alive." In Rembrandt's *Bearded Oriental* (Figure 1.6), the animated quality of the figure *and* of the lines and tones suggests vigorous life. The man's confident stance is intensified by the swift but certain strokes. Notice how the fanlike eruption of rhythmic lines emerging from the arms and waist further heightens the figure's barely contained energy. Even in the more specifically drawn forms of the head, the beard, eyes, and nose are developed with authoritative force. Despite the small scale of these forms, the lines and tones that comprise them are powerfully alive. Again, in Matisse's *Crouching Nude with Black Hair* (Figure 1.7), the assured and nimble character of the lines helps to enact the figure's dancelike action. Her forms, although anatomically inexact, are expressively right. As drawn, the lively, supple nature of these forms amplifies the artist's response to the figure's gesture.

Although the Rembrandt drawing asserts an elegant strength, while the Matisse drawing conveys a gentle pliancy, both artists share a common enthusiasm for spirited, graceful forms. But aliveness in drawing doesn't always depend on graceful harmonies. The goal in Hokusai's *Wrestlers* (Figure 1.8) seems to be the ruggedly potent, even awkward character of the two struggling figures. Their gnarled and straining forms contrast with the more graceful ones of the man who is observing on the right. He serves as an expressive counterpoint against which the tensions and stresses of the struggling wrestlers gain greater impact. Note that the wrestlers are drawn with lines that are deliberate, even crabbed, suggesting the tension of the forms, while those of the third figure are more rhythmic and flowing. This contrast can even be seen in the difference between the shapes of the wrestlers' feet (and the lines used to form them) and the feet of the onlooker. Likewise, the more or less angular shapes of the wrestlers' muscular forms, and their strong directions and interlockings, are in clear contrast to the gentler shapes of the third figure. Hokusai even manages to extract a heightened sense of drama (while simultaneously balancing the masses of the entire drawing) by emphasizing the leftward lurching of the wrestlers with the opposing tilt in the figure on the right.

Note that Hokusai, like Rembrandt and Matisse, has altered anatomical fact in order to strengthen expressive force. For example, by sacrificing anatomical accuracy in the placement of the feet of the foreground wrestler (which would show them foreshortened and hence small) Hokusai gains an expressive "rightness" by providing a more stable base for the weight of the upper body's leftward thrust. The best exponents of figure drawing *utilize* rather than eulogize anatomical facts because their purpose is to precisely *express,* not record. For the same reason, artists suspend the laws of perspective and the rules that have accumulated around the uses of line or value, composition, or the various drawing media whenever these laws and rules interfere with

their creative intentions. Such artists place their desire for freedom of inquiry, experience, and interpretation ahead of conformity to any convention or system. Although widely separated in time, place, and culture, the drawings of Rembrandt, Matisse, and Hokusai show how abstract meanings augment, and in turn gain from, representational meanings.

Another common denominator in the best figure drawings is *the economy and directness with which the artist establishes the drawing.* Invariably, master drawings are as concise and as straightforward as the artist's theme and tools permit. In fact, one of the most engaging qualities of great drawings is the great amount of figurative and dynamic content present in an economically conceived image. The choice of a medium that permits such a succinct

FIGURE 1.6
**REMBRANDT VAN RIJN** ( 1606–1669 )
*Bearded Oriental in a Turban, Half Length*
Pen and wash. 11.7 x 11.4 cm.
*Staatliche Museen Preussischer Kulturbesitz.*
*Kupferstichkabinett. West Berlin.*

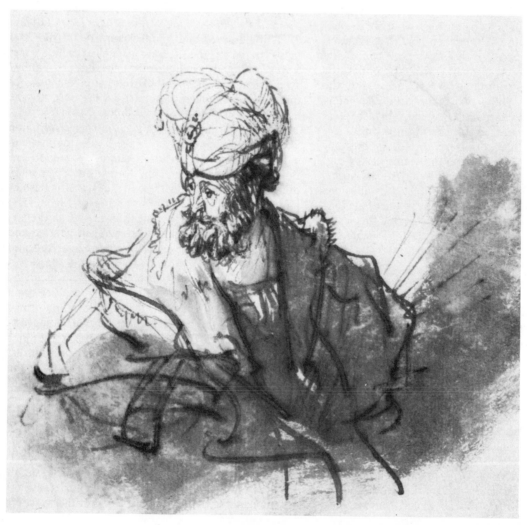

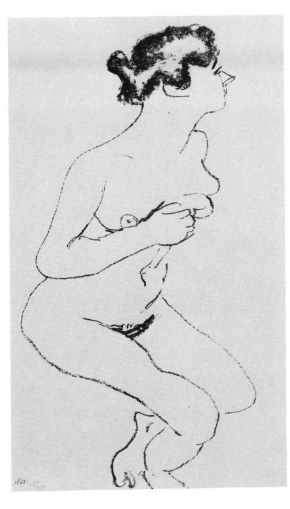

**FIGURE 1.7**
**HENRI MATISSE** (1869–1954)
*Crouching Nude with Black Hair* (1906)
Lithograph, printed in black. 16 5/8 x 8 3/4 in.
*Collection, The Museum of Modern Art, New York.*
*Larry Aldrich Fund.*

**FIGURE 1.8**
**KATSUSHIKA HOKUSAI** (1760–1849)
*Wrestlers*
Brush and sumi ink. 12 x 16 1/2 in.
*Trustees of the British Museum, London.*

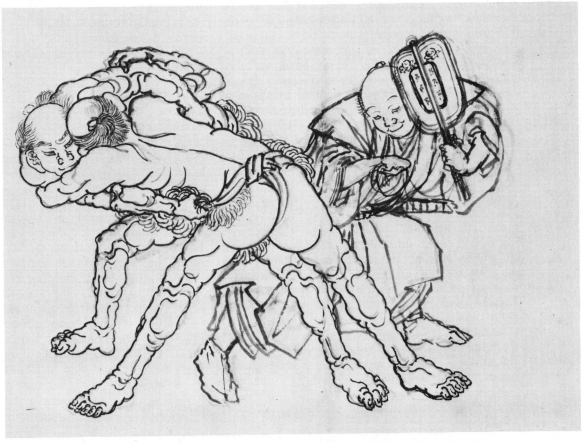

graphic statement is important. All master drawings demonstrate a sensitive interaction between the meanings and the means used.

Still another important common denominator is that *the best drawings convey a unique attitude, a temperament.* This quality stems partly from the nature of the subject's figurative and plastic considerations and partly from the artist's overall temperament—his or her general likes and dislikes—both as an artist and as an individual. A discussion of the psychological and social forces that shape an artist's point of view—how we arrive at our particular aesthetic and temperamental persuasion—is beyond the scope of this book, but we should recognize that an artist's temperament definitely determines the kinds of perceptions and responses that are made. What is perhaps less obvious is that the artist's ability to assert his or her attitude clearly is crucial to the drawing's success as a work of art. Genuine creative invention demands genuinely personal interpretations, as little deflected by outside influences as possible. The best figure drawings always show an unwavering insistence on a frank declaration of interests—on aesthetic and temperamental judgments. Such works are always eloquent in the clarity of their intent. They are keenly bold or delicate, schematic or sensual, animated or stilled. In other words, great figure drawings always incisively affirm the artist's felt convictions about a subject's important human and dynamic conditions.

The best figure drawings, even when they are highly subjective images, also reveal the artist's *knowledge of the structural and anatomical nature of human form.* However, as noted earlier, in master drawings it is always evident that these matters serve, but never dominate, the artist. In studying anatomy, or when a thorough preparatory sketch of the figure's forms is desired, it is important to make drawings that are precise and comprehensive; some artists, such as Michelangelo (Figure 1.15), elevate their anatomical studies to the level of art. This is the case when artists have integrated their interest in anatomy with their awareness of the figure's dynamic potential. Such drawings are never merely anatomical inventories, but show an inventive interplay between facts and feelings, between the figure's measurable actualities and the expressive power implicit in its forms. Structure and anatomy are essential as *liberating,* not restricting factors. And whether we accentuate or subdue their role in our drawings, we must do so with the qualities of judgment and authority that only a genuine understanding of these factors makes possible.

One of the most important realizations of such understanding is that structural and anatomical considerations, in addition to clarifying figurative conditions, can participate in a drawing's dynamic

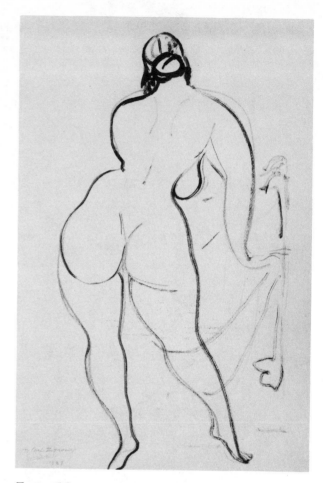

FIGURE 1.9
GASTON LACHAISE (1882–1935)
*Back of a Nude Woman* (1929)
Pencil, quill pen, and india ink. 45.5 x 30.9 cm.
*The Brooklyn Museum.*
*Gift of Carl Zigrosser.*

meanings; they can both stimulate and strengthen relational and emotive ideas. In Lachaise's *Back of a Nude Woman* (Figure 1.9), the design strategy exists among the marks *and* the human forms they denote. The "beat" of ovoid shapes and the rhythmic undulations of contour lines are the abstract counterpart of the pattern and character of the figure's forms. It is impossible to view Lachaise's drawing without responding to the dynamic nature of the lines and shapes that express in abstract, plastic terms the same activities and sensual tone of the drawing's figurative character. It is apparent that the structural aspects of Lachaise's drawing, as shown in the solid, interlocking masses and his use of anatomy to simplify some forms and to amplify others, are the product of sound knowledge, and that they interrelate with the drawing's design and expression. Here, all four factors interact to advance the same theme.

This leads us to the last common denominator. Great figure drawings reveal an authoritative and personal solution to the universal challenge that all serious exponents of figure drawing face: *the governance among the factors of structure, anatomy, design, and expression inherent in human form.* Although the degree to which each factor participates in a drawing's creation is determined by perception and intent, *all four* must be inventively integrated in forming the image. Because these four elements are the *given conditions* in figure drawing, and each is dependent on the others, none can be disregarded without weakening the quality and meaning of the rest.

## THE EMERGENCE OF INTERPRETIVE FIGURE DRAWING

Interpretive figure drawing, in the sense described earlier as conveying the felt convictions of an individual temperament, was a relatively late arrival in the history of art. But when it arrived on the scene, structure, anatomy, design, and expression were all interacting properties of the best drawings. Perhaps figure drawing's main strength, namely its ability to function as a direct means of personal inquiry and interpretation—its power as a tool for quickly finding and stating—is the reason for its delayed appearance as a major category of creative expression.

Artistic imagery from the dawn of history to the late Middle Ages (if such a sweep of time can be summarized) was largely determined by highly formalized, collective conventions. Representations of the figure, human or animal, conformed to these rigid schemas. The earliest depictions of the human figure are few and rather crude when compared to the cave paintings of bison and other animals of that period, which show a sensitivity to rhythmic line. By the Neolithic era, man had begun to leave a visual record of human activities conveying a sprightly charm (Figure 1.10), but these pictures conformed strictly to formula and were simple in concept. With the emergence of the Egyptian civilization and the civilizations of the Tigris-Euphrates valley, far more sophisticated but still rigidly stylized conventions developed for representing human form (Figure 1.11).

Although impressive humanistic developments occurred in many aspects of Greek civilization, in early Greek art formula solutions for depicting the figure showed only slight allowance for objective investigation. Not until 550 B.C. did Greek art begin to develop its grand aesthetic concepts based on objective visual inquiry and a collective ideal that saw man as physically and spiritually perfected ac-

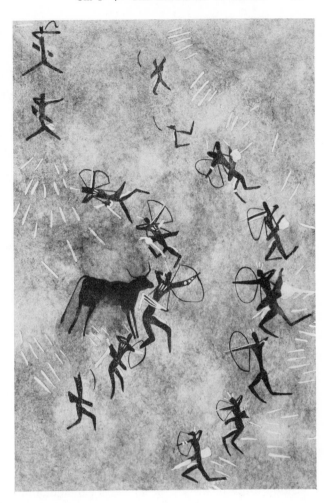

**FIGURE 1.10**
Facsimile of rock painting: A fight, apparently for possession of a bull. Khargur Tahle, Libyan Desert. *Frobenius-Institut, Frankfort am Main.*

cording to Greek societal standards. This fertile convention was flexible enough to permit a modest degree of personal interpretation, and the first individuals of outstanding mastery begin now to be known to us by name. Sculptors such as Phidias and Praxiteles and vase painters such as Epictetus and Douris leave their imprint on later Greek art. This classic style was to have a profound impact on most artists of the Renaissance, and, periodically, on many artists throughout the world, especially in the West. But despite the great heights that idealized representations of the figure—owing much to a sensitive understanding of human form—attained in later Greek sculpture and painting, drawings of the figure (done almost exclusively as vase decorations) generally show a still markedly conventionalized treatment (Figure 1.12). This is not to suggest that these drawings are less aesthetically valid or pleasing; indeed, many are of outstanding artistic merit.

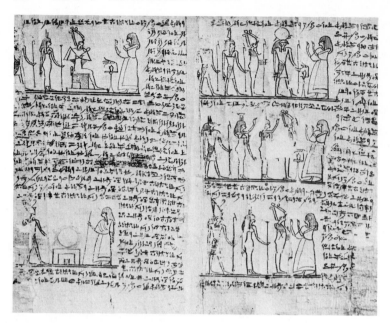

FIGURE 1.11
Hieratic, Late Period
Papyrus of Ta-Amon. *Book of the Dead
Courtesy Museum of Fine Arts, Boston.
Gift of Martin Brimmer.*

But they are less the result of inquiry and response than of a collective system, a cultural schema for depicting human forms. Virtually no drawings on flat, bounded surfaces emerged from Greek, or still later, Roman art. And with the exception of a small number of sculptors and painters, no tradition of art done in a spirit of personal interpretation developed from these cultures.

During the Middle Ages a highly symbolic convention arose in the art of manuscript illumination, which became somewhat more observational and interpretive with time. Occasionally, as in Figure 1.13, such manuscript art reached a degree of freedom from convention, but such works were the exception.

Drawing, and especially figure drawing, resulting from an investigative, humanistic, and personally interpretive attitude didn't begin to appear as a serious creative activity until the Renaissance. With the emergence of a sense of individuality, a thirst for scientific and philosophical knowledge, and a desire

FIGURE 1.12
Attic Red-Figured Style (c. 490–480 B.C.)
*Battle of Centaurs and Lapiths*
Kylix (exterior). Terracotta and brush.
*Courtesy Museum of Fine Arts, Boston.
H. L. Pierce Fund.*

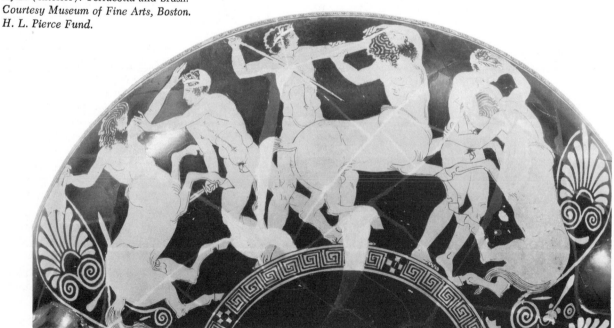

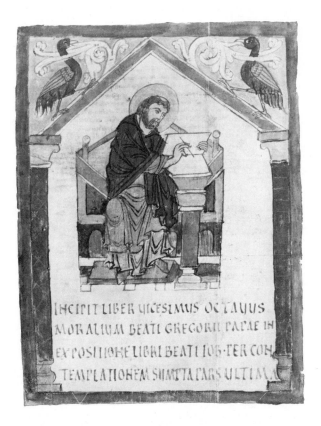

to understand the nature of the world and of man, drawing became an efficient and even necessary mode of exploration and expression. In this climate of inquiry, earlier, collective conventions of art quickly gave way to individual interpretation, and a powerful interest in drawing burst forth. Not only did this emancipation from the restrictions of formal schemas dramatically alter the motives and meanings of works in painting and sculpture: the spirit of the Renaissance can also be credited with the birth of interpretative drawing—especially figure drawing—as a serious form of creative expression.

The engraving *Battle of Nudes* (Figure 1.14), by the fifteenth-century Italian sculptor Pollaiuolo, provides an example of the emerging interest in human form during the early Renaissance period. The artist's observant attention to anatomical facts and his sensitivity to the supple, rhythmic nature of human forms represent a new level of attraction and understanding in the art of figure drawing. Although the drawing's overall style is one of deliberate, refined delineation—characteristics which typify earlier artistic attitudes—its dynamic and unified nature shows a sensitive, if muted, reciprocity between structure, anatomy, design, and expression.

By the sixteenth century the tendency toward a

FIGURE 1.13
Carolingian Illumination, 10th Century
*St. Gregory*
Manuscript.
*Courtesy Museum of Fine Arts, Boston.*
*William Francis Warden Fund.*

FIGURE 1.14
ANTONIO POLLAIULO (c. 1430–1498)
*Battle of Nudes*
Engraving. 40 x 57 cm.
*Courtesy The Fogg Art Museum, Harvard University.*
*Francis Bullard Bequest.*

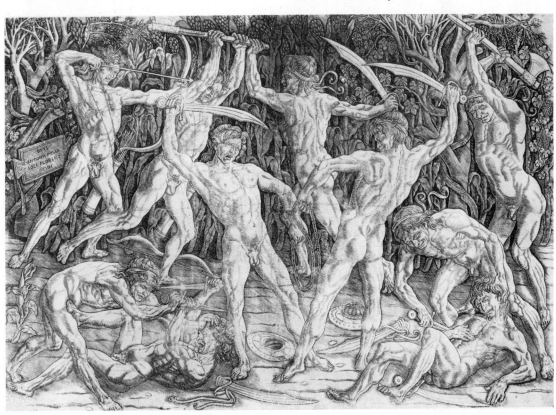

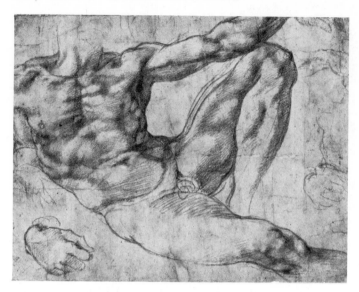

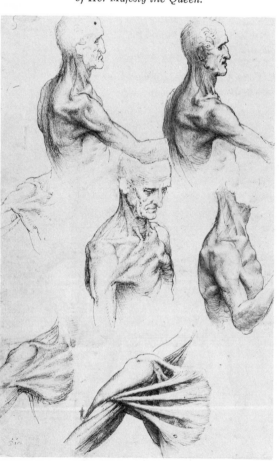

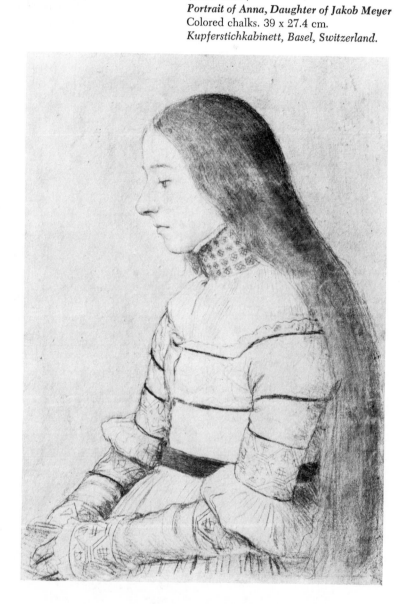

FIGURE 1.15
MICHELANGELO BUONARROTI (1475–1564)
*Study of Adam for "The Creation of Adam"*
*in the Sistine Chapel*
Chalk on tan paper. 9 5/8 x 15 in.
*Trustees of the British Museum, London.*

FIGURE 1.17
HANS HOLBEIN the Younger
(1497–1543)
*Portrait of Anna, Daughter of Jakob Meyer*
Colored chalks. 39 x 27.4 cm.
*Kupferstichkabinett, Basel, Switzerland.*

FIGURE 1.16
LEONARDO DA VINCI (1452–1519)
*Myology of the Shoulder Region*
Pen and ink, some gray washes. 19 x 24 cm.
*Windsor Castle, Royal Library.*
*By gracious permission*
*of Her Majesty the Queen.*

calculated elegance in figure drawing had been largely superseded by more uninhibited attitudes of inquiry and response. This change resulted from a growing perceptual sophistication nurtured by cross-influences among artists, the value that patrons of the arts placed on original concepts, and the ready market for major projects in painting and sculpture which required investigative, preparatory drawings. Then too, sixteenth-century art, especially in Italy, often dealt with religious or mythological themes of a monumental kind, utilizing large numbers of figures in complex settings, conditions that prompted bolder and more direct approaches to the act of drawing. Renaissance drawings continued to reflect an attraction for the humanism and grandeur of Greek and Roman art in ever more forceful terms. A comparison of Pollaiuolo's drawing of the male figure with Michelangelo's treatment of it (Figure 1.15) shows the high degree of understanding of, and feeling for, human forms that developed in later Renaissance drawing. What prompts Pollaiuolo to a somewhat demure use of structural and anatomical matters moves Michelangelo to an almost sculptural and dramatic image. Even in this preparatory study Michelangelo conveys a sense of Adam's power and grace.

Throughout the Renaissance, especially in Italy and Northern Europe, an interest in drawing the human figure flourished. Like Michelangelo's drawing, many of these figure drawings represent preparatory sketches for works in painting and sculpture. Many other drawings, like da Vinci's study of the shoulder region of a male (Figure 1.16), resulted from the intense investigatory spirit of the time. Some, such as *Portrait of Anna, the Daughter of Jakob Mayer* (Figure 1.17), by the Northern Renaissance artist Holbein, *were* intended as final graphic statements. In Holbein's drawing, the precise and subtle fluctuations of volume-revealing edges and surfaces, and his sympathetic understanding of the young woman conveyed by lines and tones as gentle as the subject and the design, provide a striking contrast with Michelangelo's dramatic and structurally rugged approach to human form. Seen together, these drawings suggest something of the range of interpretation made possible by the liberating spirit of the Renaissance.

A sensitive interest in the figure's structure and anatomy as capable of conveying powerful dynamic meanings continued to flourish in the seventeenth century. Often, drawings showed a more daring search for the figure's expressive essentials than a thorough exploration of its parts. Rosa's *Youth Pulling off His Shirt* (Figure 1.18) and Canuti's *Study of a Dead or Sleeping Man* (Figure 1.19), illustrate this more interpretive concept. It is immediately apparent that these artists have intensified the flow of

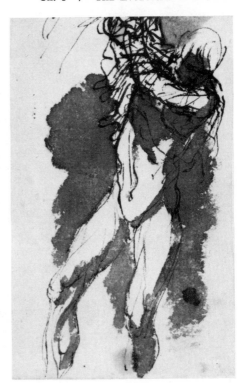

**FIGURE 1.18**
**SALVATOR ROSA (1615–1673)**
*Youth Pulling off His Shirt, Full Figure*
Pen and brown ink, brown wash.
2 3/8 x 3 1/2 in.
*The Art Museum, Princeton University.*

the figure's forms into a fluid ripple, creating a strong sense of animation and vitality. Such rhythmic movement and energy demand more than an understanding of anatomical and structural facts. They demand an awareness of the abstract possibilities—the expressive energy—of human forms, and an empathic response to them when drawing. Whether Rosa and Canuti observed or imagined their subjects, they had to feel the weight and tensions of the limbs, the fullnesses and hollows of the forms, the behavior of the figure, *as if it were their own.* For only a total identification with the figure's form and behavior could have prompted the judgments and handling that express these actions with such economy, clarity, and impact.

Another seventeenth-century artist, the great Flemish painter Rubens, was an enthusiastic student of Renaissance attitudes and techniques, but brought to them an individual stamp of vigor and tactile sensitivity. In his *Study for the Figure of Christ on the Cross* (Figure 1.20), there is the same high degree of knowledge about, and empathy with, human form that we see in the Michelangelo, Rosa, and Canuti drawings. Rubens's emphasis on the figure's action, masses, design, and character, rather than on

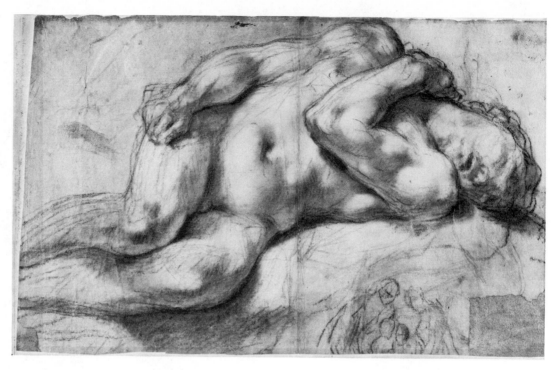

FIGURE 1.19
**DOMENICO MARIA CANUTI**
(1620–1684)
*Study of a Dead or Sleeping Man*
Red and white chalks.
*The Pierpont Morgan Library.*

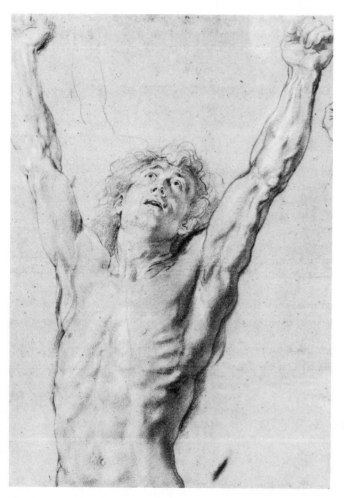

FIGURE 1.20
**PETER PAUL RUBENS (1577–1640)**
*Study for the Figure of Christ on the Cross*
Charcoal, heightened by white. 15 1/2 x 20 1/4 in.
*Trustees of the British Museum, London.*

finished surfaces, reveals the artist's identity with the figure's situation. Rubens *feels* as well as visualizes the situation he depicts.

If the Renaissance artists were attracted to the idealized forms of antiquity, seventeenth-century artists were usually more impelled toward encounters with human forms as they found them. And, as Figures 1.18, 1.19, and 1.20 show, they drew them with more tumultuous energy. But if some traces of the Renaissance interest in an idealized, heroic interpretation of man lingered on (as in the Rubens drawing), this influence is wholly absent in the drawings of the greatest seventeenth-century artist, Rembrandt.

Although Rembrandt's drawings depict individuals realistically, they possess moving visual metaphors that suggest important psychological and spiritual meanings. That is, they seek to evoke humanistic meanings through accurately observed or envisioned subjects stated in dynamic terms that amplify such meanings. No one, until Rembrandt, focused as intensively or with such penetrating clarity upon the introspective nature of ordinary people,

and few have ever expressed such insights more engagingly and with greater force. While drawings in a realistic manner and with a sensitivity to psychological subtleties had appeared earlier (Figure 1.17), few approach the power in Rembrandt's drawings to transcend their figurative content, to imply universal truths. In Rembrandt's works, even simple domestic scenes are transformed into moments that suggest deeper significance. A drawing by Rembrandt, whether of a child, a cripple, or a wealthy burgher, is at once a penetrating human observation and a daring system of expressive design.

His figure drawings do more than integrate abstract and psychological expressions with figurative material. There is instead a *fusion* of these qualities. In his *Saskia Sick in Bed* (Figure 1.21), the lines and tones are simultaneously engaged in creating the design and the mood, as well as the forms and space. Each mark is engaged in all of these functions. Consider, for instance, how the value, shape, and overall activity of the broader strokes of the background complement the value, shape, and activity of the blanket, and how, by their airy nature, they rein-

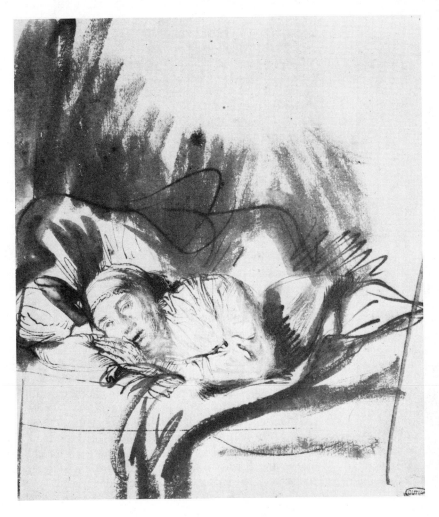

FIGURE 1.21
REMBRANDT VAN RIJN
(1606–1669)
*Saskia Sick in Bed*
Pen, washes of tone. 16.3 x 13.5 cm.
*Musée du Petit Palais, Paris.*
*Photo Bulloz.*

force the figure's substantiality. Additionally, these strokes, representing a large cast shadow, explain the light source and, by their agitated nature, serve to deepen the figure's stillness. The figure's hand is at once an expression of relaxation and a reflection of the fingerlike curved lines, large and small, that appear in the clothing and surrounding bedding. On the far left, the large, dark tone acts as a necessary "containing wall" for the vigorous undulations that course through the image, and by its dry, abrasive nature "calls" to similar textures in the background and on the bedding.

FIGURE 1.22
REMBRANDT VAN RIJN (1606–1669)
*Old Woman Bathing Her Feet*
Etching. 16.2 x 8 cm.
*Courtesy Museum of Fine Arts, Boston.*

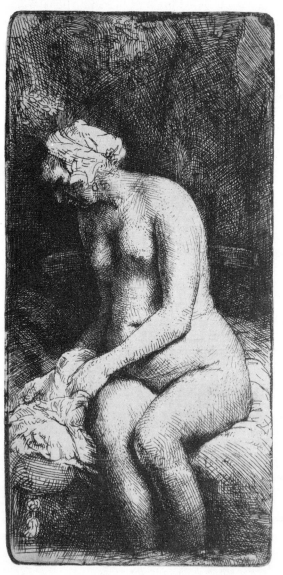

For Rembrandt, even a drawing of an old woman bathing becomes transformed into a universally understood expression of dignity and grace. In his etching *Old Woman Bathing Her Feet* (Figure 1.22), Rembrandt approaches his theme with empathy, not pity; with respect, not sentimentality. The measurable factors and the dynamic ones merge to form an affirmation of human strength and nobility, and to tell of spiritual, not physical beauty.

The eighteenth century brought a subtle but steady increase in the dynamic aspects of figure drawing. A growing interest in design and expression and a deepening need to make drawings reflect a more personal point of view continued to spur the exploration for new approaches to figure drawing.

An example of this trend can be seen in the study for *Jupiter et Antioche* (Figure 1.23), by the eighteenth-century artist Watteau. In this continuing climate of self-searching, Watteau accepts and utilizes his sensitivity to inflections of movement and modeling, revealed by the confident, supple lines, and by his emphasis on the gestural nature of the figure. Rhythmic, searching lines often weave through large segments of the figure, their action relating even distant parts to each other. For example, some of the lines in the right arm move along its entire length and appear to continue down the left arm, giving evidence of the relatedness of the two limbs. (How often, in student drawings, are limbs drawn without reference to each other!) Note how these tactile lines grow thicker and thinner as they ride upon the forms, suggesting volume, interjoinings and muscular tensions among parts, and even the presence of a light source. As they do this, the lines establish a design theme—a discernible pattern of light and heavy stresses—of the line itself, and of curving actions. These stresses and curves, in addition to the activities already noted, give the drawing an animated force at both the depictive and abstract level. Here, as in the drawings discussed earlier, the marks that form the image simultaneously depict, organize, and express. In other words, the abstract tenor of the lines is compatible with the nature of the figure's action; the vigorous dynamic and representational expressions reinforce each other. To draw such spontaneous actions tranquilly and deliberately would tend to diminish their force, and, consequently, our belief in them (compare Figure 1.14).

Yet another example of the trend toward more personal modes of expression in drawing is Tiepolo's *Reclining River God, Nymph, and Putto* (Figure 1.24). By assuming that a brilliant light source illuminates his subject, Tiepolo is able to broadly carve the forms in three values: the white of the page, a light tan tone, and a very dark brown one.

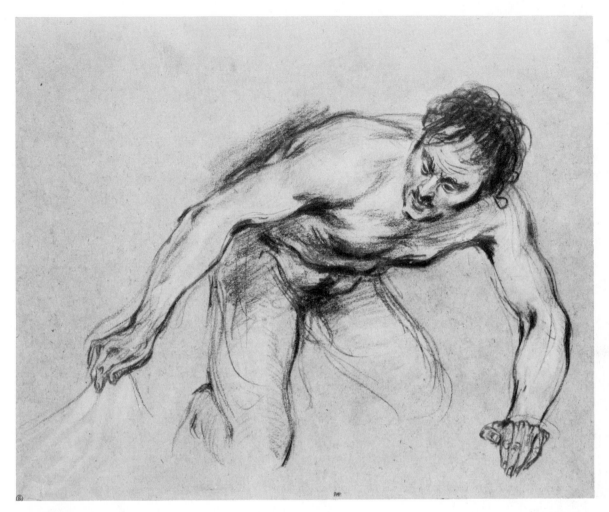

**FIGURE 1.23**
**ANTOINE WATTEAU (1684–1721)**
*Study for "Jupiter et Antioche"*
Conté crayon on toned paper. 9 5/8 x 11 5/8 in.
*Cabinet des Dessins, Musée du Louvre, Paris.*

The impressive economy and clarity with which these imagined forms are stated say much for the artist's knowledge of structure, anatomy, and perspective. The rhythmic and playful nature of the lines and shapes of tone attest to his sensitivity to the role that abstract forces perform in enhancing expressive meanings. Note, for instance, how each form is interpreted as made up of egglike components. The overall beat of such ovoids, like the pattern of dark tones that punctuates the configuration, does much to unify the image and give it a suppleness and strength that more cautious and "correct" treatment could not convey.

Another eighteenth-century artist, the Spanish painter Goya, in his series of etchings *The Disasters of War,* effectively communicates his outrage

through a powerful system of expressive design. In his *"Tampoco"* or *No More* (Figure 1.25), the atrocity described relies for its impact on more than accurate recollections of the grim event. Goya has feelingly devised dynamic activities that intensify our reaction to the barbaric scene.

The entire configuration describes a large triangular shape interrupted only by the softer shape of the lounging French officer, a wry visual counterpoint to the severe vertical lines of the hanged man. Goya's knowledge of structure and anatomy, and of the dynamic power of the visual elements, helps him to emphasize the weight of the centrally placed victim. The awful forward thrust of the head is made even more emphatic by the heavy mass of dark hair sloping downward. Fast-moving verticals add to the

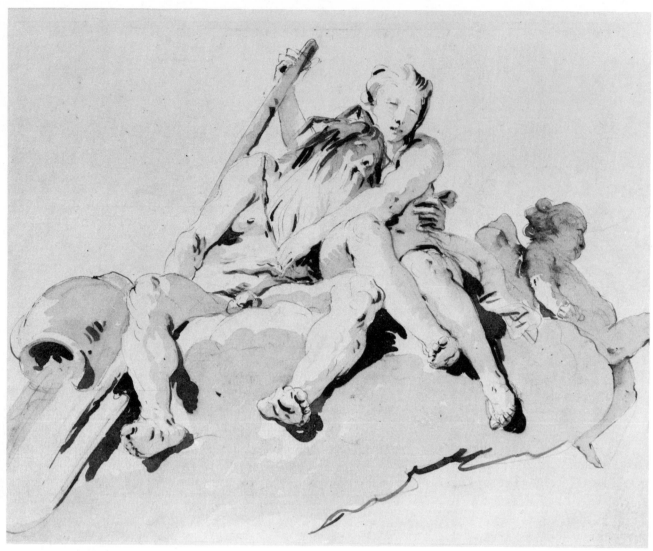

**Figure 1.24**
**G. B. TIEPOLO** (1727–1804)
*Reclining River God, Nymph, and Putto*
Brush and ink. 9 1/4 x 12 5/16 in.
*The Metropolitan Museum of Art, New York.*
*Rogers Fund, 37.165.32*

victim's weight. Even his long shirt is simplified, its edges drawn severely vertical. Although Goya gives us only a few suggestions of the body's presence beneath the shirt, we are convinced it is there; we can even guess that the hanged man's body is stocky. The fallen leggings, even the fast fall of the cast shadow below the victim's arm add to our feeling as well as seeing what has happened here. Goya further strengthens the sense of falling weight by the repetition of the vertical lines of the foliage in the distance, and by the strong vertical edge of the block against which the officer relaxes. Goya increases our initial shock of recognition by harshly contrasting the stark white of the victim's shirt with

the dark tones that surround him. Note that the only lines suggesting animation are those more gestural ones of the lounging officer. In this way, too, Goya heightens the tragic stillness of the hanged man.

Despite the deepening interest in such dynamically reinforced and more subjectively interpreted figure drawings, there were some who held to a more objective, reportorial approach to the figure's actualities, and to an interest in the aesthetics of earlier periods. The nineteenth-century artists Ingres (Figure 1.26) and Delacroix (Figure 1.27) show two extremes of aesthetic persuasion that occupied the attention of many artists of that time.

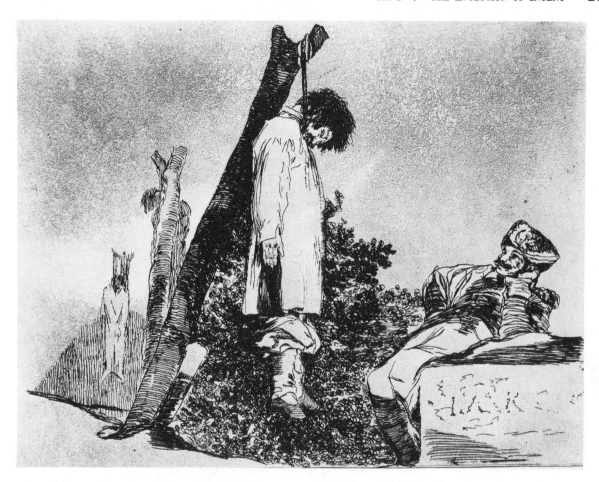

FIGURE 1.25
FRANCISCO DE GOYA (1746–1828)
*No More, from "The Disasters of War"*
Aquatint and etching. 7 1/4 x 5 1/2 in.
*Courtesy The Fogg Art Museum, Harvard University.*
*Bequest of Francis Calley Gray.*

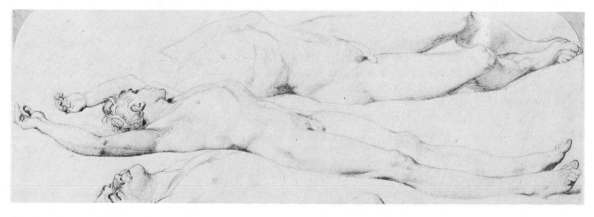

FIGURE 1.26
DOMINIQUE INGRES (1780–1867)
*Three Studies of a Male Nude* (detail)
Pencil.
*The Metropolitan Museum of Art, New York.*
*Rogers Fund, 1919.*

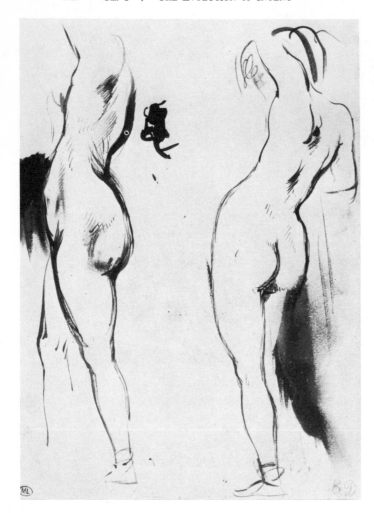

FIGURE 1.27
EUGÈNE DELACROIX (1798–1863)
*Two Nude Studies*
Pen and ink, washes of color. 19 x 14.8 cm.
*Cabinet des Dessins, Musée du Louvre, Paris.*

Ingres, the older of the two, held that "the simpler the lines and forms, the more effectively they reveal beauty and power." Figure 1.26 shows his dedication to the concept of contour—the volume-informing delineation of forms—as the desired means by which to draw. This drawing reveals Ingres' attraction to the forms of ancient Greek and Roman art. The figures are shaped by the same concern for the classic standards of beauty that attracted such Renaissance masters as Raphael (Figure 1.28). In both works, elegant and precise contours create figures of somewhat idealized proportions. In both, general structural facts and specific anatomical ones are important in the overall design of the forms. Ingres' lines, like Raphael's, are easy-paced and serenely harmonious, always engaged in subtle dynamic as well as volume-informing activities, and express a graceful order among even small anatomical details.

By contrast, Delacroix abhorred the idea of patient and deliberate contour drawing, although he too aimed for the impression of convincing volumes in space. But for Delacroix, emphasizing a volume's edges by contour lines only serves to weaken the sense of mass by calling forward those most distant parts of forms—their outlines. Instead, he advised that volumes should be grasped "by their centers, not by their lines of contour." Nor did Delacroix possess the temperament that could devote itself to explicit nuances and little harmonies. His interest lay in capturing fleeting actions by direct means. One of the boldest Romantics of nineteenth-century art, he sought the gestural, sensual qualities of the figure. In René Huyghe's view, "It is not form he studies, but rather its animating principle, its living

FIGURE 1.28
RAPHAEL (1483–1520)
*Combat of Nude Men* (detail)
Red chalk over preliminary stylus work.
14 13/16 x 11 1/8 in. (entire)
*Ashmolean Museum, Oxford.*

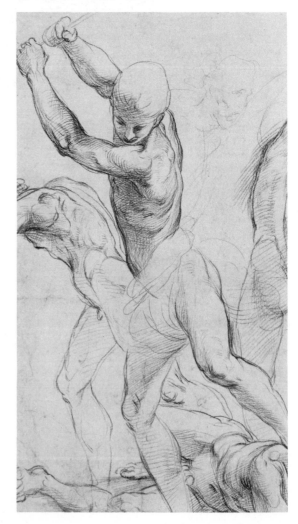

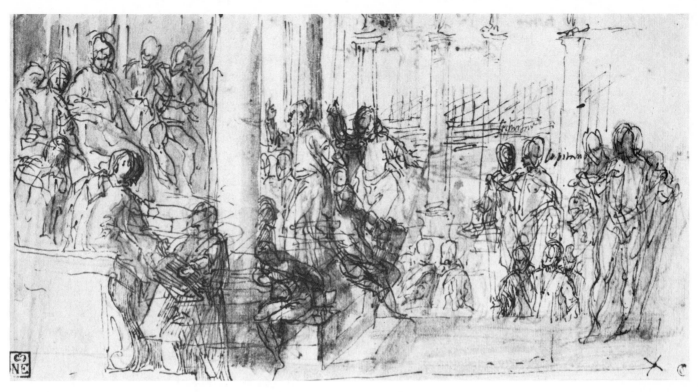

FIGURE 1.29
PAOLO VERONESE (1528–1588)
*Peter of Amiens before The Doge Vitale Michele*
Pen and wash. 19 x 27.3 cm.
*Budapest Museum of Fine Arts.*
*Collection: Poggi Estethary.*

FIGURE 1.30
FRANCESCO PRIMATICCIO (1504–1570)
*Hercules and Omphale*
11 1/2 x 17 7/8 in.
*Fonds Albertina.*

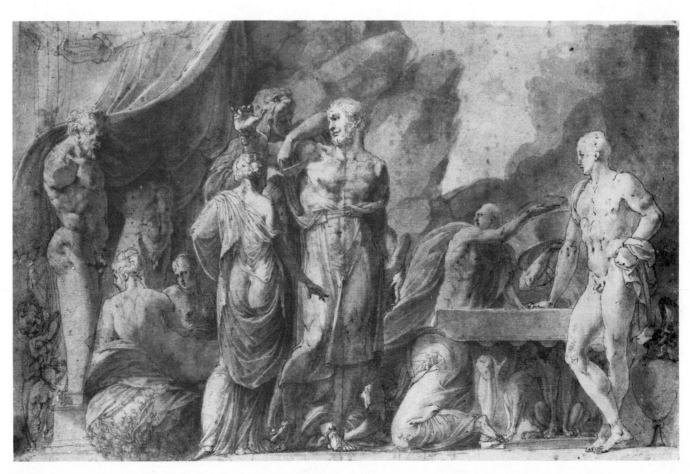

essence that he transcribes." That a passionate search for essence was an important theme in Delacroix's drawings is borne out by his advice to a student: "If you are not skillful enough to sketch a man jumping out of a window in the time it takes him to fall from the fourth story to the ground, you will never be able to produce great works."

These opposing attitudes—of a deliberate, measured delineation versus a spontaneous, gestural attack—have to some degree continued to contest with each to this day. Indeed, these differing dispositions toward the act and purpose of drawing existed long before the 1800s. They are, after all, as much determined by individual temperament as by the stylistic trends of a particular period or country. We have only to compare the drawing by Veronese (Figure 1.29) with that of another Italian Renaissance artist, Primaticcio (Figure 1.30), to recognize the fundamental differences between an explicit and a gestural approach—between the wish to explain and the wish to suggest.

Other artists, however, saw the desirable qualities of the two approaches not as opposing but actually as complementing each other. In fact, embracing both ideas, these artists emphasized at times the letter and at times the spirit of their subjects. Michelangelo, Rubens, and Rembrandt are some of the few artists for whom the seeming conflicts between the prose of delineation and the poetry of evocation are not only resolved, but become necessary, reciprocal concepts permitting a more encompassing and profound apprehension of human form and spirit. Such artists cannot accept the restrictions of either precision or suggestion. For them, the freedom to range between exactitude and impression is an essential condition of creativity (Figures 1.15, 1.20, and 1.21).

The figure drawings of the French artist Degas, regarded by many as one of the greatest figure draughtsmen of the nineteenth century, offer an interesting example of an artist's change, over the years, from a deliberate, linear mode to a strongly

FIGURE 1.31
**EDGAR DEGAS** (1834–1917)
*Study of a Nude for "The Sorrows of the*
*Town of Orleans"*
Charcoal. 35.6 x 23.2 cm.
*Cabinet des Dessins, Musée du Louvre, Paris.*

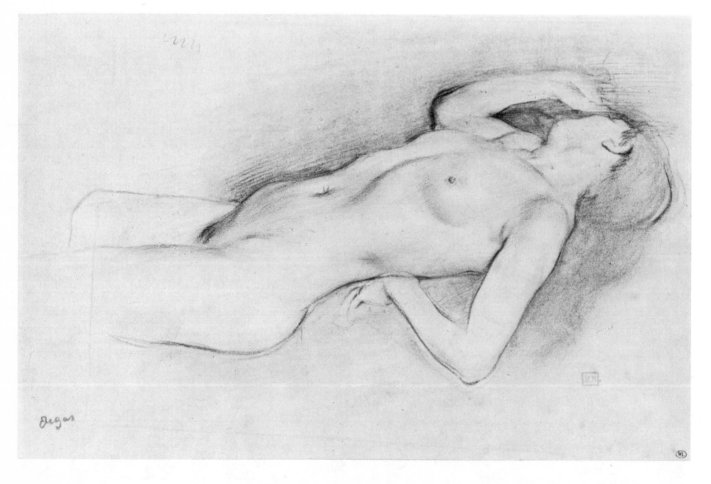

animated and almost painterly one. Early Degas drawings show his attraction to precise delineations influenced by an envisioned ideal. The later drawings show his attraction to bold and richly plastic responses to perceived or envisioned figures. As Degas' drawings became less calculated, their abstract activities gradually strengthened, and this in turn led to drastic changes in the expressive content of his work. It is impossible to say whether a change in his aesthetic interests, perhaps influenced by the work of his Impressionist fellow artists, led him from deliberate, quiet images to more spontaneous, turbulent ones. Perhaps a more philosophical change toward the figure (and life) led him from idealized to more stormy conceptions. But whether the primary stimulus was triggered by aesthetics or the experiences of living, both his abstract and figurative interests changed together, and were always congenially suited to each other.

As a young man, Degas was attracted to the classical view, as exemplified by Raphael and Degas' near-contemporary, Ingres. These influences are evident in an early drawing, *Study of a Nude for "The Sorrows of the Town of Orléans"* (Figure 1.31). But there are already some clues to the direction that Degas' drawings would take. Note the surprisingly reportorial passages in the left arm, the head, and the legs. These seem to depart from the drawing's main theme of idealized form; they seem based more on perceptions of things as they are than on conceptions. These segments appear almost awkward compared to the rhythmic flow of the torso. There is a hint of conflict between a desire to dwell on every nuance of edge, every gentle dip and rise of the terrain, and an urge to more forcefully state moving energies. The urgent tenor in the drawing of the right arm and hand; the frequent gestural accents, especially in the arms and along the figure's lower left side; the heavy accents of charcoal along the raised arm; and the fast, more calligraphic lines occurring throughout the drawing—all these suggest a wish to come to grips with issues concerning figurative and abstract forces. The result is a work in which an idealized concept of Woman, and felt perceptions of *a* woman coexist in a tenuous alliance.

Comparing this drawing with a later lithograph by Degas, *After the Bath* (Figure 1.32), we see the release of the energies hinted at in the previous drawing. There is still something of a vision present—a personal convention for human proportion. But in place of the lithe and sensuous ideal of the early drawings there is here a treatment of human forms simplified to suggest more weighty and geometrically pure forms. The drawing's dominant visual theme is movement. The hair, the curving torso, the wedgelike shape of the towel, even the pattern of the background—all exhibit a sense of motion.

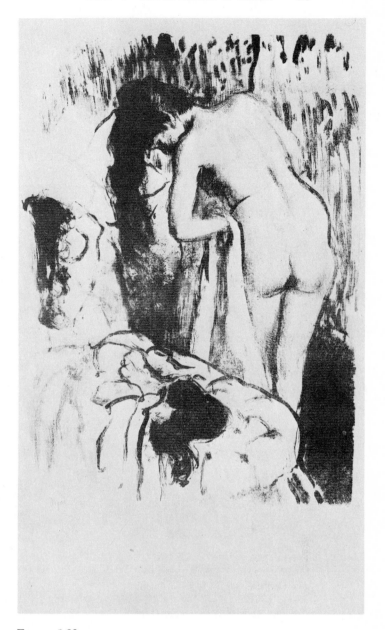

**FIGURE 1.32**
**EDGAR DEGAS (1834–1917)**
*After the Bath*
Lithograph. 14 3/4 x 11 in.
*Courtesy The Fogg Art Museum, Harvard University.*
*Bequest of Francis Calley Gray.*

There is a kind of candid camera effect, a frozen movement, in what we feel is a continuing sequence of movements. Catching the woman in the act of drying herself, Degas gives us a sense of what her prior actions were, and foretells the action to come. Notice how much stronger the abstract activities become when Degas shifts from an emphasis on denotation, as in Figure 1.31, to an evocation of the figure's essential structure and spirit. Degas intensifies

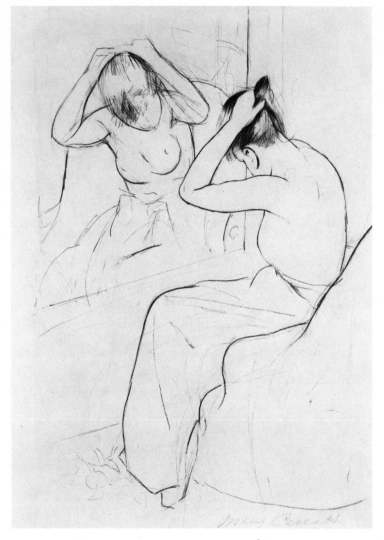

FIGURE 1.33
MARY CASSATT (1844–1926)
*The Coiffure*
15 1/2 x 17 in.
*National Gallery, Washington, D.C.*

concepts. Cassatt's *The Coiffure* (Figure 1.33), for example, shows the influence of Japanese prints on the artist. Often, the passions of the artist, finding encouragement and inspiration in the ever-expanding themes and styles of art, especially in France, were able to hit on more daring expressive modes. The drawing by Rodin (Figure 1.34) shows something of the tempo that graphic expression can attain when it is driven by strong abstract forces of motion.

So far, in broadly tracing the emergence of interpretive approaches to figure drawing, we have observed a fluctuation in emphasis between the depictive and the abstract. During the early Renaissance, emphasis focused on depiction. In the nineteenth century (and earlier), artists differed in their choice of emphasis but, as we have seen, for some of them (in any age) both qualities were, or, as in the case of Degas, became, compelling and interdependent themes. Much twentieth-century figure drawing continues to move in the direction of integrating subjective expressive needs with drawing's abstract potentialities. But, as in earlier periods, the strongest drawings, both in creative and human terms, seem to be those which reveal a sensitive interaction among the four basic factors, and between the figurative and abstract meanings they generate. The best exponents of figure drawing have always understood that each factor inevitably affects—and is affected by—the other three.

From what has been said it should not be inferred that artists favoring figurative matters are necessarily less sensitive to dynamic ones, or that artists who emphasize plastic and emotive matters are less concerned with depictive ones. In their choice of emphasis, artists cannot disregard either aspect. When they do, the drawings that result, however realistic or abstract they may be, usually lack the impact of works in which the "what" and the "how" reinforce one another. Although Goya's etching (Figure 1.25) emphasizes the figurative whereas Lachaise's drawing (Figure 1.9) stresses the abstract, both are integrated systems of depictive and dynamic themes. Their differences of emphasis are based on their different creative and temperamental intent. Similarly, although all are highly figurative works of an inquiring nature, the emphasis on gesture and emotive energies in the works of Rosa, Canuti, and Rodin; on harmonious design in Raphael, Ingres, and Cassatt; and on an integration of both of these themes in Rubens' study for the figure of Christ and in Rembrandt's drawing of Saskia, all show how a drawing's representational content can be clarified and given expressive meaning by different dynamic stresses.

Later nineteenth-century figure drawings and those of the twentieth century are characterized by

the relational play among the visual elements to create this more dynamically vigorous graphic and human statement. In Chapters Five and Six we will examine the relational and emotive dynamics of figure drawing to see what creative possibilities they hold. Here it is important to emphasize again that in all great figure drawings, every mark adds to the figural, organizational, and expressive content of the image. In these two Degas drawings the four factors interact differently, but in each they succeed in shaping forms that live.

Nineteenth-century artists frequently brought more inventive subjective interpretations to drawing. Sometimes, creative crosscurrents pointed to new their general tendency toward more daring, direct, and ever more subjective points of view, and by their broad range of interests and goals. In Schiele's drawing (Figure 1.1), the animated, swirling figures and the bold abstract life of the elements that produce them are strong intensifications of both considerations. Again, in Matisse's drawing (Figure 1.7), the dual life of the drawing's figurative and abstract themes is vigorously active.

This more personal and inventive approach to figure drawing encouraged artists to explore new ways of interpreting the human figure and of com-

municating ideas and feelings. For the German artist Kollwitz, the figure became a vehicle for expressing her (and everyone's) anguish at the pain and bereavement that war brings. As noted earlier, her drawing of a weeping woman (Figure 1.2) is a deeply moving expression of sorrow. The wavering flow that envelops the figure suggests the movements we associate with weeping. In contrast to the soft fall of the lines of the drapery and kerchief, the angular arms, the action of the fist pressed to the face, the sudden tonal contrast between the right shoulder and head, and even her scale and

**FIGURE 1.34**
**AUGUSTE RODIN** (1840–1917)
*Study of a Standing Nude*
Pencil. 23.8 x 16.7 cm.
*National Gallery, Prague.*

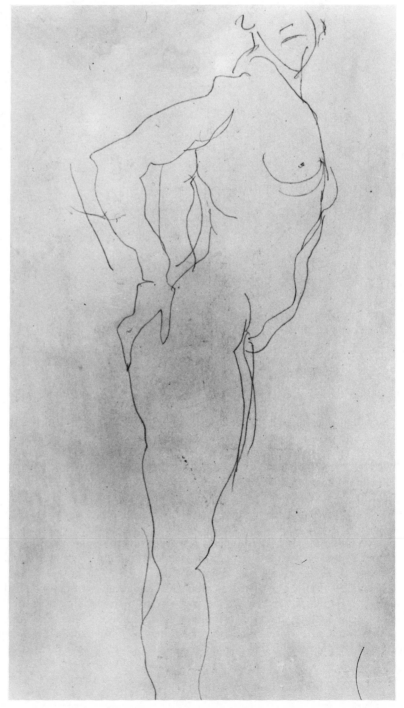

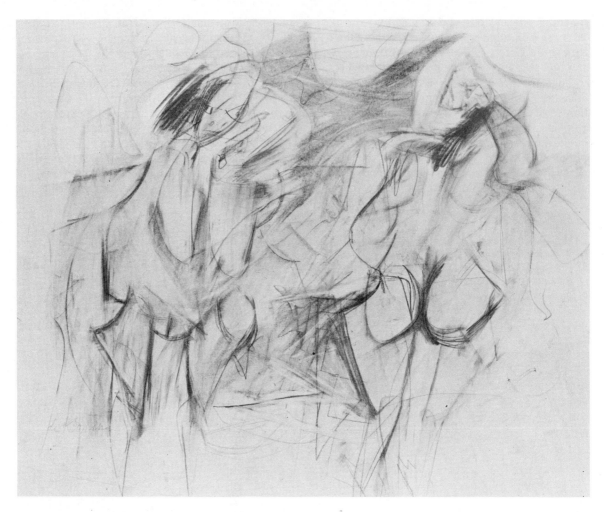

**FIGURE 1.35**
**WILLEM DE KOONING** (1904–   )
*Two Women III* (1952)
Pastel and charcoal on paper. 14 3/8 x 18 1/2 in.
*Allen Art Museum, Oberlin College, Ohio.*
*Friends of Art Fund.*

placement on the page, all intensify our understanding of the drawing's message of grief.

Some artists have always been motivated by the need to convey a moving, provocative, or perhaps amusing message. It might be compassion, as in the drawing by the Northern Renaissance artist Grünewald (Figure 1.3); it might be sensuality, as in the drawing by the late nineteenth-century sculptor Rodin (Figure 1.34); or rage and protest, as in the drawings by the twentieth-century artists de Kooning (Figure 1.35) and Rothbein (Figure 1.36).

Such artists are impelled as much by human as by visual themes. Unlike artists for whom figure drawing is first of all an act of inquiry and analysis, artists oriented toward human commentary are motivated by the need to feel as well as to find.

In the twentieth century, the factor of design in figure drawing has become increasingly important. This interest in the formal, relational ordering of the elements and of the figurative forms they produce has led to a notable characteristic of many contemporary artists: the emphasis on the two-dimensional aspects of the figure and of its environment. Although the best artists have always been sensitive to a drawing's two-dimensional design—to the relational interactions of the visual elements within the bounded area of the page, or *picture plane*—such relational activities were generally subordinated to those of the third dimension. This should not suggest that the two-dimensional designs of earlier drawings are necessarily less fully considered or sophisticated, but that their impact—their ability to

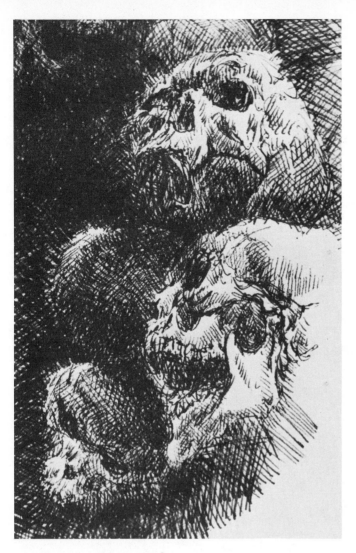

FIGURE 1.36
RENEE ROTHBEIN (1924–    )
*Study for the Nazi Holocaust Series*
Pen and ink. 5 x 7 1/2 in.
*Courtesy of the artist.*

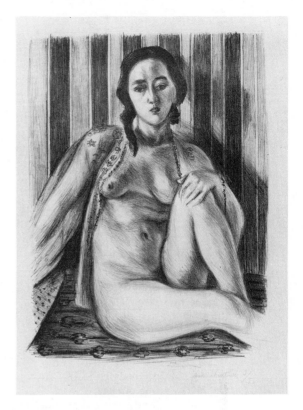

FIGURE 1.37
HENRI MATISSE (1869–1954)
*Odalisque*
Lithograph. 12 x 16 in.
*National Gallery of Art, Washington, D.C.*
*Rosenwald Collection.*

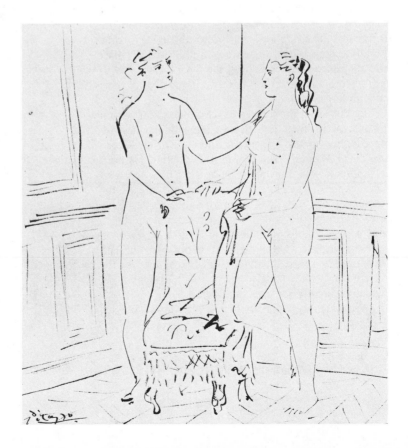

FIGURE 1.38
PABLO PICASSO (1881–1973)
*Two Nudes* (1923)
Pen and ink. 8 1/4 x 7 13/16 in.
*Museum of Art, Rhode Island School
of Design.*
*Gift of Paul Rosenberg.*

attract and dominate our attention—is intentionally reduced to avoid muffling the drawing's volumetric and spatial order.

For many recent and contemporary artists, expanding the abstract activities upon the picture plane has permitted new graphic ideas and experiences. In Matisse's *Odalisque* (Figure 1.37), bold systems of straight and curved lines, textural and tonal contrasts, and shape and pattern variations all call our attention to the drawing's surface-state. There are equally strong clues to these forms as volumes in space, but these structural and spatial statements share in, rather than dominate, the drawing's overall design. This enables us to "read" the drawing in two compatible and satisfying ways. No sooner do we experience an ordering of two-dimensional conditions than volumes emerge to offer an ordering of masses in space. This impression, in turn, subsides into the matrix of picture plane activities to start the cycle over again. This creates a pulsating ambiguity between flat and deep space, where the contrasts between geometric and organic areas and among the variously patterned textures take on different visual meanings.

Picasso's *Two Nudes* (Figure 1.38) is another example of a design-oriented drawing. In contrast to the Matisse, which relies for its design strategy on strong patterns and strongly defined, enclosed shapes, Picasso's design theme is based on subtle tensions. There is tension in the broken lines, in the lines that strongly suggest but never actually enclose shapes, in the lines and shapes that suggest vertical and horizontal directions but are themselves always diagonal, and in the overall fluctuation between the depictive and the plastic nature of the lines. Additionally, small bursts of textural activity in the hair of both figures, the chair, and the floor contrast with the austere character of the two figures and their surroundings.

In Picasso's drawing, as in Matisse's, the visual impacts of its two- and three-dimensional activities are roughly equal. This is not the case in de Kooning's *Two Women III* (Figure 1.35), which is conceived in a way that sharply restricts the sense of volumes in space. Here, the tempestuous life of the elements, occasionally breaking free of any depictive role, accomplishes two things: it creates a predominantly two-dimensional drawing, and it conveys a powerfully aggressive statement about the subject. De Kooning relies on the expressive nature of the elements' abstract state to carry the message; here, evocation largely replaces denotation.*

We have seen that in figure drawing a concern

with abstract considerations is not new. We have also seen that a sound understanding of structure and anatomy has always informed and influenced the best figure drawings. Whether it is a dominant theme, as in Figure 1.15, a spur to gestural activity, as in Figures 1.18 or 1.27, or a guideline to expressive summaries of human forms, as in Figure 1.35, it is apparent that structural and anatomical knowledge participated in the choices and judgments that shaped these images.

Sometimes structural issues and the visual metaphors of strength and energy they suggest are prominent ideas in figure drawings, as in Figures 1.15 and 1.24, where the figure's constructional, often planar, aspects are strongly in evidence. Sometimes, as in Figures 1.7 and 1.38, they are only felt, rather than seen; gentle nuances instead of bold carvings.

For many artists structural considerations are important in the early stages of developing their figure drawings. In Rubens's preparatory sketch *Studies for "The Presentation in the Temple"* (Figure

FIGURE 1.39
PETER PAUL RUBENS (1577–1640)
*Studies for "The Presentation in the Temple"*
Brown ink and wash. 21.4 x 14.2 cm.
*The Metropolitan Museum of Art, New York.*
*Gift of Mr. and Mrs. Janos Scholz.*

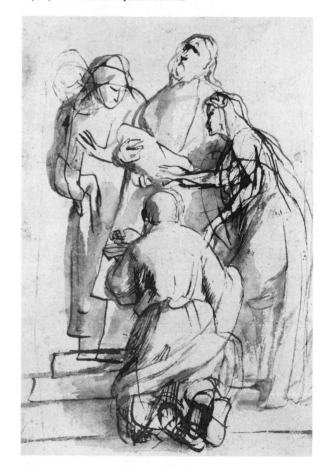

* For a thorough discussion of the concepts of evocation and denotation, see Nelson Goodman, *Language of Art* (New York and Indianapolis: Bobbs-Merrill, 1968), chap. 1.

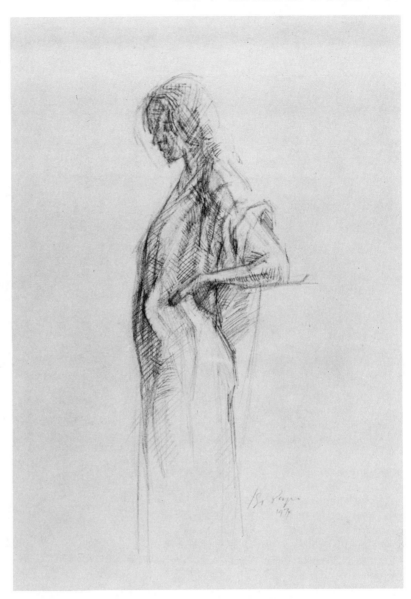

**FIGURE 1.40**
**ISO PAPO (1925– )**
*Standing Figure*
Pencil. 13 x 18 in.
*Collection of Rachel Papo, Newton, Mass.*

1.39), we can follow the artist's thinking about the placement and general character of the volumes. Many lines, especially in the three standing figures, are primarily investigative probes to establish masses. Note that some of these lines are drawn through forms, as if the figures were transparent, enabling Rubens to understand the masses in more sculptural terms. Some pale washes are broadly applied to define the large planes and the general behavior of the light. In the kneeling figure, massed lines have been placed over the washed tones, further developing the big masses. Most artists will agree that such inquiries about the structural essentials of a subject, whether actually drawn or only observed in the mind's eye, are crucial to an understanding of their subject's visual and expressive character.

Similarly, Papo, in his *Standing Figure* (Figure 1.40), uses ranks of schematic lines to establish the subject's major planes and masses. Papo's interest in understanding the architectural nature of these forms can be seen in the way the lines measure them, how lines are drawn through some forms to locate their far sides and to connect them, and how the lines are made to explore the forms' terrain. Note the surprisingly curvilinear movements among these incisively summarized and mainly angular masses. In Chapter Two we will examine this analytical, planar approach to the figure's forms. Although such structural considerations are only sometimes, as here, a dominant theme, in all good figure drawings they are always in evidence, however subtly, interacting with the other factors.

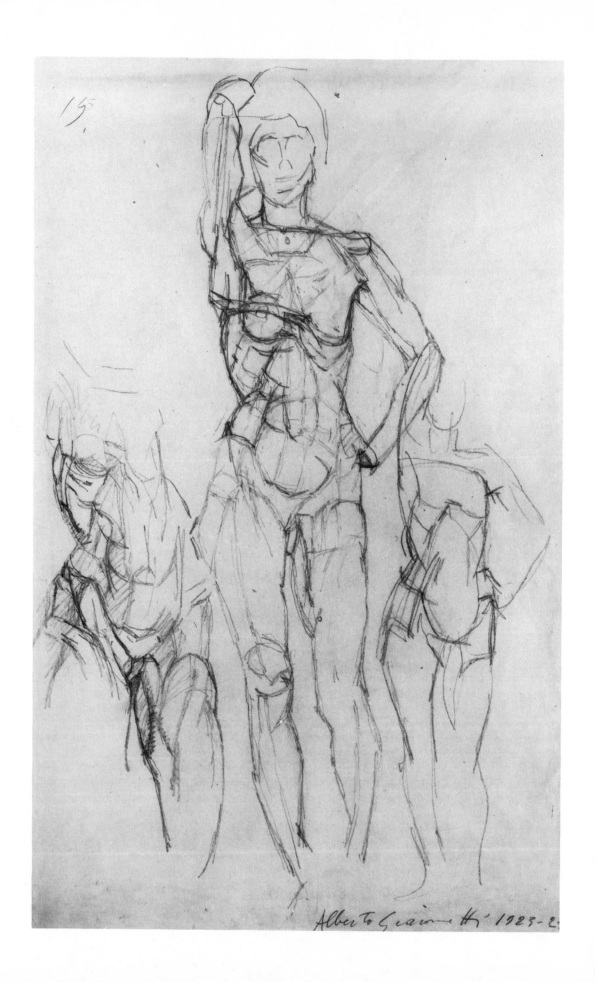

Yet another useful example of structural considerations is Giacometti's *Trois Femmes Nues* (Figure 1.41), where the figures are formed by a coming together of flat and curved planes that abut and interlock in various ways. Contrary to the beginner's tendency to rely heavily on contours—on defining a form by its outer edges—Giacometti fits together facets of the figure, only some of which form the figure's silhouette, thus reducing attention to the subject's outer boundaries. For Giacometti, the purpose is to define mass, not shape. This is especially evident in the left and central figures, where, once the drawing is under way, the emphasis shifts from the tentative sketching of outer edges (as in the figure on the far right) to a more emphatic construction of the figure's planar possibilities. As these structurally dominant drawings show, conceiving the figure as an architectural event holds important creative potential.

Every age redefines humankind. The artists of the twentieth century, creating with a sense of limitless freedom to inquire and interpret, have come forward with a multitude of definitions. These differing approaches to figure drawing, whether they tend toward an expressionistic, design-oriented, or realistic persuasion, have to contend with the same forms that confronted Michelangelo, Rembrandt, Degas, Picasso, and all the other great exponents of the figure. And this common challenge—the figure—has imposed *its* conditions on artists of every age, as they have imposed their modes of order and expression on it. The figure demands dedicated investigation, empathy, and imagination before it will reveal to the artist a personally satisfying basis for interpretation.

In this broad review, anatomy and the underlying factor of structure have been only briefly commented on; these considerations will be more fully discussed in the following chapters. Their impor-

tance in figure drawing cannot be overemphasized. But it should again be noted that structure and anatomy are tools to be utilized, not concepts to be worshipped to the exclusion of the figure's dynamic aspects, or to be regarded as obliging the artist to draw in a naturalistic mode. Our purpose in understanding these systems is to broaden, not restrict, choice; to enhance, not diminish, abstract meanings. This is the case even when anatomical forms are themselves the subject, as in Rothbein's *Study for the Nazi Holocaust Series* (Figure 1.36). In this drawing both the skulls *and* the eruptive fury of the dynamic forces cry out a warning. To lose sight of anatomy's function as both a source and agent of visually expressive inventions is to replace felt perceptions and insights with unselective scrutiny. Such an attitude tends toward taxidermy, not life.

Art is not science. Young artists today who wish to draw the figure cannot pick up the trail where Degas or Matisse stopped. They cannot begin by building upon the achievements of these artists, not only because beginning artists lack the vast factual knowledge about human form that masters possess, but also because they lack the penetrating perceptual comprehension and informed intuition that all great artists evolve over a lifetime of encountering human form and spirit. In any case, we cannot (and should not want to) adopt another's sensibility.

We must form our own interests and insights by a dedicated study of the basic factors involved in figure drawing and by a searching examination of what these factors demand of us as artists and as members of the human family. Thus our interests (a) in the figurative—the inquiring, analytical, and interpretive responses to salient actualities; (b) in design—the selecting, governing, and unifying of relational forces; and (c) in expression—the desire to heighten, provoke, and release—all require that we undertake a four-dimensional study of the figure: as a construction, a machine, a harmony, and a voice.

FIGURE 1.41
ALBERTO GIACOMETTI (1901–1966)
*Trois femmes nues* (1923–24)
44.5 x 28 cm.
Kunsthaus, Zürich, Switzerland.

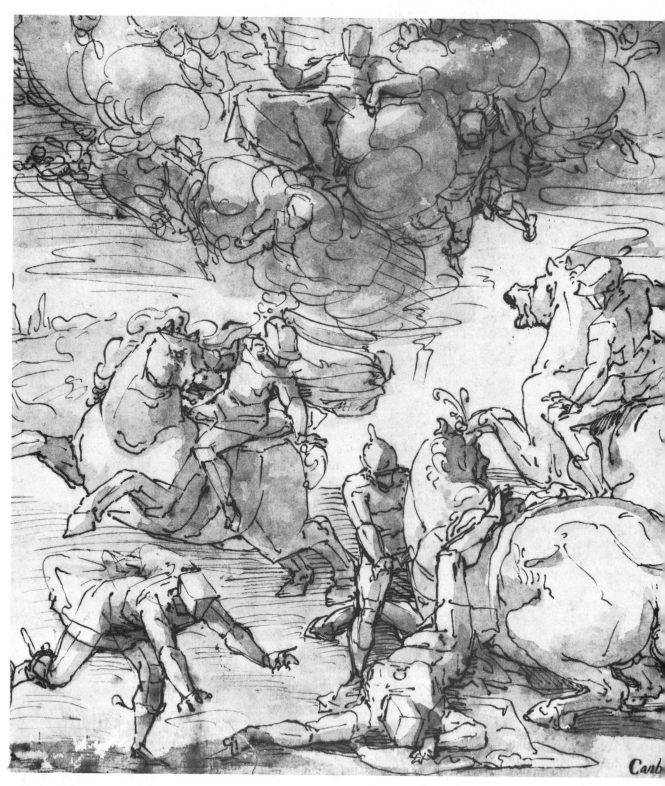

**FIGURE 2.1**
LUCA CAMBIASO (1527–1585)
*Conversion of St. Paul* (detail)
Pen and brown ink, brown wash.
*The Art Museum, Princeton University.*

TWO

# THE

# STRUCTURAL

# FACTOR

*The Figure as a Constructional System*

## SOME GENERAL OBSERVATIONS

Paul Cézanne had this advice for the art student: "Treat nature by the cylinder, the sphere, the cone. . . ."* In other words, discover the basic geometric volumes that underlie *all* forms. This is easy to do with many subjects: we recognize the cylindrical form of a silo or a cigar, and can readily see a Christmas tree as conical or a barn as block-like. But we may at first have difficulty seeing these and other geometric solids as underlying human forms. There are several reasons for this. The beginner, reacting to the figure's imposing presence, usually tries to capture it by concentrating on its surface textures and the light playing across the forms. A preoccupation with *re-presenting* such surface actualities (generally in a highly polished manner) blinds the student to the geometric core forms. Moreover, the beginner's awe of the figure, which is quite rightly regarded as complex, important, and

* *Paul Cézanne: Letters,* ed. John Rewald (London: Cassirer, 1941).

beautiful, and the subtlety with which the figure suggests its pure solids, make an analytical search for them difficult. Then, too, the beginner's tendency to assemble the image in a sequence of mostly unrelated segments makes a search for the figure's essential action, form-character, and proportions nearly impossible. As with the traveler who can't see the forest for the trees, the beginner, in concentrating on a sequence of details, misses the figure's fundamental movements and masses. One of the primary insights of sound figure drawing, then, is the need to understand the figure's forms as reducible to arrangements of simple geometric summaries.

Seen this way, human forms can be reduced to such geometric solutions as shown in Figure 2.2. As this illustration shows, the figure's forms yield to more than one kind of geometric interpretation. Some artists, such as Cambiaso (Figures 2.1, 2.5, and 2.34), favor blocklike solutions; others, such as Picasso (Figure 2.8) and Tintoretto (Figure 2.20), often reduce the figure to cylinders, spheres, and ovoids. As Figure 2.2 shows, some form-summaries are not, strictly speaking, purely geometric. So we

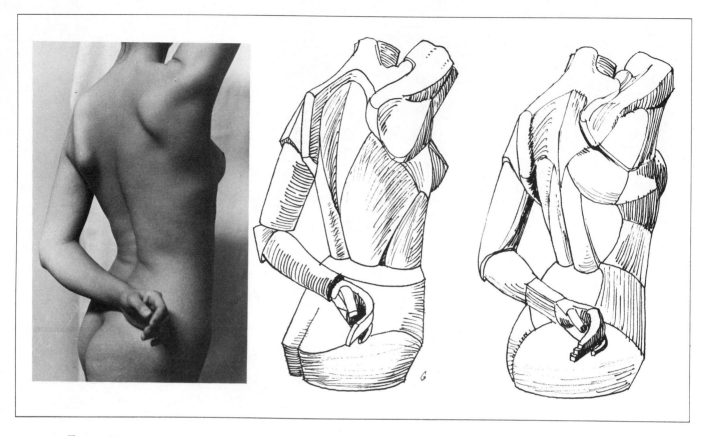

FIGURE 2.2

FIGURE 2.4

FIGURE 2.3

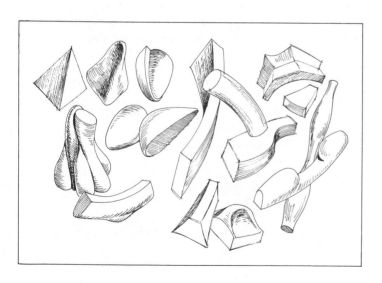

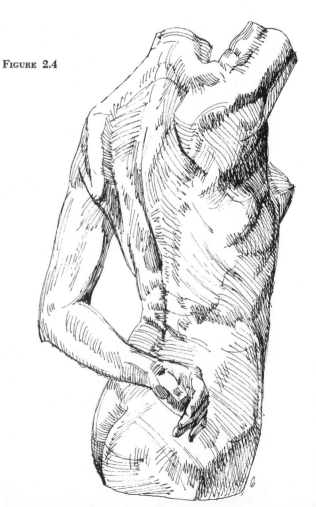

must expand on Cézanne's list of simple forms. In the human figure we can find underlying forms that suggest the pyramid, the egglike or ovoid forms, the wedge, and the bent or twisted block, as well as several variants and combinations of these and other simple forms (Figure 2.3). All of these simple masses are useful in helping us to better understand the structural nature of the figure.

Such simple solids can also be understood as *emerging from* human forms. In Figure 2.2 the figure on the left is seen as reduced to the simple forms in the analyses, but in Figure 2.4 we sense the figure to contain these pure forms within it; the forms, forcing their way to the surface, simplify the figure's surface terrain, their various joinings explaining the passages between them.

Once we understand the figure as both reducible to and emerging from simple geometric volumes, we have the reciprocal concepts that help us to understand the figure's forms in more manageable visual terms. As we can see, in his *The Conversion of St. Paul* (Figure 2.5), Cambiaso relies on just such simple masses to clarify the structure and positions in space of complex human and animal forms. In this preparatory sketch, the artist is exploring the structure and lighting of a proposed painting theme.

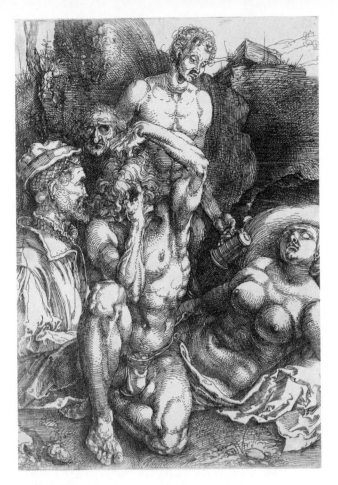

FIGURE 2.6
ALBRECHT DÜRER (1471–1528)
*Man in Despair*
Etching. 7 3/8 x 5 3/8 in.
*National Gallery of Art, Washington, D.C.
Rosenwald Collection.*

FIGURE 2.5
LUCA CAMBIASO (1527–1585)
*Conversion of St. Paul*
Pen and brown ink, brown wash. 27.7 x 40.7 cm.
*The Art Museum, Princeton University.*

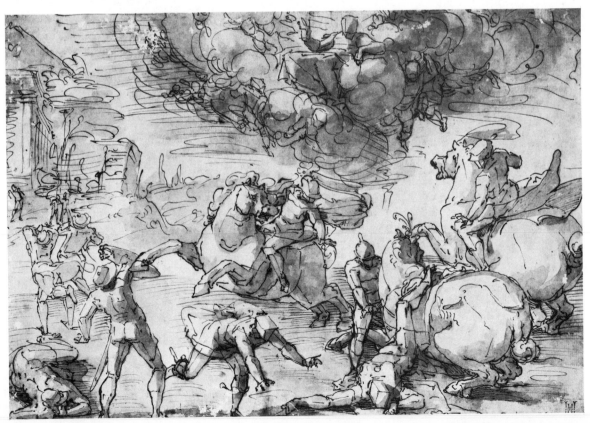

Logically enough, he reduces the subject matter to its volumetric essentials, enabling him to quickly and easily arrange the main building blocks of the form and composition. Notice how in this envisioned scene Cambiaso calls on his store of anatomical knowledge to help shape the simple volume-summaries. As Figure 2.1 clearly demonstrates, the foreshortened upper and lower segments of the fallen rider's torso, despite their blocky simplifications, strongly suggest the rib cage and pelvis.

Cambiaso's use of a light source also helps clarify the subject's main masses. Light coming from a single source will most strongly illuminate those flat or curved surface segments, or *planes,* directly facing it, leaving those planes turned away from the light source darker. Cambiaso's consistency in illuminating all the planes facing the light, which here falls from a point just over our left shoulder, provides us with an additional means for understanding the structure and placement of these forms. Note too that by this simplified means the artist is better able to quickly establish the tonal design of the work.

But this emphasis on structural clarity is often present in works intended for more than exploratory study. For many artists the figure's architectural aspects are important matters, as Michelangelo's drawing *Adam* (Figure 1.15) clearly shows. Some artists emphasize the figure's constructional aspects by frankly stressing the geometric solids that human forms hint at. In Dürer's etching *Man in Despair* (Figure 2.6), we find strong suggestions of cylinders, cones, ovoids, and only slightly less evident hints of block forms, as in the left arm and leg of the central figure. Cézanne's restatement of the figure in the simple masses he speaks of expresses a timeless monumentality (Figure 2.7), and in Picasso's *Woman Seated and Woman Standing* (Figure 2.8), the forms, boldly showing their geometric origins, create powerful, sculpturelike figures.

Other artists, such as Whistler (Figure 2.9) or Pascin (Figure 2.10), although they hold these form simplifications in mind, emphasize instead the figure's pliant, serpentine character. For such artists, structural deductions are still necessary (though largely unseen) guides in suggesting volume in simple, spontaneous figure drawings primarily concerned with rhythm and movement.

Although the need to see the structural, stable aspects of mass is fundamental to good figure drawing, perception doesn't begin or end with the noting of planes and values. We must discover our ability to respond to the abstract meanings in our subject matter *and* in the emerging drawing—the rhythms, tensions, contrasts, and affinities that constitute the dynamics of perception. Once we do, these

FIGURE 2.7
PAUL CÉZANNE (1839–1906)
*Figure of a River God*
Pencil. 125 x 223 mm.
*The Art Institute of Chicago.*

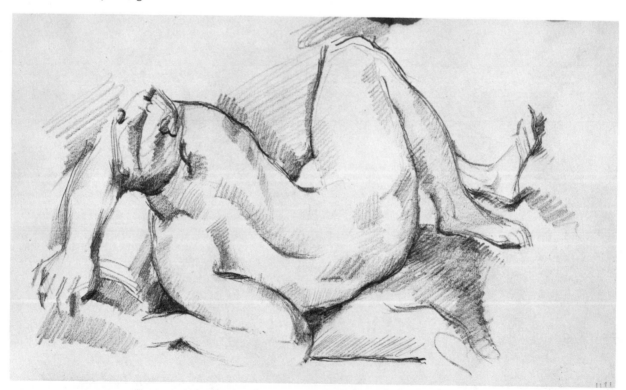

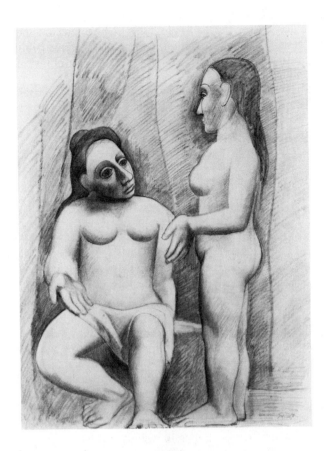

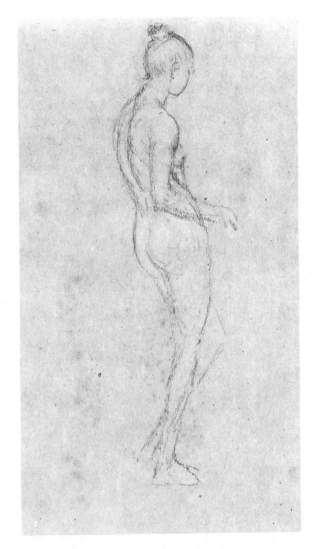

**FIGURE 2.8**
**PABLO PICASSO** (1881–1973)
*Woman Seated and Woman Standing* (1906)
Charcoal. 24 1/8 x 18 1/4 in.
*Philadelphia Museum of Art.*
*Louise and Walter Arensberg Collection.*

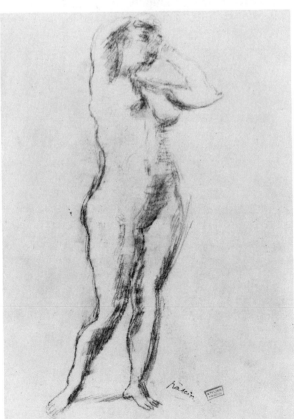

**FIGURE 2.9**
**JAMES McNEILL WHISTLER** (1834–1903)
*Standing Female Figure*
Crayon, pastel on brown paper. 10 3/4 x 6 5/16 in.
*Courtesy The Fogg Art Museum, Harvard University.*
*The David and Lucie Stone Collection.*

**FIGURE 2.10**
**JULES PASCIN** (1885–1930)
*Nude*
Pencil. 9 x 11 3/4 in.
*Courtesy The Fogg Art Museum, Harvard University.*
*The David and Lucie Stone Collection.*

inferences become as visually evident as the stable, measurable aspects of perception. Thus, the criteria that determine sound responses in drawing the figure (or anything else) must embrace the subject's structural qualities *and* its plastic, expressive ones. They are, in fact, interdependent perceptual considerations. In analyzing the structural nature of our model, we can no more disregard the energies that play among the parts, giving them order and character, than we can concentrate on such dynamic forces to the exclusion of seeing the figure's structural essentials. Neither aspect of the model's forms can be usefully understood unless they are seen as acting on each other. In failing to see the interdependence between the measurable and dynamic components of perception we fail to fertilize our constructions. When this occurs, the resulting drawings are dead blueprints rather than living graphic inventions.

But accentuating either a subject's structure or its plastic life is a valid and necessary theme for many artists. Other artists—for example, Rubens, Rembrandt, Tiepolo, and Degas—consider the structural and dynamic essentials to be equally important as visual conditions of the completed work. For these artists the figure's solid geometry is both a goal and a tool. Their drawings reflect the view that a subject's structure is an important key to its dynamics, and its dynamics a key to its structure. They realize that in disregarding a figure's plastic character they fail to grasp important structural traits. For,

in any pose, the effects of weight, the tension and pressures among parts, and the sense of forms being strained or limp are all *felt* as well as observed realities.

A drawing of the figure is not the figure itself but a graphic equivalent. If this equivalent is to convey the artist's truest response, he or she will need to negotiate between fact and feeling, between analysis and empathy. Rembrandt does this in his *Female Nude Asleep* (Figure 2.11). Limp weight is expressed by simple, blocky forms that are, considering the urgent spontaneity of Rembrandt's handling, remarkably convincing volumes. Notice how much we know about the structure of the figure's torso, left arm, and legs, and how few lines and tones are used to construct them!

But these forms do much more than convey structural essentials. By their weight and pliancy, their emphatic overlappings, and their rhythmic harmony, they *enact* as well as describe the pose. They do still more. Note how Rembrandt draws the billowing forms of the bedding to emphasize the design's "crescendo": a great burst of dynamic force at the head. Note too that Rembrandt further underscores this center of activity by placing the drawing's largest tones on and below the head, by the scale of the pillows, and by the bold lines that radiate from them. The design builds in weight and tension to the left, echoing the buildup of the figure's forms on that side. By their similarity of handling and direc-

**FIGURE 2.11**
**REMBRANDT VAN RIJN** (1606–1669)
*Female Nude Asleep*
Pen and brush in bistre ink. 13.5 x 28.3 cm.
*Rijksmuseum, Amsterdam.*

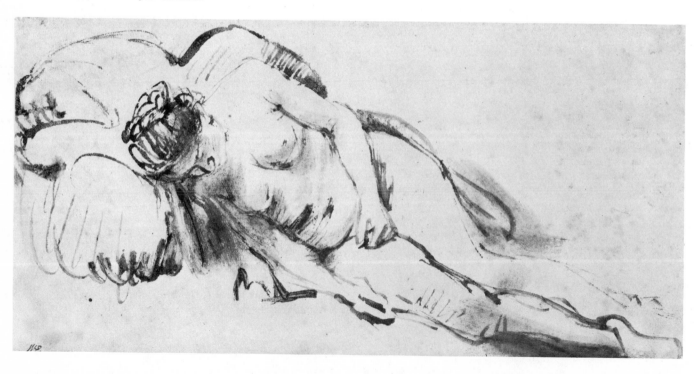

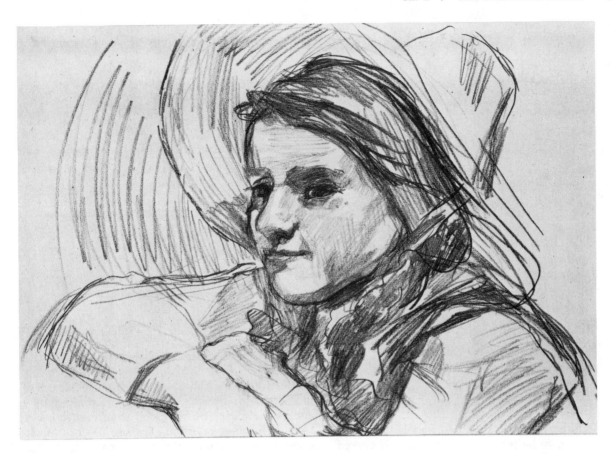

FIGURE 2.12
OSKAR KOKOSCHKA (1886–    )
*Trudl Wearing a Straw Hat*
Black crayon. 33.3 x 47.8 cm.
*Rijksmuseum, Amsterdam.*

tion, the lines that move around the figure's forms and those which express the bedding's mass and the weight of the figure upon it serve both structural and dynamic functions. These lines act as a kind of visual meter—a beat—that unites forms as it defines them.

This brief analysis only touches on some of the ways in which Rembrandt understands the interdependence of his subject's structure and design. There are other ways. For example, the dual role of the various types of edges throughout the drawing— their depictive and plastic activities—also shows the artist's grasp of the interplay of architectural and abstract matters. Indeed, much of the sleeping figure's compelling presence is due to inventive dynamic solutions that intensify the figure's structural nature.

This fusion of analytical and empathic interests is also apparent in Kokoschka's *Trudl Wearing a Straw Hat* (Figure 2.12). As in Rembrandt's drawing, we sense that Kokoschka perceives his world in dynamic, not static terms. Not only do lines produce sweeping movements in the hair, hat, and back-

ground, but even the shapes and planes that construct the young woman's forms possess an animated drive. For Kokoschka, the analysis of the subject's structure provides him with strong plastic relationships and tensions. In the same way, his responses to the subject's rhythmic character provides him with motives for emphasizing the structure in some areas and subduing it in others. Here, as mentioned earlier, structural discoveries stimulate dynamic ones, and vice versa.

In these general remarks concerning the structural factor, we have been examining the artist's need to see the underlying geometric basis of the figure's forms. Comprehending a subject's fundamental masses serves as a tool, a theme, and as a stimulus and carrier of the dynamic energies that make drawings come alive. To better understand how the artist extracts the structural character from the raw material of the figure—often obscured by conflicting light sources and always somewhat camouflaged by color, texture, and minor surface effects—we must now turn to those issues that activate these perceptions.

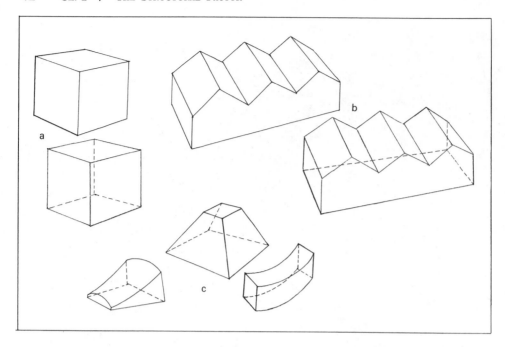

FIGURE 2.13

## A PLANAR APPROACH
## TO HUMAN FORM

For the artist the basic structural unit is the plane. Planes can here be further defined as flat or curved surfaces, or facets of a surface whose boundaries can be described by lines. Usually these boundaries represent the shape of a form, or changes in the terrain of a form's surface. For example, in Figure 2.13, the three planes (a) represent three separate surfaces which, by their positions in space, collectively suggest a cube. But in (b) the six upper planes are more readily seen as changes in the direction of a single, rooflike surface. When planes group together to form solids, they suggest other, unseen planes, as in (c).

Just as planes always result from the shape of, or changes in, a form's surface, so do we, in nature, always see planes as separated from each other by changes in color or value. The use of lines to separate adjacent planes is a convenient graphic convention, but lines rarely exist in nature, and not at all in the figure. In human forms even the finest "lines" are actually narrow hills or valleys, as, for example, in the folds and creases of your hands.

Examining your hand from several angles will show that very few planes are easily visible as neat, bounded facets. Most of the planes of the hand, like those of the rest of the human figure, are small, often curved, and generally flow into each other. In analyzing or inventing a figure's masses, artists must see the large or *major* planes first. They must train

FIGURE 2.14

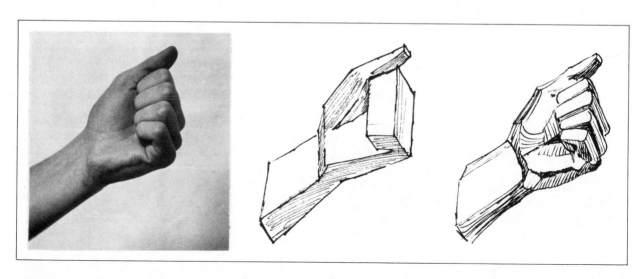

FIGURE 2.15
**DOMENIC CRETARA** (1946–   )
*Seated Figure, Back View*
Pencil. 18 x 24 in.
*Courtesy of the artist.*

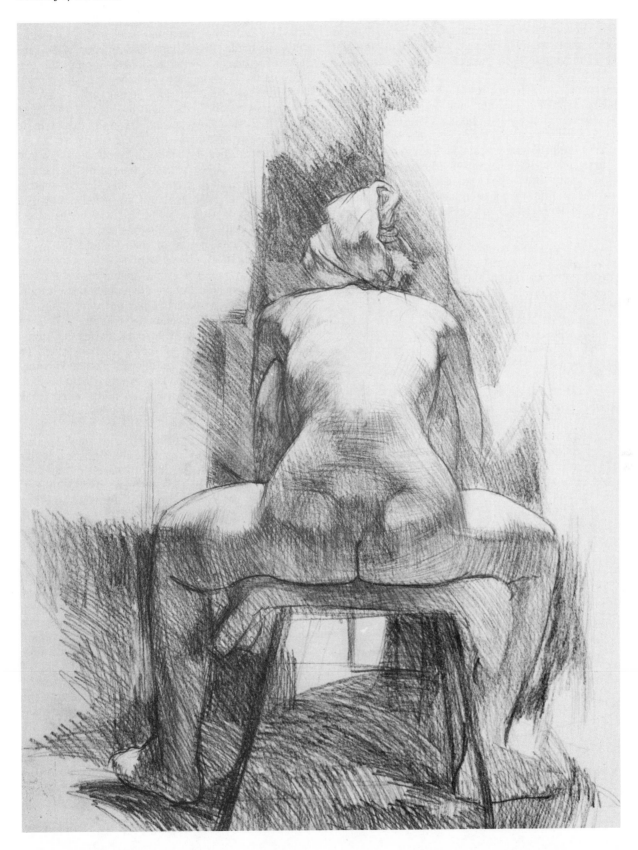

themselves to see groups of small planes as forming larger ones when they are roughly alike in their direction in relation to other groups of small planes. For example, examining our hand held in a fist, as in Figure 2.14, we see that the four fingers suggest a blocklike mass, and that the thumb and palm also offer similar blocklike masses. But to see these blocky forms we must disregard the little planar surface changes that each part of the fist is composed of. They obscure our recognition of the large planes they collectively form. In other words, we must analyze a form's structure, not by recording every plane we see, but by first making a conscious search for the form's larger planes.

Not until the shape, scale, and direction in space of these major planes are established can we, with any certainty, draw those smaller facets that comprise them. For, in constructing the major planes, we set up the scaffold to receive the small planes. To reverse the process and arrive at the major

FIGURE 2.16
JACQUES VILLON (1875–1963)
*Portrait of Félix Barré*
Black chalk over traces of blue pencil.
14 3/4 x 13 15/16 in.
*The Metropolitan Museum of Art, New York.*
*Purchase, 1963 Rogers Fund.*

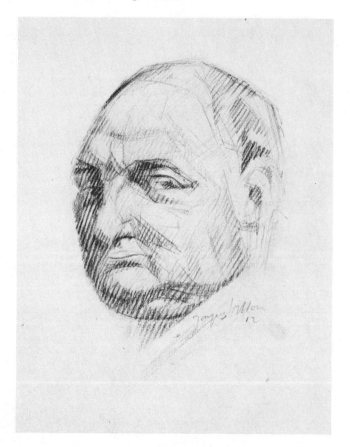

planes by accumulating small ones usually results in an overpowering flood of details that makes for fussy drawing and a weak sense of masses in space. Volumes tend to drown in a sea of details.

Like the major planes of the fist, large planes exist throughout the figure, as we saw in Cambiaso's drawing. Examining these major planes, we find that they subdivide into somewhat smaller ones—the secondary planes. Secondary planes modify the major ones to provide more specific, but still simplified, versions of the subject's actual surface-state, as in the drawing on the far right in Figure 2.14. These major and secondary planes are well illustrated in Cretara's *Seated Figure, Back View* (Figure 2.15). The artist clarifies the planes by grouping them into three tonal divisions: white (the tone of the paper), light gray, and dark gray. Note that the crosshatching lines creating these planes are usually drawn in the direction of a plane's short axis or in the direction of its position on the figure's surface, and show the flat or curved nature of each plane. Even in the headdress these groups of structural lines turn with the form. Cretara is sensitive to the abstract possibilities of such line groups. He unifies those of the figure with a network of similar but darker lines in the background, simultaneously creating a field of spatial depth and a handsome design of tonal patches. As this drawing amply demonstrates, an analytical approach to the figure's planar construction can result in compelling graphic ideas. But to find such large planes we must make intellectual, analytical perceptions and not merely record our retinal impressions.

All of the figure's forms, large or small, can be reduced to simpler, more manageable masses. Looking again at our fist, we see that each of the four clenched fingers is, in each segment, as blocklike as the fist they collectively produce. In examining any of the major planes of these smaller forms we find they subdivide into their secondary and still smaller planes. It seems the closer we look, the more aware we become of these tiny variations and the less aware we are of a form's major planes. As noted earlier, learning to see the larger planes that groups of smaller planes belong to is basic to understanding any form's structural essentials. Overlooking this constructional aspect of form is one of the common pitfalls of the beginner, who strives instead to produce volume by repeated rubbing and smudging of the drawing. But such blendings not only destroy the freshness of a drawing's forms, they destroy the forms themselves. In analyzing the figure's masses we should avoid confusing such soft blending with form clarity, and, in establishing the figure's planes, we should avoid drifting too far from the mainstreams of its major and secondary planes down the tributaries of superficial detail.

Comparing the female figure in Dürer's etching (Figure 2.6) with Rembrandt's drawing of a woman in a similar pose (Figure 2.11) shows that although Dürer has gone further in explaining the figure's structure, he does not go much beyond the secondary planes in doing so. Where he does become engrossed with surface niceties, as in the side view of the head on the left, the head just above it, and, though to a lesser extent, the right foot of the central figure, the structural character of the forms is actually less clearly stated.

The aesthetic benefits that derive from analyzing the figure in planar terms are highly regarded by many artists. Such artists intend to interpret the figure in these prismatic units, not for purposes of study, as Cambiaso does, but for creative purposes. In Villon's *Portrait of Félix Barré* (Figure 2.16), the artist's theme appears to be the realization of the psychological as well as the architectural character of the sitter through a utilization of the emotive and explanatory power of the strong masses that planar modeling provides. Planar analysis, then, is more than a tool for understanding a subject's construction; it is an important source of creative insight.

## THE INTERJOINING OF PLANES AND MASSES

Some parts of the figure appear to interlock and some to fuse. Again, our hands provide a useful example for study. Looking at your partially open hand, palm side up, notice that the thumb and its fleshy heel seem to be deeply rooted in the palm and wrist. As your bring the thumb and fingers together a bit more, each segment of the fingers, the fleshy pads of the palm, and the thumb show more strongly these embedding, interlocking, and overlapping characteristics. Opening the hand wide, each finger stretched to its limits, greatly reduces this type of structural condition. In this position the fingers seem fused with the palm, a five-lane continuation of the major plane of the palm.

In analyzing the figure's forms we must decide when parts seem to interlock and when they seem to fuse. Here, the term *form* defines the figure's major segments (arm, head, foot, etc.), and the smaller segments of which they are composed. For example, the features of the head (eyes, nose, lips, ears) and the often overlooked features that separate them (chin, cheek, forehead, temple, etc.) can all be regarded as interjoinings and fusions of small *form-units*.

A form-unit, then, is any large or small part of the figure whose mass is seen as a self-contained component—a building block—in the figure's structural state. The way each of these parts appears to

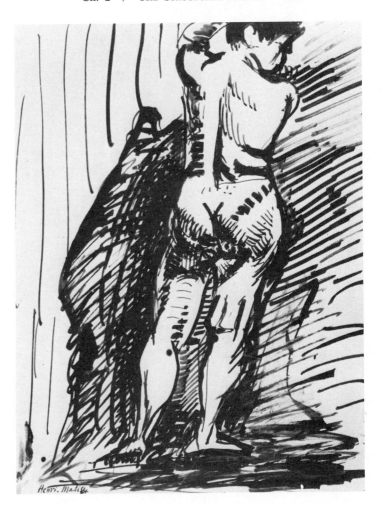

**FIGURE 2.17**
**HENRI MATISSE (1869–1954)**
*Nude Study*
India ink with quill pen. 26.4 x 20.2 cm.
*National Gallery, Prague.*

interjoin is, of course, largely determined by our anatomy and, as we have seen, by the particular arrangement of the forms. But there remains a considerable degree of freedom to interpret the interjoining of form-units according to personal preference and expressive intent. Some artists emphasize the wedging, overlapping, and embedding characteristics; others, the gentle flow of the forms; and still others strike a balance between these two general kinds of unions.

Matisse, in his *Nude Study* (Figure 2.17), drives parts together with great force. Form-units grasp and overlap each other resolutely, even aggressively. The upper part of each leg holds the lower part as if by pincers. At the neck and waist bold lines express the weight and tension of overlapped forms strongly pressed together. How different is Ingres' interpretation of a standing female figure! In

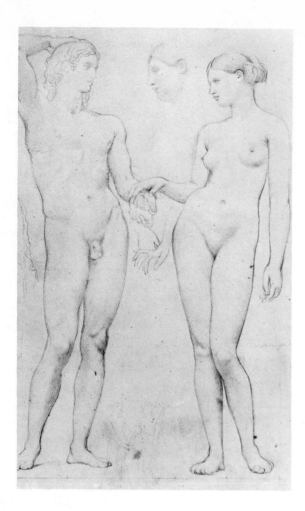

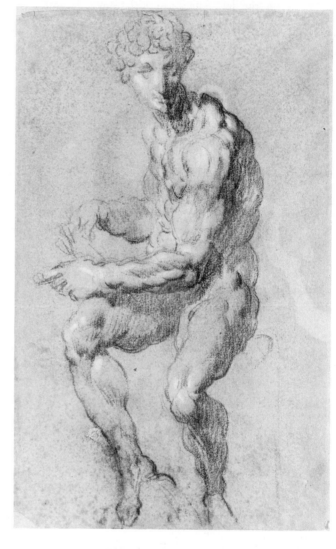

FIGURE 2.18
DOMINIQUE INGRES (1780–1867)
*Two Nudes, study for "The Golden Age"*
Pencil. 16 3/8 x 12 7/16 in.
*Courtesy The Fogg Art Museum, Harvard University.*
*Bequest of Granville L. Winthrop.*

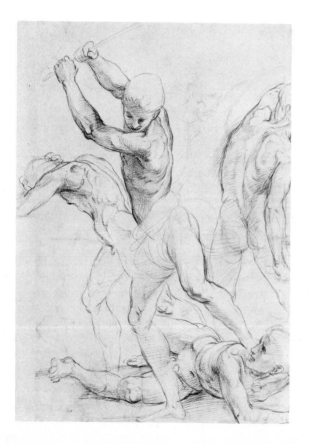

FIGURE 2.20
JACOPO TINTORETTO (1518–1594)
*Study of a Model for the "Giuliano de' Medici"*
*of Michelangelo*
Black and white chalk.
*The Governing Body of Christ Church, Oxford.*

FIGURE 2.19
RAPHAEL (1483–1520)
*Combat of Nude Men*
Red chalk over preliminary stylus work.
14 13/16 x 11 1/8 in.
*Ashmolean Museum, Oxford.*

his study *Two Nudes* (Figure 2.18), Ingres' interpretation relies on precise delineation and subtle fusions of form-units, rather than on rugged interlockings. In Raphael's *Combat of Nude Men* (Figure 2.19), there is a balance between the abrupt and fluid union of parts. Although each figure clearly shows the deep roots of the limbs embedded in the torso, and many other form-units such as those in the left arm and leg of the central figure are vigorously constructed, Raphael keeps a graceful flow moving throughout the drawing. He does this by stressing curved rather than flat planes, by simply omitting some interjoinings, as along the left side of the central figure's raised leg, and by a delineating edge as rich in rhythmic flow as it is in volume-informing fact.

Tintoretto merges the concepts of strong and subtle joinings by forceful interlockings of graceful form-units. His powerful *Study of a Model for the "Giuliano de' Medici" of Michelangelo* (Figure 2.20) is an undulating system of exaggerated interjoinings made of ovoid rather than blocklike segments. This study of a work by Michelangelo, itself a heightened interpretation of idealized forms boldly interjoined, conveys a strong sense of aliveness through the energetic way these richly modeled forms interact. Their almost serpentine ripple implies pulsating movement and great strength. It is worth noting that Tintoretto's drawing is an excellent example of structural and anatomical matters serving the factors of design and expression. Note the abstract and emotive energies of the forms and the sense of barely contained action. Segantini's *Male Nude Torso* (Figure 2.21) shows a more conservative interpretation of human forms as emerging from rounded rather than blocklike solids. But there is an impressive clarity in the way these form-units interjoin. Note how insistently the lines ride upon the changing directions of the surface. They rise and fall with the terrain, explaining the depth of every hollow, the height of every rise, and the degree of abruptness or flow in the union between the parts. A sculptor, using Segantini's drawing as a guide, could model these forms in clay and never be in doubt about the subject's volumes.

As Segantini's, Tintoretto's, and Raphael's drawings demonstrate, the impression of the rising and falling of the figure's terrain owes much to the way the lines used to model the forms move upon the surface. Such surface-probing lines, usually drawn close together, are sometimes called *cross-contour,* or cage-lines. Moving in "schools," they collectively chart a volume's surface-structure in visual terms that are easy to understand. Sometimes, as in Figures 2.7 and 2.17, these structure-seeking lines are used to indicate only the secondary planes, allowing the white of the page to create the figure's major

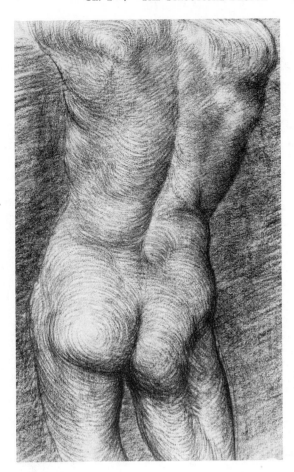

FIGURE 2.21
GIOVANNI SEGANTINI (1858–1899)
*Male Nude Torso*
Black chalk. 12 1/4 x 8 in.
*Courtesy The Fogg Art Museum, Harvard University.*
*Bequest of Granville L. Winthrop.*

planes. This often has the effect of suggesting a light source striking the forms. Usually, these straight or curved hatched lines move around the body of a long form such as an arm or leg. On flat planes they more frequently repeat the plane's short axis. However, such line-groups may run in the direction of the long axis of a plane or a form and still define surface conditions by the varying distance between lines, or by their differing thicknesses. Something of this can be seen in Figure 2.16. Less frequently, such inner contour lines are made to describe circular levels of terrain, much in the manner of the cartographer. Such a schema can be utilized for medical purposes by a computer, as in Figure 2.22.

Cross-contour lines, when they succeed in explaining the terrain of the forms they occupy, and the interjoining of planes and masses, seem not to intrude on our sensibilities as textures no matter how bold (Figure 2.17). Our first impression is of

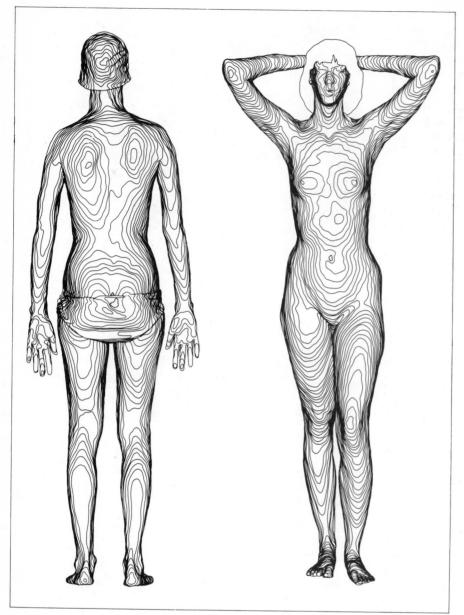

**FIGURE 2.22**
**DR. R. E. HERRON**
*Composite of Back View of Male Figure
and Front View of Female Figure*
Computer drawing.

their volume-revealing nature. Only when lines fail to explain the terrain do they strike us as strong patterns appearing upon the form itself. Notice that the lines in Figure 2.22, although they are exact registrations of levels of terrain, *do* possess a textural nature; they seem to rise to the level of the page in a decorative manner. This is so because of their mechanical, unchanging nature. A convincing realization of form requires the artist's *feel* for the changing surface as well as acute visual judgments.

All gifted artists, of whatever period or style, have, in their formative years, fully explored the structural nature of the forms around them. This has been so even when their mature work was of a severely nonobjective kind, as in the case of Albers,

whose investigations into form, color, and space phenomena reveal the same sensitivity we find in his early *Self Portrait* (Figure 2.23), a brilliant demonstration of the creative role structural considerations may play.

Whether artists stress or subdue the joining of planes and form-units, whether they favor a blocklike or egglike schema, or as in Rembrandt's drawing (Figure 2.11), a selective choosing between the two geometric mass concepts, they need to apprehend the figure's subtle forms as reducible to simpler masses that interjoin in various ways. Held in the mind's eye, unions such as those in Figures 2.2 and 2.27 help artists to understand and to explain the forms they draw.

FIGURE 2.23
JOSEF ALBERS (1888–    )
*Self-Portrait*
Transfer lithograph. 18 1/8 x 12 in.
*Collection, The Museum of Modern Art, New York.*

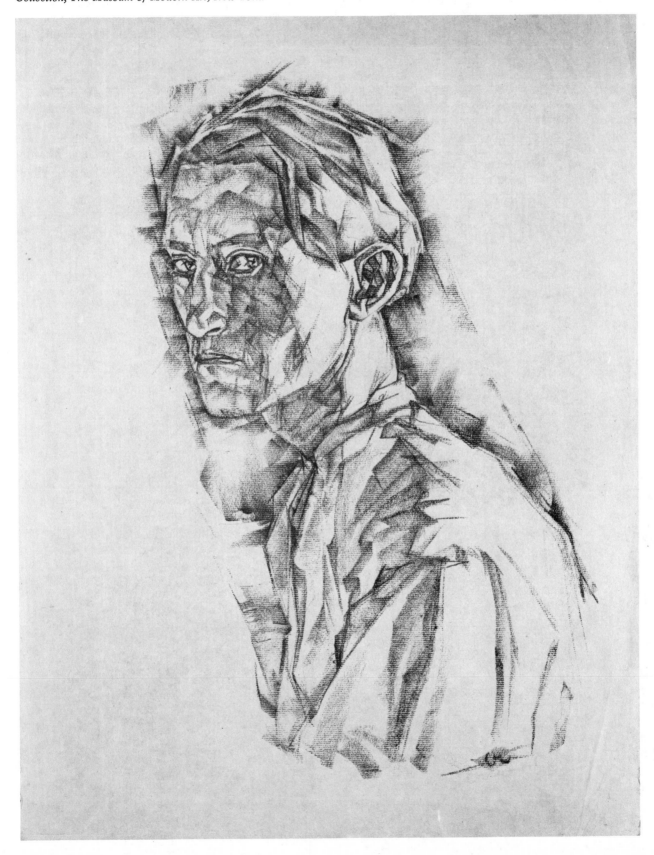

## STRUCTURE AND VALUE

Most volumetrically convincing drawings rely on values to help clarify the figure's structural nature. Indeed, the structure-seeking hatchings, as they establish the tilt of flat planes, show the turnings of curved ones, or explain how planes and masses interjoin, usually suggest light playing upon the subject. This is the case in Figures 1.40 and 2.17, where structural issues, and not illumination, are the dominant theme. But when these hatchings produce values that are accented on one side of a form and only lightly indicated, or even omitted, on the other side, we sense more strongly the presence of light upon the form. Michelangelo's *Studies of a Madonna and Child* (Figure 2.24) does this. Although it is clear in this preparatory sketch that form real-

ization is the artist's main motive, he suggests a gentle light falling from the upper left side. Michelangelo does this by only lightly modeling the planes facing to the left, while darkening the hatchings on the planes turned toward the right. Note how, on the Madonna's face and neck, the changing directions and values of the lines that constitute the planes explain how the surface facets abut and blend to form the surface character of those parts.

But the structurally sensitive artist is not *primarily* concerned with values for their illumination effects. Drawings that only imitate the existing light and dark areas of a subject—as photographs do—are merely records of light's accidental behavior. Light is indifferent. It strikes any solid in its path, sometimes explaining structure, sometimes camouflaging or even destroying it.

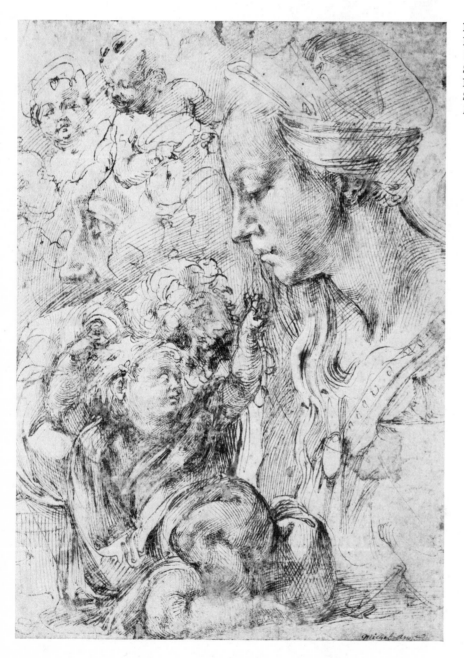

FIGURE 2.24
**MICHELANGELO BUONARROTI**
**(1475–1564)**
*Studies of a Madonna and Child*
*Pen and brown ink. 11 1/4 x 8 1/4 in.*
*Staatliche Museen Preussischer Kulturbesitz.*
*Kupferstichkabinett. West Berlin.*

and 1.6), values are necessary to describe the figure's topography. While few artists go to the opposite extreme, explaining every facet of a subject's terrain, as Segantini, Michelangelo, and Stevens do, it is highly informing for the student to make some drawings in which no deserts of empty, unexplained terrain exist.

Value, then, is able to convey light and model form. It can also distinguish among the inherent values of a subject's parts. For example, values can show the dark tone of the hair against the lighter tone of a head or hat. The inherent lightness or darkness of a form, or any of its segments, apart from the effects of light upon it, is called its *local-tone*. Artists intending to convey the local-tones of their subject matter will generally simplify them to keep from weakening value's structural role. In Watteau's *Study of a Young Negro* (Figure 2.26), the light tone of the headdress and the darker tone of

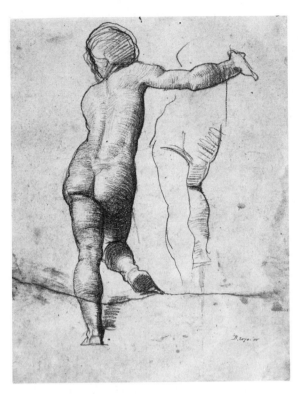

FIGURE 2.25
ALFRED STEVENS (1817–1875)
*Two Studies of a Standing Figure, Back View*
Red chalk. 18 3/8 x 6 1/4 in.
*Victoria and Albert Museum, London.*

FIGURE 2.26
ANTOINE WATTEAU (1684–1721)
*Study of a Young Negro*
Red and black chalk, heightened with white
on gray paper. 7 1/8 x 5 3/4 in.
*Trustees of the British Museum, London.*

Imagine a zebra standing before a fence made of diagonally crossed lattice which is casting strong shadows on the animal. Simply copying the shadows and stripes would result in a richly patterned zebra whose structure would be lost in the visual confusion of so many crisscrossed ribbons of tone. Or imagine a figure illuminated from several sources at once, as occurs when overhead lights are spaced across an entire ceiling, or when daylight enters through windows from several directions. The figure will be brightly lit, but most of the forms will appear flat, showing little volume-revealing value change. When artists desire a sense of light-bathed forms, most will nevertheless subordinate the effects of illumination to structural interests, as Stevens does in his drawing *Two Studies of a Standing Figure, Back View* (Figure 2.25). Here, light falls from a point high on the left side, but the illuminating role of value is secondary to its volume-informing one. The figure's right leg *is* in shadow, but the hatched lines that produce the leg's shadowed state are concerned first with modeling the form.

Such form-revealing information is of course not possible in contour drawing alone. Although contour lines can be surprisingly informing about the nature of the masses they enclose (Figures 1.5

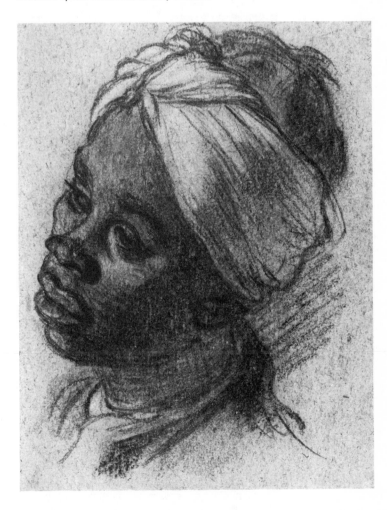

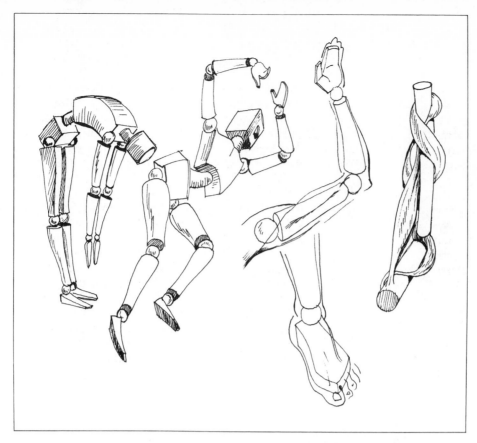

FIGURE 2.27

FIGURE 2.28

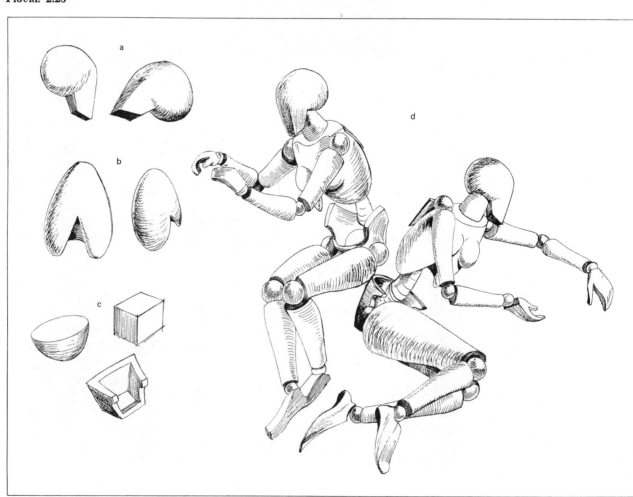

the head are indicated by simple, flat values: Watteau unifies these areas by a band of dark tone that suggests the presence of light as it models the ovoid formed by the face, headdress, and hair. Note that in modeling these three areas the artist emphasizes major and secondary planes. Note too how feelingly the value-producing line groups move upon the forms. Comparing Watteau's drawing to the similar view of the Madonna's head in the Michelangelo drawing, we see that Watteau's providing of information about the local tones of the young black are in addition to, not in place of, structural clarity. In both drawings a major interest is the experiencing of the subject's important masses.

## STRUCTURAL SUPPORTS AND SUSPENSIONS IN THE FIGURE

The skeleton provides a firm, armaturelike system of support for the figure's more pliant muscular and fatty tissues. In Chapter Three we will examine the skeleton in some detail, but here we must add to our understanding of the figure's structural nature a sensitivity to the supporting role of the skeleton beneath the drapery of muscle, fat, and skin. To better understand those rigid forms that hold and the behavior of those more flexible forms that are held, we can temporarily envision the skeleton as reduced to a simple, manikinlike system of bony

**FIGURE 2.29**
**JACOB DE GHEYN II** (1565–1629)
*Studies of Four Women at Their Toilet*
Pen and ink, some black chalk;
on gray paper. 26.1 x 33.6 cm.
*Musées Royaux des Beaux Arts, Brussels.*

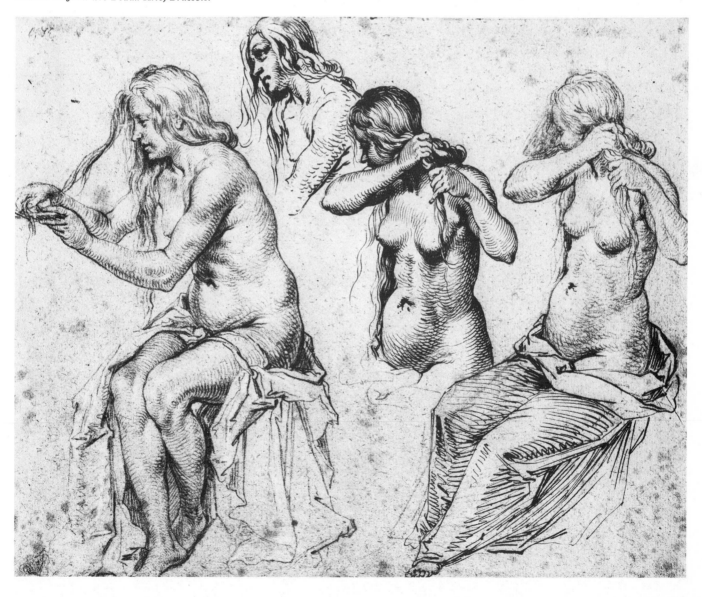

masses connected by spheres, cylinders, and wedges (Figures 2.27 and 2.28).

The three large masses of the skeleton are the skull, the rib cage, and the pelvis (Figure 2.28). Of the three, the skull is the most visible, influencing surface forms throughout the head. Reduced to its simplest geometric state, the skull can be represented by an ovoid upper segment which extends downward in front into a blocky lower segment, not unlike a police whistle (a). The rib cage is reducible to a large, egglike mass, small end up, with a pie-slice opening in its curved front plane that extends upward from the base of the egg to about its middle (b). Somewhat less visible in the figure than the skull, the rib cage is still a prominent mass, especially in the area of the wedgelike opening, and strongly influences the shaping of the upper torso. The pelvis is more deeply buried in the figure. A

complex form, it can be reduced to several simple masses: into a half-sphere, a block, a winged and slightly tapered, hollowed block, or to the forms shown in the manikins in Figure 2.28 (c). Note that the manikinlike figures (d) in our illustration show ball joints at the shoulder, elbow, knee, wrist, and ankle. These roughly correspond to the bony prominences found throughout the skeleton, occurring at the ends of the long, shaftlike bones of the limbs, or resulting from small, projecting bones, as at the knee. Most of these protuberances are visible to some degree in most poses, for example, in de Gheyn's *Studies of Four Women at Their Toilet* (Figure 2.29). Additionally, the ball joints shown in Figure 2.28d suggest the figure's mobility at these sites.

Imagining the manikinlike scaffold inside the figure on the far left of de Gheyn's drawing helps us

FIGURE 2.30
FRANCOIS BOUCHER (1703–1770)
*Seated Nude*
Red and white chalk on gray paper. 30 x 39.2 cm.
*Rijksmuseum, Amsterdam.*

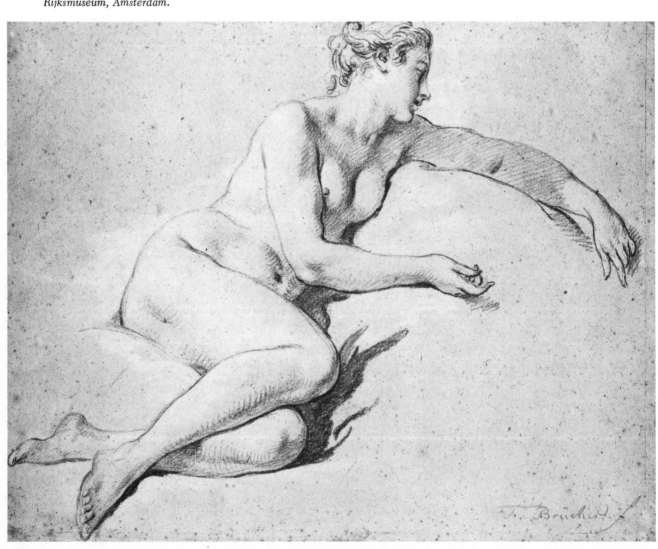

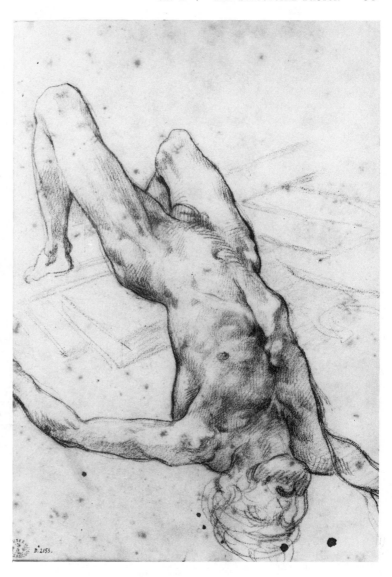

FIGURE 2.31
THÉODORE GÉRICAULT (1791–1824)
*Study for one of the figures in*
*"The Raft of Medusa"*
Charcoal on white paper. 28.9 x 20.5 cm.
*Musée des Beaux Arts, Besançon.*

sense how the muscular and fatty tissues are draped upon the skeleton; it also helps explain why the "container" of skin is stretched taut in some places, as at the knees and hips, and why it is slack in other places, as in the chest and abdomen. Note how de Gheyn, in drawing the figure's fleshy forms, suggests the inner armature of the skeleton, how he integrates firm and supple passages everywhere, avoiding form-solutions that are wooden or rubbery. He does this not only at the joints, where the bones come to the surface, but throughout the length of the limbs, and in the torso where, especially in the figure on the left, we sense the rib cage and pelvis through the heavily fleshed forms. Note too the clarity of the cross-contour lines which de Gheyn uses to convey the abrupt and flowing unions between form-units.

Likewise, in Boucher's *Seated Nude* (Figure 2.30), we sense the presence of an inner supporting system. Although this figure is rather heavily proportioned, even plump, the forms are not balloon-like or rubbery. As in de Gheyn's drawing, they show alternating firm and pliant passages that suggest the skeletal substructure. Comparing Boucher's drawing with its schematic counterpart in Figure 2.28 helps explain what holds and what is held.

Naturally, the skeleton's influence is more apparent in lean figures, especially male ones. Géricault's study for one of the figures in his painting *The Raft of Medusa* (Figure 2.31) reveals a keen understanding of the skeleton's effect upon the figure's outer casing. The rib cage and the wings of the pelvis are quite distinct. Throughout the figure the taut sheath of the skin hints at the forms below, suggesting the firm, inner structure pressing outward. Note that the head, only roughed in, looks something like the schematic skull in Figure 2.28a. Although developed much further, the head in

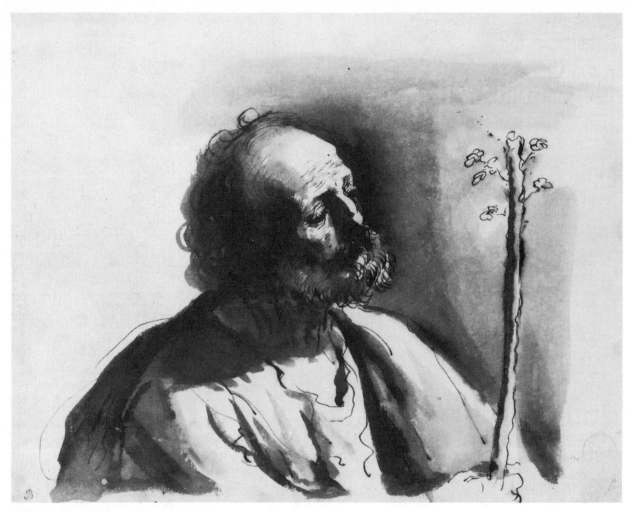

FIGURE 2.32
GIOVANNI FRANCESCO BARBIERI,
called GUERCINO (1591–1666)
*St. Joseph*
Pen and bistre ink. 16.8 x 20.7 cm.
*The Art Museum, Princeton University.*

Guercino's *St. Joseph* (Figure 2.32) is still modeled chiefly by large planes that do not surrender their dominance to the smaller details. In fact, notice that in all the structurally sensitive drawings we have been looking at in this chapter, simple form concepts underlie the modeling of forms in values. As noted earlier, knowing a form's basic planar character provides a logical basis for establishing the light and dark tones upon it. Both Géricault's depiction of small but pronounced surface changes and Boucher's modeling of large but subtly turning ones are enhanced by the artist's appreciation of the figure's underlying cubes, cylinders, ovoids, etc., shaped in part by the bony substructure. Something rings true in drawings that show the skeleton's role in forming and affecting the figure's surface forms. Such works express truths about the figure's construction and character that the mere collecting of surface data cannot achieve.

## STRUCTURAL ASPECTS OF FORESHORTENING

As with all forms in nature, those of the figure are subject to the laws of perspective. Although an examination of perspective is not within the scope of this book,* it is necessary here to comment briefly on some of its basic principles.

A basic concept of linear perspective holds that any view of any solid mass involves the foreshortening of some of its surfaces. For example, looking directly at one plane of a cube must necessarily show other of its planes to be foreshortened. In some forms we cannot see the foreshortened planes—for example, when our line of sight is cen-

* For a fuller discussion of linear and aerial perspective, see Nathan Goldstein, *The Art of Responsive Drawing,* 2nd ed. (Englewood Cliffs, N.J.: Prentice-Hall, Inc., 1977), chap. 5.

tered on the bottom plane of a cone or pyramid. More often, and especially in the forms of the figure, any view of a form, large or small, shows some of its surfaces turned away from our line of sight. Although the beginner may not be aware of it, any "easy" pose, such as a front view of a figure standing at attention, contains a great deal of foreshortening. Such a pose consists of a severely foreshortened view of the sides of the head, torso, and limbs. Depending on the eye level of the student in relation to the model, this pose will also show foreshortened views of the top or underside of various forms. For example, if the student is seated in front of the standing figure, he or she sees a foreshortened view of the *underside* of the model's nose and jaw, and a foreshortened view of the *top* surfaces of the model's feet, as in Figures 2.8 and 2.18.

The greater the degree of foreshortening, the greater the visual reduction—the shortening—of a plane's surface. *All* planes except those at a right angle to and centered in the viewer's line of sight are seen as foreshortened, as in Figure 2.33a. The more a plane's position parallels the viewer's line of sight, the less can be seen of its surface. When a plane is exactly in line with the viewer's line of sight, only its near edge is visible, as in Figure 2.33b. Curved planes, by their nature, are always seen as foreshortened (Figure 2.33c).

Naturally, what is true for a single plane holds true for the flat and curved planes of any solid mass. The variously positioned forms of the figure in any pose are better understood by first determining their location in space in relation to your line of sight, and your *eye level,* that is, the height of your eyes from the ground plane upon which you are standing, seated, or even lying. For the artist the terms *eye level* and *horizon line* are synonymous. Our eye level determines the high or low position of the horizon line in our field of vision. If we lie on the sand, looking at the sea, the horizon line is low; if we stand up, it is higher; and if we climb the lifeguard's tower, the horizon line is higher still. In Cambiaso's *Resurrection and Ascension* (Figure 2.34), it is evident that the artist has envisioned a scene occurring mainly above his (and consequently, our) eye level. Because the horizon line is low, we look down on only those few forms located below it, namely the feet and lower limbs of the three figures standing on the ground plane. All other forms in the drawing, regardless of their angle and degree of foreshortening, we see as positioned above our eye level. This is so even though we do see the top planes of some of the forms, because we understand the overall location of the figures to be above our eye level.

We have all learned, or instinctively know, that horizontal lines which are actually parallel appear to incline toward each other, meeting at an imaginary point on the horizon line. We have all noted this apparent converging of lines when walking down a corridor or street. It is equally true that any group of parallel lines projecting back into space, that is, away from the viewer at *any* angle, will appear to

**Figure 2.33**

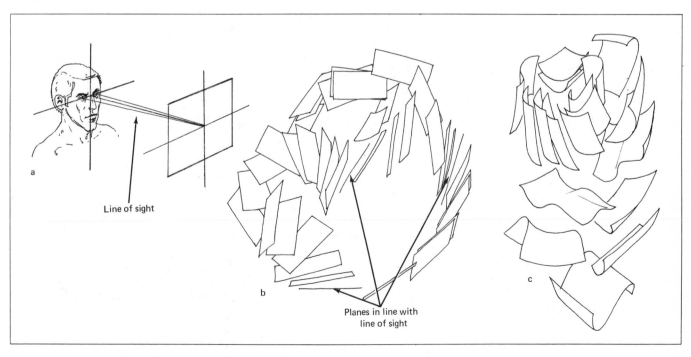

Line of sight

Planes in line with
line of sight

FIGURE 2.34
LUCA CAMBIASO (1527–1585)
*Resurrection and Ascension*
Pen, ink, and brown wash. 13 1/8 x 9 3/8 in.
*Gabinetto Nazionale delle Stampe, Rome.*

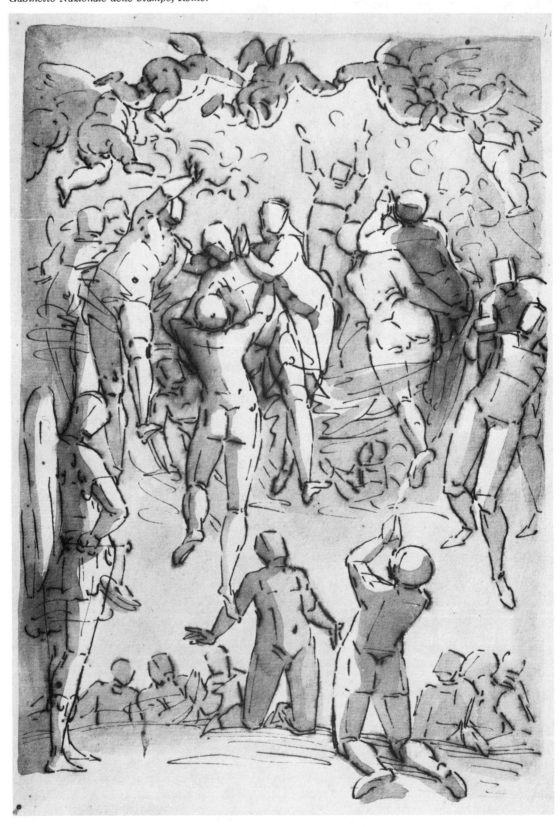

FIGURE 2.35

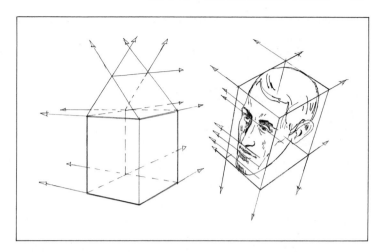

FIGURE 2.36
**NATHAN GOLDSTEIN (1927– )**
*Reclining Figure, Foreshortened View*
Red chalk. 10 3/4 x 11 1/2 in.
*Collection of the author.*

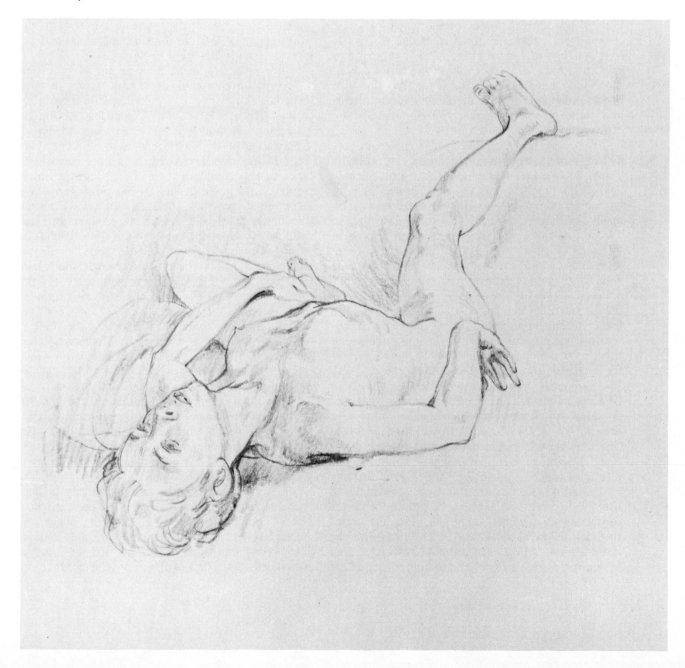

converge, as in Figure 2.35. Thus, the width of any form possessing parallel lines (edges), such as a block or cylinder, appears to diminish as it projects back toward the horizon line, or toward any imaginary point above or below it. Such forms appear. then, to taper. Forms that *actually* taper, as many of the figure's forms do, will appear to do so to a greater degree than blocks or cylinders when projecting away from the viewer, as in Figure 2.36. Note that here the position of the head and neck, the torso, and the upper and lower limbs are made easier to locate in relation to each other by the device of the near form always overlapping and "digging into" the form beyond it. The edges of the throat are overlapped and set into the torso, which in turn asserts its dominance over the upper right leg by a single line; the upper right leg does the same to the lower leg, which overlaps the foot. This dominance of the near over the far form holds true in the figure when the same foreshortened forms are viewed from either end. In Michelangelo's *Studies for the Crucified Haman* (Figure 2.37), a right arm projecting back and a left one thrust forward both show this principle at work. Comparing the two hands in the upper part of the drawing again reveals how these pincer interlockings clarify the position of forms in relation to each other.

The ability to reduce the figure's masses to geometric forms (whether these forms are actually drawn in as a preliminary substructure or are only held in the mind's eye as the work proceeds) is of particular importance in drawing views of drastically foreshortened forms. This ability is evident in Tiepolo's *Apollo with Lyre and Quiver, His Arm Upraised* (Figure 2.38). But, as we have seen, foreshortening is an ever-present phenomenon, even with forms only slightly turned away. In Cretara's *Sheet of Studies of the Female Figure* (Figure 2.39), the forms are located both above and below our eye level; and this impression is conveyed by the artist's. sensitive tapering of the forms, by the direction of the lines that model them, and by his appreciation of the geometric core that underlies each one.

Tintoretto's fragmentary sketch, *Lying Man* (Figure 2.40), because it shows several stages of development, permits us to see the unfolding of a drawing of severely foreshortened human forms. The drawing was begun by a search for the direction, and the tapering, overlapping nature of the forms, as can be seen in the barely begun drawing of the arms. On this underdrawing, a scaffold of simplified forms is established. Tintoretto then turns to refining some earlier shape judgments and begins to block in broad tones that further strengthen the sense of mass. In the most completed portions, such as the torso, he reinforces the turning nature of the

part by modeling with lines that move around the form. We sense the artist's awareness of the figure's converging lines, and his appreciation of its substructure and the geometric basis of its parts. These insights assist the expressive authority and are some of the forces driving this compelling sketch.

As the previous three drawings show, the figure's forms are more clearly located in space, and more convincingly drawn, when perspective considerations and a sensitivity to the geometric basis underlying human forms are present. Note that these drawings, although centuries apart, show a common understanding of the torso and limbs as essentially cylindrical, the head as ovate, and the feet as wedge-like. Additionally, these three artists utilize a strong light source, all model the forms in three values, and all consistently stress the overlap of the far form by the near one as a clue to their location in space. The purpose in noting these similarities is to point out that even when artists take similar steps in the construction of a figure drawing, the visual and expressive results can vary widely.

For most beginners, drawing any human form in severe foreshortening is difficult. Often the student begins to draw a foreshortened form as he or she actually sees it, but in the completed drawing the part looks as though it had been viewed from an overhead position. What began as an objective study of a foreshortened view of, say, a leg, ends in a drawing that combines some of the student's observations with some of his or her *prior knowledge* about legs: that they are long forms, have certain familiar outlines, and contain some important characteristics such as the knee and the ankle. Under the stress of analyzing the actualities before them, some beginning students abandon perceptual inquiry and fall back on stored, clichéd notions about the figure's forms. Yet the same students can probably draw severely foreshortened blocks, cylinders, and cones with considerable skill. Indeed, if the students *and* the instructor of a beginning life-drawing class were each to draw a foreshortened cylinder, it would be difficult to identify which drawing was the instructor's. But were the students and the instructor to draw a finger in the same position as the cylinder, the instructor's drawing would be immediately identifiable. What has changed? Essentially, little. The finger can be understood as a modified cylinder, one with a number of abrupt and fluid planar changes, but still conforming to a tapering, tubular core. The instructor's drawing is the one most likely to have benefited from a grasp of the subject's *essential* mass, upon which the variations—the major and secondary planes—can be modeled, the resulting forms overlapped and interjoined, and the firm and supple characteristics of the finger conveyed.

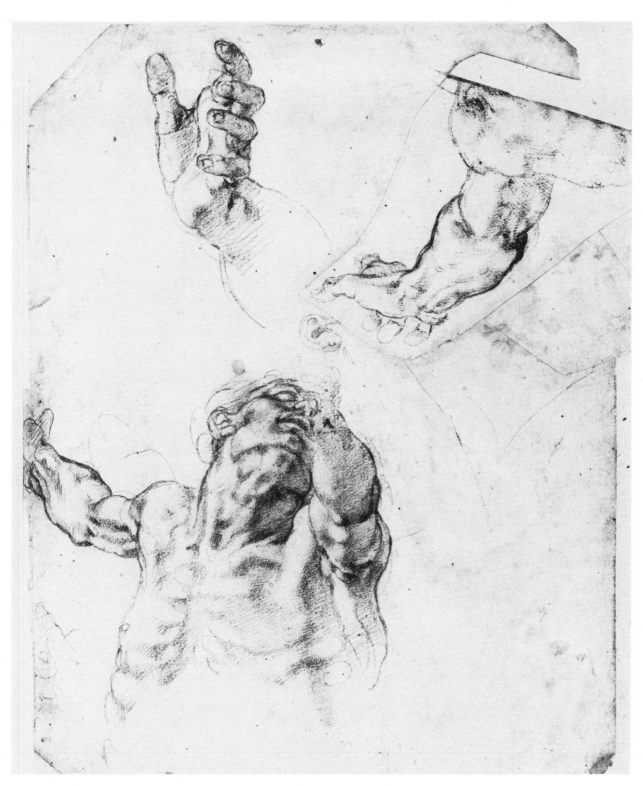

**Figure 2.37**
**MICHELANGELO BUONARROTI (1475–1564)**
*Studies for the Crucified Haman*
Black chalk. 33.3 x 22.7 cm.
*Teylers Museum, Haarlem.*

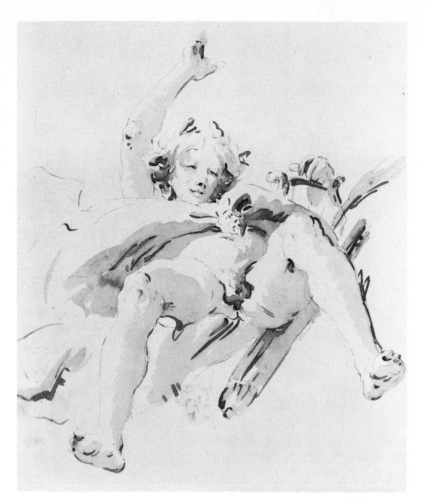

FIGURE 2.38
GIOVANNI BATTISTA TIEPOLO
(1696–1770)
*Apollo with Lyre and Quiver,*
*His Arm Upraised*
Pen and brown ink, brown wash
over black chalk. 8 5/8 x 7 1/4 in.
*The Pierpont Morgan Library, New York.*

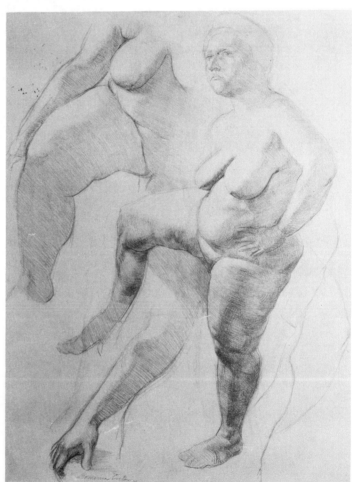

FIGURE 2.39
DOMENIC CRETARA (1946–    )
*Sheet of Studies of the Female Figure*
Red chalk on toned paper. 18 x 24 in.
*Collection of the author.*

62

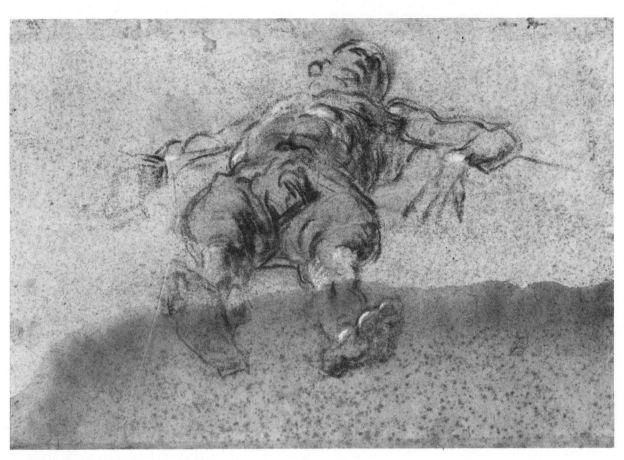

**FIGURE 2.40**
**JACOPO TINTORETTO** (1518–1594)
*Study of a Reclining Figure*
Charcoal, heightened with white on faded blue paper.
179 x 275 mm.
*The Art Institute of Chicago.*

**FIGURE 2.41**

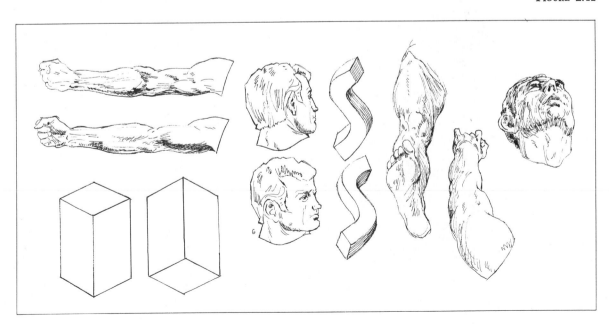

The instructor can call on another basic perceptual concept that serves structural interests. He or she knows that every volume has its definable limits—its outline, or *shape state*. By noting the shape-state of a foreshortened volume, one can more easily establish its position in space. The shape of a form—its silhouette—defines the form's position in space and conveys important clues about its structure; it represents a form's totally foreshortened planes, which is what edges are largely composed of. The beginner who means to draw the foreshortened leg but draws instead an overhead view has failed to observe the leg's shape in actuality. Forms in different positions may share a common shape, and the familiar forms of the figure will, in certain poses, offer very unfamiliar shapes (Figure 2.41). *The ability to comprehend the shape of a form or a plane as if it were a flat puzzle piece is an essential perceptual skill.*

## SEEING SHAPE, DIRECTION, AND EDGE

A helpful exercise for more objectively seeing parts as flat puzzle pieces is to hold a sheet of Plexiglas before you and, using a wax crayon, carefully trace upon it the outlines of the figure's forms, as in Figure 2.42. Such an experiment will underscore two important facts: (1) the outlines of most human forms, even when only moderately foreshortened, appear misshapen, and (2) most outlines of such forms are more complex, containing more subtle turnings, than you may have supposed.

A useful procedure for more objectively drawing the shape-state of any form or form-unit before you is what might be called *drawing in straight line segments*. All artists realize that the freely drawn gestural lines which usually begin a drawing, although necessary to establish the figure's essential rhythms, tensions, and moving energies, only weakly reflect the shape actualities of the figure's parts. To more accurately assess these shapes, many artists will then restate each shape's edges, restricting their drawing to straight lines only. They know that many poor shape judgments are hidden among the sweeping curves of the drawing's first lines, and that by translating a shape's curving edges into a series of straight line segments that collectively describe these curves, they can far more accurately define the shape's boundaries.

Such straight line drawing can be seen in Rubens's *Bathsheba Receiving David's Letter* (Figure 2.43). The mainly angular kind of lines on the left side, intended as an underdrawing, can be seen to underlie the rest of the drawing. Note especially the drawing of the originally intended position of Bathsheba's left leg. Angular edge drawing is of course a major factor in constructing the masses in Cambiaso's drawings (Figures 2.5 and 2.34), and in Papo's drawing (Figure 1.41). Picasso's *Study for the Painting, "Pipes of Pan"* (Figure 2.44) provides

**FIGURE 2.42**

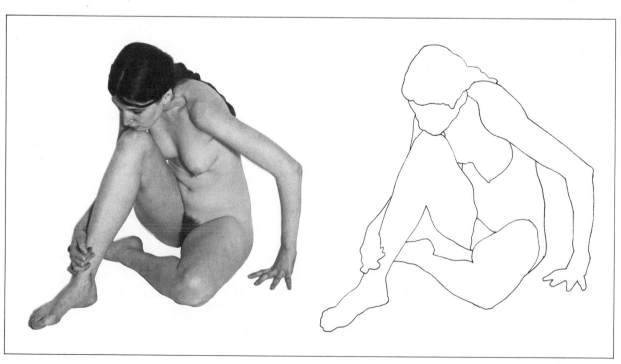

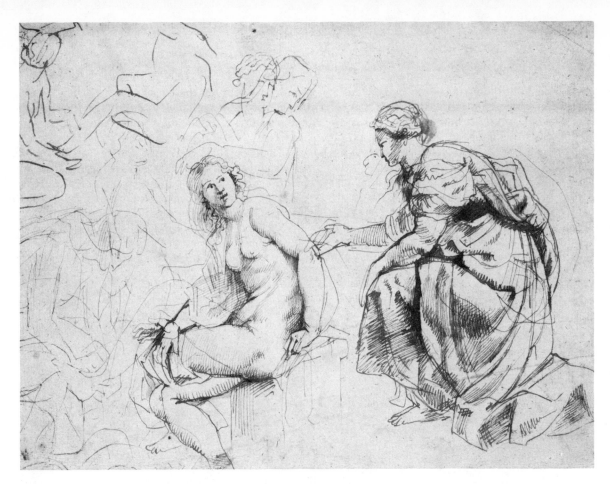

FIGURE 2.43
PETER PAUL RUBENS (1577–1640)
*Bathsheba Receiving David's Letter*
Pen and ink. 19.2 x 26.6 cm.
*Staatliche Museen Preussischer Kulturbesitz.*
*Kupferstichkabinett. West Berlin.*

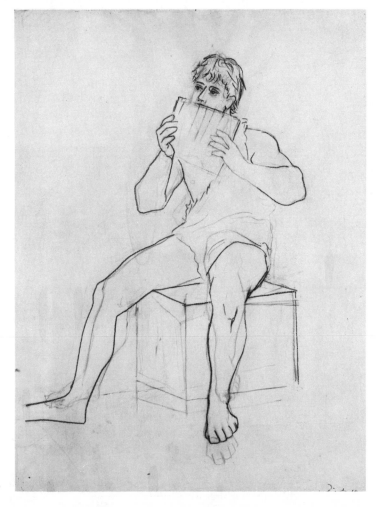

FIGURE 2.44
PABLO PICASSO (1881–1973)
*The Pipes of Pan*
Charcoal. 640 x 490 mm.
*The Art Institute of Chicago.*

a very clear demonstration of seeing curved edges as if they were composed of straight lines.

Even a simple, freely drawn curving line is almost impossible to duplicate *exactly* by again trying to freely draw it. Try it and you'll see. Restating such a line by first reducing it to the straight lines it can be broken down to, as in Figure 2.45a, will insure more accurate results. Once this is done, the lines can be reworked to soften the angles (b). Giacometti's drawing (Figure 1.41) shows this evolution from straight to curved edges.

His drawing also illustrates the point that the abutments between the figure's planes, when likewise treated in this angular way, more clearly define the figure's masses. Such abutments seldom occur with the clarity we find in Giacometti's or Papo's drawings. To see them we must search for the subtle ridges and crests that mark changes in the direction of the figure's surfaces. As with the outer contours, once the figure's inner contours have been noted, they can, if desired, be modified to any degree.

Such structurally lucid lines, in restating complex organic forms in simpler, more concrete terms, help us to better judge the location, relative scale,

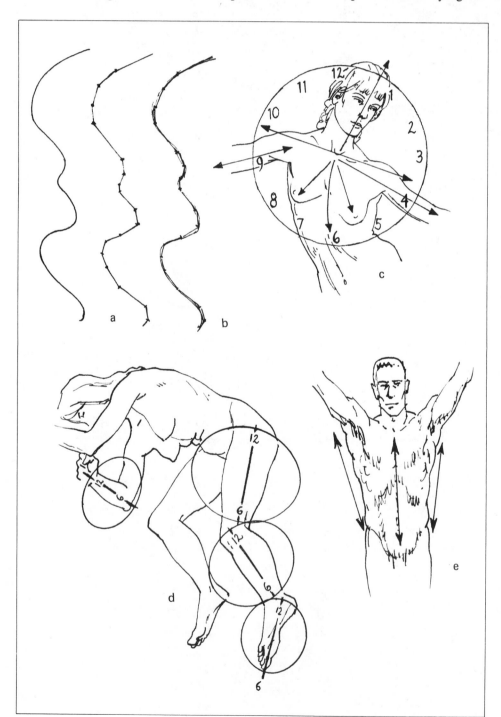

FIGURE 2.45

and design of the forms, as well as their constructional nature. Then too, these schematic, straight-line inquiries, in reducing forms to temporarily simpler states, create just those important lines of perspective that show how forms arrange themselves and recede in a spatial field. One of the most important (and first) responses to an observed (or envisioned) form is its direction in both two- and three-dimensional space. Unless we note the particular tilt of a part, and whether it advances toward us or recedes, we have overlooked the most fundamental fact of its existence in space.

A form's two-dimensional orientation is easily recognized by the simple device of imagining a clockface upon it. This helps us to judge whether an arm, head, torso, *or a segment of a form's edge* is at, say, two o'clock or three o'clock, as in Figure 2.45c. Analyzing a part's location in three-dimensional space can be done in the same way, provided we imagine the clockface to encircle the part at the angle that aligns the part's long axis with the line running from six to twelve o'clock, as in Figure 2.45d. When we are establishing these two- and three-dimensional directions, it is important to recognize the difference between the direction of a part's long axis and the several directions of that part's edges, for they may differ widely. For example, in contrast to the vertical long axis of a front view of an upright torso, its edges are inclined outward in a V-shaped manner, as in Figure 2.45e.

Related to these perspective considerations is a less evident but nevertheless important one, namely, the direction, or angle, at which cross-contour lines intersect a form in modeling it. A cross-contour line appearing at eye level will be seen as a straight line, as illustrated in Figure 2.46. Such a line will show little or nothing of a form's surface changes; in fact, it tends to deny them. However, lines drawn above and below it, because they occupy inclined planes (shown by dotted lines in our illustration) *are* form-revealing. Cross-contour lines, then, tell most about a form's volumetric nature when the direction in which they are drawn is at a right angle or at any oblique orientation to the direction of the form. This can be seen in Figure 2.43, where cross-contour lines strike the forms at various angles. The universality of this graphic strategy can be appreciated when we see the same process at work in a contemporary drawing (Figure 2.47). Notice that Bloom integrates form-realization and expressive intent by modeling the forms with lines that suggest wrinkles as well as mass. Indeed, Bloom's use of line, in showing the artist's sensitivity to anatomical and design considerations, shows a fine integration of all four factors of figure drawing.

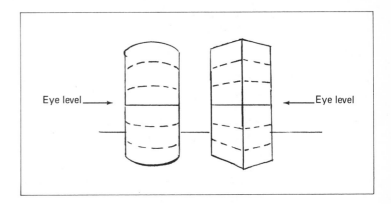

**FIGURE 2.46**

**FIGURE 2.47**
**HYMAN BLOOM** (1913–    )
*Nude Old Woman* (1945)
Brown crayon. 9 1/2 x 7 7/8 in.
*Grunwald Center for the Graphic Arts,*
*University of California, Los Angeles.*

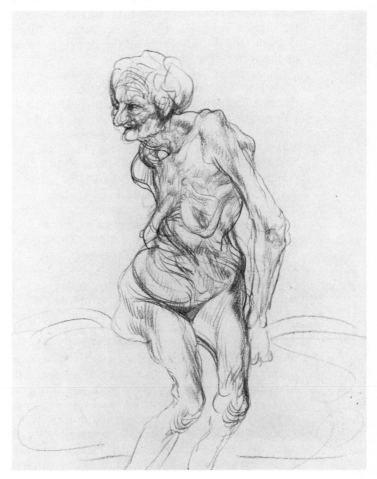

## STRUCTURAL ASPECTS
## OF THE DRAPED FIGURE
## AND ITS ENVIRONMENT

Most exponents of figure drawing convey in their works a sensitivity to the action and structural character of the anatomical forms beneath the drapery of the skin—the tensions, weight, rhythms, and masses of the bones, muscles, and fatty tissues that affect the figure's surface forms. The skin, then, can usefully be thought of as a kind of drapery. Tight-fitting for the most part, the skin still shows drapery-like folds and wrinkles and the taut and slack behavior of cloth, especially in older people (Figure 2.47). Most master figure drawings also suggest something of the general action and structural character of the figure beneath the drapery of clothed figures. In such drawings, the gestures and general structure of the limbs and torso are often clearly evident, even when the figure is voluminously draped, as in Rubens's drawing (Figure 2.43). Here there is little doubt about the position, weight, and robust character of the servant's forms. Not only does Rubens define the figure's action and structural essentials; in some areas, such as the servant's left upper arm and left leg, he actually "draws through" the drapery to reveal the general contours of the forms beneath.

Conversely, then, clothing can be thought of as a kind of loose second skin. And, like skin, it requires a firm armature to hold it up, yielding to the pull of gravity wherever it is free of support. Occasionally, drapery will be as taut as skin usually is. When this is the case, it will reveal almost as much about the forms it covers as skin does. Even a loose garment will reveal something about the nature of the forms beneath; for instance, in cases where forms interrupt the fall of a fold, or create folds where they press against the drapery, or in cases where the drapery clings to the top surfaces of forms. These conditions can be seen in Rubens's drawing (Figure 2.43) and in da Vinci's *Study of Drapery* (Figure 2.48).

Beginners should be as attentive to the ways in which drapery reveals the body's action and masses as they are to the ways in which the body's surfaces reveal deeper anatomical forms. This search for *the forms below* provides a useful basis for selecting among the many folds and creases in a subject's drapery. They can, as Rubens does, emphasize those folds that reveal the figure's gesture and form, and omit or subordinate those folds which obscure or confuse such actions and masses. Note that Rubens explains the drapery's intricate topography by the same means with which he models the servant's (and Bathsheba's) forms; namely, by reducing forms to

their major and secondary planes, by the direction of the hatchings upon the planes, and by clarifying the way form-units interconnect.

Every drawing teacher has seen student works in which an interest in structural analysis, design, perspective, and proportion diminished sharply when the student turned from drawing the figure's forms to drawing the drapery upon it. Often there is an even greater deterioration of inquiry and association—of visual involvement—when the student goes on to draw the indoor or outdoor matter surrounding the figure. These drawings reveal the student's declining interest in forms other than human ones. But it is fundamental to good figure drawing to recognize the structural and dynamic opportunities in drapery and in the masses and spaces that make up the figure's environment. Indeed, no creatively important sensitivity to the figure's architectural or expressive character is possible without a comparable sensitivity to these matters in all other forms in nature. Although we may prefer one kind of subject matter to another, until we can appreciate the visual potential of all kinds of subject matter we don't fully understand the possibilities of one in particular. Just as all forms can be reduced to simple geometric masses, so do they all suggest plastic, expressive energies. Genuine perceptual sensitivity can respond to virtually any combination of manmade or natural forms. As John Steinbeck observed, "Love is a chain of love."

An analysis of the folds in any draped material shows that they conform to a few characteristic masses and movements (Figure 2.49). Usually, a fold can be reduced to three planes: an ascending plane, a flat or curved top plane, and a descending plane (a). Sometimes the ascending and descending planes are overlapped by the top plane, as in (b). Sometimes the valleys separating folds are broad and flat, sometimes they are narrow and concave, as in (c). When the latter is the case, the folds appear to roll in a wavelike manner. Unless interrupted by other forms or folds, the folds will radiate from a point at which a form interrupts their fall (d). When drapery is held at two points, both sets of radiating folds will dovetail as the individual folds intercept each other (e). Tubular drapery, such as sleeves or pant legs, tends to fall in circular dovetail patterns, a series of zigzags, or in opposing V-shaped folds, as in (f). Occasionally, especially when the drapery is somewhat loose, Y-shaped folds will occur (g). When stretched tight, valleys may disappear as folds push together (h). When tubular drapery is bent, or when any material is "caught" in the bending of the figure's forms, folds rush away from the point of tension (i). All other fold arrangements are variants

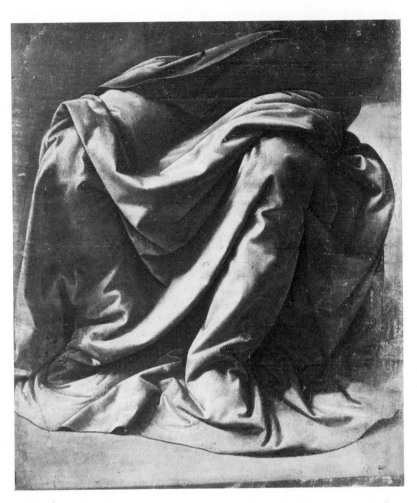

**Figure 2.48**
**LEONARDO DA VINCI (1452–1519)**
*Study of Drapery*
Brush, gray wash, heightened with white,
on linen. 26.5 x 23.3 cm.
*Cabinet des Dessins, Musée du Louvre,
Paris.*

**Figure 2.49**

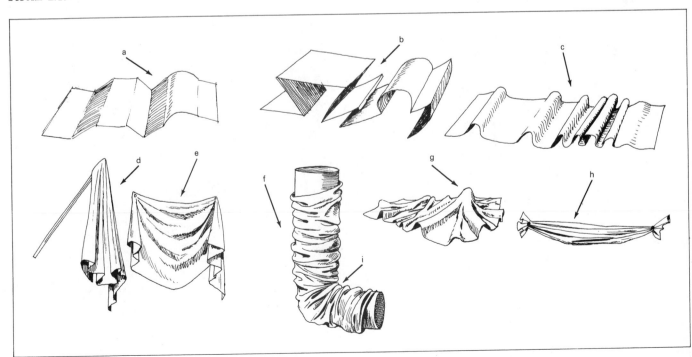

FIGURE 2.50
REMBRANDT VAN RIJN (1606–1669)
*St. Augustine in His Study*
Quill and reed pens and ink. 18.3 x 15 cm.
*Devonshire Collection, Chatsworth. Reproduced by
permission of the Trustees of the Chatsworth Settlement.*

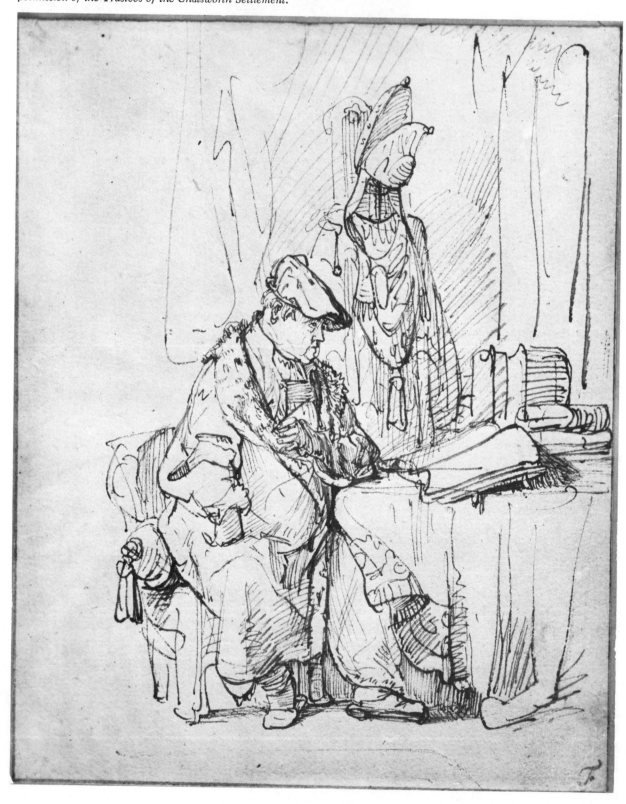

of the foregoing kinds, and the folds in soft materials such as silk will show more rhythmic, wavelike movements, while harder materials such as cotton will show a more angular, faceted behavior.

In master drawings, the folds, whether of silk, wool, *or* skin, reveal the artist's understanding of their structure, weight, and gestural character. Although the figure is often more fully drawn than some of the drapery and surrounding environment, in the best drawings nothing is drawn indifferently. Drawings that show a lessening of care to anything within their boundaries suffer a lessening of responsive involvement—of meaning. In the previous chapter it was noted that the best figure drawings hold to a point of view and to a consistent quality of response. Here it must be stressed that whatever the point of view, and even though some parts of a drawing may be more fully developed than other parts, the consistency of our inquiry and concern must extend to *everything* that constitutes our subject matter.

This is well illustrated by Rembrandt's *St. Augustine in His Study* (Figure 2.50). In addition to his remarkable grasp of the measurable matters of direction, shape, scale, and value, Rembrandt never fails to feel the structural forces and plastic energy of his subjects. Examining the animated interplay of *all* the forms in this drawing, we can appreciate Kenneth Clark's observation that "here was one of the most sensitive and accurate observers of fact who has ever lived, and one who, as time went on, could immediately find a graphic equivalent for everything he saw."*

Figure 2.50 serves as a useful visual summary of the main points we have been discussing in this chapter. Here we find a resolute constructing by major and secondary planes, the underlying geometric solids these planes suggest, a rich variety of

* Kenneth Clark, *Landscape into Art* (New York: Transatlantic Arts Inc., 1961), pp. 30–31.

**FIGURE 2.51**
NICOLAS POUSSIN (1594–1665)
*Bacchus and Ariadne*
Pen, bistre ink washes, on pinkish paper.
15.6 x 25 cm.
*Courtauld Institute of Art, London.*

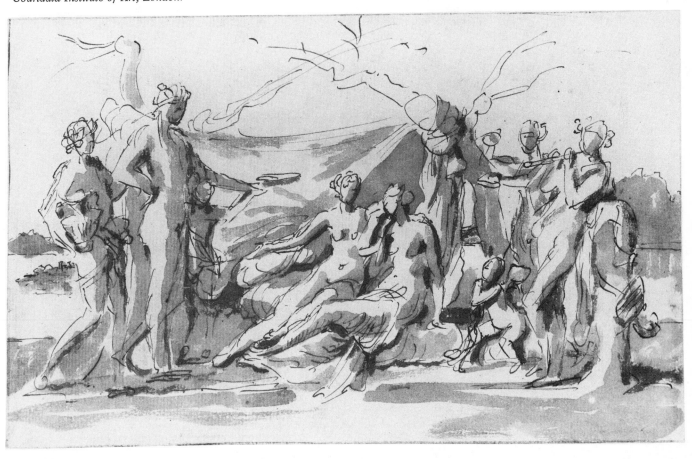

interjoinings, the sense of firm and fluid segments of form, convincing foreshortening, and clues to the figure's forms revealed by the drapery. Note the heavy, almost water-soaked character of the drapery. And, as this drawing so clearly shows, the term *drapery* can be extended to include such diverse items as hats, pillows, book pages, and, of course, skin. Rembrandt treats the vestments, tablecloth, chair, and robe with the same kind of inquiry and caring as he does the head and hands. Every form in this work is structurally lucid and all are depicted in a state of lively, complemental interplay. For Rembrandt, structural analysis is indeed a key to graphic invention.

Glancing at the drawings in this book, you notice that most of them depict little, if any, of a subject's immediate surroundings. Sometimes a few lines or tones suffice to suggest some masses and a sense of space. But even in the most abbreviated of statements about a figure's environment, the *quality*

of the artist's visual judgments does not waver. Artistic freedom does not include the right to disregard a consistency of involvement and intent. Again, this does not mean that each part of the drawing must be carried to the same degree of completion; drawings which do so are sometimes rather dull. It does mean that in drawing the figure's drapery and surroundings, a single kind and quality of interpretation should be discernible despite differences in the degree of emphasis. Degrees of completion and even of clarity may vary, but concentration and caring may not.

Poussin's *Bacchus and Ariadne* (Figure 2.51) and Millet's *The Diggers* (Figure 2.52) illustrate two very different but consistently held attitudes toward structure. Poussin's brief sketch probes the harmonious design possibilities of the subject's major masses. Here, the structural factor serves a lyrical visual idea. But for Millet the weighty substantiality of the draped figures, of their shovels, and of the

FIGURE 2.52
JEAN-FRANÇOIS MILLET (1814–1875)
*The Diggers*
Etching. 9 3/8 x 13 1/4 in.
*S.P. Avery collection.*
*Prints Division, The New York Public Library.*
*Astor, Lenox and Tilden Foundations.*

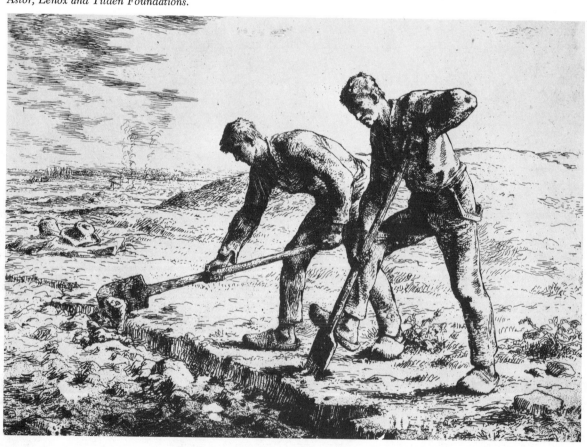

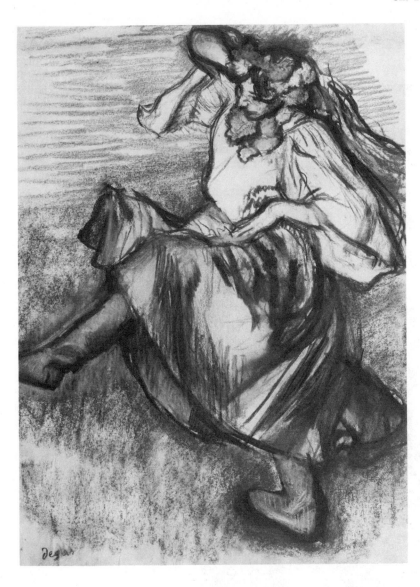

FIGURE 2.53
EDGAR DEGAS (1834–1917)
*Russian Dancer*
Pastel. 24 3/8 x 18 in.
*The Metropolitan Museum of Art,*
*New York.*
*Bequest of Mrs. H. O. Havemeyer,*
*1929.*

earth itself is a dominant theme. And the way both artists go about calling out these differing qualities is instructive. In Poussin's drawing, planes and masses are airy, open, and flowing; in Millet's, they are firm, enclosed, and deliberate. Poussin's lines are animated, the tonal changes are gentle and in flux; Millet's lines are short jabs, the tones fixed and boldly contrasting.

Note how differently they treat the drapery. For Poussin the flowing drapery serves as a means of connecting groups of figures; its graceful sweeps embrace the entire configuration decoratively. For Millet the drapery is coarse and volume-revealing; it tells about the forms it covers and of its own density and weight.

In drawing drapery, artists often suggest the differences in the weight and texture of different fabrics. Each material has its own structural character;

all fold in different ways. Each has its own style of accommodating itself to the forms it covers. Depending on the type of material, the snug or loose fit, and the figure's action, the drapery can be an important expressive tool. In Degas' *Russian Dancer* (Figure 2.53), the dancer's animated movements are intensified, not obscured, by the drapery's actions. Note that Degas makes a relative distinction in the weight and texture of the blouse, the heavier skirt, and the leather boots. Observe also that hair, as Degas shows, has a draperylike behavior. Sometimes, as in de Gheyn's *The Bird Catcher* (Figure 2.54), the drapery carries virtually the **entire** responsibility for presenting the figure. Although only one arm is bare and the blouse and trousers fit loosely, we sense the body's forms and can tell that the figure is an adult, powerfully built male.

Perhaps the most imposing truth about the figure is its vital substantiality—its presence as a living organism. This appreciation of the figure's spirit and substance has motivated the search for structural truths in realistic imagery, and has provided an avenue of approach for more subjective graphic inventions. An outstanding example is the *Study for Sculpture* by Henry Moore (Figure 2.56). If extracting the structural essentials from the live or imagined model is a kind of abstracting, so is our transposing of these essentials into lines, tones, and textures on a flat surface. Abstraction, it seems, is at the heart of any work of art. The best exponents of figure drawing are the most adept at recognizing the simultaneity of their marks as referring to both physical facts and to the abstract activities that give human forms a living presence.

We have seen how structural considerations, in addition to clarifying volume and space, serve to stimulate the dynamic activities that enliven the

FIGURE 2.54
JACOB DE GHEYN II (1565–1629)
*The Bird Catcher*
Pen and brown ink on gray paper. 16.5 x 13 cm.
*Museum Boymans-van Beuningen, Rotterdam.*

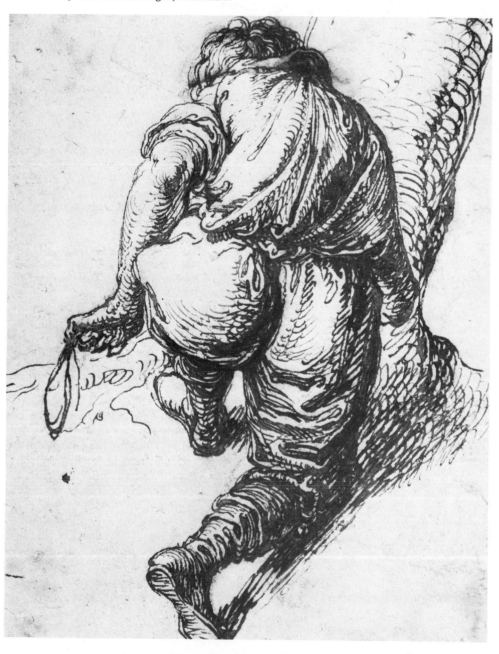

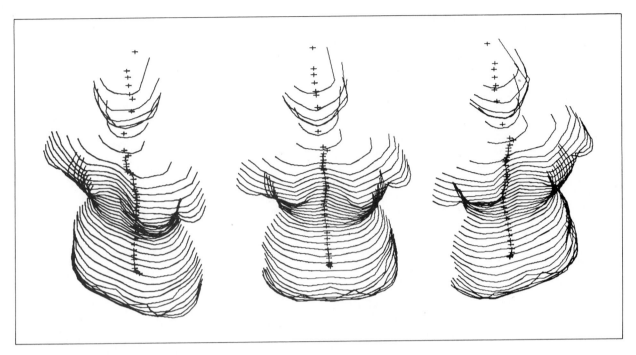

**FIGURE 2.55**
**DR. R. E. HERRON**
*Three Back Views of a Seated Female Figure*
Computer drawing.
*Courtesy, Texas Institute for Rehabilitation and Research,*
*The Texas Medical Center, Houston.*

forms we draw. Thus, in this chapter, we have come by way of the structural factor in figure drawing to one of the most important themes of Chapter One, namely, that the best figure drawings are not *re*-presentations, but *equivalent presentations:* graphic organisms that parallel living figures by coming alive *in their own terms.* An interest in the structural nature of one's subject is the perfect antidote to a fussy concern with surface details and a visually logical pursuit; we cannot begin to communicate a subject's volumetric state until we understand it. Unless such understanding occurs, superficial details are all one *sees.* But figure drawings that are living graphic organisms emerge from felt perceptions of a subject's structural and dynamic truths, and not from a scrutiny of surfaces. As Henri Matisse put it, "Exactitude is not truth."*

* From an article by Matisse in the Philadelphia Museum of Art Exhibition Catalogue, 3 April–9 May, 1948, pp. 33–34.

## SUGGESTED EXERCISES

The following exercises can be done in any order and may be adjusted to suit your own needs and curiosities. When an exercise calls for more than one drawing, try to vary the time you spend on each from a minimum of twenty minutes to a maximum of one hour. Use any medium and suitable surface, but avoid the harder graphite (lead) pencils, which promote timidity and tight handling. As you do these drawings, try several combinations of materials and vary the sizes of your works. However, avoid making very small-scale drawings. Little drawings tend toward cautious handling and are usually more difficult to control by virtue of their smallness. A useful range for these drawings is between 10″ × 14″ and 18″ × 24″.

1. Make three drawings of your hand. In the first, limit the drawing to simple geometric forms such as the block and the cylinder. Show how these forms fit together in a simple, manikinlike manner. In the second drawing, analyze the forms of your hand for the major and secondary planes, relying mainly on line, and emphasizing straight-line segment drawing

wherever strong curves are found. Where it becomes necessary to use tonalities to clarify various overlappings, use cross-contour or hatched lines that ride upon the flat or curved planes in directions that convey the angle—the tilt—of the planes. Emphasize the various interjoinings of forms by trying to see how the form units come together. In the third exercise, draw your *gloved* (or mittened) hand, stressing the tensions in the fabric produced by the hand's position. Emphasize the larger masses and actions of your covered hand. This should be the most fully realized drawing of the three, but avoid fussy rendering of textures and surface details. Instead, tell more about the larger forms of the drapery and about the forms they cover. Imagine that a sculptor will use your third drawing as a guide for a piece of sculpture. Ask yourself whether or not he could "read" every passage of the terrain in your drawing.

2. Rework or redraw several of your figure drawings to show a bold summarizing of planes, forms, and form units. Stress simple form-solutions and simple interjoinings, in the general manner of Figures 1.41, 2.17, and 2.34. Emphasize flat and curved planes; at the edges, only straight and simple, C-curved lines. This emphasis on straights and C-curves promotes decision making based on your analysis of the essential nature of each plane, form, and edge segment. Such drawings are often admirably resolute; they show the strength and authority we associate with affirmative choices—even when they are wrong! Imagine a light source falling on the forms and simplify the drawing's tones to three values: the white of the page, a light gray, and a dark gray. But use values sparingly, only where you feel they will help clarify volume and space. In doing so, avoid hard, "cut out" shapes of tone. Instead, apply them freely and keep them open-edged, loose.

3. Draw several imaginary figures in action, in the manner of Cambiaso (Figures 2.1, 2.5, and 2.34). Your drawing should reflect Cambiaso's bold analytical attitude, rather than his particular technique of drawing.

4. Rework or redraw several of your life drawings in the ovoid manner of Tintoretto's drawing (Figure 2.20). Again, concentrate on the artist's method of analysis, not on his style of drawing. Referring to the anatomical illustrations in Chapters Three and Four will help you to restate the forms of your drawings in this way.

5. Using Figure 2.28 as a guide or point of departure, devise your own manikinlike system of simple forms and redraw several of your life drawings using these forms to help reshape and clarify the basic character of the figure's masses. Continue with these drawings, working tonally, developing their manikinlike forms into more human ones. Referring to the anatomical illustrations in Chapters Three and Four will help to develop a system of simple forms, and will help you to carry them further.

6. Using the manikin system you have devised in Exercise 5, invent several line drawings that show your figures in various severely foreshortened positions. Select one of these views and carry it further, using three values and absorbing the manikin forms into the developing figure-forms.

7. Again using the manikin forms developed in Exercise 5, make several line drawings of imagined figures in various standing and seated poses. Use line sparingly and lightly. When these drawings are fairly well realized, draw simply draped clothing over them. Assume the drapery to be made of a rather heavy, limp material that will produce large but simple folds. You will find that drawing the folds of the drapery will lead you to rely more on values. This is because it is difficult to show the gradual inclination of a curved plane by line alone. Again, select a light source, modeling with three values, but develop these values by hatchings that move upon the form, rather than by smudges of tone.

8. Using the Ingres drawing (Figure 2.18) as your subject, redraw it three times: first, as if you were positioned high up and saw the figures far below you; second, as if you were lying on the ground *just in front* of the two figures; and third, as if you were standing in a position somewhat to one side of the figures, where one figure slightly overlaps the other. In all three drawings the forms can be reduced to somewhat more simplified masses.

FIGURE 2.56
HENRY MOORE (1898–    )
*Study for sculpture "Madonna and Child"*
Grease crayon, touches of pen, gray wash background on white paper. 9 x 7 in.
*Courtesy The Fogg Art Museum, Harvard University. Gift of Meta and Paul J. Sachs.*

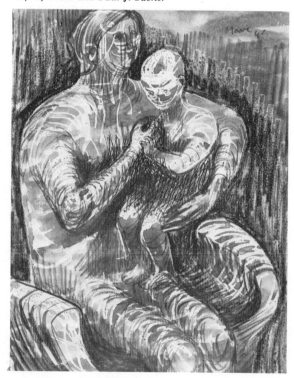

9. Make several line drawings from the live model. Begin to draw with a Giacometti-like search for the direction of parts, their shape, and their major planar character (Figure 1.41), developing each drawing to a point that conveys the figure's *general* structural character. Avoid using line in a bold, dark manner here, as you will work over this stage of the drawing. Still using line, proceed by drawing, in fewer, more continuous lines, across the forms with cross-contour lines that move in various directions. For example, cross-contour lines may be drawn downward from the top of the head to the chin, neck, or even down the chest to the toes; across the chest, or obliquely upon an arm or leg. Another example of computer drawing (Figure 2.55) shows one method by which you can investigate the changing nature of the subject's surface. Here, the figure's surface structure is revealed by cross-section contours that bisect the figure at fixed intervals. As noted earlier, when such lines are drawn upon flat or curved planes turned away from a light source and omitted on planes that face the light, a sense of form *and* illumination emerges, as in Figures 2.19, 2.24, and 2.25. Imagine the cross-contour lines you draw to be produced by an ink-soaked insect who leaves a trail that discloses the hills and valleys of the figure's changing terrain. Now, too, you should restate the figure's outlines in this more tactile frame of mind. Continue drawing in a manner that regards the Giacometti phase of the work to be a kind of scaffold that is now being draped with the heavier, supple forms that characterize a drawing by Rubens (Figures 1.20, 1.39, 2.43). Finally, model the forms further by suggesting a light source, in the mode described above.

10. Using Rembrandt's *St. Augustine in His Study* (Figure 2.50) as a general guide, draw an observed view of a draped figure in an interior. Try to give the sense of firm and fluid masses that show strong rhythmic and tensional behavior. Give the sense of drapery's limp and clinging character to any materials or objects that permit such an interpretation. In so doing, do not lose sight of the need to grasp the essential structural character of *all* the forms, as well as the direction, shape, scale, and location of each.

11. Redraw Poussin's *Bacchus and Ariadne* (Figure 2.51) in the general manner of Millett's *The Diggers* (Figure 2.52); and redraw the Millet etching in the general manner of the Poussin drawing. You may not be able to decipher all of the planes and forms in the Poussin, and should make any changes you wish.

12. Draw a life-size self-portrait that emphasizes the planar nature of your facial forms, as in Figure 2.16, but develop the forms by hatchings and cross-contour modeling that run in the direction of each plane's long or short axis, as in Figures 2.4, 2.12, and 2.29.

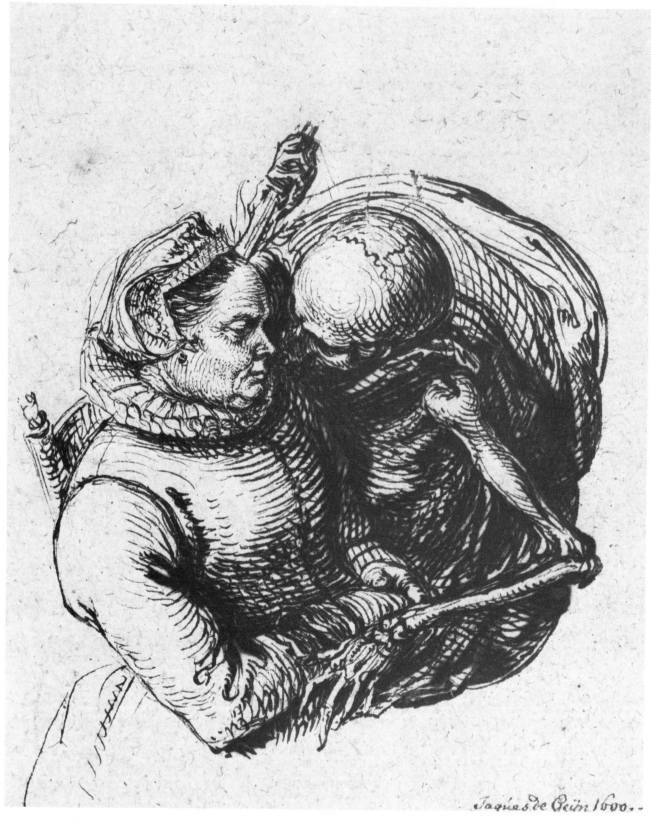

Jaques de Gein 1600.

**FIGURE 3.1**
**JACOB DE GHEYN II** (1565–1629)
*Allegory of Death*
Pen and ink on gray paper. 16 x 13 cm.
*Rijksmuseum, Amsterdam.*

# THREE

# THE

# ANATOMICAL

# FACTOR

*Part One: The Skeleton*

## SOME GENERAL OBSERVATIONS

In the previous chapter we saw that structural considerations uncover the essential nature of the figure's masses. Here, we will see how anatomical factors explain the inner forms and forces that shape them. The ability to analyze the figure's structure is greatly affected by a knowledge of artistic anatomy (a far simpler study than medical anatomy). Students who disregard the study of anatomy restrict their drawing to a kind of rote recording of bumps and hollows they don't really understand. Without basic anatomical information they lack the means to select from or alter what they see. They can neither experience nor endow their drawings with the expressive authority that all good exponents of figure drawing enjoy.

No one can say just how much structural analysis is sufficient for good figure drawing, nor prescribe how large or small a part anatomical considerations should play. The role of these interacting factors is of course determined by our perceptual, temperamental, and creative interests. But because both fac-

tors must participate in forming images that come alive, both must be well understood by the art student. It is no accident that the best figure drawings show a strong working knowledge of anatomy.

In this chapter and the next we will examine those anatomical facts of most importance to the artist. But we will do so in a rather unorthodox way. The approach to anatomical matters we take here is an attempt to bridge the often troublesome gaps between the clinically precise anatomy text, the living model, and the demands of creative figure drawing.

Too often art students are unable to apply their knowledge of anatomy to the living individual before them. Most anatomical illustrations are dispassionate diagrams of the human mechanism. Their precision is needed to pinpoint articulations, insertions, and so on. Such illustrations are not intended to convey the living spirit of human forms or to suggest anatomy's creative potential. There have been notable exceptions. Many of da Vinci's anatomical drawings suggest the figure's provocative dynamics. For example, in his muscle study, *Myology*

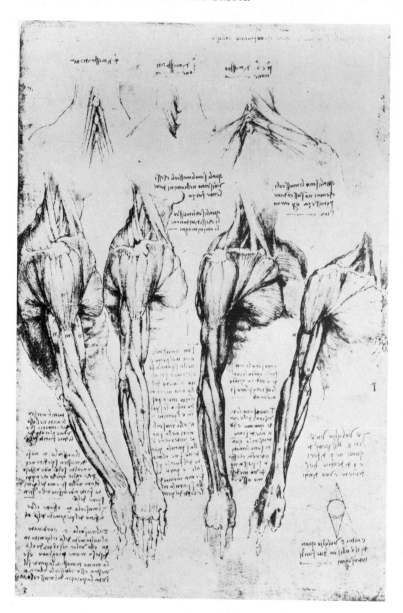

FIGURE 3.2
**LEONARDO DA VINCI** (1452–1519)
*Myology of Shoulder Region*
Black chalk. 29 x 19 cm.
*Windsor Castle, Royal Library.*
*By gracious permission*
*of Her Majesty the Queen.*

*of the Shoulder Region* (Figure 3.2), we sense da Vinci's response to visual and expressive energies as well as to the anatomical aspects of the forms. But most contemporary anatomy texts do not attempt more than an accurate and concise presentation of the figure's mechanical facts. The best of these texts* are indispensable sources of much useful information, but they do not discuss the role this information may play in figure drawing. The student is still left wondering for what purposes and to what degree such knowledge is to be used, and how a knowledge of anatomy is to aid in expressing the figure's energies, tensions, vitality, and character.

* For a listing of anatomy texts, see the bibliography.

May anatomical facts be intentionally ignored or altered? Should the student clarify or exaggerate bones and muscles that the figure only hints at? Will a concern with anatomical detail intrude on a drawing's design or mood, or may it assist these considerations? In what ways can anatomy play a part in a drawing's visually expressive life—its dynamics? In not addressing these important questions the traditional anatomy book unintentionally presents a danger for the student: it implies that anatomical clarity and accuracy are "responsibilities" of the artist, are artistic goals. Although specific anatomical facts are important, they can be intimidating. Some students feel their creativity stifled by the demands that anatomical accuracy imposes. In studying from a text exclusively concerned with scientific anatomical facts, the student often becomes self-conscious about making any changes. Then, too, a concentration on precise visual data strikes many students as dry, remote from the pulsating and provocative people before them. Their initial, intuitive grasp of the figure's dynamics seems not to fit the facts, seems not to be a part of the figure at all. But when such material is integrated with examples of anatomy's possibilities as a source of creative invention, as a tool and servant of interpretive interests, students can more effectively pursue their study of this vital information.

Our purpose in this and the following chapter, then, is twofold: to examine the more important aspects of the figure's skeletal and muscular systems, and to consider some ways in which a knowledge of anatomy can benefit our perceptual understanding of the figure and serve our creative interests.

## THE SKELETON

If the beginner in life drawing regards the skeleton at all, it is probably at those places in the figure where it presses against the surface, markedly affecting the terrain. Even then, such passages are only tolerated as complicating, lumpy interruptions of the otherwise smooth-flowing forms. They disconcert the student, who knows they represent parts of masses beneath the skin, but has no way of knowing their form, function, scale, or, consequently, their representational or expressive importance.

But the master figure artist welcomes this evidence of the skeleton throughout the figure. He or she realizes the structural importance of the skeleton as both an armature and a protective container for the figure's muscles and organs. Its armaturelike nature aids the artist's understanding of a figure's gestures as well as its proportions; its large, container-like forms helps in establishing the major masses of the head and torso. The skeleton's influence on the figure's forms helps the artist understand the pressures, weights, and tensions acting from within on the figure's container of skin. In some passages, such as the shoulders or hips, the planar character of various bones helps the artist to better understand the interjoinings of various surface form-units. Additionally, the recurring presence of hard skeletal forms at the surface helps to explain the skeleton's role as a firm scaffold for the supple drapery of the figure's softer tissues. Such passages, of a more angular nature, serve as visual counterpoints to the figure's more rounded masses, as in Figure 3.4, where we see a pattern of "hard and soft" areas that serve both structural and plastic goals.

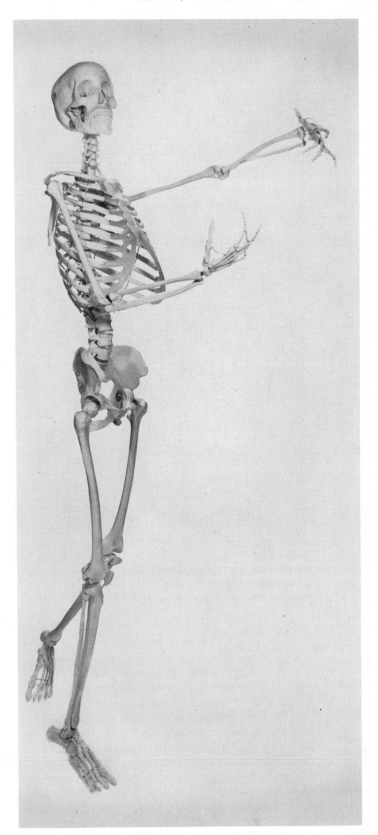

Figure 3.3

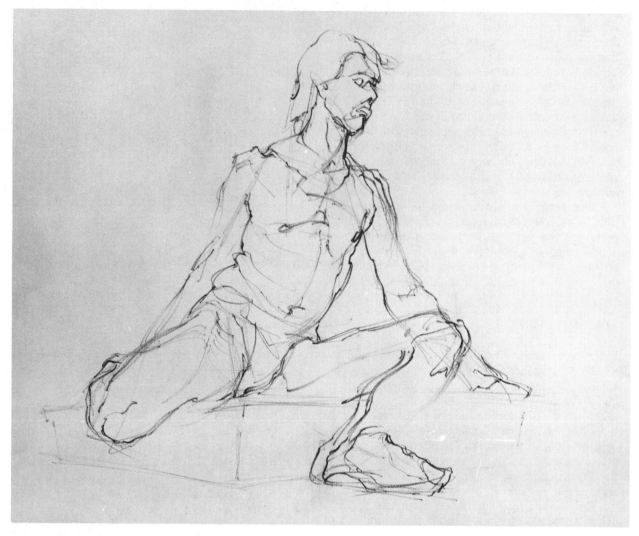

**FIGURE 3.4**
**ALEX McKIBBIN** (1940–    )
*Male Figure, Seated*
Black chalk. Courtesy of the artist.

Knowing it is the skeleton, more than the muscles, that accounts for a figure's stance (Figures 3.4, 3.61, and 3.62) and reveals the directions and lengths of its parts in a stick figure manner, is important in analyzing the pose before us, or in constructing one from our imagination (Figure 3.5). And knowing something about the form and purpose of the bony masses beneath the figure's surfaces, particularly in those passages where they are much in evidence, is important in giving our drawings the ring of truth. The skeleton contributes greatly to the figure's unique rhythms, its allover pattern of firm and supple passages, its interwoven qualities of power and pliancy.

## THE SKULL

The skull consists of twenty-two bones, most of them in pairs (Figure 3.6). All but the jawbone, or *mandible,* are connected to each other by suture (dovetailed) joinings. For the artist, the skull is best regarded as composed of two major masses: the ovoid brain case, or *cranium,* consisting of eight bones, and the blocklike formation constituted by the fourteen facial bones. Six of the cranial bones are of structural importance: the *frontal,* the two *parietals,* the two *temporals,* and the *occipital.* The *sphenoid,* located mainly on the underside of the cranium, is of some interest only at the temples, where it appears to be an extension of the temporal bone. Of the fourteen facial bones, only the two *zygomatics,* the two *maxillae,* the two *nasal,* and the already mentioned *mandible* are of visual and structural importance.

Several planes and masses of particular importance in the front view are: the convex plane of the frontal bone (forehead); the small, inclined planes of the nasal bones, forming a short base for the projecting cartilage underlying the nose; the blocky masses of the zygomatic, or cheek bones, forming pronounced overhanging ledges; the curved and for-

ward tilting plane of the maxilla, or upper jaw; and the squared-off "horseshoe" of the mandible. Also important are the ridges of the downward sloping and rather squarish eye sockets, which, in the living model, are in evidence both above and below the eye. Other landmarks often visible in the fleshed forms are the *superciliary ridge,* a slight thickening in the outer, upper corner of the eye socket; that segment of its lower ridge alongside the nasal bone; and the *canine fossa,* a shallow depression below the eye socket, often quite pronounced in lean-faced individuals (Figure 3.7a).

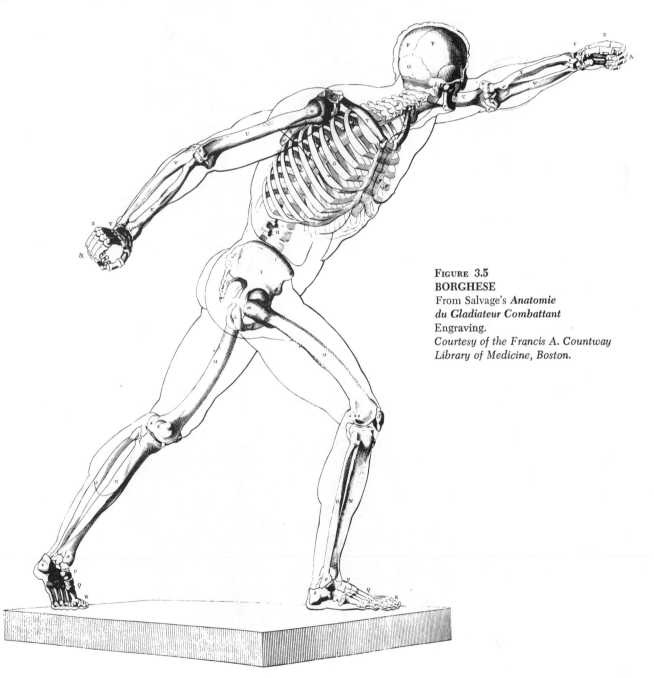

FIGURE 3.5
BORGHESE
From Salvage's *Anatomie du Gladiateur Combattant*
Engraving.
*Courtesy of the Francis A. Countway Library of Medicine, Boston.*

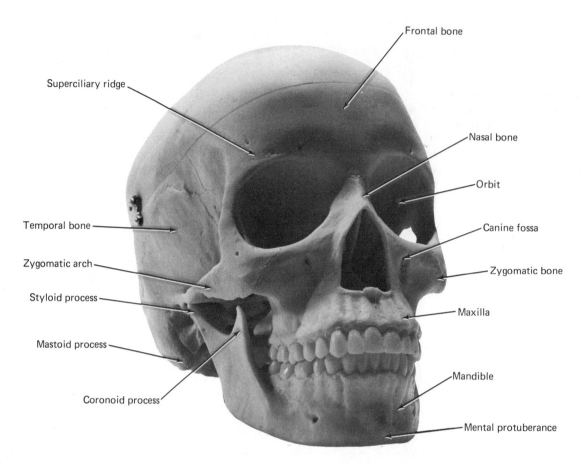

Figure 3.6

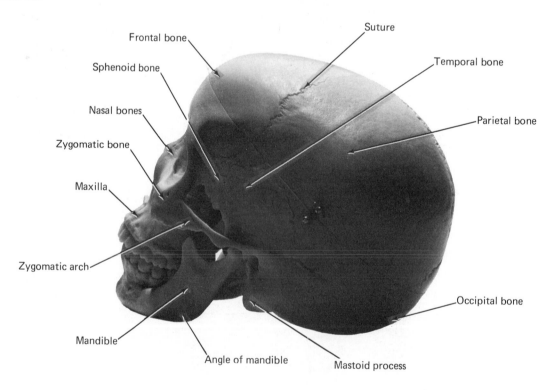

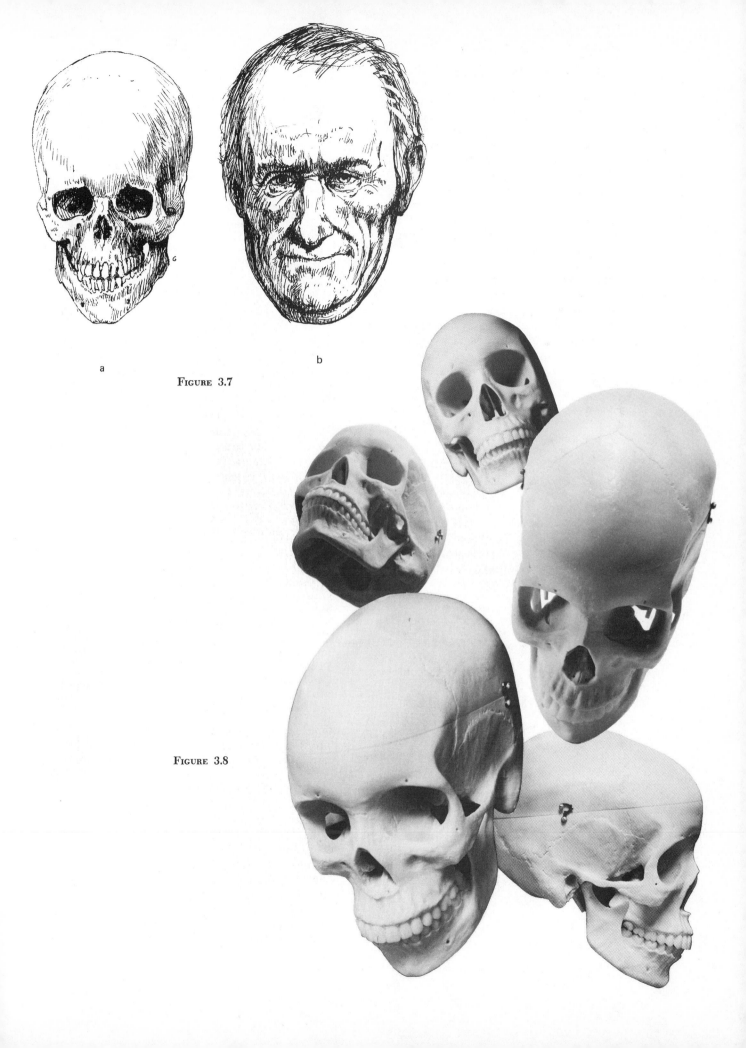

a       b

FIGURE 3.7

FIGURE 3.8

From the side view, the contour of the cranium is accounted for by the frontal, parietal, and occipital bones. The shallow indents of the temporal and sphenoid bones (temples), when overlaid by muscle, produce the rather flat planes of the side of the head. Below the temporal bone and joined with the outer ridge of the eye socket, a horizontal ridge of bone called the *zygomatic arch* connects the temporal to the zygomatic bone. In this view, too, the forward thrust of the maxilla and the angular nature of the mandible, the one moving bone of the skull, are substantial influences on the living forms. Note that the occipital bone extends backward somewhat, and that the *mastoid process* provides a small protuberance.

Understanding the skull's basic structure is essential in constructing the head in its various posi-

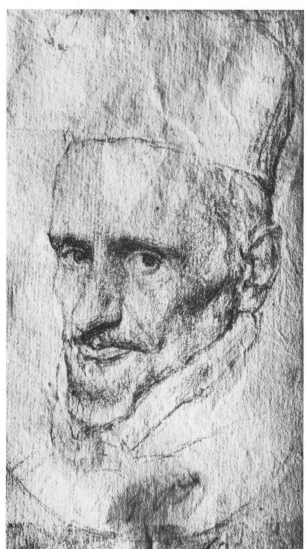

FIGURE 3.9
**LLOYD LILLIE** (1932–    )
*Study of a Woman's Head*
Pencil. 9 x 12 in.
*Courtesy of the artist.*

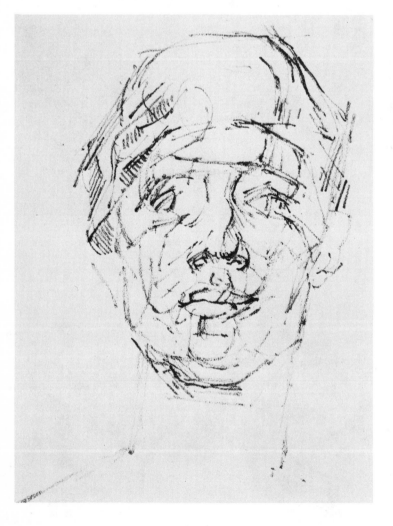

FIGURE 3.10
**DIEGO VELASQUEZ** (1599–1660)
*Cardinal Borgia*
Chalk.
*Real Academia de Bellas Artes de San Fernando, Madrid.*

tions (Figure 3.8). Unlike the limbs or the torso, which are more heavily overlaid by muscular and fatty tissues, the skull, even in heavily fleshed heads, exerts a strong influence on the surface forms (Figure 3.7b). This is particularly true of the cranium's mass, whose egglike form is always evident, whether the head is viewed from the front, side, or top. In Lillie's *Study of a Woman's Head* (Figure 3.9), the artist's appreciation of the skull's effect on the living forms is felt in the strong linear rhythms created by lines "chasing" each other along ridges and valleys, and in the rugged carving and interjoining of form-units. Note the downward tilt of the eye sockets, and of the underlying presence of the zygomatic, nasal, and maxilla bones. Note, too, the influence of the angular mandible on the drawing of the jaw. Here the factors of structure and anatomy are energetically interrelated by an animated line quality that suggests a strong and vibrant individual.

Again, in Velasquez's *Cardinal Borgia* (Figure 3.10), there is a convincing presence of a skull underlying the surface forms. In this preparatory sketch (one of the two or three drawings known to be by the hand of the great Spanish master) we can easily trace many of the cranial and facial bones. Note how clearly Velasquez defines the zygomatic bone and ridge, the superciliary ridge, and the overhanging ledge of the frontal bone.

## THE SPINAL COLUMN

The spinal column, comprised of twenty-four movable vertebrae and two immobile segments—the *sacrum* and *coccyx*—connects the three large, bony masses of the skeleton: the skull, rib cage, and pelvis. The vertebral column emerges from its base in the pelvis and, tapering as it rises, undergoes four curves along its route to the base of the skull. The four curves, as can be seen in Figures 3.11, 3.12, and 3.13, are convex in the seven *cervical* vertebrae, concave in the twelve *thoracic* vertebrae, convex in the five *lumbar* vertebrae, and concave in the sacrum and coccyx.

Although the spine represents the central axis of the torso, and tall columns of deep muscle flank it on either side, making a deep, vertical valley all along the back, its presence at the surface is intermittent and not often pronounced. The central spurs of the spinal column (Figures 3.11, 3.12, and 3.13) protrude mainly at the base of the neck, at the upper part of the thoracic region, and, when the back is bent, as in stooping, throughout the lumbar region. In most poses the *sacral triangle,* a flattish, dimpled area marking the location of the sacrum, is clearly evident.

Because the spinal column connects the skeleton's large masses, major pivotal or bending movements of this moderately flexible chain of vertebrae can occur only between these masses. Thus, the large bony masses are moved by the movements of the vertebrae between them. Movements of the head are initiated in the cervical vertebrae, and movements of the thorax and pelvis, in the lumbar vertebrae. The first and second cervical vertebra, the *atlas* and *axis* respectively, because of their special construction, allow for rotating and pivoting movements of the head (Figure 3.13). The spine's construction, in addition to its rotating and bending actions between the large masses, also allows for a slight curving of the thoracic vertebrae in extreme bending of the rib cage to the side.

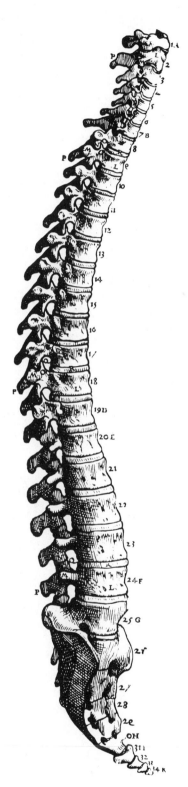

**FIGURE 3.11**
**ANDREAS VESALIUS (1514–1564)**
Plate 10 from *De humani corporis fabrica,* Book I
Engraving.
*Courtesy of the New York Academy of Medicine.*

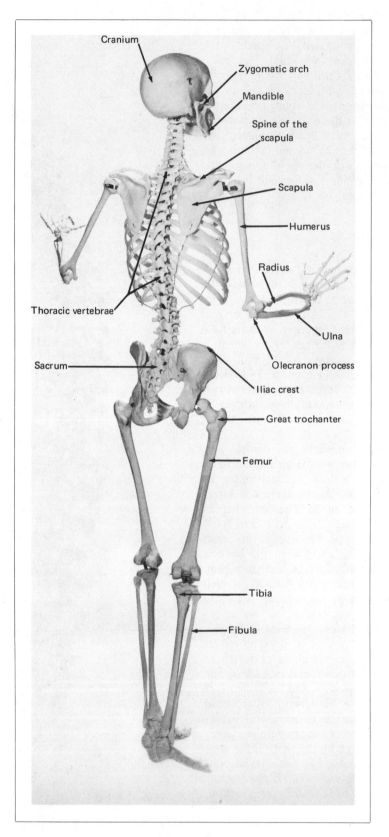

Figure 3.12

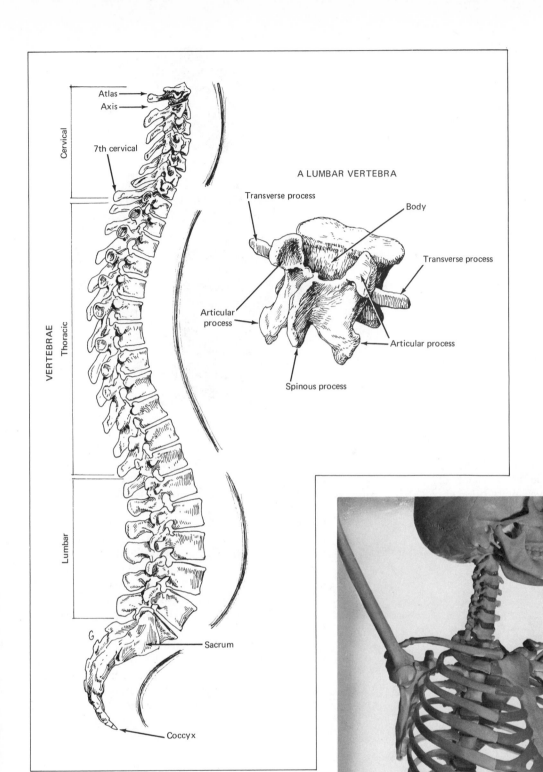

Atlas

Axis

Cervical

7th cervical

VERTEBRAE

Thoracic

Lumbar

Sacrum

Coccyx

A LUMBAR VERTEBRA

Transverse process

Body

Transverse process

Articular process

Articular process

Spinous process

FIGURE 3.13

FIGURE 3.14

## THE RIB CAGE

Like an egg, small end up and somewhat wider in the front than in the side view, the thoracic cage is composed of twelve pairs of ribs, the twelve thoracic vertebrae with which the ribs articulate, and the *sternum,* or breast bone (Figure 3.14). The ribs swing downward and out from either side of the vertebral column for a short distance, then turn sharply to curve toward the front, still turned downward. At no point do the ribs themselves turn upward toward the sternum bone; their upward "homing in" on the sternum is completed by extensions of cartilage, as shown in Figure 3.14.

Counting downward, the eighth rib marks the widest point of the rib cage from the front view. Because in the back view the sharp forward turn of the ribs occurs at about the same point in each rib, there is a discernible change in the direction of the ribs along a slightly curved vertical line. These lines, marking the abrupt change in the large planes of the back, are called the angles of the ribs. With the arms at rest, the medial (inner) edge of the *scapula* (shoulder blade) falls into a rough alignment with this angle (Figure 3.15). The resulting flattish construction of the back of the rib cage, still evident in the fleshed figure, is unique to humans and accounts for our ability to lie flat on our backs.

The upper seven pairs of ribs, called *true ribs,* are each directly attached to the sternum by individ-

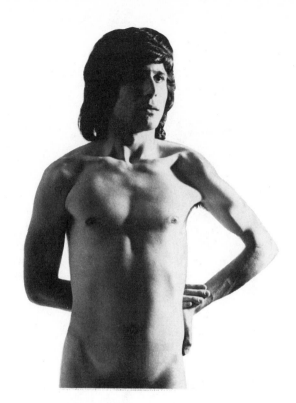

FIGURE 3.16

ual straps of costal cartilage. Of the lower five pair, called *false ribs,* the cartilaginous straps of the eighth, ninth, and tenth ribs all join to form a common, thick band that connects to the lowest part of the sternum. The resulting thick rim of cartilage forms a V-shaped opening (wider in the male torso) in the lower half of the rib cage, called the *thoracic arch,* a frequently pronounced landmark in the fleshed figure (Figure 3.16). The last two pairs of ribs, called *floating ribs,* are smaller in length and terminate well within the body, making no sternal contact.

The dagger-shaped sternum, viewed from the side, tilts obliquely downward and forward from its highest point, at the pit of the throat. It is about seven inches in length and is comprised of three fused segments. Each of the segments is tilted to a slightly different degree, turning more sharply downward in the lower two segments. The sternum is widest in the uppermost segment, the *manubrium,* notched on either side to receive the clavicles (collar bones), and notched at the top to form part of the familiar indentation of the pit of the throat (Figure 3.17). The *body,* or central segment of the sternum, like the manubrium, is indented along both sides to receive the cartilage extensions of the ribs. In length, the body is almost twice that of the manubrium. The lowest and smallest segment of the sternum, the *xiphoid process,* is not usually seen in the fleshed figure. Its lower tip marks the top of the rib cage's V-shaped cartilage-rimmed arch.

FIGURE 3.15

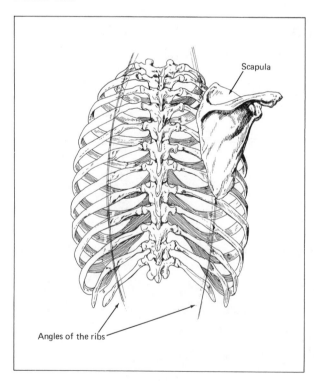

Scapula

Angles of the ribs

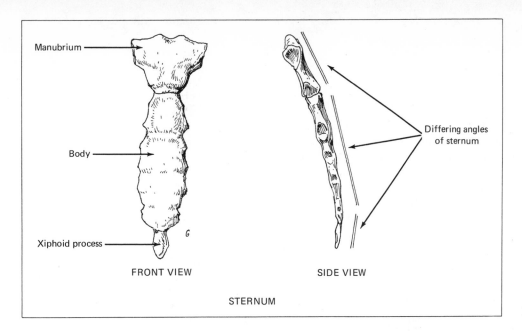

Manubrium

Body

Xiphoid process

Differing angles
of sternum

FRONT VIEW

SIDE VIEW

STERNUM

FIGURE 3.17

FIGURE 3.18

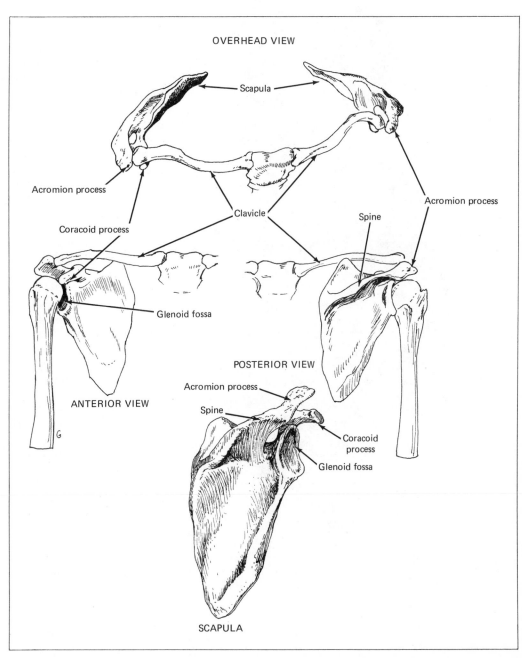

OVERHEAD VIEW

Scapula

Acromion process

Acromion process

Coracoid process

Clavicle

Spine

Glenoid fossa

POSTERIOR VIEW

ANTERIOR VIEW

Acromion process

Spine

Coracoid
process

Glenoid fossa

SCAPULA

## THE SHOULDER GIRDLE

From an overhead view, the bones that comprise the shoulder girdle look rather like a cupid's bow. The bow is formed by the S-shaped *clavicles* in front and the *spine of the scapula* and its *acromion process* in back (Figure 3.18). The scapula is a trowel-shaped, bony plate with a handle-like projection, its spine, near the top. Its medial (nearer to the body's mid-

FIGURE 3.19

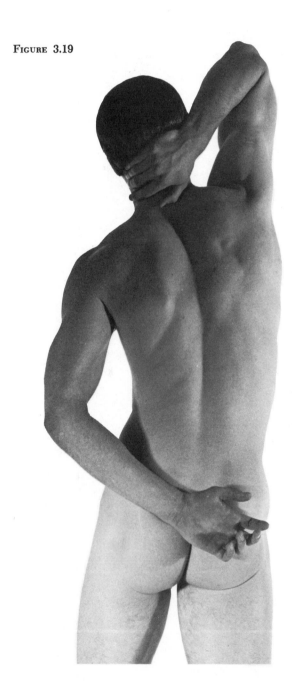

line) edge is nearly vertical, its lateral (further from the midline) edge is markedly oblique, and its upper edge inclines downward toward the bone of the upper arm. Near the top, its projecting spine, beginning at the medial edge, rises above the slanted upper edge and, at its extremity, turns sharply forward to meet the outer end of the clavicle. This outer end is called the *acromion process*. In meeting, the acromion process is located just a little beneath the outer tip of the clavicle (Figure 3.18). With the arms at rest at one's sides, the height of the scapulas (about 6½ to 7 inches) equals their distance apart at their pointed lower ends. At the lateral upper edge of the scapula, just below its junction with the clavicle, is the *glenoid fossa,* a rounded socket which receives the head of the *humerus,* the bone of the upper arm.

Because the scapulas are attached to the skeleton only at their junction with the clavicles, they are free to swing upward, as when we raise our arms above our heads, and outward, as when we clasp our hands behind our back. This can be seen in Figure 3.19, where the left scapula, its medial edge and pointed end very evident, pushes outward; while the right scapula, less visible because of the muscles that encase it in this position, has moved in an upward arc, its pointed end near to the upper torso's edge. Being slightly hollowed on its inner surface, the scapula rides easily over the rounded form of the rib cage. However, when the arm is raised, the scapula remains stationary until the arm approaches a horizontal position. Once the arm is raised above the line of the shoulders, the scapula begins its swing outward to the side of the rib cage. This outward movement is clearly shown in Michelangelo's *Studies for the Libyan Sibyl* (Figure 3.20). Note, on the figure's left side, how the spine of the scapula is turned forward to articulate (meet with) the clavicle. On the right side, although the arm is raised, its backward movement brings the scapula nearer to the spinal column, causing deep muscles (the rhomboids) to bulge into the vertical folds seen on that side.

In this remarkable anatomical study, Michelangelo's knowledge of the interaction of bone and muscle is clearly expressed by his structural vocabulary, that is, by his ability to show the volume of specific form-units and their interjoinings. Evident here, too, is a sensitive understanding of the design—the harmonies and tensions—of human anatomy. Note also the expressive power of these heroic forms: an engaging contrast between the energy suggested in their athletic development and the delicate modeling that caresses them into being. Here again is an example of the four factors brilliantly interacting.

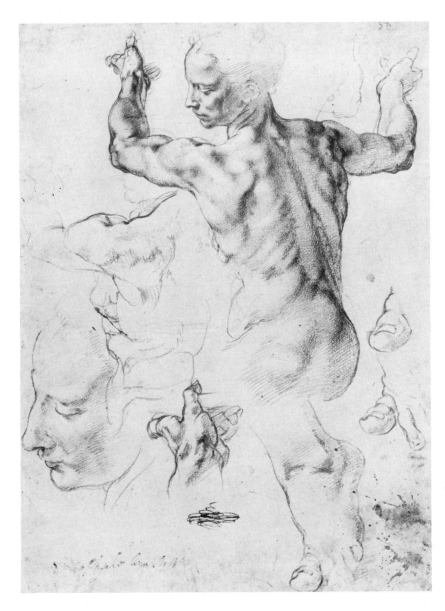

FIGURE 3.20
MICHELANGELO BUONARROTI
(1475–1564)
*Studies for "The Libyan Sibyl"*
Red chalk. 11 3/8 x 8 3/8 in.
*The Metropolitan Museum
of Art, New York.
Purchase, 1924 Joseph Pulitzer
Bequest.*

## THE PELVIS

The pelvis, its upper part flared out in a dishlike manner and its lower part in a more tubular way, is the single bony mass of the lower trunk. It surfaces in only two places: at the base of the spine (the sacral triangle) and at the hips, where the *anterior-superior iliac spines* are visible as bony projections in the front and side views, and the *posterior-superior iliac spines* are seen as bony arcs or curved furrows (depending on the lean or muscular state of the figure) in the back view (Figures 3.21 and 3.22). The anterior-superior iliac spine projections, especially visible in the female figure (Figure 3.23), are at the leading edge of the *iliac crests,* the

thickened rims of the winglike hip bones which, with the sacrum, form the basinlike container for the intestines and reproductive organs. In very lean figures certain poses reveal most of the iliac crests.

There are notable differences of proportion between the male and female pelvis. In the female, the pelvis is wider, shallower, and less massive in bulk, the pubic arch more rounded and wider, the sacrum shorter and wider, and the pelvic cavity larger. The male pelvis is thicker and more angular overall (Figure 3.22). From the side view the male pelvis appears to tilt forward to a lesser degree than the female pelvis does; note the pronounced backward tilt of the lower trunk in Figure 3.23.

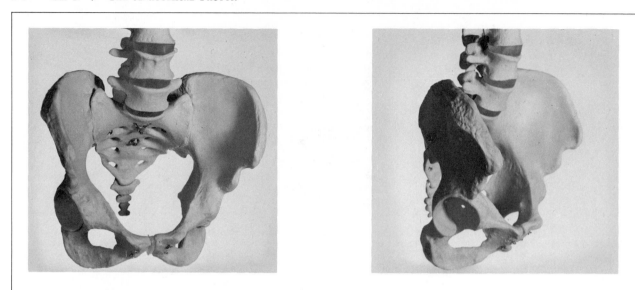

**Figure 3.21**

**Figure 3.22**

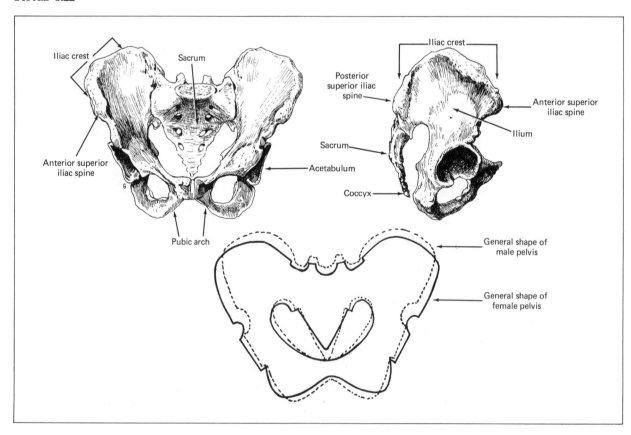

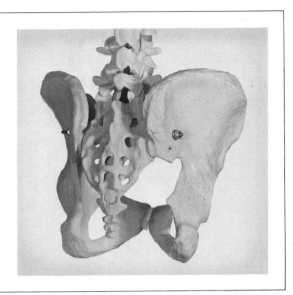

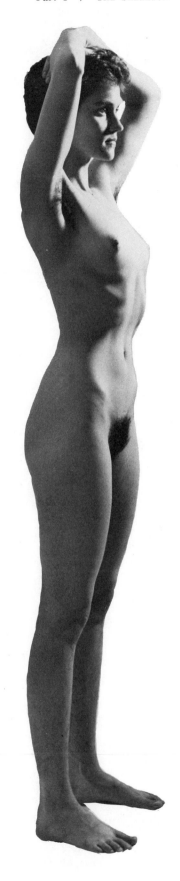

FIGURE 3.23

FIGURE 3.24
**KÄTHE KOLLWITZ** (1867–1945)
*Two Nudes*
Charcoal. 24 x 19 in.
*National Gallery of Art, Washington, D.C.*
*Rosenwald Collection.*

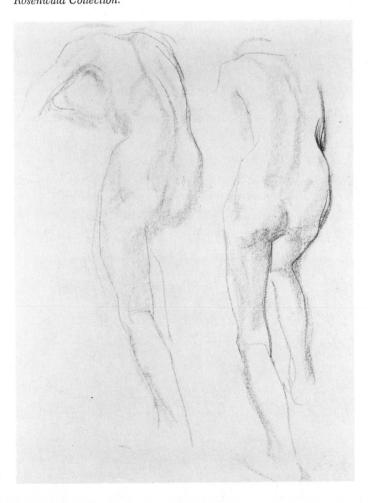

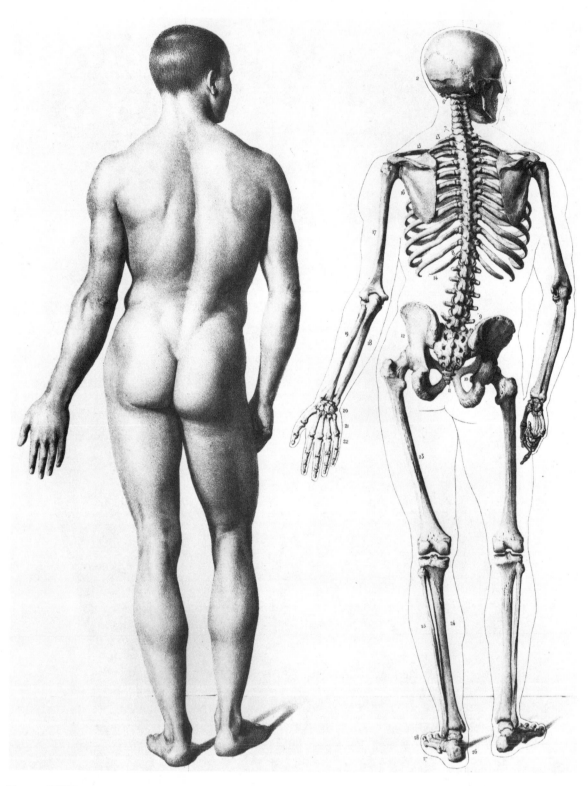

**Figure 3.25**
**DR. J. FAU**
*The Anatomy of the External Forms of Man,*
*Plate 3*
*London, Hippolyte Bailliere, 1849.*
*Courtesy of Countway Library.*

96

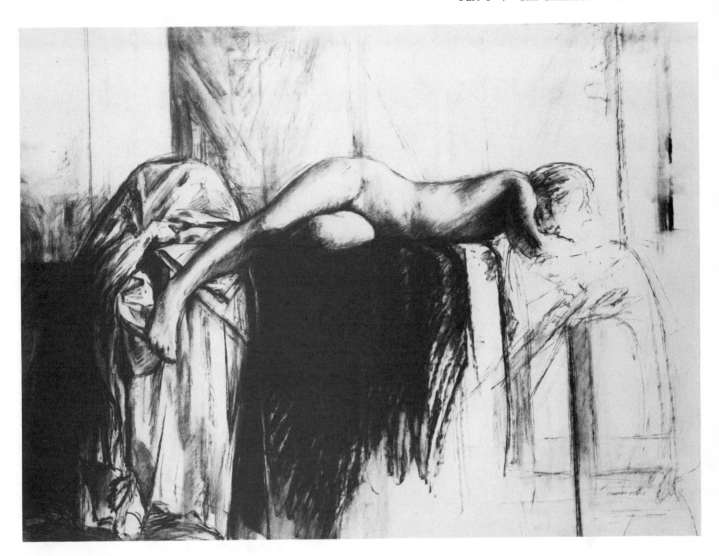

FIGURE 3.26
SIDNEY GOODMAN (1936–    )
*Model on a Draped Table, 1977–8*
Charcoal. 29 x 41 in.
*Photo courtesy of Terry Dintenfass, Inc., New York.*
*Photo by eeva-inkeri.*

Although deeply embedded in the musculature and fatty tissues of the lower trunk, the pelvis exerts its blocky influence on the living forms. Kollwitz, in her *Two Nudes* (Figure 3.24), makes use of the angular character of the pelvis to shore up her fluid treatment of the figure's forms, and to bolster a design theme of straight and curved lines. Note how often the skeleton surfaces in these brief sketches.

The pair of irregularly shaped iliac bones, which, with the sacrum, comprise the pelvis, are fixed and no movement occurs among them. Indeed, the position of the pelvis, which, in the side view, appears to continue the direction of the lumbar vertebrae, does not alter much, even when the torso

is curved forward as when, with our legs held straight, we bend over to touch our toes. But if there is only moderate movement in such forward (or backward) motions, there is more pronounced freedom of movement in the front view, where the pelvis can tilt markedly to the left or right. The pelvis will always tilt upward on the supporting leg side, as in Figure 3.25.

Despite the subtle clues in the living form to the mass and position of the pelvis, noting its form and angle is essential to seeing the character of any pose. This is so even in reclining poses. Goodman, in his *Model on a Draped Table* (Figure 3.26), clearly explains the figure's shift from a side view in the upper

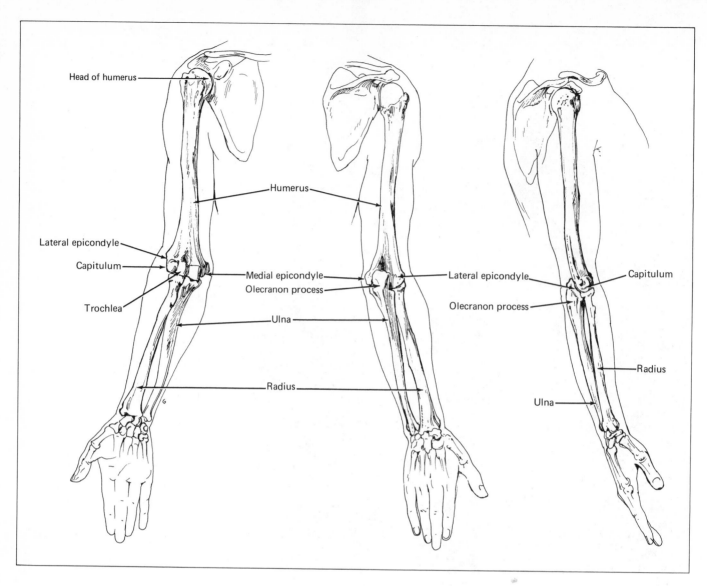

**FIGURE 3.27**

**FIGURE 3.28**

body to a front view in the lower by showing the effect on the surface forms of the angle and mass of the pelvis.

## THE ARM

There are three major long bones in the arm. The longest and thickest is the *humerus,* the bone of the upper arm; in the lower arm, the *radius* and *ulna* are roughly parallel, with the ulna positioned slightly higher. In the fleshed figure the *medial* and *lateral epicondyles* of the humerus (the protuberances at the bone's lower end) are generally visible, as are the styloid processes, the protuberances at the extremities of both the radius and ulna (Figure 3.27). At the shoulder, the ball-like head of the humerus is often visible, despite the fullness of the deltoid muscle (Figure 3.31).

A versatile joint at the elbow allows for bending and rotating movements by the lower arm. In

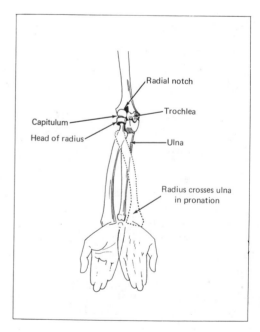

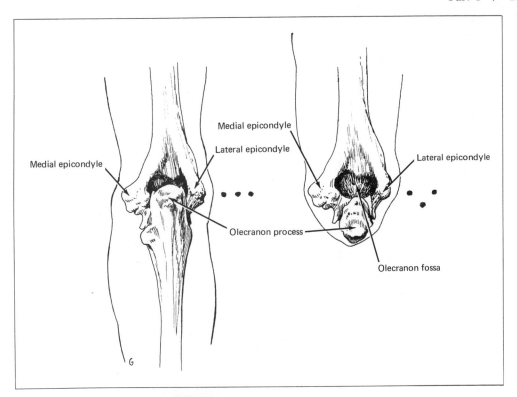

FIGURE 3.29

FIGURE 3.30

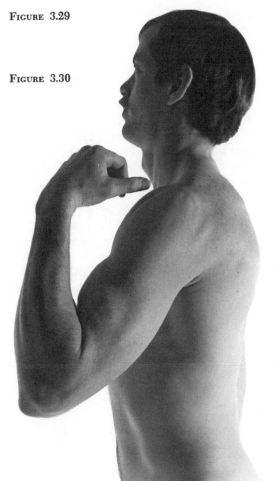

FIGURE 3.31

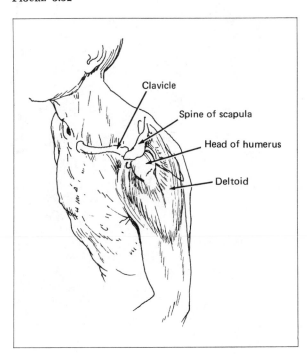

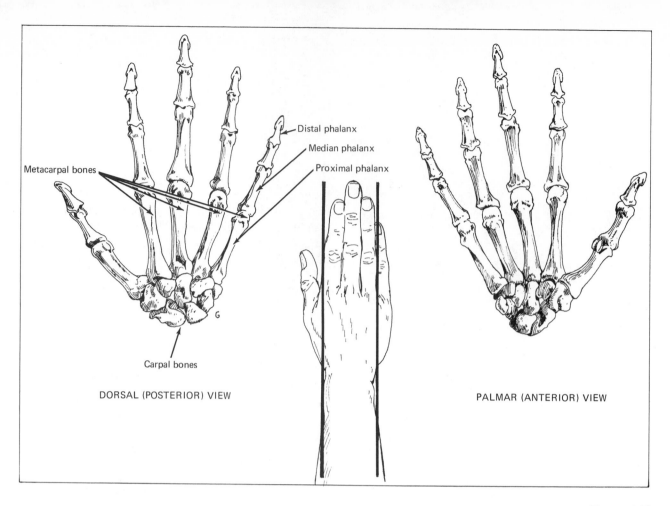

Distal phalanx
Median phalanx
Proximal phalanx

Metacarpal bones

Carpal bones

DORSAL (POSTERIOR) VIEW

PALMAR (ANTERIOR) VIEW

FIGURE 3.32

bending, the ulna moves around the *trochlea,* a spool-like ending on the humerus. In rotating actions the rounded end of the radius revolves within the radial notch of the ulna and rotates upon the *capitulum* of the humerus in a ball-and-socket manner (Figure 3.28). When the palm of the hand is turned face up (supine), the radius and ulna are parallel; when the palm is turned face down (prone), the radius crosses over the ulna (3.28).

At the wrist, the rounded head of the ulna (on the little finger side) is visible in the prone position (palm down); when the hand is supinated (turned palm upward), this rounded projection disappears. At the elbow, a posterior view of the extended arm shows the *olecranon process,* a pronounced, blocky mass at the end of the ulna, to be in a rough horizontal alignment with the medial and lateral epi-

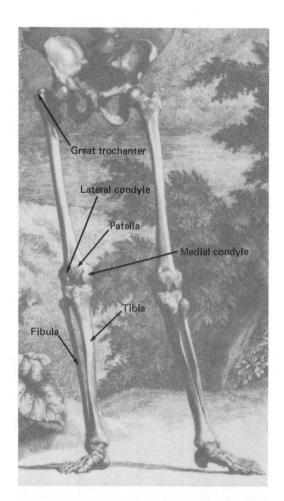

Great trochanter

Lateral condyle

Patella

Medial condyle

Tibia

Fibula

FIGURE 3.33
BERNARD ALBINUS (1697–1770)
*Skeleton, Front View* (detail), from *Tabula sceleti et musculorum corporis humani* (1747).
Engraving.
*The Francis A. Countway Library of Medicine, Boston.*

condyles of the humerus. When the arm is bent, the three protuberances form a V-like arrangement, and the olecranon process becomes an even larger projecting form (Figures 3.29 and 3.30). Figure 3.31 shows the arrangement of the clavicle, spine of the scapula, and humerus bones at the shoulder, where the head of the humerus is sheltered beneath the junction point of the other two bones.

There are twenty-seven bones in the wrist and hand. In the wrist, eight *carpal* bones form a ball-like mound just below the heads of the ulna and radius. Embedded in the palm are the five *metacarpal* bones. The heads of these slender, curved bones (the knuckles) are visible when the hand forms a fist; when the fingers are extended, these protuberances all but disappear. There are fourteen *phalanges* (finger bones). Of the three bones in each finger, those nearest the wrist (the proximal phalanges) are longest; those next (the medial phalanges) are two-thirds the length of the proximal

phalanges; and the bones of the fingertips (the distal phalanges) are two-thirds the length of the medial phalanges (Figure 3.32). The thumb is composed of only two phalanges, the joint between them falling on a line with the metacarpal heads.

Most beginners draw the hands (and feet) too small. Actually, the length of the hand is about four-fifths that of the head. Likewise, in width, the hand covers most of the face. When the fingers are extended and held together, the outer edges of the index and ring fingers line up with the edges of the arm at the wrist (Figure 3.32).

## THE LEG

There are four bones in the leg and twenty-six in the foot. In the upper leg, the *femur,* the longest bone in the body, provides the only bony joining between the torso and the lower limb. At the knee is

**FIGURE 3.34**

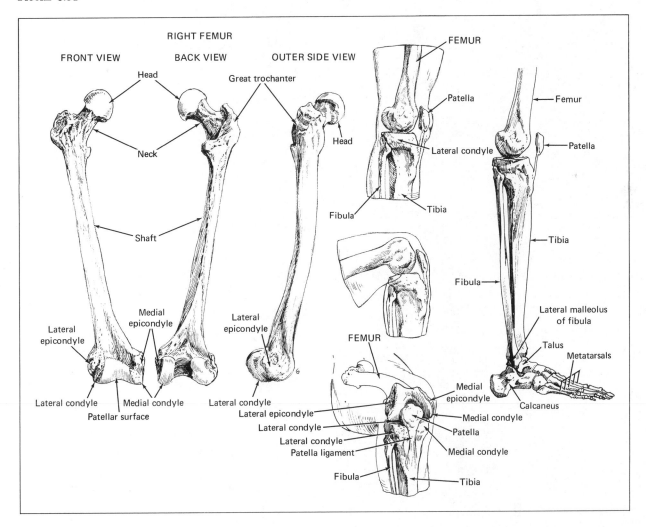

the *patella* (the kneecap), a roughly triangular, shieldlike bone. In the lower leg are the *tibia* and *fibula,* in a fixed, parallel position (Figure 3.33).

The femur is sometimes visible in the area of the hip, where the *great trochanter,* a blocky outcrop of bone, shields the femur's slender neck and rounded head. This head is received by the hollowed *acetabulum* of the pelvis in a ball-and-socket joint that permits a considerable freedom of movement of the upper leg. The femur is always in evidence at the knee, where the medial and lateral *condyles,* the thick rims at the femur's inferior (lower) end, and the raised hills at the center of

these bony rims, the *epicondyles,* come to the surface in the fleshed figure, as is shown in the "see through" drawings of the bent legs in Figure 3.34.

Seen from the front, the two femurs incline downward to meet at the knees; seen from the side, the femur describes a subtle convex curve. Something of these movements can be seen in Figures 3.3 and 3.5. At the broad, lower base of the femur the medial and lateral condyles articulate with the tibia. The femur's *patellar surface,* a smooth depression between the condyles, permits the patella to move in straightening the leg. The patella is always a pronounced landmark in the straightened leg, pro-

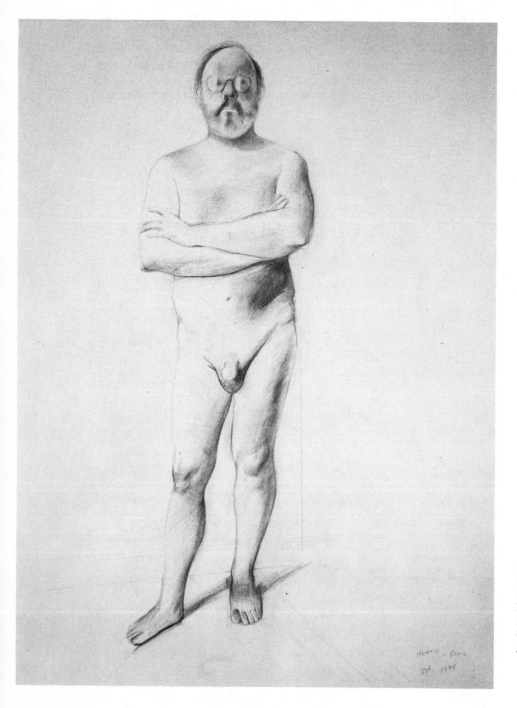

**FIGURE 3.35**
DAVID HOCKNEY (1937–    )
*Henry Nude, Paris*
Pencil. 21 3/4 x 19 1/2 in.
*Photo courtesy of André Emmerich Gallery, New York.*
*Photo by Bettina Sulzer.*

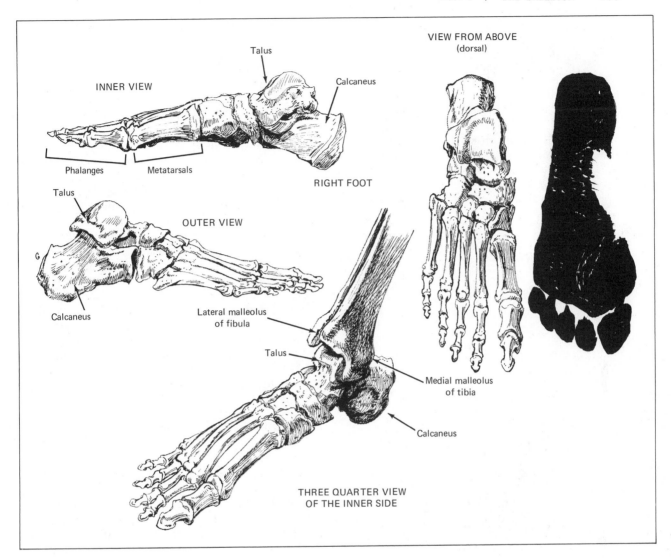

INNER VIEW

Talus

Calcaneus

RIGHT FOOT

Phalanges    Metatarsals

VIEW FROM ABOVE
(dorsal)

Talus

OUTER VIEW

Calcaneus

Lateral malleolus
of fibula

Talus

Medial malleolus
of tibia

Calcaneus

THREE QUARTER VIEW
OF THE INNER SIDE

**Figure 3.36**

truding at the knee even in heavy-set individuals, where muscular and fatty tissues encroach upon it, as occurs in Hockney's *Henry Nude, Paris* (Figure 3.35). Here, too, we can see the diagonal axis of the femur in the figure's supporting leg. Note that the olecranon process of the ulna also strongly projects despite the heavily fleshed arms. In passing, we should consider the clarity of all the forms in this seemingly simply modeled figure. By modeling the darkened planes in massed lines that encircle forms or show the tilt of a plane, the artist economically constructs the figure's masses in an effectively form-revealing way.

Only the tibia articulates with the lower end of the femur, its broad, flat head meeting with the femur's equally broad base. When the leg is bent, the patella settles in among the protuberances of the femur and tibia, becoming almost lost to view. The

tibia's shaft, triangular in cross section, produces a long vertical plane and ridge at the surface, the familiar shinbone. One of the few places in the figure where the bone lies beneath the skin unprotected by muscular tissue, the shinbone is a prominent landmark in the lower leg. The fibula, acting like a flying buttress, supports the broad upper head of the tibia by pushing up against the underside of the tibia's lateral condyle (Figures 3.33 and 3.34).

Of the seven *tarsal* bones of the ankle, the spool-like *talus* sits astride the *calcaneus,* the blocky, backward projecting heelbone that provides one end of the arch of the foot, the other end being comprised of the forward ends of the *metatarsals* and *phalanges* (Figure 3.36). The talus is engaged in the raising and lowering of the foot. The remaining tarsal bones collectively form the upper part of the ankle's inclined ramp connecting the leg and foot.

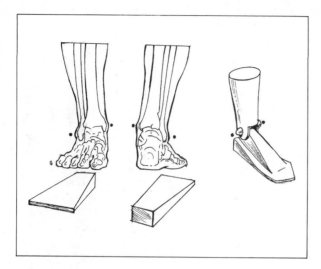

FIGURE 3.37

FIGURE 3.38

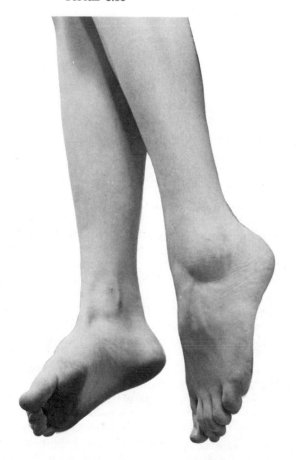

The curved metatarsals correspond to the metacarpals of the hand, but their more evident curve more emphatically influences the fleshed forms of the foot. As any footprint shows, the points of contact with the ground are greater on the outer side of the foot (Figure 3.36). The arch of the foot is more visible on the medial side view, the form of the foot rising almost vertically on that side, and its base lifted from the ground between the metatarsals and the calcaneus. A sizable protuberance produced by the *medial malleolus* of the lower tibia marks the juncture of the tibia and the talus. On the lateral side the foot is flat upon the ground all along its base, its form rising at a marked angle. In the front view the protuberance of the *lateral malleolus* of the fibula can be seen to be lower than its counterpart on the inner side of the ankle. The foot is narrower and higher at the heel, wider and lower at the toes, its essential mass being wedgelike (Figure 3.37). The blocky nature of the four small toes, the result of each turning downward at its ending, and the upward turning of the large toe, can be seen in Figure 3.38, which also shows the foot's wedgelike character, the backward projecting calcaneus, and, in the lower foot, the lateral malleolus.

## SKELETAL PROPORTIONS

No system of measurements can replace sensitive perceptual inquiry. Any system of skeletal proportions is of limited value since it refers to varying lengths of parts seen in the same plane, as when the figure is standing at attention. Knowing that the femur is twice the length of the skull is less helpful when the upper leg is seen in severe foreshortening; and the fact that the humerus is half again the length of the radius and ulna may confuse the beginner who observes the reverse to be the case, as in Figure 3.39. However, knowing certain relationships of scale and location *is* often useful in clarifying what is observed, and especially in guiding what is invented. A prior knowledge of the skeleton's proportions can assist perception but should never dictate to it. For example, in drawing the figure in Figure 3.39, knowing that the foot is almost as long as the lower arm (from the elbow to the wrist), or that the length of the rib cage is half again that of the pelvis helps establish scale relationships because these parts are more or less in parallel alignment and at a right angle to our line of sight. When parts *are* foreshortened, as the upper legs are here, knowing their length relative to other parts serves as a guide in modeling them so as to appear in proportion.

The measurements that follow should be regarded as general, not precise. Several different

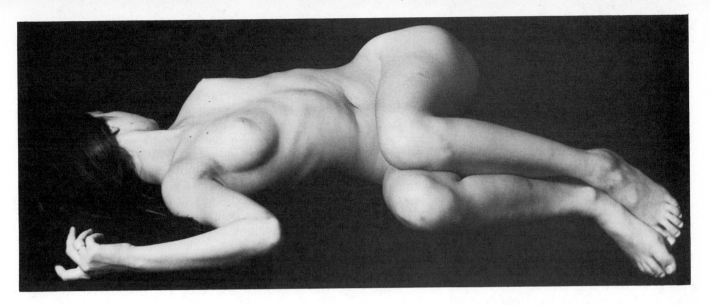

FIGURE 3.39

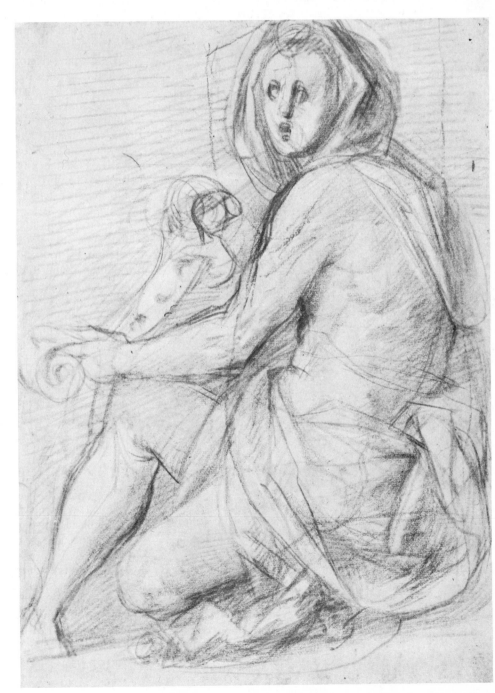

FIGURE 3.40
Copy after the *Sibyl* of
**JACOPO DA PONTORMO**
(1494–1556)
Red crayon on buff paper.
11 1/4 x 8 1/8 in.
*Courtesy The Fogg Art Museum,
Harvard University.*
*Bequest of Charles A. Loeser.*

canons of proportion have been devised in the past. Some, like the heroic proportions of Michelangelo's *Adam* (see Figure 1.15) or those used by the Mannerists such as Pontormo to elongate the figure (Figure 3.40), were designed to endow the figure with certain expressive qualities. Other canons, resulting in the more plebeian proportions of the figures by Goya (see Figure 1.25) or Pascin (Figure 3.41), were necessary for their more earthy expressive interests. The proportions offered here represent *average* calculations. But we should bear in mind that human adults may vary from less than five feet to about seven feet in height; they may be big-boned or frail, and may be powerfully or subtly muscled. More important, we should recognize that the artist, unlike the anthropologist, does better to support his perceptions with intuition than with calipers.

FIGURE 3.41
JULES PASCIN (1885–1930)
*Marion* (1929)
Charcoal and oil on canvas. 92 x 73 cm.
*Musée des Beaux Arts, Grenoble.*
*Gift of Hermine David and Lucie Krohg, 1937.*

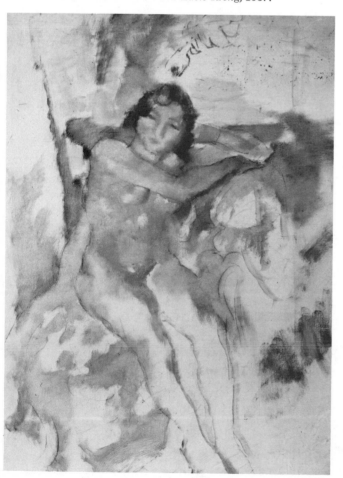

The traditional unit of measure in the skeleton is the skull. Although, as noted above, different systems of proportion have been developed, such as the one devised by the nineteenth-century anatomist Salvage, who based a system of measurement on the division of the figure into eight units (Figure 3.42), the average figure universally is about seven and one-half skull-lengths, rarely less than seven or more than eight. In both the male and female (Figure 3.43), measuring one skull-length down from the skull strikes a point at the tip of the xyphoid process in front and just above the lower end of the scapula in back. Measuring one more skull-length down strikes a point just below the highest point of the iliac crest in the male skeleton, and just at the highest point of the iliac crest in the female skeleton. Another skull-length down strikes a point about two inches below the great trochanter in both the male and female skeletons, and just at the carpal bones when the arm is held alongside the body. As Figure 3.43 shows, each of the remaining three and one-half skull-lengths falls between, rather than on, useful landmarks. However, this changes if we now begin to measure skull-lengths from the base of the foot upwards. The first length brings us to a point halfway to the knee, a second measure strikes the patella, a third evenly divides the femur, and a fourth skull-length strikes the top of the great trochanter.

It is useful to know which bones are roughly the same in length. As Figure 3.44 illustrates, the sternum, scapula, clavicle, pelvis, ulna, radius, and skeleton of the foot all measure just over or under one skull-length. The bones of the wrist and hand are about three-fourths of a skull-length, as are the sacrum and coccyx together. The rib cage, humerus, tibia, and fibula are likewise similar in length, about one and one-half skull-lengths.

Some additional proportions worth noting are shown in Figure 3.45. It is one skull-length from the seventh cervical vertebra to the lower tip of the scapula, and one skull-length from that point to the iliac crest. Another skull-length down strikes a point just below the great trochanter. The midpoint in the male skeleton is just at the pubic bone; in the female it is slightly above the pubic bone. Hence (fashion illustrations notwithstanding), the female's legs are slightly shorter relative to the height of the figure than is the case in the male figure. Both feet when placed together at the heels but pointed outward measure about one skull-length in the front view.

The three anatomical plates by the famous Renaissance anatomist Albinus (Figures 3.46, 3.47, and 3.48) show in accurate detail the skeletal forms, proportions, and locations discussed in this chapter, and serve as a visual reference and summary.

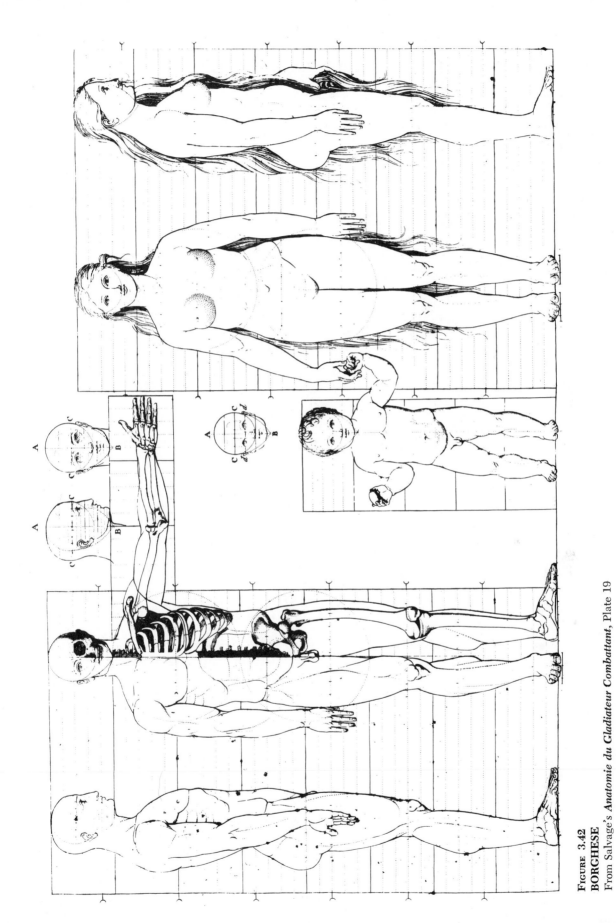

**Figure 3.42**
**BORGHESE**
From Salvage's *Anatomie du Gladiateur Combattant*, Plate 19

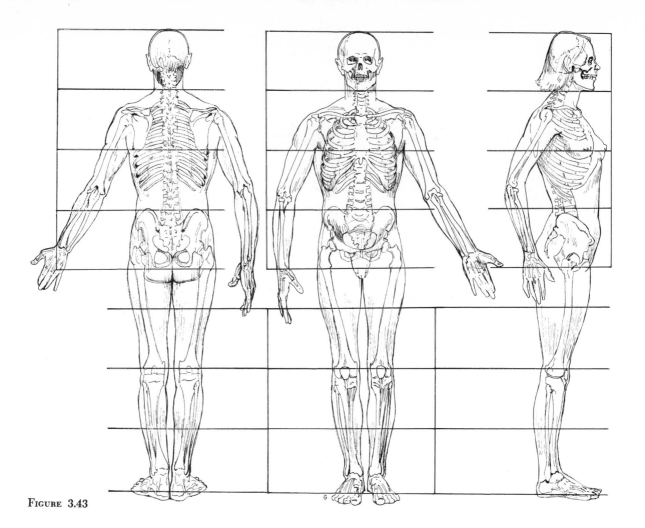

FIGURE 3.43

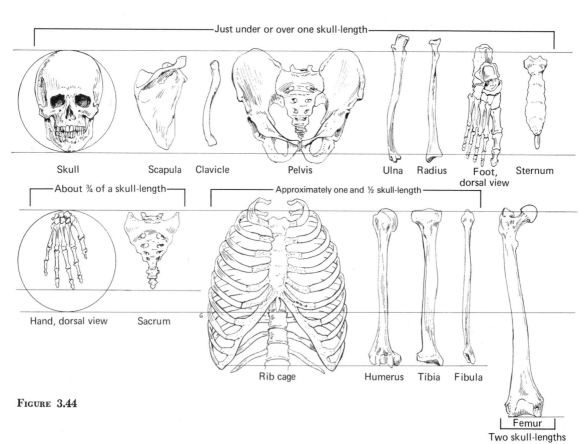

Just under or over one skull-length

Skull    Scapula  Clavicle    Pelvis         Ulna  Radius  Foot,      Sternum
                                                          dorsal view

About ¾ of a skull-length          Approximately one and ½ skull-length

Hand, dorsal view    Sacrum         Rib cage        Humerus  Tibia  Fibula

FIGURE 3.44

Femur
Two skull-lengths

108

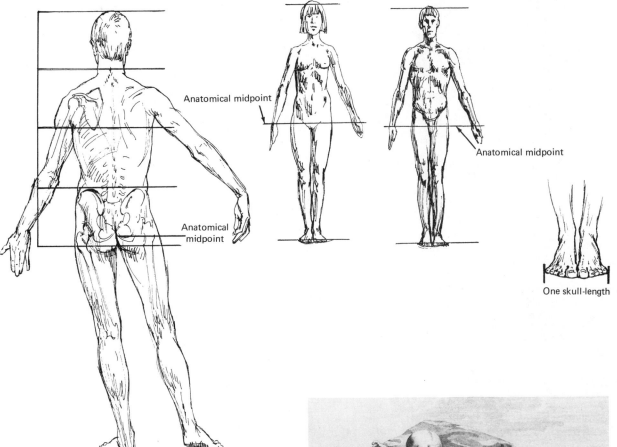

Anatomical midpoint

Anatomical midpoint

Anatomical midpoint

One skull-length

**Figure 3.45**

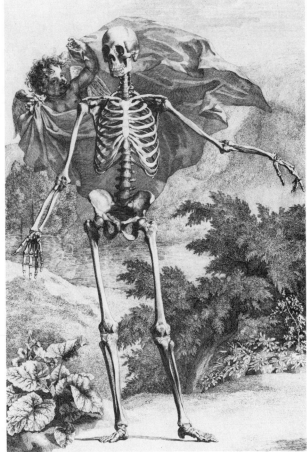

**Figure 3.46**
**BERNARD ALBINUS** (1697–1770)
*Skeleton, Front View*
Engraving.
*Courtesy of the Francis A. Countway Library of Medicine, Boston.*

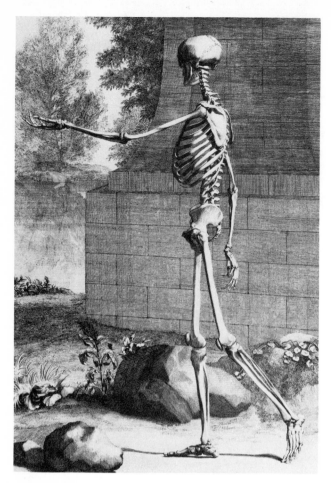

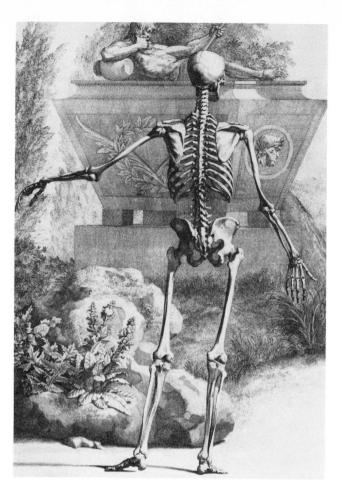

**FIGURE 3.47**
**ALBINUS**
*Skeleton, Side View*

**FIGURE 3.49**
**DOMINIQUE INGRES (1780–1867)**
***Three Studies of a Male Nude***
*Pencil. 7 3/4 x 14 3/8 in.*
*The Metropolitan Museum of Art,*
*New York.*
*Rogers Fund, 1919.*

**FIGURE 3.48**
**ALBINUS**
*Skeleton, Back View*

Figures 3.46, 3.47, 3.48 are from ***Tabula sceleti et
musculorum corporis humani*** by Bernard Albinus.
*Reproduced by permission of The Francis A. Countway
Library of Medicine, Boston.*

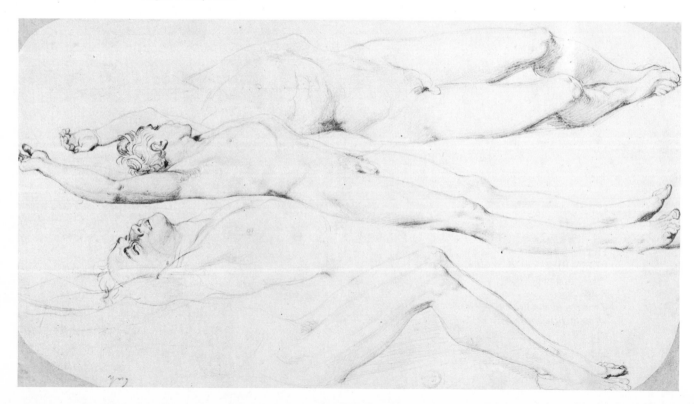

## THE SKELETON
## IN FIGURE DRAWING

A knowledge of the skeleton stimulates and guides good figure drawing. In Ingres' *Three Studies of a Male Nude* (Figure 3.49), the elegant flow of the forms is enhanced by the artist's response to the skeleton's influence on the living forms. The protuberances at the joints and elsewhere serve to keep the forms from becoming too fluid and fast. Ingres uses bony landmarks like commas, to provide visual pauses that establish a measured pace and to clarify the figure's construction. Hence, for Ingres, the skeleton serves to guide the drawing's design as well as the figure's structure. Note the skull's influence on the forms of the head, the knowledgeable drawing of the bones at the elbows, wrists, knees, and ankles, the clearly visible mass of the rib cage, and, at the hips, the tilt of the pelvis and the influence of the great trochanter.

It is important that we recognize the skeleton's potential for contributing to a drawing's essential character—to structural, plastic, and emotive matters. Indeed, in some poses, the skeletal frame is a very imposing aspect of what we see. Comparing Figures 3.50 and 3.51 with their "see through" counterparts in Figure 3.52 helps explain the skeleton's omnipresent effects on the forms in these poses.

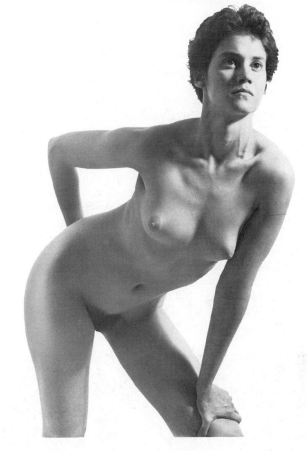

FIGURE 3.51

FIGURE 3.50

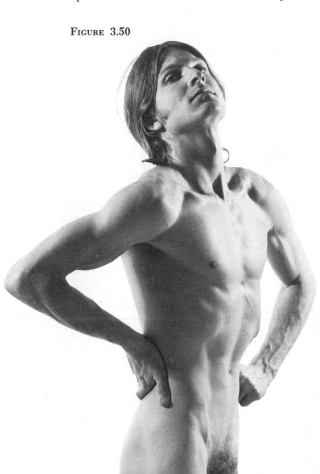

FIGURE 3.52

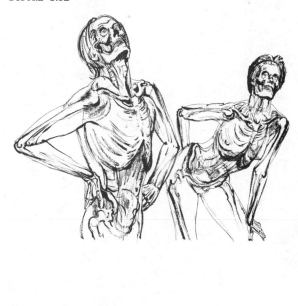

As Figure 3.51 shows, the skeleton's presence is not necessarily more evident in the male figure. Recognizing the general masses of the rib cage and pelvis in Figure 3.51 is fundamental to an understanding of this pose. In the poses of Figures 3.50 and 3.51, the skeleton's role in forming planes and form-units produces strong energies—rhythms and tensions—that hold great potential for enlivening a drawing. Then, too, we should take into account the expressive power—the physiological drama—of the skeleton pressing and pulling upon its encasing muscles, fat, and skin. That this anatomical tug-of-war can stimulate strong expressive meanings is especially evident in the drawings of Michelangelo (see Figures 1.15, 2.37, and 3.20). A contemporary response to the skeleton's role in shaping surface form is Bloom's *Seated Figure* (Figure 3.53). Indeed, here the skeleton, whether sensed or seen, is one of the drawing's major themes.

Nadelman's structurally insistent *Head and Neck* (Figure 3.54) is based on a sound knowledge of the forms of the skull. Hardly an accurate visual account of the skull's influence on the fleshed forms, the drawing does convey a strong architectural idea stimulated by the skull's structural character. But the same skeletal forms can suggest entirely different interpretations.

Although structurally powerful, the main thrust of Rothbein's woodcut *Angel of Death* (Figure 3.55) is toward an enigmatic but moving expression. The artist's knowledge of the skull's forms enables her to alter and order them in a way that creates a provocative image—one that is both skeletal and fleshed, tangible and ethereal, foreboding and compassionate.

Even in drawings where the anatomical factor plays a minor visual role, the knowledgeable artist is able to integrate skeletal facts with creative needs. In Golub's *Standing Figure, Back View* (Figure 3.56), the drawing of the spinal column and sacral triangle not only helps explain the form of the figure's back, but also intensifies the curved, forward "rush" of the torso, and contributes to the pattern and density of the drawing's linear design.

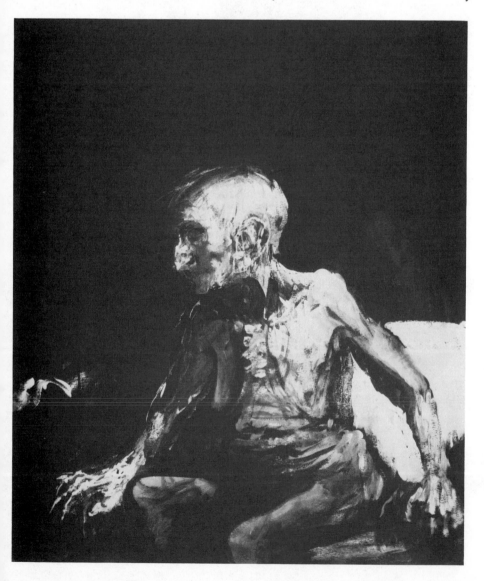

FIGURE 3.53
HYMAN BLOOM (1913–   )
*Seated Figure*
Gouache. 18 3/4 x 16 1/8 in.
*Courtesy of Terry Dintenfass, Inc.,
New York.*

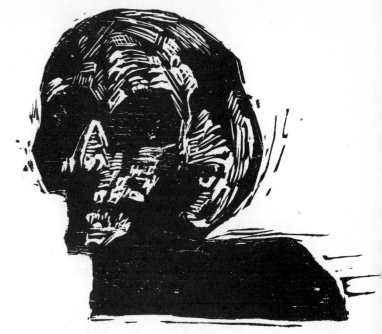

FIGURE 3.55
RENEE ROTHBEIN (1924– )
*Angel of Death*
Woodcut. 6 3/4 x 8 in.
*Collection of the author.*

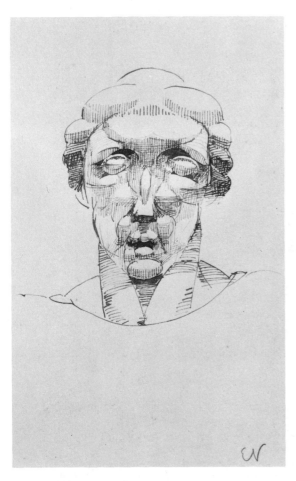

FIGURE 3.54
ELIE NADELMAN (1882–1947)
*Head and Neck*
Pen, black and brown inks on beige paper.
11 1/8 x 7 1/2 in.
*The Metropolitan Museum of Art, New York.*
*Gift of Lincoln Kirstein, 1965.*

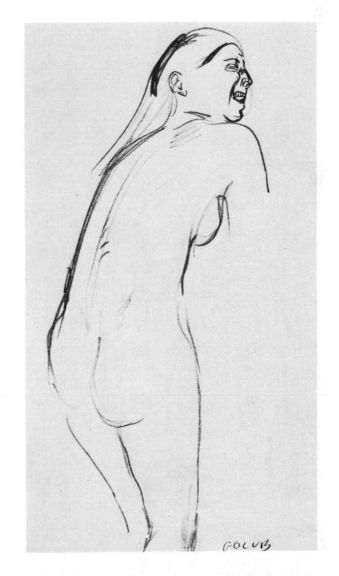

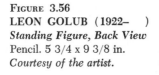

FIGURE 3.56
LEON GOLUB (1922– )
*Standing Figure, Back View*
Pencil. 5 3/4 x 9 3/8 in.
*Courtesy of the artist.*

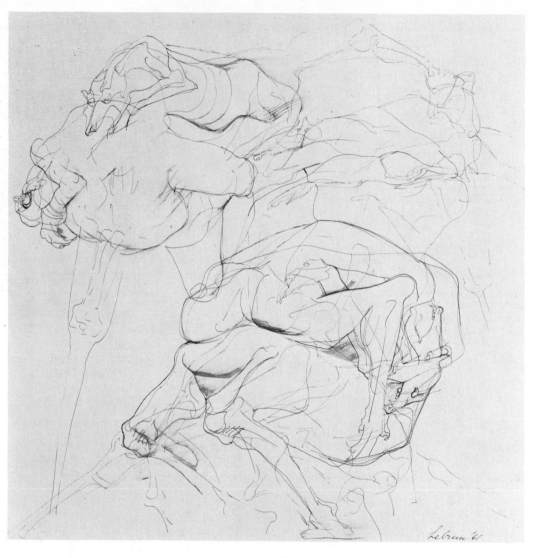

FIGURE 3.57
RICO LEBRUN (1900–1964)
*Three-Penny Novel—Beggars into Dogs* (1961)
Pen and ink. 37 1/4 x 29 7/8 in.
*Worcester Art Museum, Worcester, Mass.*
*Anonymous gift in memory of Bertha James Rich.*

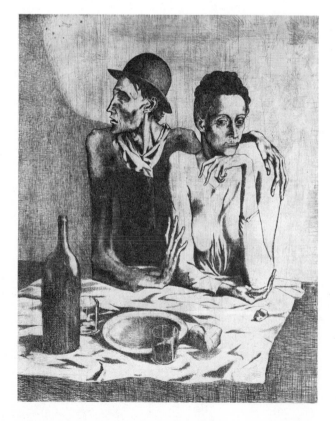

FIGURE 3.58
PABLO PICASSO (1881–1973)
*The Frugal Repast*
Etching. 46.3 x 37.7 cm.
*National Gallery of Art, Washington, D.C.*
*Rosenwald Collection.*

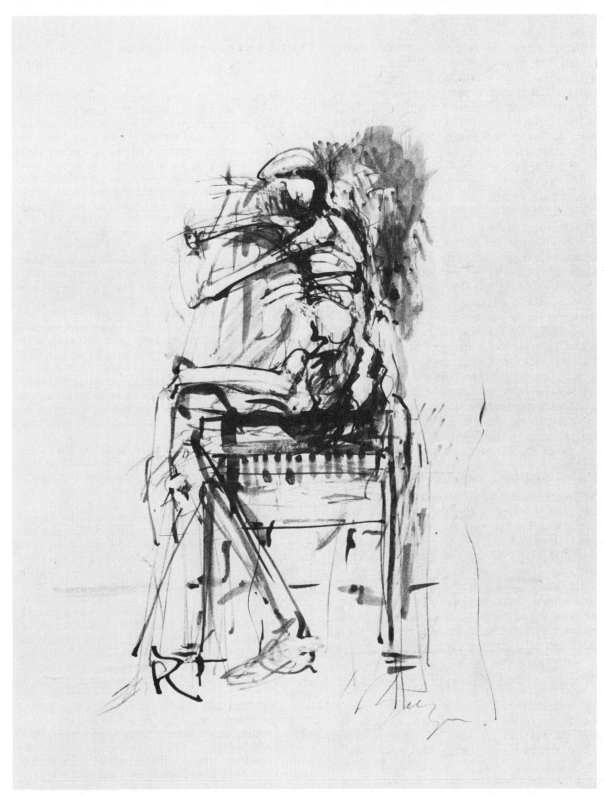

Figure 3.59
JOHN BAGERIS (1924–    )
*Seated Skeleton I*
Sepia and black ink, some gouache. 10 x 13 in.
*Collection of Mrs. Lucy Stone, Cambridge, Mass.*

Although in most drawings the skeleton is suggested but not shown as such, Lebrun's *Three-Penny Novel—Beggars into Dogs* (Figure 3.57) makes the skeleton itself a part of the subject, as do de Gheyn and Bloom (Figures 3.1 and 3.53). Here, drawn in swift, delicate lines, femurs, tibias, scapulas, and other indefinable bones add to the drawing's quiet terror.

In Picasso's etching *The Frugal Repast* (Figure 3.58), the skeleton's presence is felt throughout the drawing of both figures, and sometimes appears in surprising clarity, as at the shoulders, arms, and hands. Note the shallow depression of the temporal bones in both heads, the lateral end of the clavicle in the man's right shoulder, and the lateral epicondyle at the elbow. Note, too, the bones of the wrists and hands of both figures. But Picasso's interest in the skeleton is not clinical, and these anatomical niceties are not included merely for accuracy. Picasso's emphasis on the skeleton serves the interests of design and expression. As an agent of design it enriches edges and forms with engaging linear and planar activities, and, by the artist's subtle distortions of skeletal facts, helps emphasize the squares and L shapes formed by the torsos and arms. As an expressive agent, the skeletal presence, by stressing the figures' lean but strong and graceful bodies, seems to evoke the durability of man in the face of his mortality.

It seems fitting to end this brief review of some ways that the skeleton may bolster and amplify the structure and meaning of figure drawing, or can serve as the subject itself, with Bageris's *Seated Skeleton I* (Figure 3.59). In this engaging interpretation of the skeleton, Bageris extracts powerful structural and dynamic meanings which, in drawings of the living forms, operate more subtly under the figure's fleshy cloak. But, as this drawing amply demonstrates, a knowledge of the skeleton's masses can provide a rich source of intense dynamic energies. Although this drawing represents one artist's version of the skeleton's limitless potential for both suggesting and participating in structural and dynamic meanings, we can benefit from the artist's X-ray glimpse of forces at work within the figure's bony armature. In drawing the figure, we need to penetrate the surfaces in order to experience the masses and movements that shape them from within. We may come away with a very different set of responses than the explosive ones in Bageris's drawing, but a sensitive awareness of the forms and forces below the surface—and the anatomical knowledge that enables us to make such a penetration—is necessary if we are to avoid the trite and the commonplace.

## SUGGESTED EXERCISES

Clearly, the more we know about the skeleton, the more convincingly we can establish the figure's masses in space, utilize (as we saw in Chapter Two) the skeleton's role as an armature and influencer of surface forms, and can benefit from its structural, relational, and expressive potential. To do this, we should make a serious study of the skeleton. Examining and making studies of illustrations and photographs of the skeleton, as in Figure 3.60, is extremely important. And, because no single anatomy text can fully communicate the form and location of every bone (or muscle), the student should own at least two good anatomy books, and make a study of others. But even the best anatomical illustrations cannot compare with the clarity and quality of understanding provided by examining and drawing from the skeleton itself.

When the school or class cannot provide a skeleton for study, drawings can be made from specimens in museums of natural history or in local medical schools. Best of all, the student can purchase all or part of a skeleton from a medical supply house. This is not as difficult or expensive as it may seem. When necessary, several students can purchase a skeleton on a cooperative basis. In addition to authentic skeletons, there are available today very accurately detailed, life-size plastic skeletons, or parts of skeletons. These, too, can be purchased from medical supply manufacturers or suppliers. All the photographs of the skeleton shown in this chapter were made from one of these replicas, in this case, a product of Medical Plastics Laboratory (see the bibliography).

Because most anatomical illustrations of the skeleton are of the traditional, standing front, back, and side view, one of the immediate advantages of drawing from the skeleton itself is the freedom to pose it in ways that enable you to study various foreshortened views of the bones, as in Figure 3.61. Equally important, the structural character of the bones and how they fit and relate to each other is more fully experienced than is possible when they are studied in illustrations and photographs. Huntington's *Skeleton Study* (Figure 3.62) is an example of the richness of form available in drawing directly from the skeleton. This drawing also serves here to suggest the degree of accuracy and development of masses you should aim for in your more extended anatomical studies. Although the wired skeleton is limited in its movements, and some bones, in certain places, will not occupy their correct position (note the skeleton's right patella in Figure 3.61), the importance of familiarizing yourself with the way the bones look from various angles more than compensates for these minor restrictions and inaccuracies.

Of less accuracy and detail are the inexpensive twelve- to fifteen-inch plastic skeletons and life-size skulls available at most hobby and art stores. While not to be compared with the quality of the life-size replicas, these little skeletons are quite useful for studying the

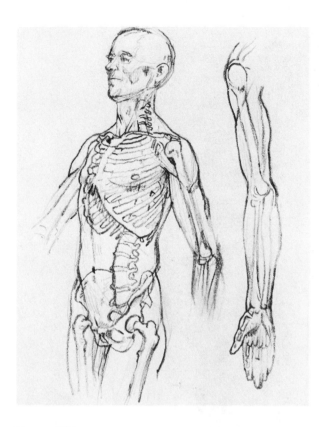

Figure 3.60

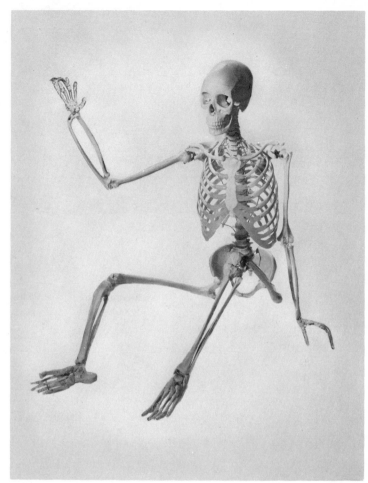

Figure 3.61

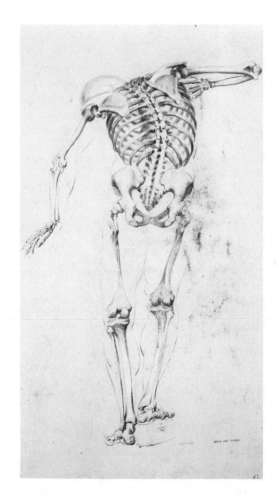

Figure 3.62
DANIEL HUNTINGTON (1816–1906)
*Skeleton Study*
Charcoal, crayon, and white chalk.
15 1/8 x 9 3/4 in.
*The Brooklyn Museum.*
*Gift of the Roebling Society.*

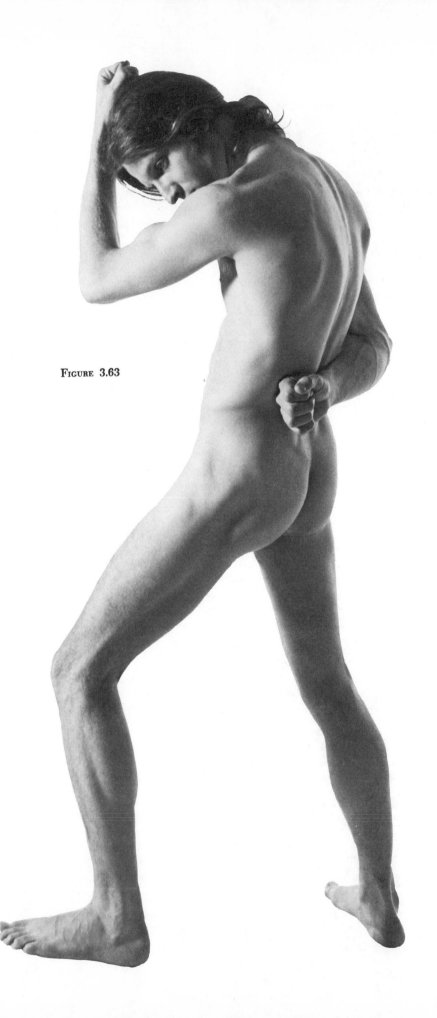

Figure 3.63

general relationships of scale and location, and are superior in some respects to the wooden manikins for use as models. Likewise, the inexpensive plastic skulls, despite their inferiority to those available from medical suppliers, are useful in studying the skull from various angles, and as an armature for muscle studies made by applying muscles made of plasticine.

The following exercises suggest some ways of studying the skeleton. When necessary, they may be simplified to more nearly suit your drawing skills. Some of these exercises may suggest other ways of learning to understand the skeleton's forms and proportions, and to stimulate your interest in its creative possibilities. Don't hesitate to explore any approach to familiarizing yourself with this important aspect of the human figure. The only wrong way to regard the skeleton is with a casual eye, born of the misconception that what is not actually visible on the figure's surface is less important than what can be seen by the naked eye.

In doing these exercises use any erasable medium and any compatible drawing surface. Unless otherwise indicated, avoid making your drawings smaller than 10″ × 14″ or larger than 18″ × 24″. Very small drawings do not permit a comfortable handling of details in extended studies, and very large ones are more difficult to keep in proportion. And, in most of these exercises, objective accuracy is an important consideration. Although none of these exercises are restricted to a given time period, none can be usefully experienced in less than thirty to forty-five minutes; some may take you considerably longer. Because your aim here is to familiarize yourself with skeletal facts, you may wish to develop these exercises in several drafts on tracing paper. By placing a first draft under a fresh sheet of tracing paper you can quickly redraw it, making corrections more easily than by extensive erasures on the same sheet. Furthermore, reversing the tracing paper to examine the drawing helps one to quickly see errors in scale, shape, structure, and location.

1. By referring to a skeleton, to anatomy texts, or to the illustrations in this chapter, draw a twelve-inch-high detailed study of the skeleton as it would appear from the pose shown in Figure 3.63. Note the skeletal clues in the figure. Your drawing should approach the degree of precision in Figure 3.64.

2. Using a manikinlike system of simple forms such as those you devised for Exercise 5 in Chapter Two, lightly sketch one front and one back view of the pose shown in Figure 3.63. These drawings should be at least twelve inches high. If necessary, make a simple stick-figure model out of wire or pipe cleaners to help you establish the two views. Or, if working in a studio classroom, have the model take the pose in Figure 3.63 long enough to allow you to rough in the essentials of the required two views. Next (working on a tracing paper overlay would be useful here), draw the skeleton as it would appear in the two views, allowing your schematic underdrawing to guide you in establishing the foreshortening of various bones, their scale, and their placement. Make these drawings rather generalized and simplified. For example, the rib cage need not be drawn rib by rib, but should suggest its egglike mass and perhaps something of the straplike nature of some of the ribs.

3. Rework or redraw several of your figure drawings, thinning down the forms to exaggerate the skeleton's influence on the surface forms. The results should suggest emaciated figures.

4. Using the skeleton or any other visual reference material to assist you, draw either a three-quarter view, an overhead view, or a worm's-eye view of any of the Albinus skeletons (Figures 3.46, 3.47, and 3.48).

5. Working from the skeleton itself or any of the illustrations in this chapter, draw any standing view of the skeleton as it would appear if wrapped in a thin, semitransparent material that clings to the forms. Show the material stretched taut in some places and loosely draped in others. The entire skeleton need not be covered, and the material may wrap around some forms several times, thickening them.

6. Working from the skeleton itself, make the following series of carefully observed drawings:
   a. Several studies of different views of the skull.
   b. Several studies of different views of the shoulder girdle. Be sure to include a view that looks down upon the shoulder girdle. In the study of the back view, include the entire scapula.
   c. Several studies of the bones of the torso, including at least one foreshortened view.
   d. Several studies of the bones of the arm and hand. In at least one of these drawings the lower arm and hand should be pronated (Figure 3.65).
   e. Several studies of the bones of the leg and foot, showing the pelvis in at least one of these (Figure 3.65). One of the studies should show the leg bent at the knee.

7. Using Figures 3.66 and 3.67 as models, and any water-based medium in combination with your pencil or chalk, make a drawing of each pose in which you extract strong structural and dynamic ideas and energies, as Bloom and Bageris have done in Figures 3.53 and 3.59 (see also Bageris's *Seated Skeleton II*, Figure 7.12). Don't hesitate to alter, omit, or add anything that will help make your drawings intensely personal responses to the subjects. Because these drawings should mirror *your* reactions to the two poses, the Bloom and Bageris drawings should be regarded more as examples of the creative freedom possible than as goals to emulate.

8. Make a line drawing, in a broad and free manner, of four or five skeletons dancing, leaping, or floating around the page. Simplify the forms as much as you wish. Here, the point is to experience the gesture and design possibilities of the skeletal forms. Allow skeletons to overlap or to interpenetrate each other —as if the forms were transparent. Contours may be simplified into straight and curved segments or can exaggerate the ins and outs of a form's edge. Try to create interesting rhythms and shapes. Do so not by arbitrarily distorting the bones, but by permitting gesture and design responses to influence your

XXXVI

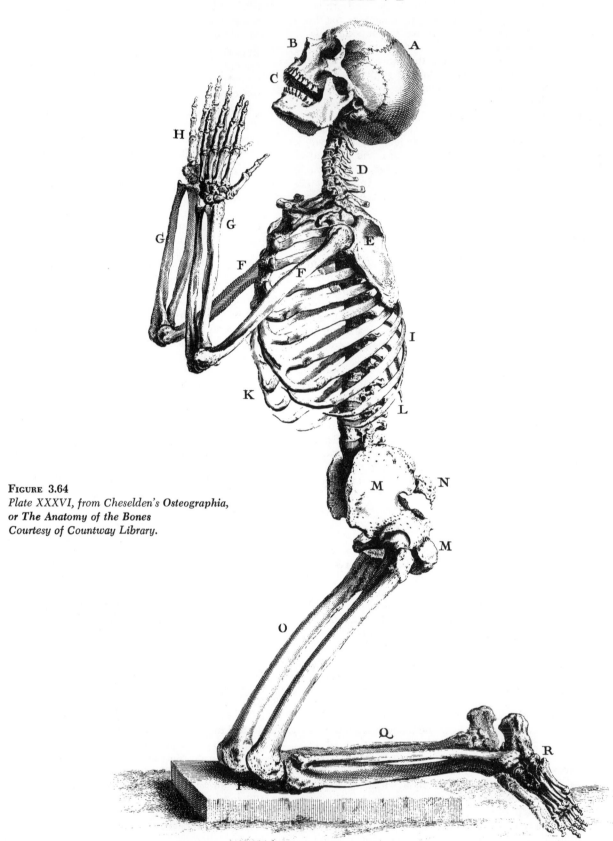

**FIGURE 3.64**
*Plate XXXVI, from Cheselden's Osteographia,
or The Anatomy of the Bones
Courtesy of Countway Library.*

general handling and style of drawing. These drawings may be more two- than three-dimensional in conception, or may allude to solid masses by modeling the forms with hatched lines.

9. Invent a skeleton that is related to our human one but differs from it in proportion and, to some slight extent, in design. You can think of your drawing as a representation of the skeleton of a prehuman "missing link" or as some humanlike skeletal system of an inhabitant of another planet. Insist on making each bone so structurally clear that a sculptor could construct this skeleton by using your drawing as a guide.

10. Using the skeleton you invented in the previous exercise as a model, draw it again, this time in an action pose that produces some markedly foreshortened forms. Suggest what the figure might look like in the life state by giving it a lean cover of skin. Without the musculature and fat to help support and shape this skin, it will of course behave much as tight-fitting clothing would, if draped upon a human skeleton. Again, insist on volumetric clarity, modeling the forms in any manner that will make them emphatically three-dimensional.

11. Draw a skeletonlike figure intended as an illustration for a magazine article on famine. Here, anatomical accuracy may be subordinated to an imaginative image that expresses the article's dire theme. Forms may be unfocused, fragmented, or distorted to the point of abstraction.

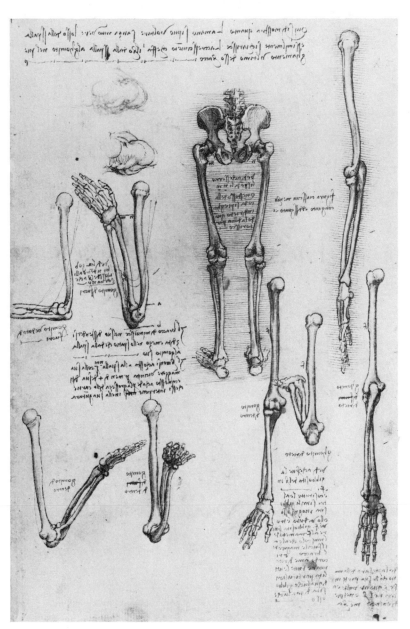

FIGURE 3.65
**LEONARDO DA VINCI (1452–1519)**
*The Extremities*
Pen and ink. 29 x 20 cm.
*Windsor Castle, Royal Library.*
*By gracious permission of Her Majesty the Queen.*

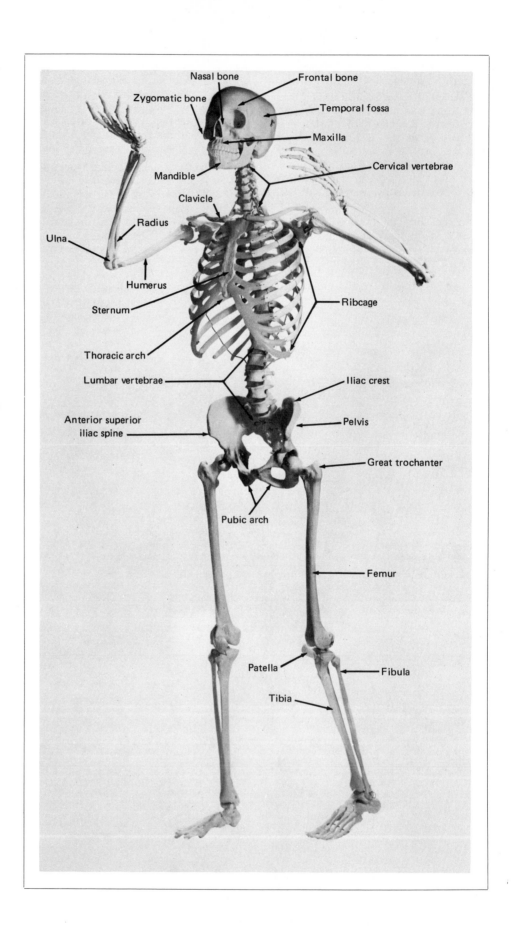

FIGURE 3.66

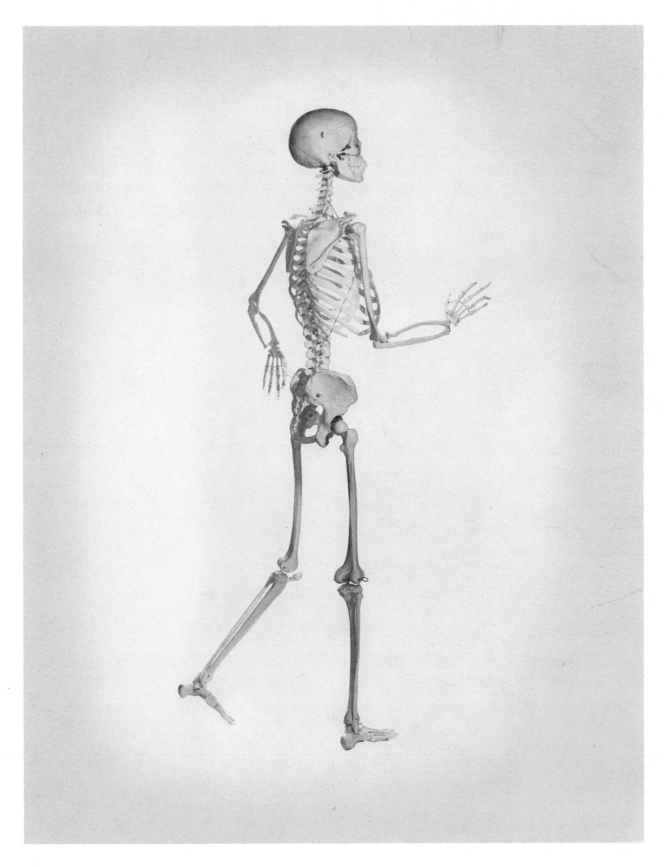

FIGURE 3.67

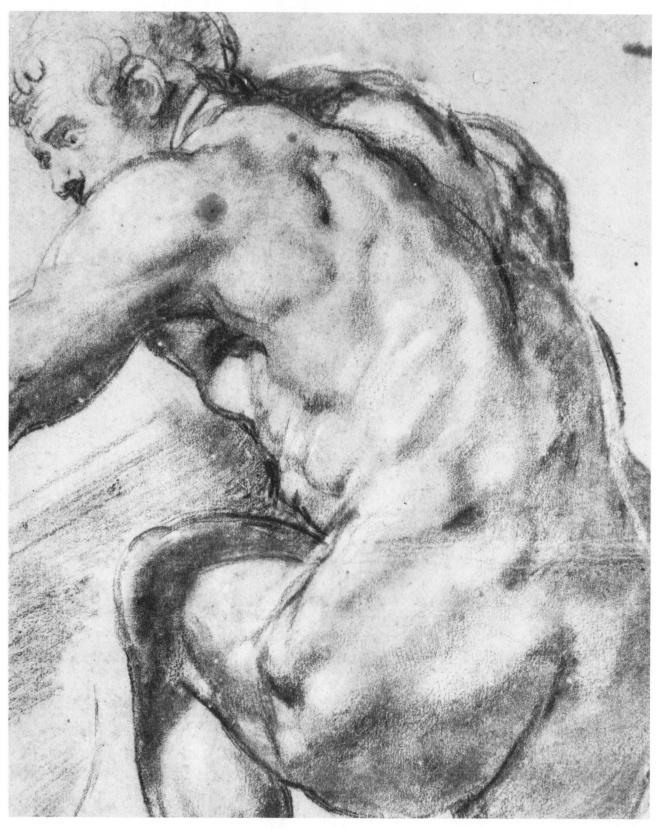

FIGURE 4.1
PETER PAUL RUBENS (1577–1640)
*A Nude Man Kneeling* (detail)
Black and white chalk.
*Museum Boymans-van Beuningen, Rotterdam.*

# FOUR

# THE ANATOMICAL FACTOR

*Part Two: The Muscles*

## SOME GENERAL OBSERVATIONS

In this chapter we will examine three main themes concerning the muscles and the ways in which a grasp of major anatomical facts assists creative figure drawing. One theme examines the location, function, and form of those muscles most influential in shaping the figure's living forms; a second theme considers their morphological role—how the muscles affect the body's surfaces; the third theme explores how the muscles may serve as agents that stimulate graphic inventions concerning structure, design, and expression. This last theme accompanies the first two (a) to provide some immediate examples of how a knowledge of anatomy assists creative ends, and (b) to point out that the artist's obligation is not to anatomical accuracy, but to certain visually expressive truths.

In this anatomical survey, visualizations carry the main burden of communication. Although important features concerning attachments and surface effects are described, the sense of the overall disposition and character of the muscles is best studied through the anatomy illustrations and the reproduced drawings, photographs, and sculptures.

One of the more distressing errors in the drawings of some beginners shows the head, neck, and limbs as only tenuously attached to the trunk. Similarly, the upper and lower parts of a limb are drawn as if each part ended before the next began. This tendency toward what may be called the sausage-link syndrome probably stems from the following assumptions by the student: Because the figure's forms are thinnest at the joints and appear most swelled between them, and because the segments must be free to bend, each segment must therefore be self-contained, its muscles terminating short of the joint. But, if this were true, the body would be immobilized. It is only by muscles crossing over joints to attach to bones on the other side that mobility is possible. Muscles attach to bone or to other tissues by *tendons*—tough, nonelastic tissues located at the ends of the long muscles and at the edges of broad ones. Muscles function as levers in moving bones by acting across the joints, which in turn act as points of support (Figure 4.2).

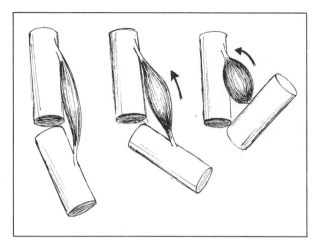

FIGURE 4.2

Although the figure's fleshy forms, mainly shaped by muscle, *do* taper at the joints, it is not the result of a bundle of muscles ending where another one begins, but of muscles thinning down to cords and sheets of tendon that often interlace with other muscles as they move across joints in both directions. Instead of sausage-link attachments, the head, neck, and limbs are deeply embedded in the torso by muscles and tendons woven far beyond the apparent end of any single part. Thus, throughout the body, most of the muscles appear braided in various ways. Something of the interlaced nature of the figure's muscles and the deep embedding of the limbs can be seen in Figure 4.1.

Muscles work by contracting their fleshy fibers, or *bodies.* In contraction the muscle body is drawn together, growing shorter and thicker. To do this, one attachment of the ends of a muscle must be fixed, the other movable. A muscle's *origin* is the

point of fixed attachment; its *insertion* is the movable point of attachment. In Figure 4.2 the muscle's upper attachment is the origin because it pulls the lower form toward the upper one. But Figure 4.2 omits an important feature of muscle movements. No muscle acts alone. Whenever a muscle or group of muscles contracts, other *opposing* muscles are activated to modify or regulate the action of the contracting ones (Figure 4.3).

This arrangement of muscles in opposition to each other is a necessary anatomical condition, allowing not only for fine-tuned regulation of actions, but also for the controlled return of parts after their movement. For example, in the lower arm the *flexor* muscles bring the fingers together in a fist, the *extensor* muscles extend the fingers, and the *supinator* muscles enable the hand to rotate. But all these muscles are engaged in each of these actions, either in contracting or expanding functions. Additionally, these three muscle groups, working in complicated harmony, permit the many combinations of movements of the lower arm and hand.

In general, then, for any bodily movement to occur, some muscles must work by contraction while other muscles, related to the function of the moving part, are to some degree relaxed. This is the case whether it is the bending of a finger or of the torso. Knowing which muscles are at work in a pose and which are relaxed can help us decide which surface forms to emphasize. Normally, artists more strongly indicate (and even exaggerate) those muscles actively engaged in producing an action, modifying or even omitting those muscles which are relaxed. To give equal attention to every muscle (unless for purposes of study) can actually lessen the viewer's understanding of the gestural nature of a pose, and can result in a drawing that, in Leonardo da Vinci's

FIGURE 4.3

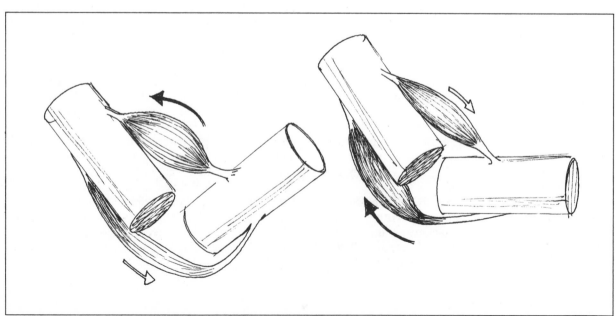

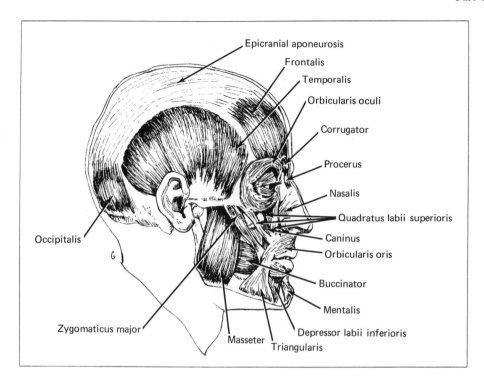

**FIGURE 4.4**

words, will look "more like a bag of nuts than a human figure."*

We can better understand the behavior and form of many of the figure's muscles (and bones) by testing their function in our own bodies. Where feasible, try to isolate and operate the muscles under discussion in the following sections. The advantages, for study, of a little privacy and a full-length mirror are obvious.

## MUSCLES OF THE HEAD

While the skull, as we saw in Chapter Three, is an ever-present influence on the surface forms of the head, the muscles of the head play a less important role. Most of the facial muscles are small, thin, or deeply embedded in fatty tissue; likewise the thin muscles of the cranium have little effect on the fleshed forms. But a few of the muscles shown in Figure 4.4 do affect contours or surface conditions, and warrant special attention.

The *masseter,* from its origin at the underside side of the zygomatic arch to its insertion at the angle of the mandible, is one of the most visible muscles of the head, accounting for the obliquely turned bulge running from the corner of the jaw to

**FIGURE 4.5**

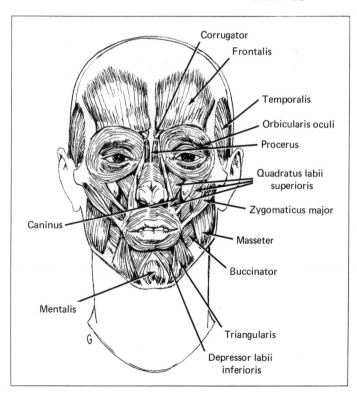

* Leonardo da Vinci, *The Treatise on Painting,* trans. A. Philip McMahon (Princeton, N.J.: Princeton University Press, 1956), vol. 1, p. 125.

the cheekbone. The lines of its body, if extended, would embrace the eye socket.

The fan-shaped *temporalis,* along with the masseter, operates the closing and biting movements of the mandible. The temporalis originates and largely fills the recessed plateau of the temporal fossa, passing under the zygomatic arch to insert into the coronoid process, the forward prong of the mandible (see Figure 3.6). Far less visible than the powerful masseter, the temporalis is nevertheless an influence on the surface form of the temple, producing a slight bulge in the otherwise recessed area of the temple (Figure 4.5).

The *frontalis,* a flat, broad muscle divided vertically, is of interest because it wrinkles the brow horizontally and lifts the eyebrows. Although its form contributes little to the contour of the forehead, its upper, curved origin, high on the frontal zone, will often show if the hairline is high enough. The frontalis inserts into the skin of the brow and nose (Figure 4.5).

The *corrugator,* originating at the medial end of the superciliary arch and inserting into the skin of the eyebrows, is a small muscle that strongly affects the surface of the forehead in frowning expressions. It forces the vertical wrinkles of the brow and causes the eyebrows to bunch up near the nose (Figures 4.5 and 4.6).

Encircling the mouth is an elliptical muscle, the *orbicularis oris,* which has the unique distinction of having no bony points of attachment. Instead, it

originates among some nine small muscles around the mouth, most of which seem aimed at the mouth, and inserts into the skin surrounding the lips. Contractions of this muscle produce all the closing, pursing actions of the mouth (Figure 4.5). Repeated contractions account for the permanent radiating creases often seen in the elderly. The *orbicularis oculi* is also a circular muscle, encompassing the eye and operating the opening and closing of the eyelids. Here again, radiating creases, the familiar crow's feet, testify to its encircling contractions (Figure 4.5).

Originating from the zygomatic arch and inserting into the corner of the mouth, the *zygomaticus major* provides an important oblique line of abutment between the planes of the side and front of the face, as can be seen in Figure 3.10 and in Holbein's *Cardinal John Fisher* (Figure 4.6). Note in the latter the effects of the frontalis and corrugator muscles, and Holbein's sensitivity to bone and muscle throughout the head.

## SURFACE FORMS OF THE HEAD

The forehead consists of the area represented by the frontal bone and closely corresponds to its form. In planar terms, the forehead can be divided into a broad, bulging center plane, often sloping somewhat backward, and a smaller plane near each temple which abuts the center plane at a point about one-

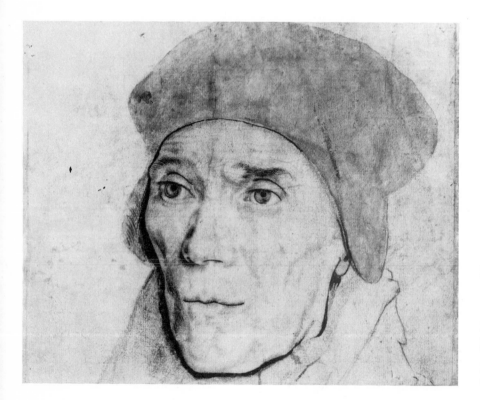

FIGURE 4.6
HANS HOLBEIN the Younger
(1497–1543)
*Cardinal John Fisher* (detail)
Red and black chalk, brown ink washes,
pen and India ink on primed paper.
*Windsor Castle, Royal Library.*
*By gracious permission*
*of Her Majesty the Queen.*

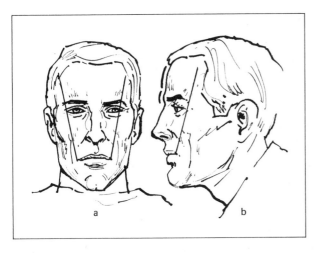

**Figure 4.7**

third in from the outer edge of the eyebrow. Each line of abutment is tilted at an angle that, if extended, would cause it to strike the corner of the mouth (Figure 4.7a). Often, the rounded form of the frontal bone causes the central plane of the forehead to appear rounded to within an inch above the brows. Here the thickened ridge of bone above the eye sockets forms smaller bulges at the outer corner of the brow, and again near the nose (Figure 4.7b).

The eyeball is deeply set into the orbital cavity, the eyelids acting as upper and lower "awnings." Because most light sources are located above us, the upper eyelid usually casts a shadow upon the upper part of the eye. The upper lid, the larger and more clearly defined of the two, is the more mobile.

When the eyes are shut the upper lid covers most of the visible eyeball. The eyelids closely follow the curve of the eyeball, the upper lid appearing to overlap the lower one at the outer corner of the eye. In the front view the crest of the curved lower margin of the upper lid is near to the nose; in the lower lid the crest of the curve is away from the nose (Figure 4.8a). In the side view the eyelids align on an angle dropping backward (b). Like the forehead, the eyelids can be reduced to three planes each (c). In the front view the eyes are placed almost one eye-length apart (d). A line drawn downward from the inner corner of the eye will strike the outer edge or outer portion of the nostril (d).

The nose, wedgelike and projecting at an inclined angle from the general plane of the face, can be reduced to four major planes: a central plane (the bridge of the nose), often widening at the junction of the nasal bone and the *lateral cartilage,* and again at the bulb of the nose; and two side planes, inclined obliquely downward from the central plane. The plane of the base of the nose, free of the plane of the face, may be horizontal or show a slight upward or downward tilt, and is roughly triangular in shape. The nostrils are located nearer to the edges of the triangle than to its midline (Figure 4.9a).

The medial partition separating the nostrils, the *septum,* represents the lowest point of the nose in both the front and side views. The nostrils curving upward at an angle, in providing the smaller, beveled planes of the end of the nose, modify the general plane of the base (Figure 4.9b). Both the bulb of the nose and the nostrils may be either rounded or angular, reflecting the character of the cartilage

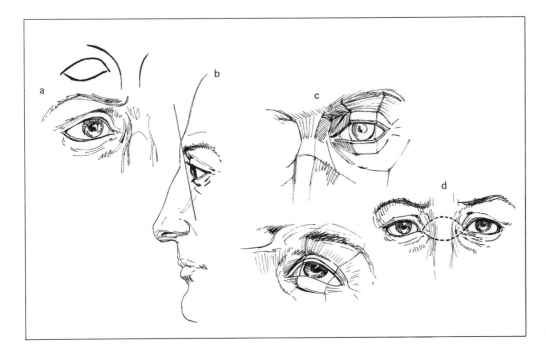

**Figure 4.8**

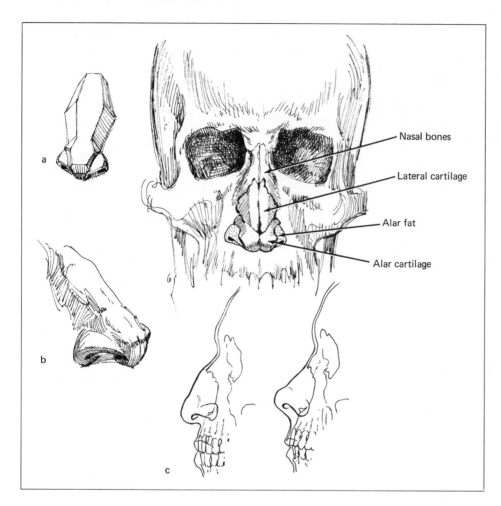

Nasal bones

Lateral cartilage

Alar fat

Alar cartilage

Figure 4.9

Figure 4.10

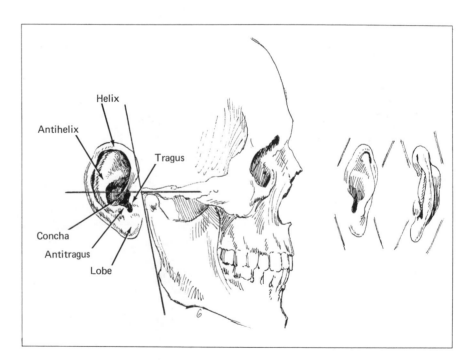

Helix

Antihelix

Tragus

Concha

Antitragus

Lobe

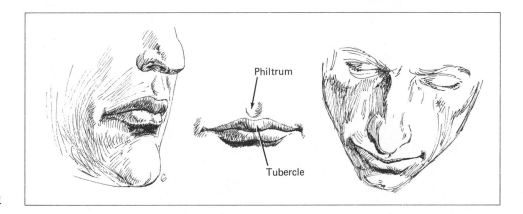

**FIGURE 4.11**

underlying these forms. Sometimes a central groove is visible at the tip of the nose, marking the junction of the two *alar cartilages* which shape the end of the nose and part of the nostril openings. In the side view, a change in profile is most likely at the junction of the nasal bone and lateral cartilage, and again, at the bulb of the nose (Figure 4.9c).

The ear (Figure 4.10) is located behind the upper angle of the mandible and is vertically centered on the zygomatic arch. In a side view of the head, the ear is roughly aligned between the eyebrow and the base of the nose. Ovoid in shape, its major features are the *concha,* the hollow in the lower half of the ear; the *helix,* the rolled outer edge of the ear; the *antihelix,* the Y-shaped, inner curved form that is parallel with the helix near the bottom of the ear but turns away from it as the two forms rise; the *tragus* and *antitragus,* the two facing "bumps" near the bottom of the concha; and the *lobe,* which may vary from a barely rounded form to a pronounced pendant. The shape of the ear varies greatly, but generally the helix emerges near the antitragus and above the earlobe. The helix describes a simple C curve and turns sharply inward to the upper end of the concha, about halfway down the ear. Seen from the front, the upper half of the ear is turned slightly downward toward the concha, the lower half, upward, and the antihelix obscures part of the helix.

The lips (Figure 4.11), centered horizontally on the midline of the head, occupy a position a little nearer to the nose than to the chin. Usually, the upper lip is slightly more forward than the lower, and is characterized by the *tubercle,* the swelled, central portion, and the two slightly curled wings.

Together, these three segments form a wide-spread M-shaped form. When closed the lips are in contact at every point, making one lip appear thin where the other is thick. The lower lip forms a wide-spread W-shaped line where it meets the upper lip, but this shape only sometimes characterizes the form of the entire lower lip. In the front view the upper lip appears to extend a bit more at the corners of the mouth than the lower lip does. When viewed from above, the overall curve of the lips upon the curved surface of the face becomes apparent. As Figure 4.11 shows, reducing the lips to a severely simplified planar state produces two major planes in the upper lip and three places in the lower one.

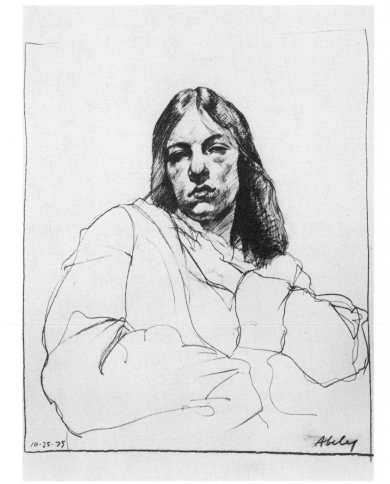

**FIGURE 4.12**
**SIGMUND ABELES** (1934–    )
*After Her Eye Operation*
Charcoal and pencil. 22 x 30 in.
*Courtesy of the artist.*

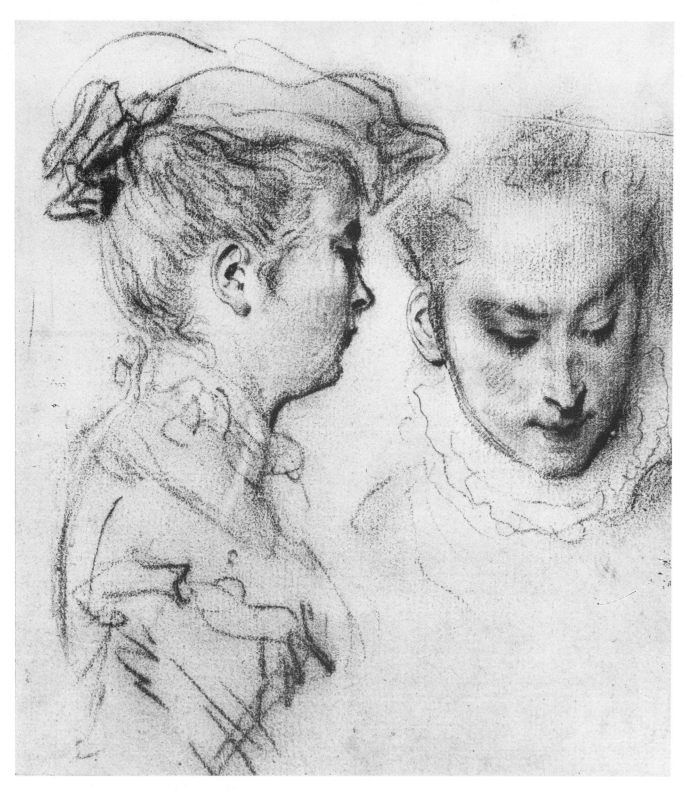

**FIGURE 4.13**
ANTOINE WATTEAU (1684–1721)
*Two Studies of the Head of a Young Woman*
Red and black chalk.
6 3/4 x 6 1/8 in.
*Trustees of the British Museum, London.*

There are three areas which are not actually part of the lips but are important considerations in modeling them: the small, fleshy mounds near the corners of the mouth; the *philtrum,* or groove below the nose, whose oblique margins strike the two peaks of the upper lip; and the furrow under the lower lip, which in some individuals may be a pronounced oblique plane that softens as it broadens to either side of the mouth, enveloping a large part of the lower portion of the face. This can be seen in Abeles's *After Her Eye Operation* (Figure 4.12), where only the forward end of the mandible protrudes through the otherwise darkened curving plane beneath and to either side of the mouth. Abeles's knowledgeable drawing of the head also illustrates another useful relationship: In almost every individual, the corners of the mouth are located where a line drawn upward toward the eyes would strike their centers, as shown in Figure 4.11.

A careful study of the Abeles drawing shows that the artist is well aware of the surface anatomy of the features discussed above *and of the areas separating them.* Notice, for example, how convincingly he defines the foreshortened plane of the underside of the chin and how deftly he establishes the abutment of the central plane of the nose with the curved plane of the forehead.

Watteau, in his *Two Studies of the Head of a Young Woman* (Figure 4.13), demonstrates a masterful grasp of the forms of the head, here expressed with an astonishing economy and grace. Note how the skull's presence is everywhere in evidence, how the lips and ears are simply stated, and how, in the head on the right, the side planes of the nose are suggested. And, as in Figure 4.12, we know a great deal about the form of the segments that separate the eyes, ears, nose, and mouth.

When drawing the head, the beginner too often concentrates almost exclusively on the features just described, leaving the terrain between them largely unregarded. The results often show modeled features floating on a flat enclosure representing the shape, but not the structural nature of the head. A far better attitude toward the forms of the head is to recognize that *every part is an important feature,* a unit of form that interjoins others, usually in a quite harmonious way. In most faces, as you can readily observe, the creases in the forehead "imitate" the eyebrows, the curved eyebrows "anticipate" the nose, the folds in the skin near the nostrils spread out to "measure" the mouth, the fleshy mounds at the corners of the mouth "parenthesize" it. This rhythmic play, so pronounced between the form-units of the head, is a characteristic to be found throughout the figure to varying degrees.

Although the areas of the cheek, temple, chin, and forehead do not offer boundaries and masses as

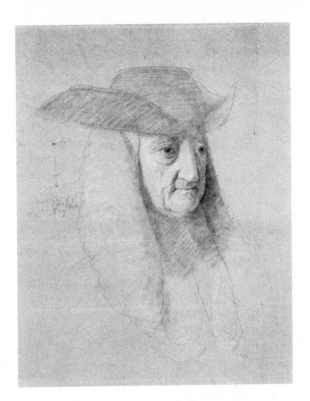

FIGURE 4.14
JOHN SINGLETON COPLEY (1738–1815)
*Head of the Earl of Bathurst, Lord Chancellor*
Black and white chalk. 26 x 19 1/2 in.
*Courtesy Museum of Fine Arts, Boston.*
*The Karolik Collection.*

clearly defined as, say, those of the nose or mouth, it is important to appreciate the skull's influence in these large areas, and to regard them with the same sensitive concern we give to the smaller features. Because fatty deposits, sometimes considerable, are often the dominant factor in forming the terrain of the cheek and chin, the planes and form-units in these areas may vary widely. Nevertheless, in the cheek, the zygomatic bone and arch and even the canine fossa are often visible, even in heavily padded faces. And despite the familiar double chin and jowls in some corpulent figures, traces of the mandible's angularities are never altogether obscured (Figure 4.14).

## MUSCLES OF THE NECK

In the anterior (front) view (Figures 4.15 and 4.16), the contours of the neck are formed by the *sternomastoids.* Each originates at the sternum and inner end of the clavicle, sweeping gracefully upward to insert into the mastoid process of the temporal bone. The fullness of the longer *sternal* body contrasts with the straplike *clavicular* branch. The sternomastoids oppose each other in turning the head left or right, but act in unison to raise and

133

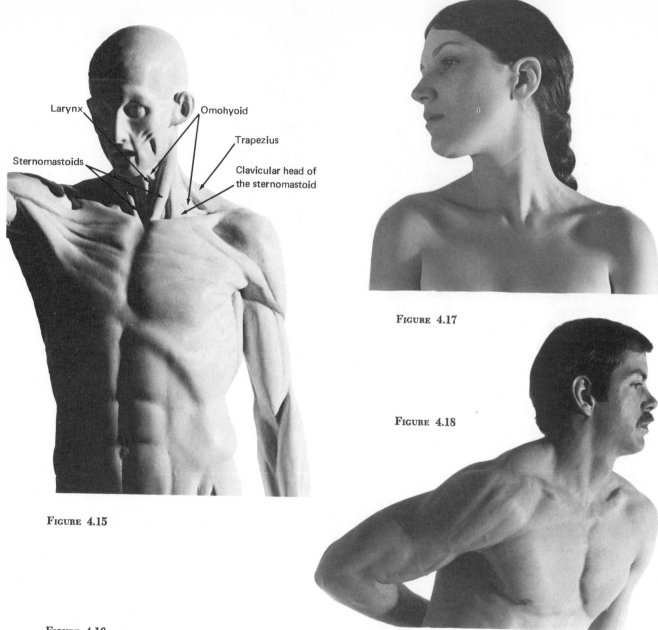

Larynx

Omohyoid

Trapezius

Clavicular head of
the sternomastoid

Sternomastoids

FIGURE 4.15

FIGURE 4.17

FIGURE 4.18

FIGURE 4.16

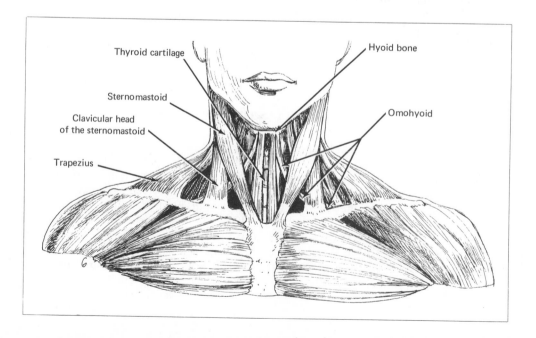

Thyroid cartilage

Hyoid bone

Sternomastoid

Omohyoid

Clavicular head
of the sternomastoid

Trapezius

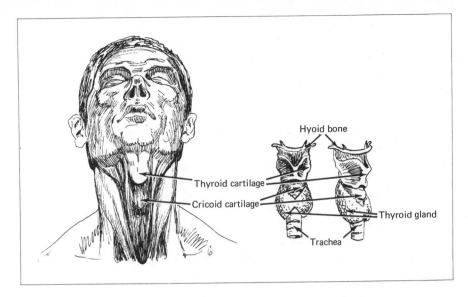

FIGURE 4.19

lower the head. Their tendonous attachments at the pit of the throat are always visible, even in necks otherwise devoid of muscular detail. The entire muscle becomes boldly evident when the head is turned far to one side, as in Figure 4.17.

Emerging from behind and about halfway down the length of the sternomastoid is the *trapezius,* providing an oblique line that ends near the lateral (outer) tip of the clavicle. The trapezius is a muscle of the back, but in the anterior (front) view it provides the triangular wedge that fills in the area between the contour of the neck and the clavicles, into which it makes one of its several insertions.

Between the sternomastoids is a triangular area, its apex at the pit of the throat, its base abutting the base of the plane of the underside of the chin (Figures 4.18 and 4.19). Most of the space between the sternomastoids is filled by the swallowing apparatus and by the larynx, whose lower part is formed by the ring-shaped *cricoid cartilage* (Figure 4.19). The U-shaped *hyoid bone* is located at the common baseline between the aforementioned triangular area and the plane of the underside of the chin. Directly below the hyoid bone is the *thyroid cartilage,* its protrusion forming the familiar Adam's apple (Figure 4.20).

FIGURE 4.20

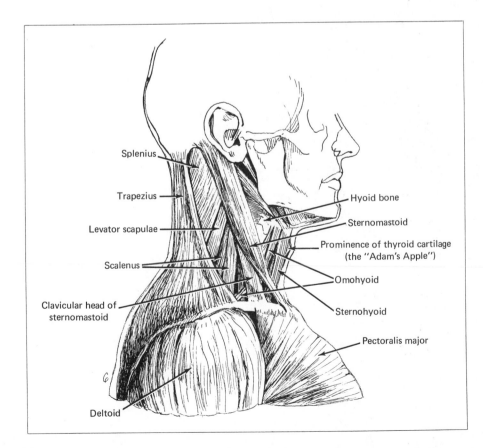

In the side view (Figures 4.18 and 4.20), the contours of the neck are formed by the trapezius on the posterior side (back) and, in the anterior view, by the larynx, the sternomastoid, and the *sternohyoid,* a muscle that depresses the hyoid and larynx. The space between the trapezius and sternomastoid is filled by three muscles, somewhat recessed and thus not often visible. They are the *scalenus,* the *splenius,* and the *levator scapulae* (Figure 4.20). The scalenus and splenius act in movements of the head; the levator scapulae raise the scapula. Note that the scalenus is rather vertically placed, but the other two muscles are decidedly oblique. Emerging from under the forward edge of the sternomastoid are several muscles of only passing interest to the artist. The *omohyoid* is of importance as the only muscle to intrude on the triangular hollow between the trapezius and sternomastoid (Figures 4.15 and 4.16), and for its occasional appearance behind the sternohyoid, itself visible when the chin is thrust forward, and, usually, in the elderly, where the sternohyoids appear as curved cords that run from the underside of the chin toward the pit of the throat.

Viewed from the posterior, the contours of the neck are again formed by the sternomastoids, the lines of the trapezius cutting diagonally across them, making the neck appear shorter. In contrast to the pronounced surface activity often found in front and side views of the neck, the back view tends to be simpler, the neck's cylindrical basis more insistent.

Here it is important to remind ourselves that our examination of specific anatomical facts should mainly serve to broaden creative freedom, not to restrict it. At first glance, Michelangelo's drawing of the neck in the detail from *Studies for the Crucified Haman* (Figure 4.21) appears flawlessly accurate, but a closer inspection shows that the artist has exaggerated the scale of the sternomastoids and the forms of the larynx region. Indeed, the muscular clarity throughout this figure and in all of Michelangelo's figure drawings, more typical of the leaner, *ectomorphic* type, is unlikely in the massively proportioned figures favored by the artist. Michelangelo seems always to give his figures the anatomical definition of lean, muscular types and the proportional heft of the athletic, *mesomorphic* types.

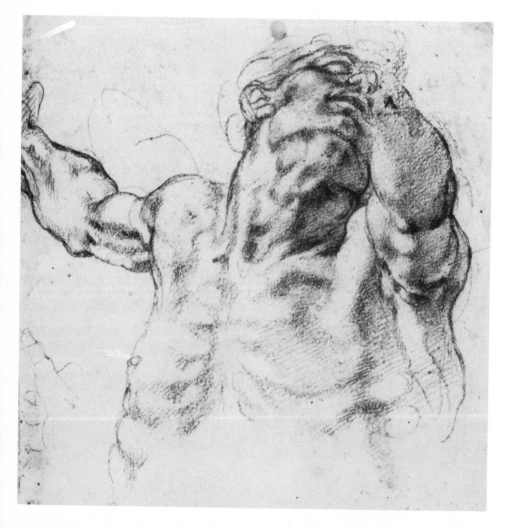

FIGURE 4.21
MICHELANGELO BUONARROTI
(1475–1564)
*Studies for the Crucified Haman*
(detail)
Black chalk.
*Teylers Museum, Haarlem.*

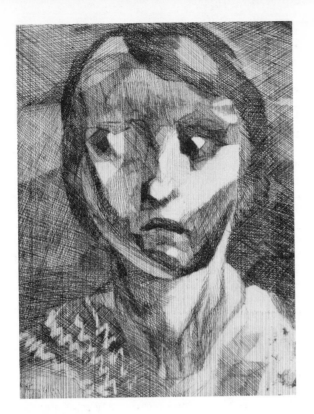

FIGURE 4.22
JACQUES VILLON (1875–1963)
*Head of a Young Girl* (2nd state, 1929)
Etching. 6 x 7 3/4 in.
*Print Department, Boston Public Library.*

By contrast, Villon's *Head of a Young Girl* (Figure 4.22) seems to be less concerned with anatomical matters. Yet the forms, despite their Cubist-like interpretation, are anatomically sophisticated. In both of these drawings a knowledge of anatomy serves as a source of structural, plastic, and emotive inventions.

## MUSCLES OF THE TORSO

In the anterior (front) view (Figures 4.23, 4.24, and 4.25), the clavicles can be seen as firm bars of attachment for the muscles of the neck, shoulder, and chest, gracefully springing from them in all directions. The clavicle's superior (upper) surface receives the trapezius and sternomastoid muscles; its lateral, inferior (lower) surface holds the *deltoid,* the powerful encasing muscle of the shoulder; and, on the medial underside of the clavicle, the *pectoralis major,* the great muscle of the breast, com-

FIGURE 4.24

FIGURE 4.23

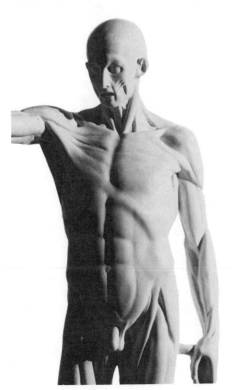

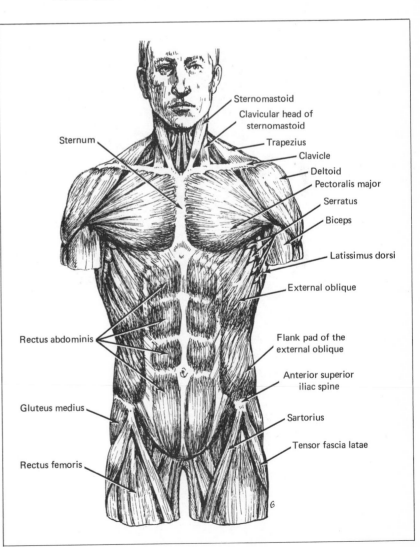

FIGURE 4.25

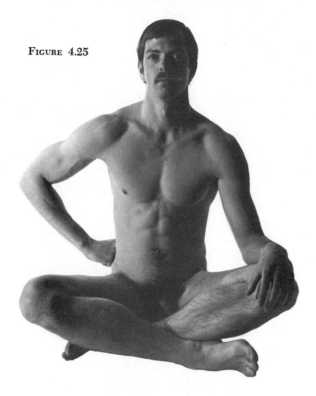

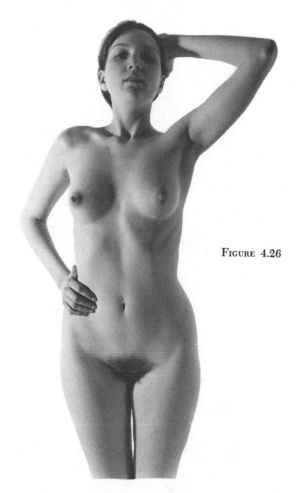

FIGURE 4.26

pletes the clavicle's muscular encirclement. The pectoralis major, in addition to its origin on the inferior surface of the clavicle, also emerges from the anterior of the sternum, and from the costal cartilage below it. Thus its origins roughly describe three sides of a square. Its insertion into the upper part of the humerus, instead of providing the fourth side of the square, draws the upper and lower boundaries of the muscle together to a point at the armpit, creating the impression of a triangle. The muscle twists at its narrowest point, just before inserting into the anterior surface of the humerus. As a result, its lower fibers attach at a higher point on the humerus than do the higher fibers, giving the muscle bundles of the pectoralis major a fanlike radiating rhythm.

These bundles of muscle fiber, also characteristic of the deltoid, give both of these prominent muscles a rich surface character (Figure 4.18). Note, in Figures 4.23 and 4.24, that one muscle bundle of the pectoralis, the one nearest the deltoid, is separated from the rest by a narrow crevice. Note, too, how the pectoralis major slips under the deltoid on its way to insertion, and that the large crevice between these muscles grows wider near the clavicle. Like the pectoralis muscle, the deltoid, from its origin at the clavicle to its insertion almost halfway down the humerus, is somewhat fanlike in character. Together, these muscles create powerful forms of much grace and energy.

The mammary gland occupies the lower, outer corner of the pectoralis major in both the male and female figure. In the male there is a general angularity to the entire muscle, the glandular and fatty tissues of the mammary gland only subtly softening the area of the breast (Figures 4.21 and 4.25).

In the female, the fuller breasts descend below the bottom margin of the pectoralis major. The form of the breast begins at the xiphoid process, but its influence can be seen as far up as the base of the manubrium. The breast is fullest at the lower, outer side (Figure 4.26). A common error in drawing these forms is placing them too high on the chest. Actually, there is as much height to the breast as to the pectoral region above it. An overhead view shows the breasts to be turned outward, the nipples located to the outside rather than centered on the forms (Figure 4.27). Thus, in the front view the nipples are decidedly to the outside of center. Only when one breast is in profile will the nipple on the opposite breast appear centrally positioned.

Below the pectoral muscle the torso's front view contour is taken up by the *latissimus dorsi*. Appearing at the armpit, it descends vertically, but because it thins as it descends and turns backward slightly at the end of its course, it is lost from sight a few inches above the waist. Actually a large

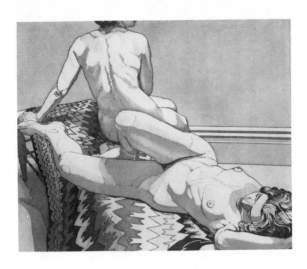

FIGURE 4.27
PHILIP PEARLSTEIN (1924– )
*Two Nudes on an Old Indian Rug*
Etching and aquatint. 23 3/4 x 29 5/8 in.
*Courtesy Museum of Fine Arts, Boston.*
*Lee M. Friedman Fund.*

FIGURE 4.28
PETER PAUL RUBENS (1577–1640)
*Study for the Figure of Christ on the Cross*
(detail)
Charcoal, heightened by white.
*Trustees of the British Museum, London.*

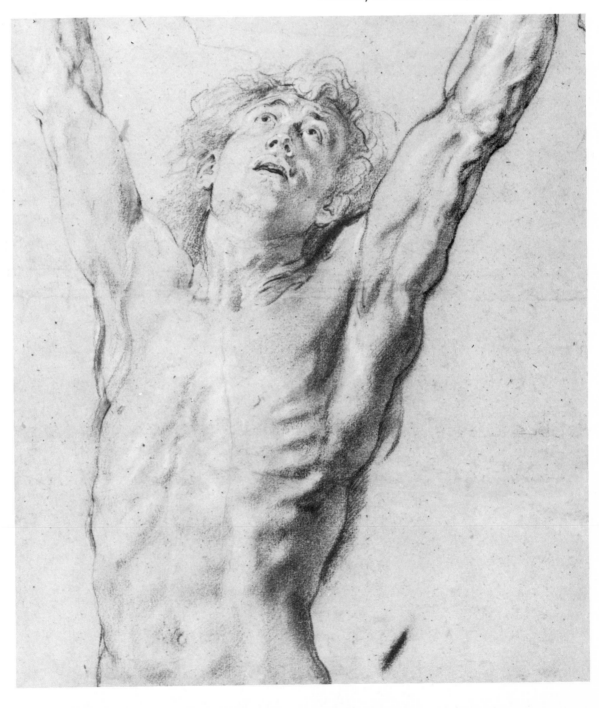

muscle enveloping the back, in the anterior view only its thickened forward edge is visible. This muscle contributes to the V shape of well-developed male torsos, especially when the arms are raised (Figures 4.28 and 4.29).

Slipping out from under the latissimus dorsi are four or five small, fleshy pads, or *digitations,* of the *serratus magnus.* This is a large but mainly deep muscle which originates on the lateral surface of the first eight or nine ribs, and inserts into the spinal border of the scapula by passing between it and the ribs. It operates the forward movement of the scapula. These fleshy pads are interlaced by thin digitations of the *external oblique,* a muscle that fills

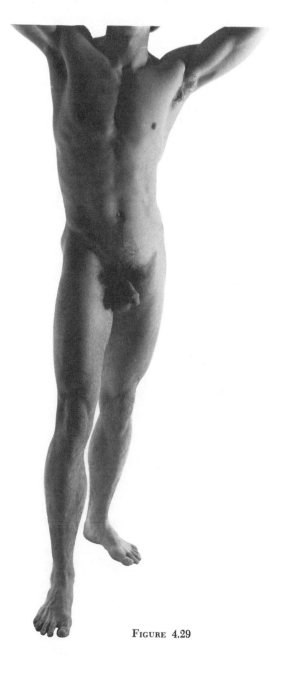

FIGURE 4.29

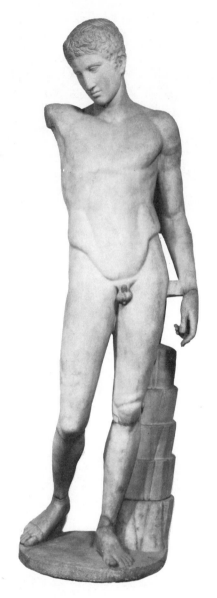

FIGURE 4.30
Classic Greek (450–440 B.C.)
*Westmacott Athlete*
Marble.
*Trustees of the British Museum, London.*

much of the area between the abdominal cavity and the latissimus dorsi. The external oblique continues the front-view contour of the torso, dropping backward from its high point near the thoracic arch until it reaches the waist, and turning somewhat outward below the waist. A thin muscle, the external oblique thickens markedly near its termination at the iliac crest. This thickened, fleshy mound at the root of the thigh, much favored by Greek and Roman sculptors, is called the *flank pad* of the external oblique (Figures 4.24, 4.29, 4.30, and 4.31).

The *rectus abdominus* muscle fills the surface

area of the abdominal cavity (Figure 4.24). It is divided vertically by tendons into two rows of four fleshy pads, themselves separated horizontally by tendons. These tendonous borders separating each horizontal pair of muscle pads become more chevronlike as they ascend. The lowest border, at the navel, is a true horizontal, but each succeeding border tends to peak more at the torso's midline. Note that the lowest group is twice the length of any of the rest. The abdominal group originates at the crest of the pubic bone and inserts into the cartilage straps

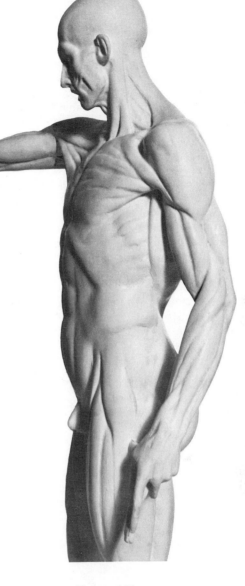

of the fifth, sixth, and seventh ribs. This group of muscles bends the spine forward, constricts the abdomen, and elevates the pelvis.

In the side view of the torso (Figures 4.31 and 4.32), note the shape and scale of the chest mass in relation to the smaller, backward-tilting pelvic mass.

**FIGURE 4.31**

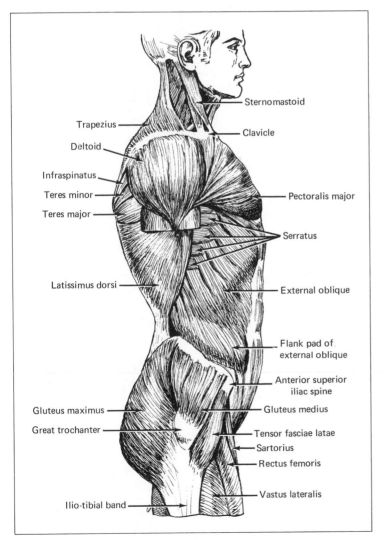

- Sternomastoid
- Trapezius
- Clavicle
- Deltoid
- Infraspinatus
- Teres minor
- Teres major
- Pectoralis major
- Serratus
- Latissimus dorsi
- External oblique
- Flank pad of external oblique
- Anterior superior iliac spine
- Gluteus maximus
- Gluteus medius
- Great trochanter
- Tensor fasciae latae
- Sartorius
- Rectus femoris
- Vastus lateralis
- Ilio-tibial band

**FIGURE 4.32**

In this view the trapezius, in its upper, vertical segment, roughly aligns with the forward edge of the latissimus dorsi. In its lower, forward-curving segment the trapezius glides into the forward edge of the deltoid, the two edges forming a lazy S curve. There is a rough similarity in the shape and tilt of the pectoralis major and the flank pad of the external oblique. The latter's lower furrow appears to turn to meet the latissimus dorsi. Note the direction of the serratus digitations in relation to the angle of the interlacing fleshy ribbons of the external oblique, the ribbons aiming at the deltoid above and at the waist below. Notice also the undulating character of the torso's anterior contour. This is formed at the top by the bold swell of the pectoralis major, followed by the thoracic arch, after which the subtle rise and fall of the muscle pads of the rectus abdominus provide the rest of the contour. Note that the backward-curving line of the lower abdomen appears to continue around the buttocks, the two edges suggesting a backward-tilting egg whose hidden upper margin would reach the waist.

In Figure 4.32 three scapular muscles come into view: the *infraspinatus,* in a line with the top of the deltoid; the *teres minor,* in the center; and the *teres*

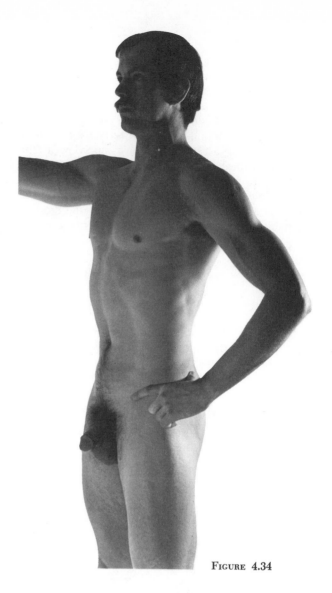

FIGURE 4.34

FIGURE 4.33
MICHELANGELO BUONARROTI (1475–1564)
*Study for a Christ on the Cross*
Black chalk. 12 1/2 x 8 3/4 in.
*Teylers Museum, Haarlem.*

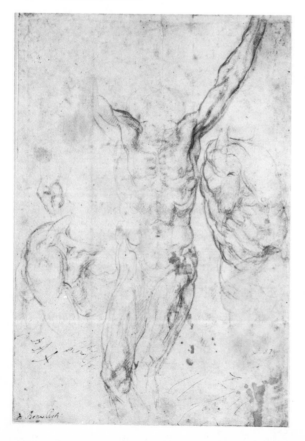

*major,* at the bottom of the group. Their common upward curve repeats the curve of the top margin of the deltoid. All three muscles originate on the scapula and insert into the greater tuberosity of the humerus, or high on its shaft. These muscles lengthen considerably when the arm is extended forward or raised high, even appearing in the front view (Figure 4.29). In Michelangelo's *Study for a Christ on the Cross* (Figure 4.33), the teres major is visible on the central figure's left side as a pronounced swelling behind the armpit. In this informing study, notice the flank pads and the sternal attachments of the pectoral muscle on the central figure, and the latissimus dorsi and digitations of the serratus magnus and external oblique in the side view. As this drawing demonstrates, when the arms are raised, the clavicles are almost entirely hidden. This can also be seen in Figures 4.21 and 4.29.

The three-quarter view of the torso in Figure 4.34 serves here to give us a better visual idea of the front and side views discussed so far. Notice that the ribs and costal cartilage that forms the thoracic arch are still much in evidence, even in a well-muscled figure. That these bony landmarks also survive the musculature and fatty deposits of the female figure can be seen in Figure 4.26.

In the posterior view of the torso (Figures 4.35 and 4.36) the trapezius appears as a four-pointed geometrical shape. The long, lower segment aims downward where it terminates at the last three thoracic vertebrae; the topmost segment appears driven into the occipital bone, and the two side segments reach to the acromion processes of the scapulas. These scapular attachments and the clavicular attachments seen in the front view are the places of insertion of this large muscle. The trapezius, involved in movements of the scapulas and the head, originates at the occipital bone and among all the spinous processes up to the last thoracic vertebra.

An important characteristic of the trapezius affecting the figure's surface form is its several tendonous areas. The largest is a spearhead-shaped tendonous plateau that reaches to the occipital bone above and ends at the second or third thoracic vertebra. The seventh cervical vertebra, the last outpost of the skeleton of the neck, is located at the center of this flat sheet of tendon. Two smaller but important tendonous areas related to the trapezius

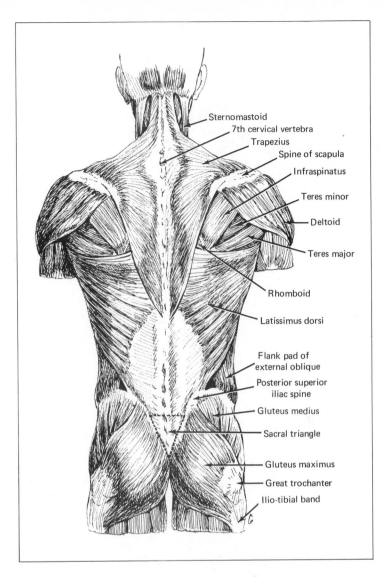

- Sternomastoid
- 7th cervical vertebra
- Trapezius
- Spine of scapula
- Infraspinatus
- Teres minor
- Deltoid
- Teres major
- Rhomboid
- Latissimus dorsi
- Flank pad of external oblique
- Posterior superior iliac spine
- Gluteus medius
- Sacral triangle
- Gluteus maximus
- Great trochanter
- Ilio-tibial band

FIGURE 4.36

FIGURE 4.37

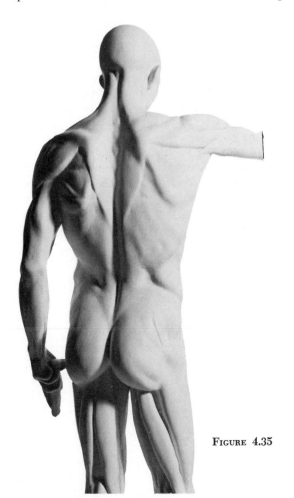

FIGURE 4.35

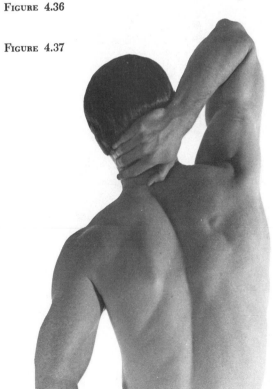

separate this muscle from the deltoids and cover the scapulas' spines. In poses where the arms are placed behind the torso, as in Figure 4.37, the hills of muscle can be seen descending to the valleys of tendon, despite that fact that the tendon in these areas covers the protruding spines of the scapulas. When the arms are placed in front of the torso, the general mass of the scapula asserts itself, as we see in the right arm of the figure in Figure 4.38. When, as in these two examples, the arm is raised high, the scapula's movement toward the figure's side tends to obscure the scapula somewhat, whether the arm is before or behind the figure. But when the arm is held low, the scapula's form becomes easier to see. Note that a pronounced backward positioning of the arm, such as that of the left arm in Figure 4.37, causes the pointed base of the scapula to protrude. Note, too, in Figure 4.37, the sharp crease and bold planes in the upper back as a result of the arms' placement, and, in Figure 4.38, the clarity of the large, spearhead-shaped tendonous sheet mentioned above.

Abutting the trapezius at the scapular spine, the deltoid's lower margin cuts across the three scapular muscles as it leaves the torso to insert into the humerus. Note the enveloping nature of the latissimus dorsi, its upper edges curving upward as it too goes to its insertion into the humerus (Figure 4.36). Below, the latissimus dorsi originates among thoracic and lumbar spinal processes and from the iliac crest. Here, too, a very large diamond-shaped tendon is bounded by the oblique fleshy ends of the latissimus dorsi and by the gluteal muscles, whose curved, tendonous attachments to the iliac crests emphasize the presence of these bony masses. A little of the flank pad of the external oblique is also visible in the back view.

Two areas in the back are affected by layers of deep muscle. The rhomboid, almost entirely hidden by the trapezius, extends from its origin on the spinal column—from the seventh cervical to the fourth or fifth thoracic vertebra—to its insertion into the inner border of the scapula. It operates the scapula's upward and backward movements. When contracted in pulling the scapula up or toward the spinal column, it forms quite pronounced vertical bulges that greatly affect the torso's posterior surface. In well-muscled figures, the influence of the rhomboid overtakes that of the trapezius even when such backward movements of the scapula are only slight. Note the vertical bulges on the left side of the figure's back in Rubens's *A Nude Man Kneeling* (Figures 4.1 and 4.39). In Figure 4.37, the small "dot" alongside the vertical bulges caused by the contracting rhomboid marks the superior, medial corner of the scapula.

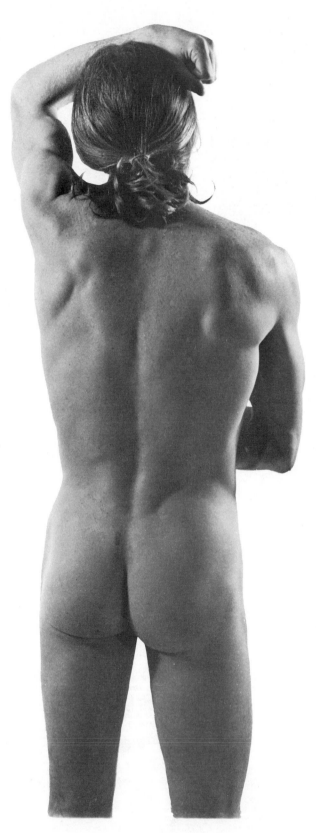

FIGURE 4.38

The *erector spinae,* a group of muscles running on either side along the length of the spinal column, are also deep muscles that affect surface form. In the fleshed figure, especially in the lower back, they suggest vertical columns flanking the long spinal valley of the back (Figures 4.37 and 4.38).

As we can see, the anatomical forms of the torso are especially bold and rhythmic. Interweavings, eruptions, and abutments of masses play all around the torso, producing forms whose design suggests continuity from part to part. One problem remaining for students with a sound grasp of artistic anatomy is deciding how much of this rich visual activity to include in their drawings. The answer, of course, varies with the intent. In drawings made expressly for anatomical study, the more anatomical material explored, the better. But even here, care should be taken to see how the torso's anatomy both creates and clarifies structural essentials, and what plastic and emotive sensations they may suggest. In Pontormo's preparatory sketch *Studies for a Pietá* (Figure 4.40), anatomical facts help explain the character of the torso's massive and rugged structure. But it is Pontormo's sensitivity to the design and expressive possibilities of the various digitations, the muscles at the shoulder, and the directions of edges and shapes that create dynamic activities throughout the drawing. In Chapter Five we will explore some ways in which anatomical formations stimulate dynamic activities such as these. But here we should note that it is the artist's appreciation of the tensions and energies alive in the torso, as well as its precise anatomical nature, that guides his or her choices of what to stress and what to subdue, and thereby influences both the drawing's purpose and handling.

Whenever objective anatomical study is not a drawing's major purpose, its kind and degree of participation will be determined by visual expressive interests. In Boccioni's *Muscular Dynamism* (Figure 4.41), anatomy plays a large role, but not for purposes of study or even for structural clarity. As the title indicates, the drawing evokes the muscles' potential for exertion and action. Note the great amount of anatomical detail still discernible in amplifying the figure's power and movement: deltoids, scapula, spinal valley, even a suggestion of the deep erector spinae tell us of the artist's understanding of anatomy, despite the drawing's rather abstract manner.

Often, much of the torso's anatomy (as well as the rest of the figure) is obscured by considerable amounts of fatty tissue, a consideration to be discussed later in this chapter. But even when this is the case, artists with a sound knowledge of anatomy are able to draw figures whose underlying bone and

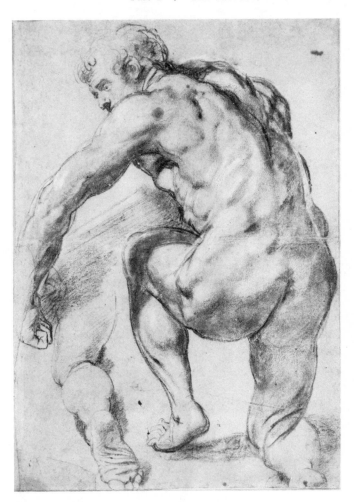

FIGURE 4.39
PETER PAUL RUBENS (1577–1640)
*A Nude Man Kneeling*
Black and white chalk. 52 x 39 cm.
*Museum Boymans-van Beuningen, Rotterdam.*

muscle we believe in—that are alive and convincing as figurative presentations and as expressive graphic inventions. In Degas' *Standing Nude Woman, Back View* (Figure 4.42), there is no doubt about the figure's skeletal and muscular properties, although Degas is sparing in his use of anatomical detail.

## MUSCLES OF THE ARM

We have seen that the bones of the lower arm rotate to permit the hand to face up (supinate) or down (pronate), and that the radius and ulna are parallel in supination but crossed in pronation. This freedom to rotate creates a great number of possible contours of the arm. When the hand is fully rotated, the thumb describes almost a full circle. Comparable

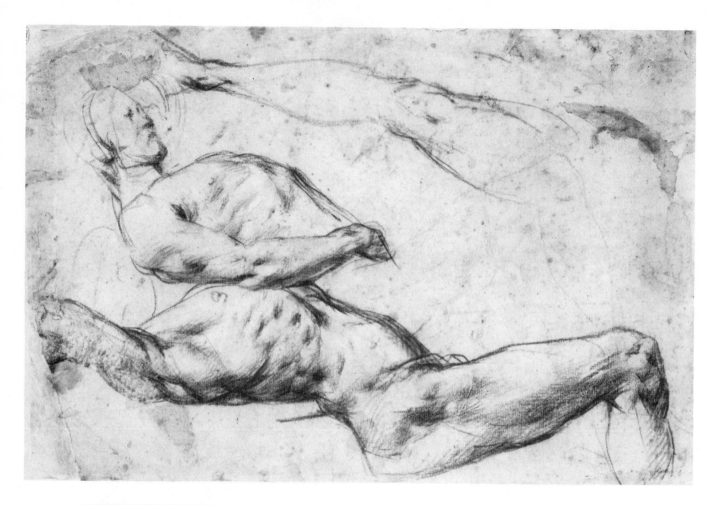

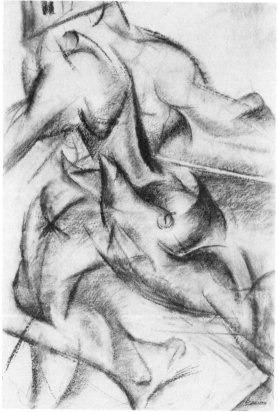

Figure 4.40
**JACOPO DA PONTORMO** (1494–1556)
*Studies for the Pietà*
Chalk. 18 x 24 cm.
*Museum Boymans-van Beuningen, Rotterdam.*

Figure 4.41
**UMBERTO BOCCIONI** (1882–1916)
*Muscular Dynamism* (1913)
Charcoal. 34 x 23 1/4 in.
*Collection, The Museum of Modern Art, New York.*

FIGURE 4.42
EDGAR DEGAS (1834–1917)
*Standing Nude Woman, Back View*
Black chalk on tan paper. 42.5 x 27.7 cm.
*Cabinet des Dessins, Musée du Louvre, Paris.*

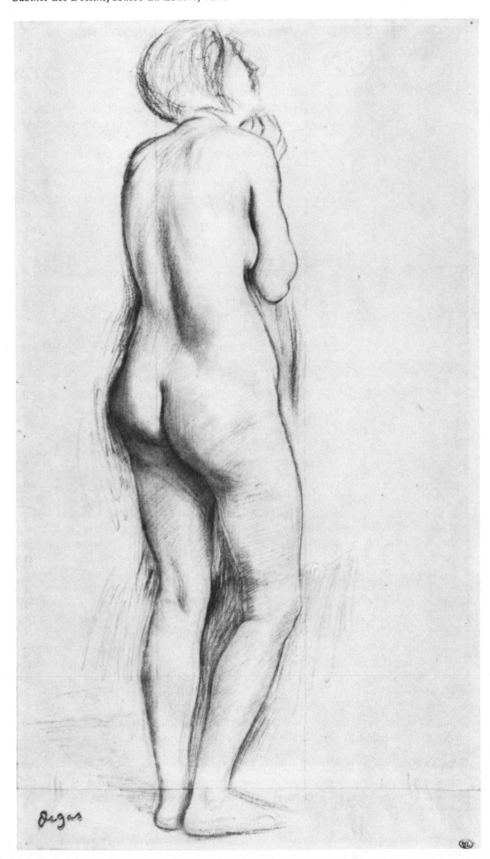

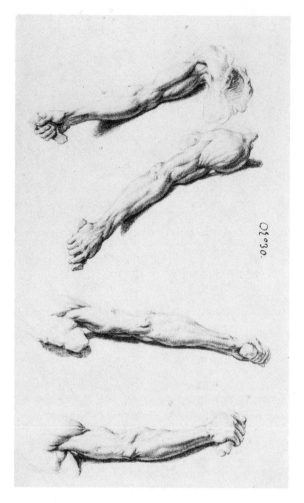

**Figure 4.43**
**JACOB DE GHEYN II(1565–1629)**
*Study of Arms*
Black chalk. 36 x 23.1 cm.
*Rijksmuseum, Amsterdam.*

changes in the location of the arm's muscles, and the form and contour changes that different views of the arm or various stages of rotation produce, require a more careful study of this limb. De Gheyn, in his *Study of Arms* (Figure 4.43), examines just such changes. No doubt the changes due to this freedom of movement add to the apprehension some students feel in approaching the arm's muscle system. However, the anatomy of the arm is no more difficult than that of the torso. The upper arm is composed of only a few muscles, and the lower arm's many muscles conveniently separate into three visual and functional groups, making it far easier to understand the form and mechanics of that part. In the hand, as in the head, only a few muscles are of practical interest to the artist.

As you can see in Figure 4.44a (and in all the illustrations of the supinated arm), when the arm is held with the palm face up, the short axes of the

basic masses of the upper and lower arm are in opposition. In this position the upper arm is seen to be narrow and the lower arm, wide. When the palm is turned down (b), the upper arm is wide and the lower arm is narrow. In the supine position the upper arm, especially in well-developed figures, tends to be flatter on the sides than on the top and bottom. The lower arm is somewhat more rounded in its upper portion, but toward the wrist it develops a blocky character: broad, flat planes on top and bottom, and narrow, flat planes on the sides. Although the hand can be aligned with the lower arm, when relaxed it turns naturally inward, toward the body.

Mechanically, the scapula and the scapular muscles participate in some operations of the arm and are part of it, but visually, the arm, at least in the anterior view, begins with the deltoid. Notice in Figures 4.43 and 4.44 that the contour of the deltoid does not curve out farthest at the top, but lower down, nearer to its insertion point a little above the origin of the *brachialis,* a muscle that flexes the arm. The brachialis is overtaken in mass by the *biceps* and *triceps* to such a degree that in the supine anterior view the lateral contour of the arm passes directly from the deltoid to the triceps, the single muscle of the posterior of the upper arm. But note that a small portion of the brachialis reappears at the medial lower portion of the biceps. In the medial side view this small segment of the brachialis is of some importance, but in the anterior view the brachialis has scant influence on the arm's surface form.

In the supine anterior view, the biceps is centrally located on the upper arm, flanked on either side by the triceps. The biceps, as the term suggests, has two heads, originating at two places on the scapula: the short head (on the medial side) from the coracoid process; the long head (on the lateral side) from the edge of the glenoid cavity. These heads unite under the deltoid and emerge in the familiar long and rather squarish muscle, which in contraction becomes more or less ovoid. The biceps inserts into the radius by a tendonous cord sometimes visible just above the bend of the arm, and by a thin tendonous sheath, or *fascia,* along the upper medial surface of the lower arm, where it acts as a kind of binder for the flexor muscles of the lower arm. The biceps participates in supination; when we bend our arm and rotate our hand, the biceps will contract when the hand is supine and relax when it is prone.

The superficial muscles of the lower arm are basically either *flexors,* muscles that draw the fingers together in a fist, or *extensors,* muscles that extend the fingers. Additionally, some of these muscles work to supinate or pronate the lower arm and hand. There are two large muscles, one a flexor and one an extensor, that are engaged in rotation. The *supinator longus* and the *extensor carpi radialis longus* together form a discernible mass that warrants our thinking of the lower arm as composed of three muscle groups. When the arm is supinated the former continues the contour above the elbow; the latter, below it. When pronation occurs (Figure 4.44b), these muscles unite to form a graceful spiral that begins with their emergence from the humerus, the fleshy bodies seeming to push the triceps and brachialis aside. The curve ends halfway down the lower arm in two tendons that begin a straight descent toward their respective insertion points. The supinator longus attaches to the end of the radius; the extensor carpi radialis longus attaches to a metacarpal bone. Note that in the supinated anterior view, the biceps' fascia and the *pronator teres* form a distinct X just below the elbow toward the inside

edge of the lower arm. The pronator teres originates on the medial epicondyle of the humerus, inserting into the radius, which it pronates.

The medial epicondyle is a common point of origin for four more muscles, all flexors: the *flexor carpi radialis, palmaris longus, flexor digitorum sublimis,* and the *flexor carpi ulnaris*. The last-mentioned muscle provides the medial contour of the lower arm down to the wrist (Figure 4.44a). The fleshy body of each of these four muscles tapers to a tendon at about the same point, about halfway down the forearm. In the living model these bodies are not seen separately but as a united form. In the supine position of the hand only two groups of muscles are of importance in substantially affecting surface form: the *thenar* muscles of the thumb, and the *hypothenar* muscles of the heel at the little finger side.

FIGURE 4.44

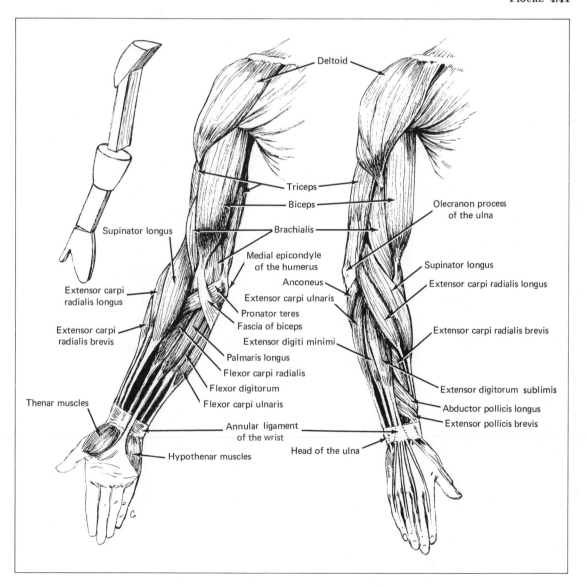

Deltoid

Triceps
Biceps
Brachialis

Olecranon process
of the ulna

Supinator longus

Medial epicondyle
of the humerus
Anconeus

Supinator longus

Extensor carpi radialis longus

Extensor carpi
radialis longus

Extensor carpi ulnaris

Extensor carpi
radialis brevis

Pronator teres
Fascia of biceps

Extensor carpi radialis brevis

Extensor digiti minimi

Palmaris longus

Flexor carpi radialis

Flexor digitorum

Extensor digitorum  sublimis

Thenar muscles

Flexor carpi ulnaris

Abductor pollicis longus
Extensor pollicis brevis

Annular ligament
of the wrist

Hypothenar muscles

Head of the ulna

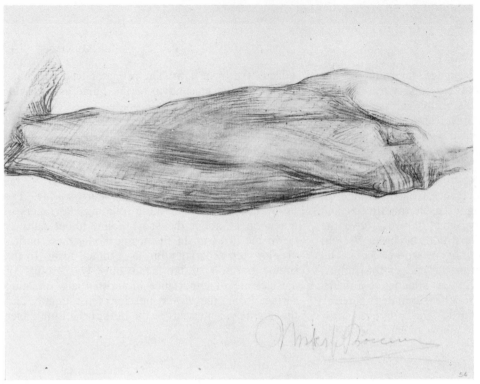

FIGURE 4.45
UMBERTO BOCCIONI (1882–1916)
*Study of a Man's Forearm* (1907)
Pencil on buff paper. 8 1/4 x 11 5/8 in.
*The Lydia and Harry Lewis Winston Collection.*

FIGURE 4.46
LEONARDO DA VINCI (1452–1519)
*Myology of Shoulder Region*
Black chalk. 29 x 20 cm.
*Windsor Castle, Royal Library.*
*By gracious permission of Her Majesty the Queen.*

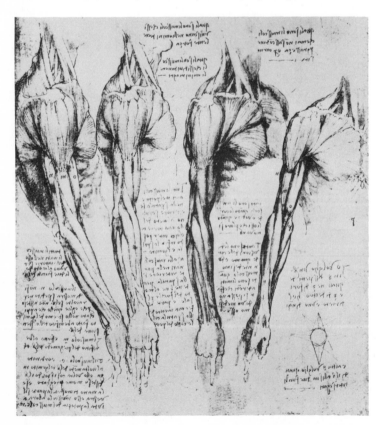

In the pronated anterior view, the triceps and the olecranon process of the ulna are prominent. Three small extensor muscles located in the lower part of the forearm share the diagonal orientation of the two large supinators. They are: the *extensor carpi radialis brevis,* the *abductor pollicus longus,* and the *extensor pollicus brevis.* The first of these extends the fingers of the hand, the latter two operate the thumb. The abductor pollicus longus is the most visible of the three.

The *extensor digitorum,* originating on the lateral epicondyle of the humerus, emerges from under the extensor carpi radialis longus and runs vertically alongside the three smaller extensor muscles just described, sending one tendon to each of the four fingers. These are the familiar radiating cords on the back of the hand. Running between the *extensor carpi ulnaris,* which bends the hand to the ulna side and extends the wrist, and the extensor digitorum, with which it shares its tendon, is the slender *extensor digiti minimi,* seldom seen on the surface. Beyond the extensor carpi ulnaris, near the elbow, the *anconeus,* which also originates on the lateral epicondyle, inserts nearby into the olecranon process and to the posterior end of the ulna. Despite its short run the anconeus creates a marked, triangular plane on the surface, and in the pronated arm appears as a focal point for the longer extensors (Figure 4.45).

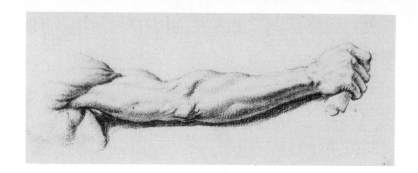

**FIGURE 4.47**
**JACOB DE GHEYN II** (1565–1629)
*Study of Arms* (detail)
Black chalk.
*Rijksmuseum, Amsterdam.*

Returning to Figure 4.44a, note that a subtle furrow extends from the bend in the arm to the thumb, separating the external group, the extensors, whose common point of origin is the lateral epicondyle of the humerus, from the internal group, the flexors, whose common point of origin is the medial epicondyle. An exception in the lateral group is the supinator longus, which is a flexor muscle and originates higher on the humerus. The extensor group appears higher on the forearm and more rug-

gedly shaped than the mass of the flexors opposite it. Between the two groups, just above the wrist, are two recessed flexors of little effect on surface form, except for the tendon of the *extensor pollicus longus,* which runs the length of the back of the thumb (see Figure 4.44b). Note that the lateral contour of the supinated front view of the arm is rich in its changes of direction while the medial contour is relatively subdued in changes, making it reducible to a simple curve.

**FIGURE 4.48**

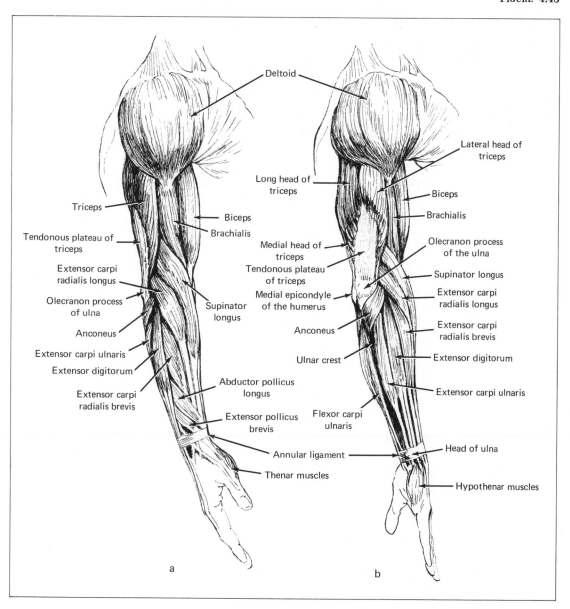

151

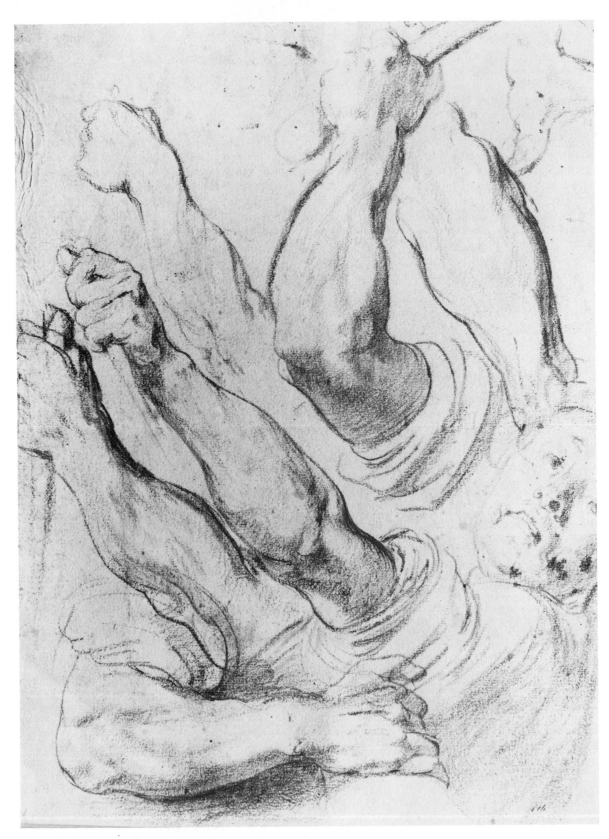

FIGURE 4.49
PETER PAUL RUBENS (1577–1640)
*Studies of Arms and a Man's Face*
Black chalk. 40.5 x 31 cm.
*Victoria and Albert Museum, London.*

As Figures 4.46, 4.47, and 4.48 illustrate, the supinator group, gracefully bridging the upper and lower arm, is more in evidence in the lateral outer side view. Note that this view of the supinated arm shows a reversal of the basic masses of the arm shown in Figure 4.44. Now the upper arm is wider than the lower. With the hand pronated 180 degrees, the forearm undergoes a twist, changing direction more in its lower than upper half. The upper arm turns even less, about 90 degrees, and the deltoid turns least, about 40 degrees.

As Figure 4.48b shows, between the extensor carpi ulnaris and the flexor carpi ulnaris is a pronounced furrow called the *ulnar crest*. This long depression is easily seen in the fleshed figure and marks the boundary separating the two opposing muscle groups. This corresponds to the furrow seen in the anterior view. The anconeus slips into this hollow to insert into the ulna.

From the arm's side view, the triceps, with its characteristic high fleshy mound and low tendonous plateau, becomes an important influence on the surface forms, especially in pronation. As the term indicates, the triceps is composed of three heads. The medial head originates on the posterior and medial portion of the humerus; the middle, or long head, below the glenoid cavity; and the lateral head, below the tuberosity of the humerus. All three share a broad, tendonous sheath that inserts on the olecranon. In a well-developed arm it is easy to discern, the inverted, V-shaped mound of the triceps muscle and the flat plane below it. The triceps extends the arm and is the antagonist to the biceps. Note that the pronated view (Figure 4.48b) turns the upper arm to reveal more of the triceps.

From behind (Figures 4.49 and 4.50), the deltoid cuts across the triceps, turning out of sight before its insertion. The teres major and latissimus

**FIGURE 4.50**

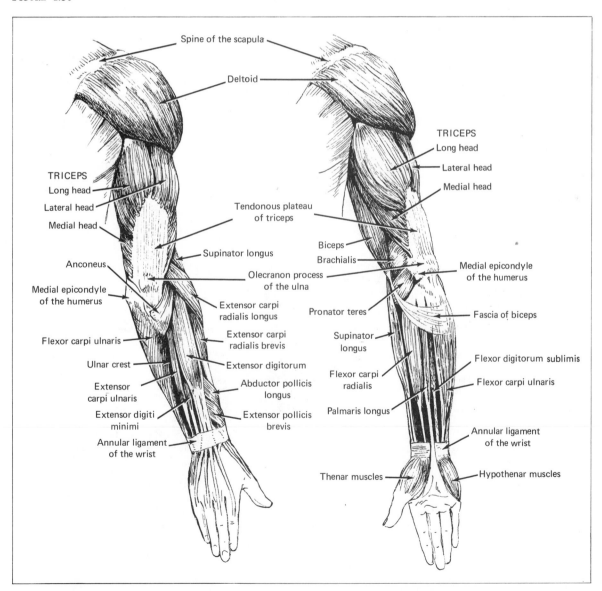

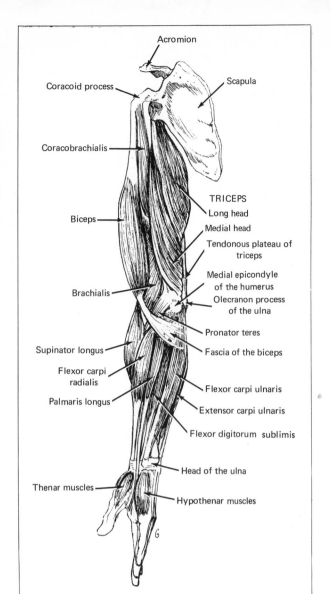

Acromion

Coracoid process

Scapula

Coracobrachialis

TRICEPS
Long head
Medial head
Tendonous plateau of triceps

Biceps

Medial epicondyle of the humerus

Olecranon process of the ulna

Brachialis

Pronator teres

Fascia of the biceps

Supinator longus

Flexor carpi radialis

Flexor carpi ulnaris

Palmaris longus

Extensor carpi ulnaris

Flexor digitorum sublimis

Head of the ulna

Thenar muscles

Hypothenar muscles

FIGURE 4.51

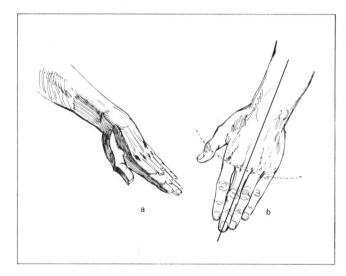

a

b

FIGURE 4.53

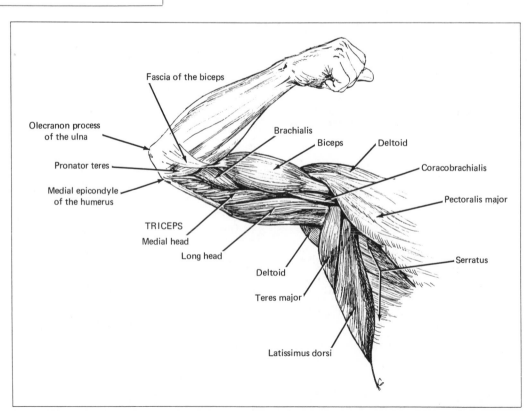

Fascia of the biceps

Olecranon process of the ulna

Brachialis

Biceps

Deltoid

Pronator teres

Coracobrachialis

Medial epicondyle of the humerus

Pectoralis major

TRICEPS
Medial head
Long head

Deltoid

Serratus

Teres major

Latissimus dorsi

FIGURE 4.52

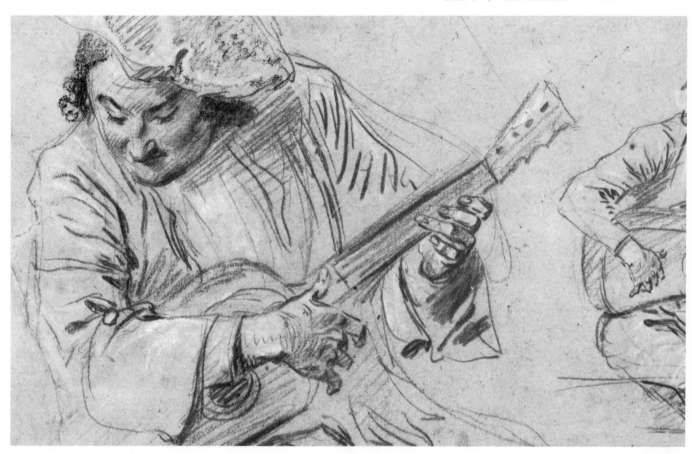

FIGURE 4.54
ANTOINE WATTEAU (1684–1721)
*Two Studies of a Man Playing a Guitar* (detail)
Red, white, and black chalk on tan paper.
Detail size 5 1/2 x 9 in.
*Trustees of the British Museum, London.*

dorsi aim for the armpit, meeting the inner contour of the upper arm provided by the medial head of the triceps.

In the supine view, the upper ends of the anconeus and the extensors carpi ulnaris, digitorum, and carpi radialis brevis all come together and sink beneath the extensor carpi radialis longus. Note the pronounced form of the medial epicondyle of the humerus, and how the position of the lower arm swings outward in this view.

In the pronated posterior view, the biceps and its fascia attachments come into view. Again, note the arm's greater degree of rotation below than above. Now the position of the lower arm swings slightly inward.

From the medial side view (Figure 4.51), the *coracobrachialis* can be seen between the biceps and triceps. Originating on the coracoid process of the scapula and inserting at about the middle of the shaft of the humerus, it becomes visible when the arm is extended or raised. When the arm is bent (Fig-

ure 4.52), the coracobrachialis and the brachialis, appearing below the biceps, form a curve that appears before and after the swelled center of the biceps.

The arrangement of the muscles in Figure 4.52 shows the long and medial heads of the triceps, the teres major, the biceps, the coracobrachialis, and the latissimus dorsi all interlaced at their entry into the armpit. The brachialis, aimed in the same direction, dies out before reaching the armpit.

In considering the structure of the hand, we should take into account the bones of the wrist. Following the blocklike character of the lower arm, the ball of the bones of the wrist gives way to the corrugated plane of tendons on the back of the hand. This plane becomes a rather angular ramp when the hand is lower than the wrist, especially if the fingers are turned up (Figures 4.53a, 4.54, and 4.55). An overhead view of the hand (Figure 4.53b) shows the middle finger to be straightest, the others turning toward it. Note that the knuckles (the heads of the

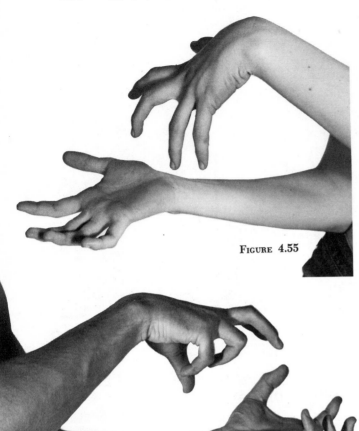

Figure 4.55

Figure 4.56

metacarpal bones) line up with the last joint on the thumb. The fingers tend toward rhythmic arrangements, whether at rest or in action (Figures 1.5, 4.55, and 4.56). The top and side planes of the fingers are rather flat, giving the fingers a more angular and stepped appearance above, and, because of the fatty pads beneath the phalanges, a softer character below (Figures 4.56 and 4.57).

The graceful nature of the arm and hand are well illustrated in Flaxman's *Two Young Women Sewing* (Figure 4.58). In the figure on the right the artist "draws through" the sleeve to delineate the major aspects of the arm's form, the better to draw the drapery upon it. Note in both figures the full deltoids, the rounded upper and more angular lower segments of the lower arm, and the sure sense of their mass. Flaxman's awareness of the design possibilities of arms and hands together is evident in their rhythmic action upward, answering the gentle, descending curve of the two draped figures.

The arms in Pascin's *Reclining Nude* (Figure 4.59) are knowingly expressed. The bulging on the figure's right arm of the supinator and extensor muscles, the strong protrusion of the olecranon, and the interplay of muscles on the inner upper arm are the results not only of observation, but of sound anatomical understanding. Indeed, the slow, caressing line, emphasizing and simplifying as it moves, tells us of the artist's anatomical sophistication. Nowhere in this delicate, sensual drawing does the line fail to show Pascin's grasp of structure; nowhere does it falter in conveying his response to the arms' (and figure's) dynamic qualities.

Figure 4.57

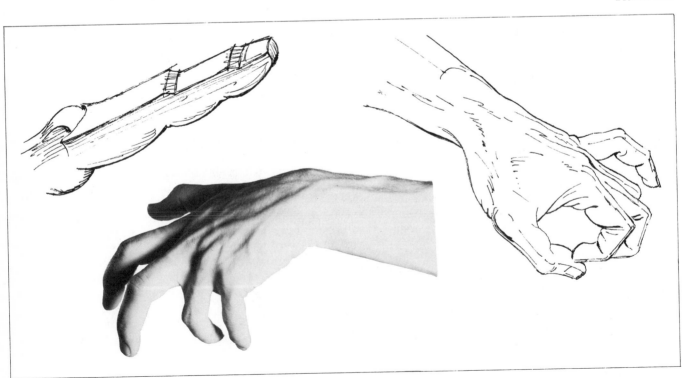

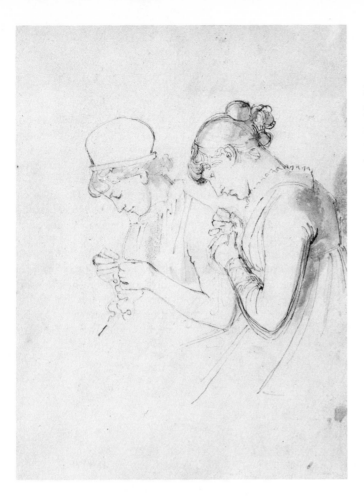

FIGURE 4.58
JOHN FLAXMAN (1755–1826)
*Two Young Women Sewing*
Pencil and pen wash. 7 x 9 in.
*Courtesy Museum of Fine Arts, Boston.*
*Anonymous gift and William A. Sargent Fund.*

FIGURE 4.59
JULES PASCIN (1885–1930)
*Reclining Nude* (1928)
Charcoal. 19 7/8 x 25 1/2 in.
*Collection, The Museum of Modern Art,*
*New York.*
*Gift of Mr. and Mrs. Peter A. Rubel.*

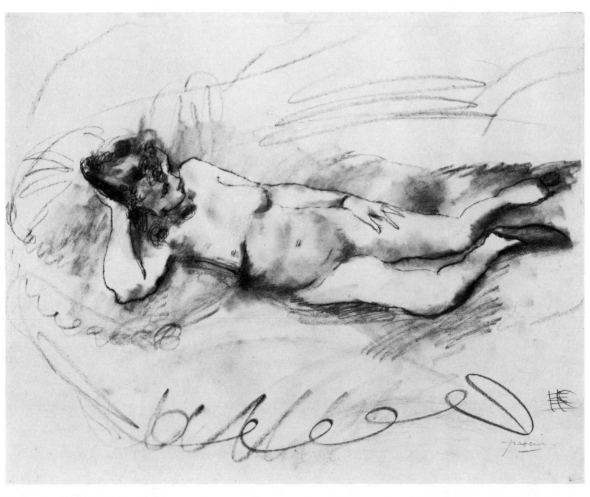

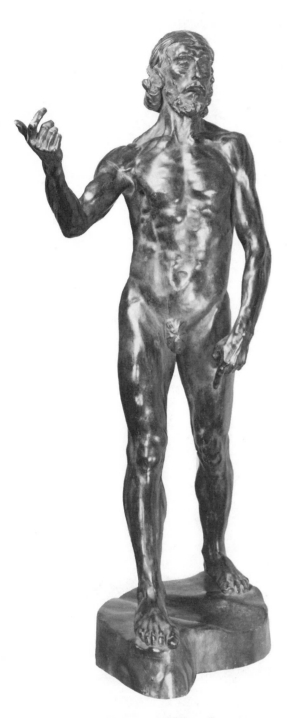

FIGURE 4.60
AUGUSTE RODIN (1840–1917)
*St. John the Baptist* (1878)
Bronze. Height 31 1/2 in.
*Courtesy The Fogg Art Museum,
Harvard University.
Bequest of Grenville L. Winthrop.*

## MUSCLES OF THE LEG

As we have seen, the pelvis provides the strong bony base that supports and permits movements of the upper body. Similarly, the bones and muscles of the lower extremities require the pelvis as a fixed base for attachments to enable the legs to move.

In the anterior view (Figures 4.60 and 4.61), the *gluteus medius,* originating on the lateral surfaces of the ilium and the iliac crest, begins the contour of the leg. The gluteus medius inserts upon the great trochanter of the femur, which, because of the bulk of the surrounding muscles, often appears at a low point in the fleshed form of the leg, rather than at a rise. An exception occurs in the leg bearing the figure's weight in a standing pose, where the mass of the great trochanter does influence the surface form

FIGURE 4.61

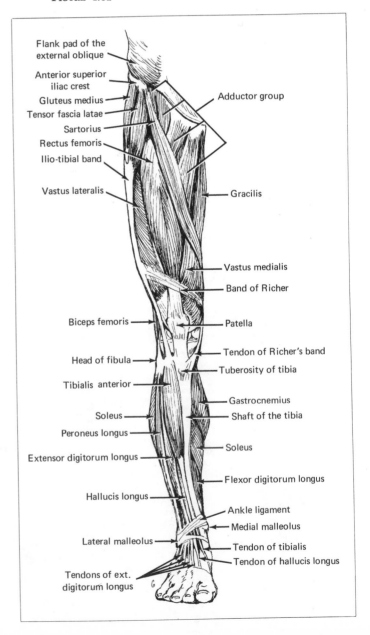

Flank pad of the external oblique
Anterior superior iliac crest
Gluteus medius
Tensor fascia latae
Sartorius
Rectus femoris
Ilio-tibial band
Vastus lateralis
Adductor group
Gracilis
Vastus medialis
Band of Richer
Biceps femoris
Patella
Head of fibula
Tendon of Richer's band
Tuberosity of tibia
Tibialis anterior
Gastrocnemius
Soleus
Shaft of the tibia
Peroneus longus
Soleus
Extensor digitorum longus
Flexor digitorum longus
Hallucis longus
Ankle ligament
Medial malleolus
Tendon of tibialis
Tendon of hallucis longus
Lateral malleolus
Tendons of ext. digitorum longus

(Figure 4.62). This is an example of an occasional occurrence in the figure: What are prominent out-croppings of bone in the skeleton often become sites of depressions in the living model (as we saw in our examination of the scapula).

The oblique direction of the gluteus medius is duplicated by the *tensor fasciae latae,* arising from the anterior tip of the iliac crest and inserting into the *ilio-tibial band* at a point just below the great trochanter. The tensor fasciae latae is a small but substantial muscle often affecting the surface terrain. It forms, with the *sartorius,* an inverted V shape. The sartorius likewise originates at the upper tip (or spine) of the iliac crest. It spirals downward grace-fully to its insertion at the upper, medial surface of the tibia. In doing so, it divides the centrally lo-cated extensor muscles from the *adductor* group on the medial side (those muscles which rotate the leg inward). The sartorius, then, is an important muscular landmark, most easily seen when the leg and foot are turned slightly inward (Figure 4.60). Near the top of the leg the sartorius may appear cordlike; below, it creates a subtle depression be-tween the extensor and adductor muscles.

Occupying the entire anterior surface of the upper leg, and thus providing its contour, is the *quadriceps femoris,* a muscle system important for its effect on the surface form. Actually, we see only three of the four muscles of this group, one being deeply embedded. They are the *rectus femoris,* originating on the lower iliac spine; the *vastus lat-eralis,* and the *vastus medialis,* both vastus muscles arising from nearby points near the top of the femur. All three muscles are extensors and share a common tendon that fits over the patella. Their individual masses are substantial and generally visible to some extent, especially when the leg bears the weight of the figure. The fleshy portion of the vastus lateralis ends well above the knee, but the vastus medialis, swelling out and obscuring the lower part of the sartorius, "crowds" the knee to insert low on the side of the common tendon. Note the *band of Richer,* a tendonous sheath obliquely stretching across this muscle group. Not visible itself, the re-stricting tendon causes these muscles to bulge out above it when they are relaxed, as in the right leg in Figure 4.29, and the left leg in Figure 4.63.

On the medial surface of the upper leg, isolated by the sartorius, are the adductor muscles. Rarely seen individually in the living forms because of the fatty deposits in this region, the adductors influence the surface as a group, providing the armature for the rounded bulge high on the inner thigh (Figure 4.64). Of this group, the *gracilis,* emerging at the pubic bone and inserting high on the inner side of the tibia, is of importance in providing the inner contour of thigh in the front view.

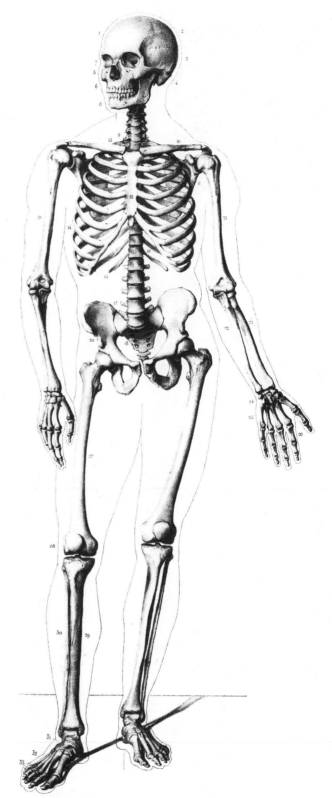

**FIGURE 4.62**
**DR. F. FAU**
*The Anatomy of the External Forms of Man, Plate 2*
*Courtesy of Countway Library, Boston, Mass.*

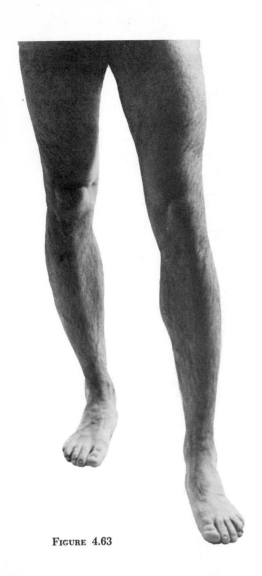

FIGURE 4.63

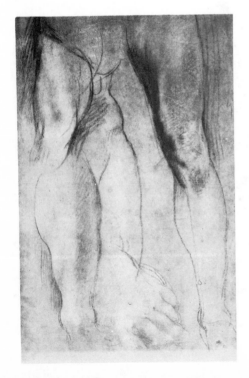

FIGURE 4.64
FEDERIGO BAROCCI (1526–1612)
*Studies of Legs*
Chalk. 41.7 x 27.3 cm.
*The Art Museum, Princeton University.*

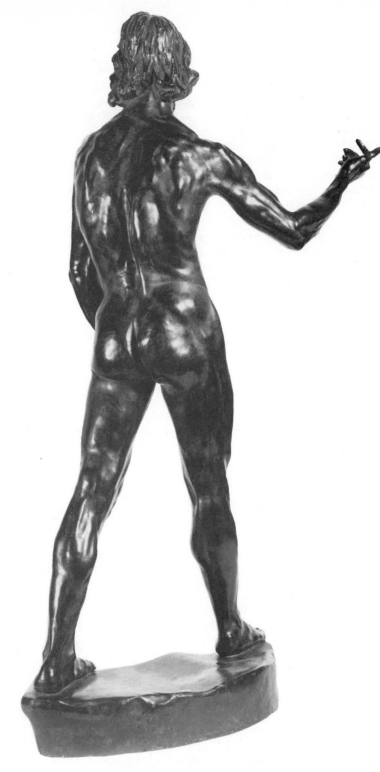

FIGURE 4.65
AUGUSTE RODIN (1840–1917)
*St. John the Baptist* (1878)
Bronze, Height 31 1/2 in.
*Courtesy The Fogg Art Museum,*
*Harvard University.*
*Bequest of Grenville L. Winthrop.*

In the lower leg the muscles suggest two masses: those grouped from the anterior edge to the tibia, and those of the calf. In front, the *tibialis anterior,* in its curving tilt, echoes the spiral of the sartorius. Positioned on the lateral side of the shaft of the tibia, it is one of the more visible muscles of the lower leg, its long tendon inserting into the big toe, its fleshy upper half swelling when the foot is flexed (moved upward). Between the tibialis anterior and the lateral contour, provided by the *soleus,* a calf muscle, are the other three muscles of the anterior group. Often visible in various turning, extending, and flexing actions of the foot, they are the *extensor digitorum longus,* the *peroneus longus,* and, emerging between the lower portions of these muscles, the *peroneus brevis.* The extensor digitorum longus originates high on the tibia and fibula, the other two, on the fibula only. All three muscles insert into the foot, the extensor digitorum longus sending tendons to all but the big toe.

On the medial side of the tibia the medial head of the *gastrocnemius,* the large muscle of the calf, provides the highest segment of the contour of the inner lower leg. The soleus, appearing again on the medial side, continues the contour, and the *flexor digitorum longus* completes it. This small muscle, emerging from under the soleus, inserts into the foot, its tendon joining those of two deep muscles to pass behind the tibia's medial malleolus. Note that the fleshy portions of the muscles of the lower leg, like those of the lower arm, taper as they descend, their tendons running down together until they radiate in the extremity. Note, also, that the medial malleolus is higher than the lateral malleolus.

The leg's deep "roots" become apparent in the back view, embedded not much below the waist (Figures 4.65 and 4.66). The attachment of the gluteus medius upon the iliac crest marks the highest point of the leg's penetration into the trunk. The *gluteus maximus* reaches almost as high, emerging from the posterior surface of the ilium and from the sacrum and coccyx. It inserts just below the great trochanter and into the ilio-tibial band. Note the oblique angle of the top, bottom, and medial margins of the buttock muscle, but its vertical lateral margin. Note also the lazy S-shaped depression along the outer edge of the gluteal muscles, the great trochanter marking the center of the indented area. This subtle hollow is often seen in the fleshed figure.

The straight descent of the gracilis contrasts with the rich curve of the vastus lateralis overlaid by the ilio-tibial band on the lateral side of the leg. The three hamstring muscles, all originating on the lower pelvis, function in pulling back or bending the leg. The gluteus maximus overlaps their common point of origin. Both the *semimembranosus* and *semitendinosus* insert into the medial surface of the tibia,

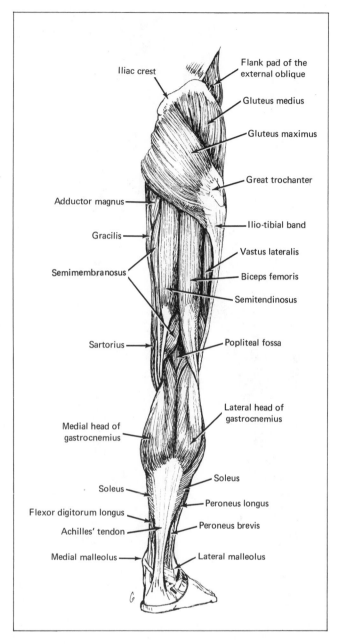

FIGURE 4.66

but the *biceps femoris* inserts into the fibula. In thus parting from their parallel descent, to insert into opposite sides of the lower leg, they produce a pincerlike effect on it. Note that the semimembranosus appears again just above the back of the knee, and the *adductor magnus* fills the space alongside the gracilis, below the buttock.

In the back view of the lower leg, the gastrocnemius, originating at the medial and lateral condyles of the femur, also parts at the back of the knee, resulting in a hollowed area, the *popliteal fossa.* This hollow shows only when the leg is bent,

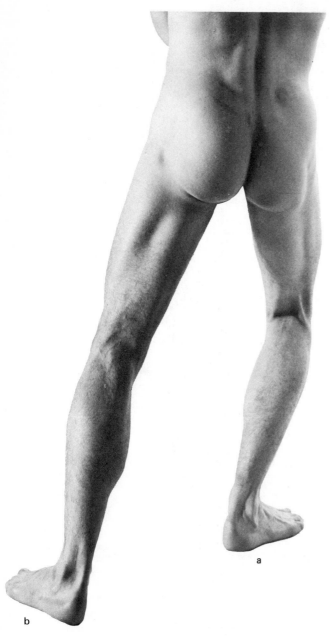

FIGURE 4.67

as in Figure 4.67a; when the leg is straight, the area appears somewhat convex, the result of fatty tissue in this location (Figure 4.67b).

As this illustration shows, the hamstring muscles are almost never seen individually, but appear in the fleshed figure as a rounded mass. The two heads of the gastrocnemius constitute the major fleshy form of the back of the lower leg. The soleus, originating on both the tibia and fibula, runs down from under the bottom of the medial bulge of the gastrocnemius, and along the outer edge of its lateral bulge. As in the leg's front view, the flexor digitorum longus emerges from under the soleus, continuing below the ankle where it turns forward and out of view. The gastrocnemius and soleus joint to the broad but tapering *Achilles' tendon,* which inserts into the calcaneus, the heel bone.

From the lateral side view (Figures 4.68 and 4.69), the gluteal muscles converge on the great trochanter. The ilio-tibial band, a long and tapering sheath of tendon attached to the lateral condyle of the tibia, forks at the top to receive the fleshy fibers of the gluteus maximus and the tensor fasciae latae. The direction and cordlike character of the iliotibial band's lower portion parallels that of the lower end of the biceps femoris. Note that the biceps femoris appears in rough alignment with the peronus longus. From this view the contour of the posterior (back) of the upper leg begins with the gluteus maximus, continues with the long, simple curve of the biceps femoris, and is completed by the semimembranosus. In the lower leg the gastrocnemius and the Achilles' tendon provide the posterior contour.

In the lateral side view, the rectus femoris above and the vastus lateralis near the knee account for the upper leg's anterior contour. In the lower leg,

FIGURE 4.68
**LEONARDO DA VINCI** (1452–1519)
*Myology of Lower Extremity*
Black chalk, some pen and ink. 29 x 20 cm.
*Windsor Castle, Royal Library.*
*By gracious permission of Her Majesty the Queen.*

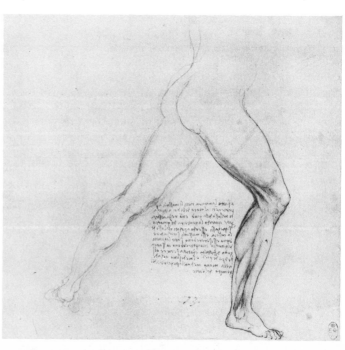

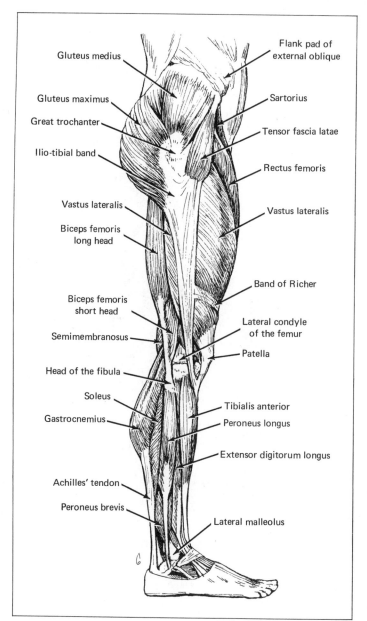

Gluteus medius

Gluteus maximus

Great trochanter

Ilio-tibial band

Vastus lateralis

Biceps femoris
long head

Biceps femoris
short head

Semimembranosus

Head of the fibula

Soleus

Gastrocnemius

Achilles' tendon

Peroneus brevis

Flank pad of
external oblique

Sartorius

Tensor fascia latae

Rectus femoris

Vastus lateralis

Band of Richer

Lateral condyle
of the femur

Patella

Tibialis anterior

Peroneus longus

Extensor digitorum longus

Lateral malleolus

FIGURE 4.69

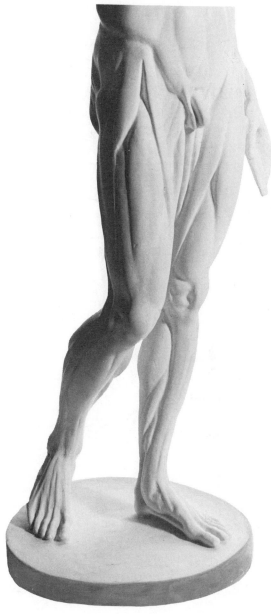

FIGURE 4.70

the tibialis anterior alone carries the anterior contour to the ankle. At the knee, the forms of the patella and the head of the tibia influence the contour. Note that in this view the sweeping curve of the front of the upper leg appears to continue through the gastrocnemius, creating a large, reversed, lazy S-curved movement.

In this (as in any other) view of the leg, the muscles of the lower leg are more in evidence than those of the upper leg. The soleus is often discernible as separate from the gastrocnemius, and the two peroneal muscles are also sometimes visible (Figure 4.68).

From the medial side view (Figures 4.70 and 4.71) the sartorius, gracilis, semintendinosus, and semimembranosus all converge on the tuberosity of the tibia. Note the broad expanse of the tibia visible in the lower leg. Note, too, the similar angle of the upper part of the sartorius and the soleus. The fatty pad beneath the patella affects the surface form of the knee in this view, and the calcaneus, thrusting backward, affects the contour of the foot.

In the foot, as in the hand, muscles play a minor role. Here, the important surface characteristics are the result of bone, tendon, and fat. On the lateral (little toe) side, the lateral malleolus of the fibula

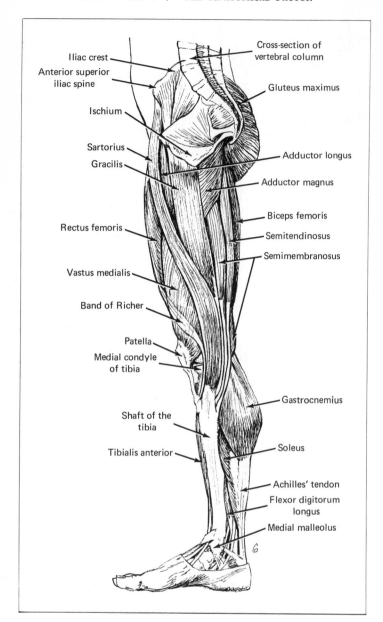

- Iliac crest
- Anterior superior iliac spine
- Ischium
- Sartorius
- Gracilis
- Rectus femoris
- Vastus medialis
- Band of Richer
- Patella
- Medial condyle of tibia
- Shaft of the tibia
- Tibialis anterior
- Achilles' tendon
- Flexor digitorum longus
- Medial malleolus
- Cross-section of vertebral column
- Gluteus maximus
- Adductor longus
- Adductor magnus
- Biceps femoris
- Semitendinosus
- Semimembranosus
- Gastrocnemius
- Soleus

**FIGURE 4.71**

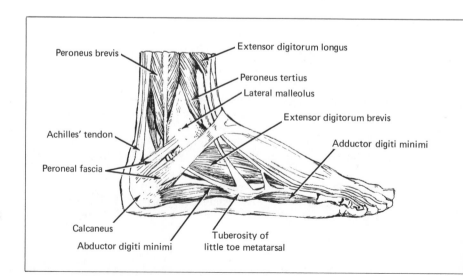

**FIGURE 4.73**
**JOSÉ CLEMENTE OROZCO(1883–1949)**
*Legs* (1938)
Charcoal on light gray paper. 25 7/8 x 19 5/8 in.
*Collection, The Museum of Modern Art, New York.*
*Inter-American Fund.*

**FIGURE 4.72**

- Peroneus brevis
- Achilles' tendon
- Peroneal fascia
- Calcaneus
- Abductor digiti minimi
- Extensor digitorum longus
- Peroneus tertius
- Lateral malleolus
- Extensor digitorum brevis
- Adductor digiti minimi
- Tuberosity of little toe metatarsal

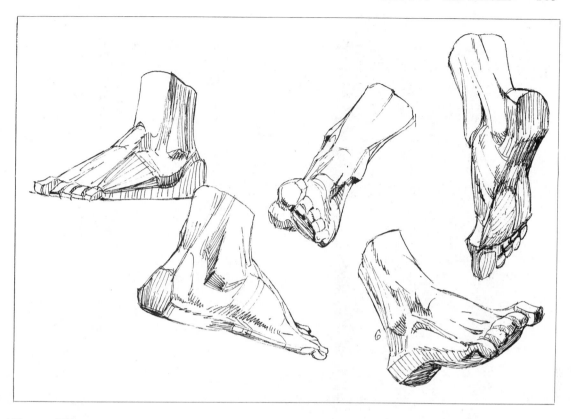

**FIGURE 4.74**

is a prominent landmark, the tendons of the per-oneal muscles turning around from behind (Figure 4.72). Less evident, the small bump about midway between the heel and the little toe represents the tuberosity of the fifth metatarsal; it also marks the insertion of the tendon of the peronus brevis. The *extensor digitorum brevis,* positioned parallel with the long axis of the foot, appears as a subtle mound in front of the lateral malleolus.

On the medial side of the lower leg the medial malleolus, the tendons curving around it, the tendon of the tibialis anterior, and the pronounced masses

of the heel and ball of the foot are characteristic features. From either side view the arched curve of the bones of the foot is an important trait, and from below, the considerable mass of the fatty pads behind the toes and at the heel, and the tendency of the toes to "aim" for the second, straightest toe should be noted (Figure 4.73).

Reduced to simple geometric masses (Figure 4.74), the arch bears a resemblance to the ramp of the hand. Note the "walkway" on the outside, and note also the straight drop on the inside of the foot.

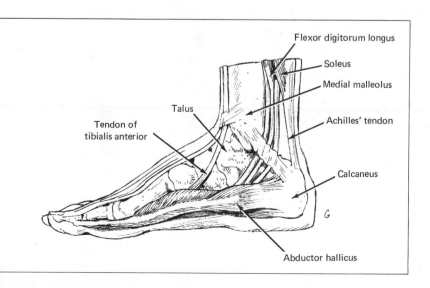

Flexor digitorum longus

Soleus

Medial malleolus

Talus

Achilles' tendon

Tendon of
tibialis anterior

Calcaneus

Abductor hallicus

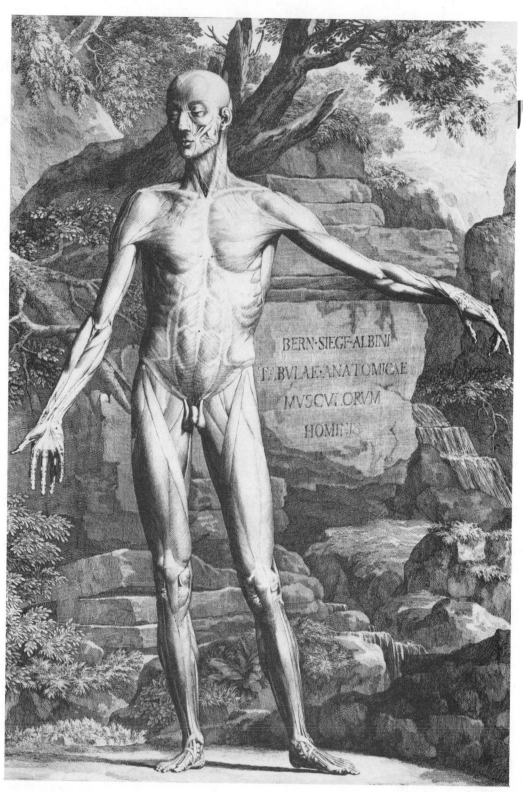

FIGURE 4.75
BERNARD ALBINUS (1697–1770)
*Muscles, Front View*
Engraving.

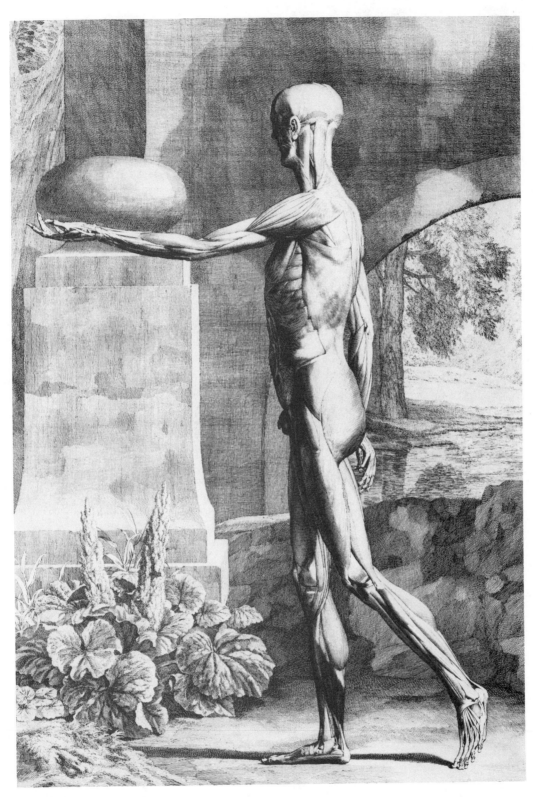

Figure 4.76
ALBINUS
*Muscles, Side View*

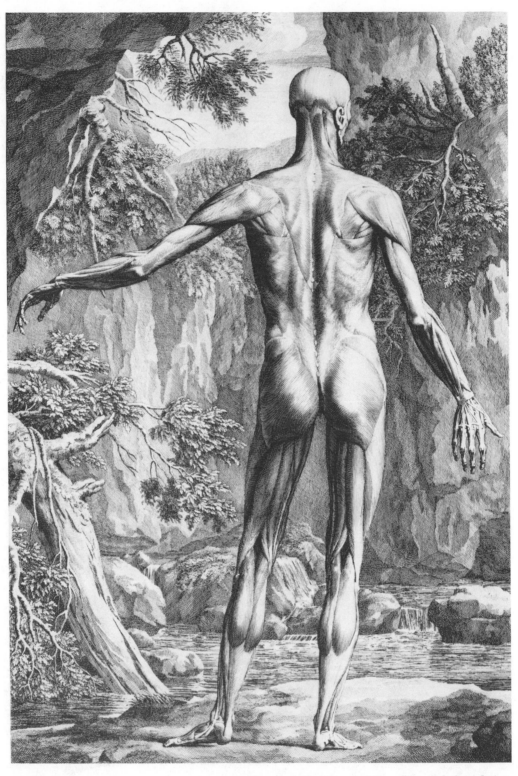

**FIGURE 4.77**
**ALBINUS**
*Muscles, Back View*

Figures 4.75, 4.76 and 4.77 are from *Tabula sceleti et musculorum corporis humani* by Bernard Albinus. *Reproduced by permission of The Francis A. Countway Library of Medicine, Boston.*

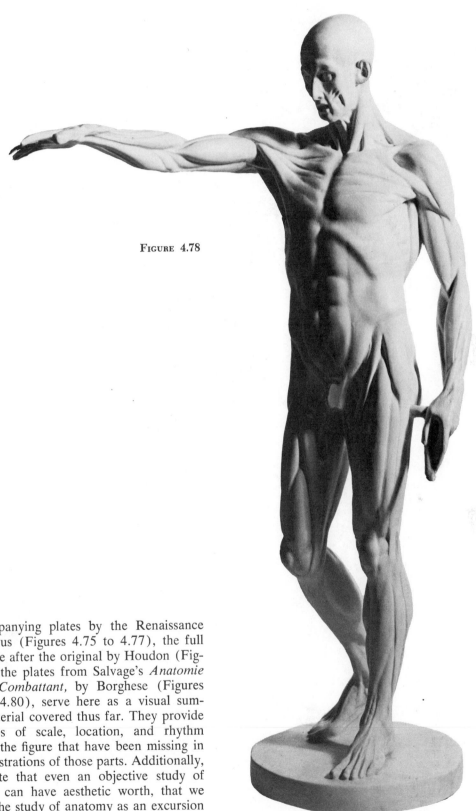

FIGURE 4.78

The accompanying plates by the Renaissance anatomist Albinus (Figures 4.75 to 4.77), the full anatomical figure after the original by Houdon (Figure 4.78), and the plates from Salvage's *Anatomie du Gladiateur Combattant,* by Borghese (Figures 3.5, 4.79, and 4.80), serve here as a visual summary of the material covered thus far. They provide the relationships of scale, location, and rhythm among parts of the figure that have been missing in the previous illustrations of those parts. Additionally, they demonstrate that even an objective study of anatomical fact can have aesthetic worth, that we needn't regard the study of anatomy as an excursion which excludes art.

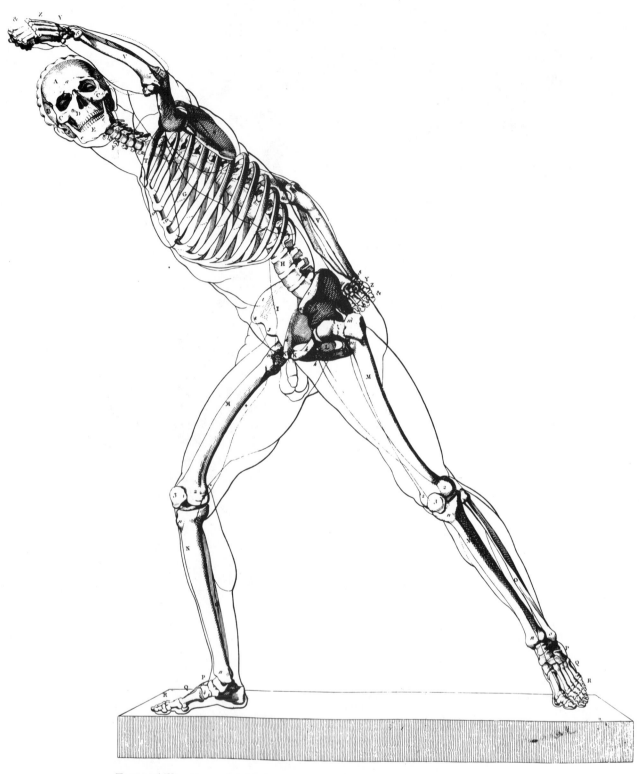

**FIGURE 4.79**
**BORGHESE**
From Salvage's *Anatomie du Gladiateur Combattant*
*Courtesy of Countway Library, Boston, Mass.*

170

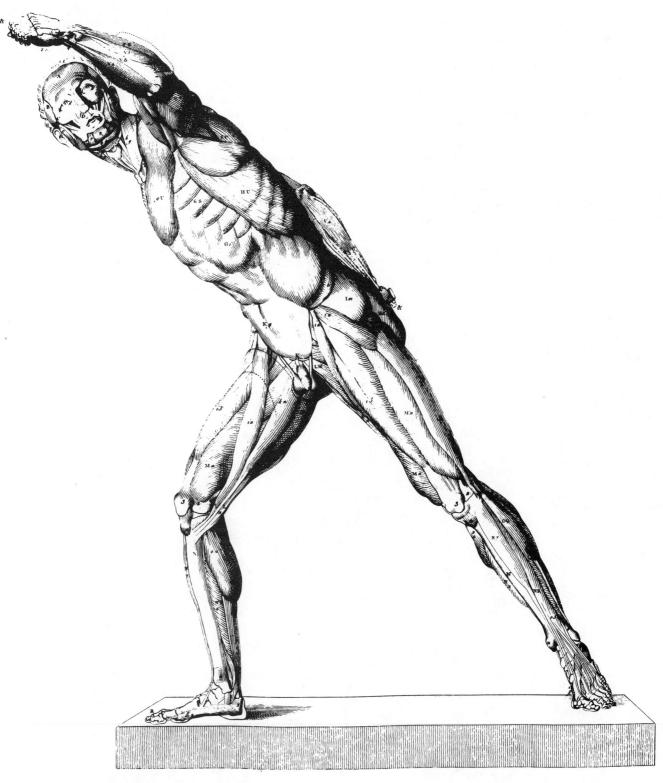

**FIGURE 4.80**
**BORGHESE**
From Salvage's *Anatomie du Gladiateur Combattant*
*Courtesy of Countway Library, Boston, Mass.*

171

## SKIN AND FAT

In the living figure the skin and fatty tissue modify the musculature of even the thinnest person.* Although the skin represents a fairly even covering, it is slightly thicker in some locations, such as the palm of the hand, the sole of the foot, and the upper part of the back. Additionally, its limited freedom of movement, the result of a loose attachment to the tissues beneath it, also varies somewhat. For example, the skin covering the top of the head, along the anterior and posterior median lines of the torso, on the palms of the hands, on the feet, and even on the inner side of the lower parts of the extremities, is less mobile than the skin on the face, around the waist, and at the joints.

* Paul Richer, *Artistic Anatomy,* trans. R. B. Hale (New York: Watson-Guptill Publications, 1971), pp. 78–81.

Superficial body fat is also unevenly distributed, and to a far greater extent than the skin. These differences in the thickness and flexibility of the body's covering, sometimes so pronounced as to create surface forms that are quite independent of the anatomical forms below, should alert us to the error of regarding skin and fat as uniformly softening the terrain of bones and muscles.

Generally, fatty deposits are heavier on the torso than on the limbs, and heavier on the upper than the lower parts of the limbs. Normally, more abundant amounts of fat are present in the female figure, softening or leveling the valleys, padding or grading the hills, and providing the graceful surface undulations characteristic of that sex. In young children and in the excessively overweight, fatty tissue not only effaces the forms below, but also creates substantial forms of its own. These rolls of fat usually appear to encircle the forms they are on, as

FIGURE 4.81
FRANCOIS BOUCHER (1703–1770)
*Cherubs*
Black chalk, heightened with white on light brown paper.
8 5/16 x 9 1/4 in.
*The Metropolitan Museum of Art, New York.*
*Gift of Charles K. Lock, 1960.*

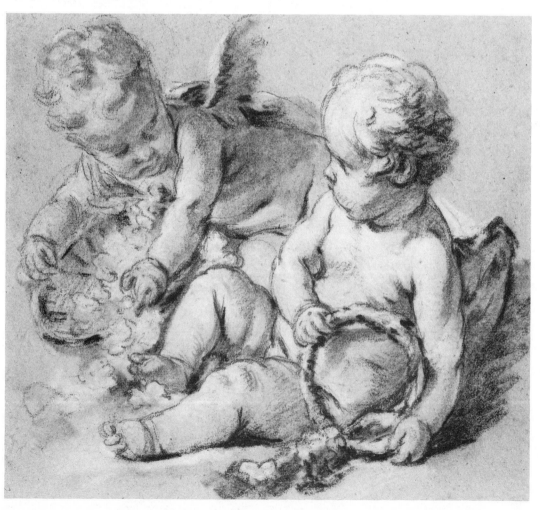

FIGURE 4.82
PETER PAUL RUBENS (1577–1640)
*Fall of the Damned*
Chalk. 29 1/2 x 20 in.
*Trustees of the British Museum, London.*

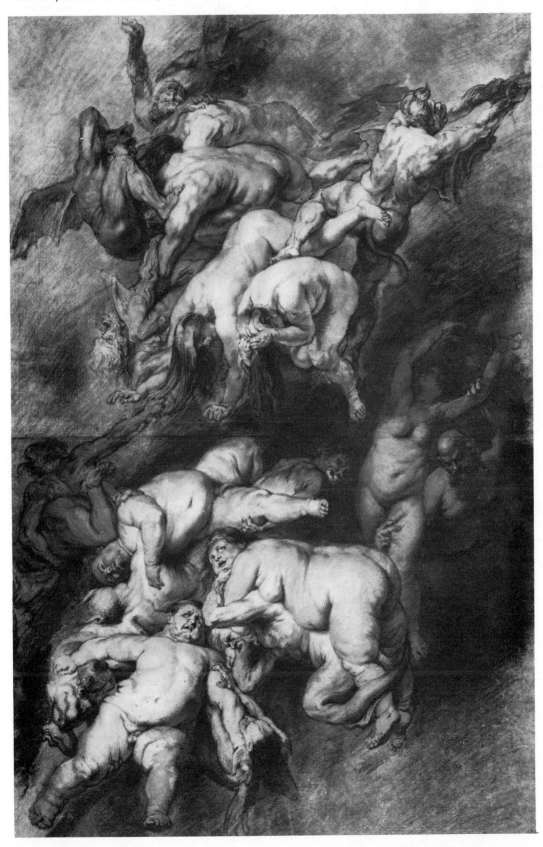

173

may be seen in the legs of the seated child in Boucher's *Cherubs* (Figure 4.81) and in the obese figures in Rubens's *Fall of the Damned* (Figure 4.82).

The amount of fat beneath the skin varies considerably. In areas such as the ears, the eyelids, and the bridge of the nose, there is no subcutaneous fat. Minimal amounts are present on the back of the hand, the foot, the sternum and clavicle area, and at the wrists and ankles. Ample deposits are found on the lower part of the face, the torso, especially at the breasts, abdomen, and buttocks, and on the upper parts of the limbs. Although fatty deposits are far greater in the female breast, fat is present in the male breast also.

In the typical female figure, fat liberally invests the upper posterior part of the thighs and the buttocks. Above and behind the wings of the pelvis it fills in the depressions in the muscular terrain, accounting for the large, inclined plane that begins at the buttocks and extends almost to the waist (Figure 4.83). In so doing, the fat obscures the hollow surrounding the great trochanter and the upper margins of the pelvis. No such long plane exists in the average male figure. Compare the squarish buttocks, the hollow at the site of the great trochanter, the curving margins of the pelvis, and the columns of deep spinal muscles which give this region a far different character in the male (see Figure 4.67).

Another drawing by Boucher, *Reclining Nude* (Figure 4.84), provides a good example of the modifying effects of fat. Here, despite the obscuring of the musculature, the stronger forms beneath still have an effect, however muffled, on the surface terrain. The figure's heavy forms are not arbitrarily cylindrical or without clues to the anatomical forms below the surface. They subtly suggest the vastus muscles, the trapezius, the extensors and flexors of the arm, the tibia, the manubrium, and so on. A sound knowledge of anatomy enables an artist to know which bones and muscles will continue, though muted, to influence surface structure and which will be effaced by fat. Such knowledge is apparent in Hockney's drawing of a middle-aged figure (Figure 3.35).

Gravity, too, plays a role in altering the position and shape of the figure's forms. In Boucher's drawing the weight of the abdomen causes it to overlay the upper leg. In Figure 4.82, gravity's effect on the breasts, abdomen, arms, and legs is emphatically stated.

## FURTHER OBSERVATIONS ON SURFACE FORMS

Let us now examine more specifically how bones and muscles influence the padded surfaces of the

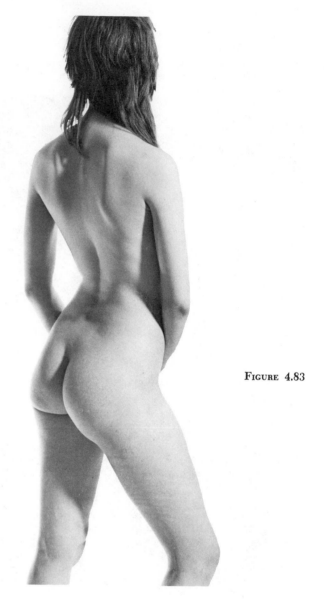

FIGURE 4.83

figure, and go on to see how some artists have utilized anatomical fact to enhance expression.

In Figure 4.85, the vertical furrows in the brow reveal a contraction of the corrugators. Light and dark planes encircling the eyes suggest the eye sockets. Above, the ledge of the brow protectively overhangs the eyes. A highlight running from the corner of the figure's right eye to the corner of the mouth divides the front and side planes of the head. The mandible's angularity is revealed by the lower contour of the head and by the planes at the chin. At the right shoulder the head of the humerus is forced to the surface by the pressure upon the arm supporting the torso. Above this protuberance the spine of the scapula and the lateral end of the clavicle join to form the rugged surface at the top of the shoulder. Compare the mass and form of the working deltoid with the relaxed deltoid of the left arm.

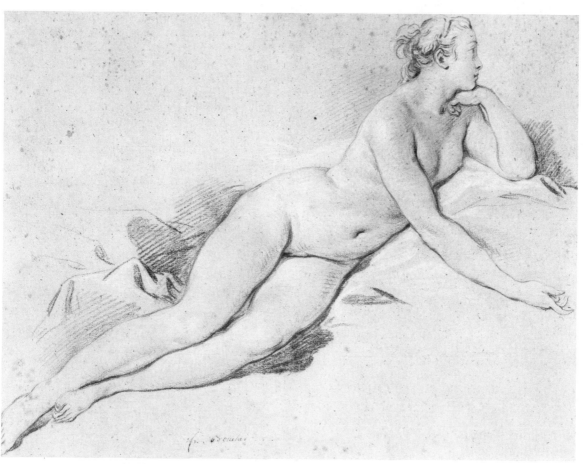

FIGURE 4.84
FRANCOIS BOUCHER (1703–1770)
*Reclining Nude*
Sanguine chalk, heightened with
white on brown-gray paper.
12 7/16 x 16 3/8 in.
*Courtesy The Fogg Art Museum,*
*Harvard University.*
*Bequest of Meta and Paul J. Sachs.*

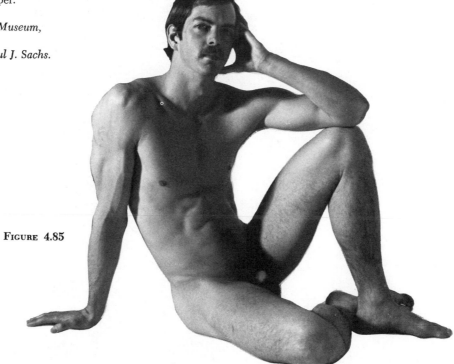

FIGURE 4.85

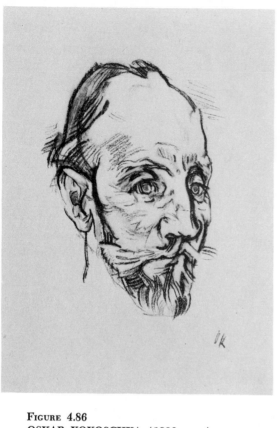

**FIGURE 4.86**
**OSKAR KOKOSCHKA (1886–    )**
*Portrait of Josef Hauer* (1914)
Black chalk. 41.1 x 30.9 cm.
*Staatsgaleria Moderner Kunst, Munich.*
*Gift of Sofie and Emanuel Fohn.*

Here the abdominal muscles are clearly seen and together form a kind of block, sitting slightly ahead of the planes to either side of it—the block running from below the pectorals to the pubic area. Just above the left knee a highlight indicates the medial condyle of the femur. In the lower left leg the gastrocnemius and the tibialis account for the back and front contours respectively, but note that the same muscles provide the contours in the foreshortened right leg. At the hips the buttock muscles form a segment separate from the mass of the leg, the result of the tensor fascia latae's insertion into the ilio-tibial band.

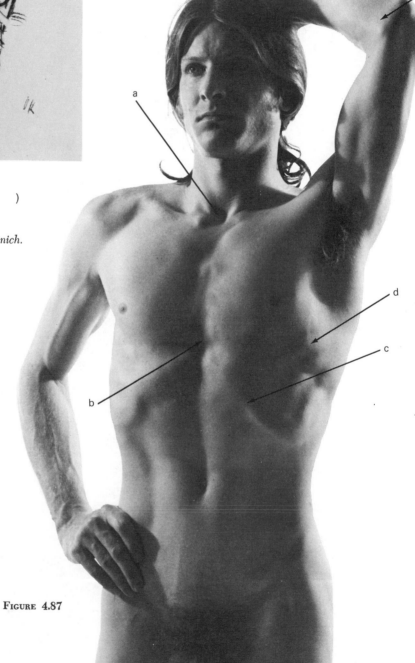

**FIGURE 4.87**

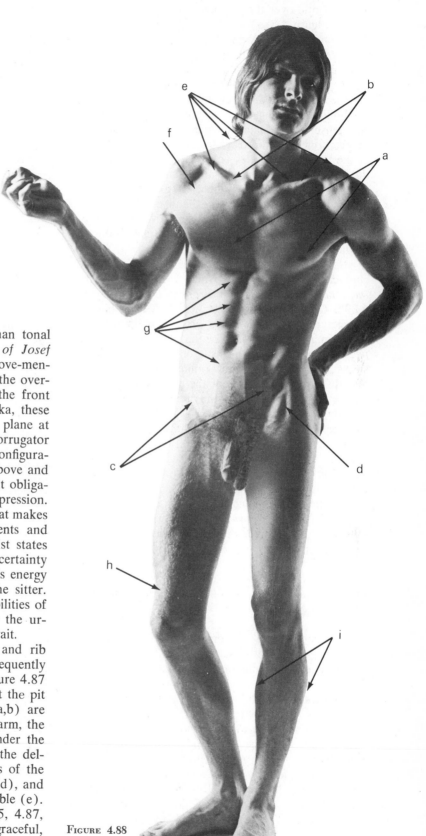

Kokoschka, relying more on linear than tonal divisions between planes in his *Portrait of Josef Hauer* (Figure 4.86), indicates the above-mentioned construction of the eye and socket, the overhanging brow, and the division between the front and side planes of the face. For Kokoschka, these anatomical facts and those of the flattened plane at the temple, the wrinkles caused by the corrugator and frontalis muscles, the knowledgeable configurations of the ear and nose, the bony ridges above and below the eyes, and so on, do not represent obligations to objectivity, but opportunities for expression. The structural and anatomical knowledge that makes possible these rugged masses and movements and the authoritative vigor with which the artist states the forms of the head impart a force and certainty that we respond to. In sensing the drawing's energy and strength we sense these qualities in the sitter. Note that the artist utilizes the design possibilities of the hair on the head and face to intensify the urgency of the rhythms that animate the portrait.

On the torso, the clavicles, sternum, and rib cage (especially the thoracic arch) are frequently visible even in simple standing poses, as Figure 4.87 demonstrates. Often, as here, the hollows at the pit of the throat and at the xiphoid process (a,b) are deeply carved. In this view of the upraised arm, the biceps and triceps seem to emerge from under the "cap" formed by the pectoralis major and the deltoid. Note the similarity between the angles of the thoracic arch (c) and the serratus muscles (d), and that both epicondyles of the humerus are visible (e).

In a well-developed male (Figures 4.85, 4.87, and 4.88), the pectoral muscles form a graceful,

FIGURE 4.88

fleshy mantle over the rib cage, ending in a "cupid's bow" (Figure 4.88a) similar to the one formed by the clavicles (b). A third cupid's bow occurs at the torso's lower boundaries, formed by the flank pads of the external oblique and the abdominal muscles (c). Some additional observations worth noting are the torso's median furrow ending at the navel; the hollow marking the emergence of the sartorius and tensor fascia latae muscles (d); the diamond shape formed by the clavicles and the sloping lines of the trapezius muscles (e); the hollows separating the deltoids from the pectoral muscles (f); the muscle pads of the abdominal muscles (g); the constricting of the leg muscles by the band of Richer (h); the gastrocnemius muscle visible on both sides of the lower left leg (i); and the wedgelike character of the feet.

Some of the above-mentioned landmarks and characteristics are seen in Michelangelo's *Study for the Nude Youth over the Prophet Daniel* (Figure 4.89). Of particular interest here is Michelangelo's exaggeration of the youth's chest. To do this, he subtly increased the width of the rib cage, making it necessary to increase the scale of the serratus, latissimus dorsi, and external oblique muscles, while slightly reducing the scale of the pelvic area. Michelangelo also stresses the massive upper body by selecting a pose that shows the widest dimension of the chest and a narrow view of the hips. Note the clarity of the peroneus longus (a) leading to the knee, itself so well explained by the heads of the fibula (b), tibia (c), and femur (d), and by the patella (e) and the patella ligament (f).

Michelangelo is completely in control of the hierarchy of his forms—of small forms being subordinate to the bigger ones they collectively constitute. His involvement with anatomical and dynamic matters never supersedes his grasp of the essential structure of the figure's forms. The chest, despite all of the surface detail, is still seen primarily as massive and blocklike; the limbs, as essentially cylindrical.

All good figure drawings show the hierarchical order by which we all see the things around us. If you glance up for one or two seconds and then try to draw what you saw, you will realize that your first impressions dealt mainly with generalities: There was a small, ornately framed painting near the door, the view from the window showed several wind-blown trees and part of an old building, the lanky student across the room seemed to be asleep. Far more visual inquiry is necessary to draw these scenes in any telling way. But these initial impressions of the essential nature of the forms we see are important, and always survive in the works of the masters. They never permit details to devour the masses of which they are a part.

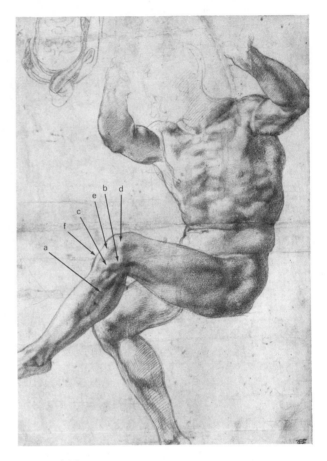

FIGURE 4.89
MICHELANGELO BUONARROTI (1465–1564)
*Study for the Nude Youth over the Prophet Daniel,*
*in the Sistine Chapel Ceiling Fresco*
Red chalk. 13 3/16 x 9 3/16 in.
*Courtesy The Cleveland Museum of Art.*
*Gift in memory of Henry G. Dalton by his nephews*
*George S. Kendrick and Harry D. Kendrick.*

In Chapter Two we saw that small form-units can be seen as either emerging from simple structural masses or as being reduced to such simple masses. But in either case, the large masses should prevail. Here, we should understand that these small form-units are shaped by bone, muscle, and fat. Cambiaso poises his drawing *Hercules* (Figure 4.90) just at that intriguing point where we wonder if specific surface forms are being absorbed by larger geometric ones or are emerging from them. Cambiaso's drawing provides an excellent example of the interaction of the structural and anatomical factors.

As we examine Figure 4.90, it is instructive to see which anatomical landmarks and forms the artist selects as modifiers of the drawing's simpler masses. In the head, the curved frontal bone and the zygomatic bone and arch are clearly indicated; in the neck, the sternomastoids, the pit of the throat, the larynx, and the flow of the trapezius to the deltoid are suggested by a few select shorthand marks that denote both the edges and structure of these forms. In the torso, complex muscles such as the external oblique and pectoralis major are reduced to the most general shape and form clues. Yet these shorthand lines are rich in detail. The hollow near the deltoid, the lumpy surface effects of the sternum and the thoracic arch, the nipples, the midline ending at the navel, and at least a hint of the interaction of the muscles at the side of the torso are all shown. And, in the limbs, although Cambiaso conceives them as essentially tapered blocks, again, each modifying mark *tells*. In the figure's right arm he suggests the swell of the deltoid and supinators, the bones of the lower arm at the wrist, and (in the figure's left arm) the biceps, the tendons of the lower arm, and the muscles at the base of the palm. In the leg he sorts out the tendon, muscle, and bone that construct the knee; he shows the gastrocnemius, soleus, tibia, peroneus longus, and hints at other muscles on the lateral side of the lower leg. The construction of the feet indicates the bones of the ankle and the downward arc of the tendons to the toes. A careful study of this drawing reveals even more anatomical details than those just mentioned. Cambiaso's *Hercules* is an impressive feat of economy based on a sound grasp of the human figure's general structure and the specific anatomical reasons for it.

The scapula provides one of the most pronounced landmarks of the back. As Figure 4.91 shows, the scapula's mechanical function as part of the arm brings it gliding over the ribs toward the side when the arm moves up and forward. In this view we can make out the two tendonous plateaus of the back: above, the smaller one, between the trapezius muscles; below, the large diamond-shaped one, its margins defined by the latissimus dorsi muscles and the iliac crests. Here, because of the thick masses of the gluteal and flank pad muscles attaching to them, the location of the iliac crests is marked by curved valleys, not hills. With the rib cage bending forward, several ribs come to the surface, their downward curve pronounced. The teres major and latissimus dorsi form a sweeping curve along the torso, and, at the hips, the gluteus medius muscles overhang those of the buttocks.

In the legs, the muscles of the posterior upper leg form a single muscular mass (Figure 4.91). On the outer side the form of the vastus lateralis is visible, strapped down by the ilio-tibial band. At the knee the tendonous cords of the ilio-tibial band and the biceps femoris are in sharp relief (a,b). On the inner side of the knee the tendon of the semitendinosus is visible (c). Note that in the lower legs the curve of the lateral contour occurs higher than the curve of the medial one. In this pose the two

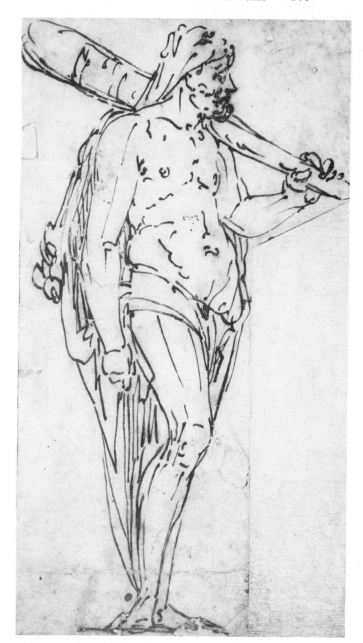

FIGURE 4.90
LUCA CAMBIASO (1527–1585)
*Hercules*
Pen and ink. 10 3/4 x 5 15/16 in.
*Courtesy The Fogg Art Museum, Harvard University.*
*Gift of Mrs. Herbert Straus.*

heads of the gastrocnemius (d), the Achilles' tendon (e), and, on the left foot, the tendon of the peroneus longus (f), are all noteworthy surface characteristics. The position of the right foot allows us to see that the foot is decidedly more narrow at the heel than at the toes. Notice that the shadow on the back stops just at the angle of the ribs, where they turn more sharply to the front.

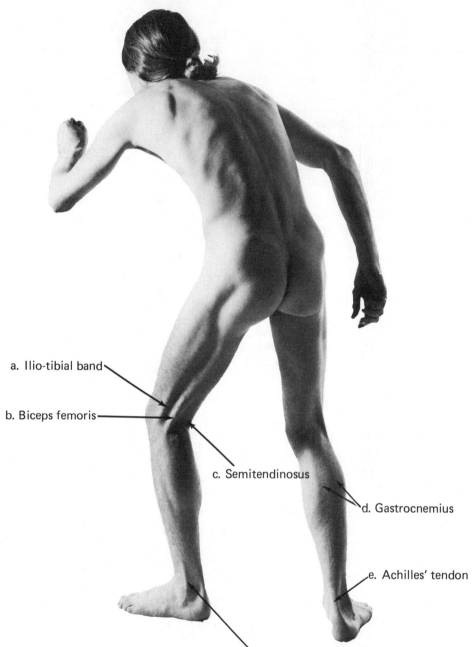

a. Ilio-tibial band

b. Biceps femoris

c. Semitendinosus

d. Gastrocnemius

e. Achilles' tendon

f. Tendon of the Peroneus longus

Michelangelo's brilliant study of the back (Figure 4.92) is a rugged landscape of muscle. But despite the gnarled terrain, the forms never lose continuity, the harmonious flow that human forms always possess. For example, the deep rhomboids overtaking the form of the trapezius, because of the left arm's position, create bulges that are in rhythmic accord with the surrounding hills and valleys. Note the clarity of the seventh cervical vertebra, the lower margin of the trapezius (not often seen), and the lower tendonous plateau.

In this drawing, accuracy sometimes gives way to creative intent and instinct. Perhaps it is Michelangelo's interest in the dramatic landscape of the back that accounts for the exaggerations and changes in the muscles of the lower back, and for every muscle appearing to be in contraction. After all, the freedom to interpret forms in any way that is visually logical and expressively accurate is a basic creative necessity. Da Vinci, who was fascinated by the study of anatomy, recognized this necessity when he advised: "He who finds it too much, let him

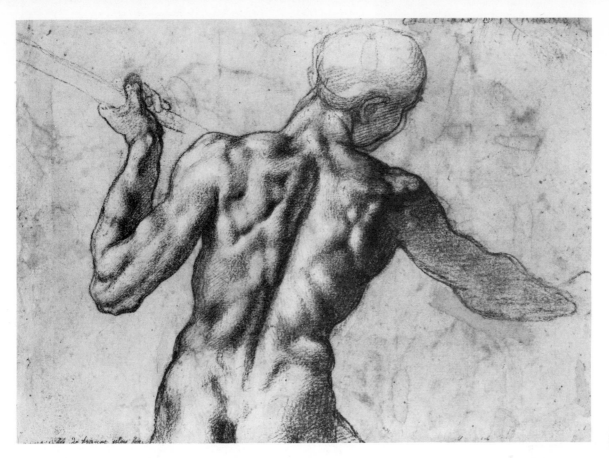

FIGURE 4.92
**MICHELANGELO BUONARROTI** (1475–1564)
*Male Torso, Seen from the Back*
Charcoal and lead white. 27.2 x 19.9 cm.
*Albertina Museum, Vienna.*

shorten it; he who finds it too little, add to it; he
for whom it suffices, let him praise the first builder
of such a machine." But even if anatomical considerations are to play a minor role in your drawings, a working knowledge of the fundamental anatomical actualities must still precede their use if they
are to have artistically useful meanings.

When the female torsos of Figures 4.26 and
4.93 are compared with the male torso of Figure
4.87, various differences can be noted. Obvious and
subtle differences are seen, such as the greater
scale and heft of the rib cage and the wider opening in the thoracic arch in the male, and the greater
investment of fatty tissue in the breasts, the longer
waist, and the wider pelvic area in the female. There
are subtler differences in proportion too. In the female the neck appears longer, the muscles throughout the figure are somewhat smaller in heft, and the
bones are more delicately fashioned, showing fewer
abrupt eruptions at the surface. But these smoother,
more rhythmic lines are due in great part to the
leveling and grading effects of the female's slightly
greater endowment of fatty tissue. Even so, the female figure discloses much of its bony and muscular
systems, and these are, of course, substantially the
same in both sexes.

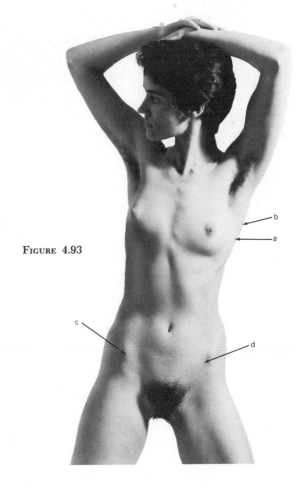

FIGURE 4.93

181

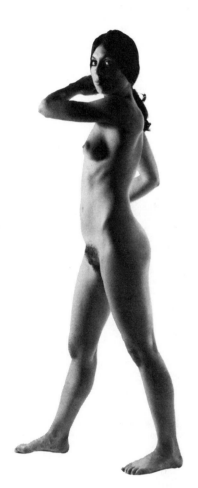

Figure 4.94

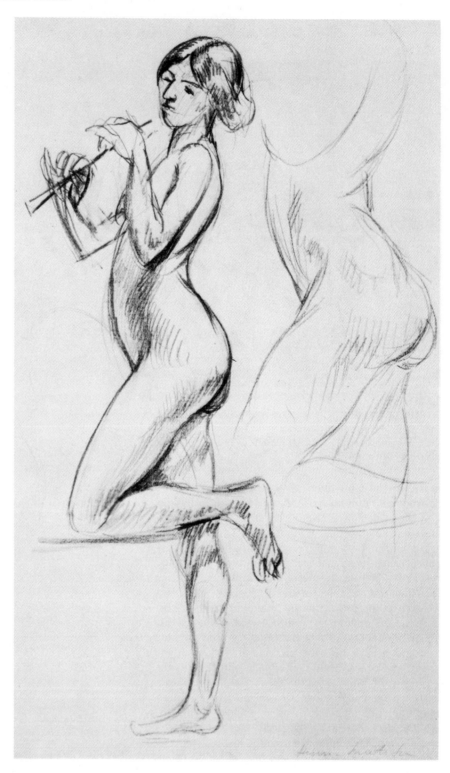

Figure 4.95
HENRI MATISSE (1869–1954)
*Two Sketches of a Nude Girl Playing a Flute*
Pencil. 13 3/4 x 8 1/2 in.
*Courtesy The Fogg Art Museum, Harvard University.*
*Gift of Mr. and Mrs. Joseph Kerrigan.*

In Figure 4.93 the points of emergence and insertion of the sternomastoid, as well as its form, are very clear. With the arms upraised, the sternal attachments of the pectoral muscles become visible. In this position the clavicles rise sharply and become somewhat obscured by the overlapping deltoids and pectorals, and the latissimus dorsi (a) and teres major (b) come into view. The breasts, despite the uplifted arms, remain low on the chest. Note how the flank pad and the gluteus medius muscles provide the widening contours running from the waist over the iliac crests, to the legs, and how the anterior iliac spines (c,d) project at points which, with the nipples, form the four points of an imaginary rectangle. The subtle mound below the navel is a characteristic of the abdomen in even the most slender female figure.

In Figure 4.94 the continuity of the scapular area with the arm is clear, as is the scale and fullness of the deltoid and the triangular arrangement of the bony projections at the elbow. The thickened rim of the thoracic arch provides the upper enclosing boundaries of the abdominal muscles, which are lost below the waist in the rounded form of the abdomen. The graceful curve of the torso, continued by the backward tilt of the pelvis, is typical of the side view of the female figure. A similar but more open curve characterizes the upper leg, its front contour turning sharply inward on approaching the knee to overhang the straighter lower leg, set a bit behind the upper one. Again, note the sharp relief of the anterior iliac spine. Usually, in the female, the muscles of the legs are seen at the surface as collective, rounded masses. Only at the approaches to the knee and ankle do tendons break the smooth flow of the forms.

Matisse, in his *Two Sketches of a Nude Girl Playing a Flute* (Figure 4.95), evokes just those characteristics described above. The artist emphasizes the graceful arc of the torso, treats the legs as tapering cylinders (whose contours reveal Matisse's sure knowledge of anatomy), draws the upper leg as overhanging the lower, and suggests the more angular nature of the elbows. In the figure on the right, Matisse notes the gluteus medius and external oblique, and suggests the collective form of the muscles on the upper part of the uplifted leg, as well as the long, inclined contour running from the buttocks to the waist, a characteristic feature of the female's lower torso.

In the figure on the left, Matisse extracts and intensifies these particular traits to support the drawing's theme of the female figure's potential for powerful visual rhythms. The more visual obstacles placed in the path of a straight or curved movement, the more time we need to make the visual

trip. And here the speed of the figure's forms is necessary to the drawing's vigorous nature. In the torso on the right, Matisse does slow down—both the speed of the movements *and* of the lines—forsaking some of the figure's serpentine qualities in favor of its sculptural ones. Thus, the same artist, on the same page, adjusts anatomy's role to serve differing intentions.

In the torso sketch, Matisse employs an even-handed treatment of the figure's structure and rhythmic energy, while in the full-figure sketch, he emphasizes movement rather than mass. This difference in stress points to the heart of the serious artist's constant concern to invent a personal "recipe" of response from these two basic ingredients of perception. As was observed in Chapter One, these ought not be mutually exclusive considerations. Here the masses in the figure on the left seem to gain strength from the vigor of the actions they undergo; in the torso on the right the rhythms seem all the more impressive because they carry along so many factual aspects of the figure's structure and surface anatomy (note the presence of the gluteus medius and the external oblique). Both figures in the drawing are structurally lucid and dynamically alive, but the treatment of movement and mass differs.

Some artists, such as Boucher (Figure 4.84) or Pascin (Figure 4.59), emphasize rhythmic energies; others, such as Cretara or Villon (Figures 2.15 and 2.16), stress the figure's architecture. But all artists utilize both of these interacting truths about the figure in whatever combination they find necessary.

Whether our drawings emphasize motion or mass is determined in part by our response to a particular subject's substance and spirit, and in part by our personal expressive purpose. Every view of the figure offers graphic ideas rich in both design and structure. In Figure 4.96 the bony armature persists through the layers of muscle and fat, affecting the surface form, while these layers produce surface forms of their own. At the same time, supple undulations, shapes, and values set off strong patterns of harmonies and contrasts. These impressions of structure and design are continually interacting. For example, the median furrow, reinforced by the cartilage of the thoracic arch, is a structural fact; its visual "pull" with the tendon of the left sternomastoid is a dynamic one. Similarly, the left upper arm and left upper leg are simultaneously understood as cylindrical volumes and as forms that move obliquely forward, cancelling out each other's direction. They create an hourglass spatial cavity that echoes the hourglass shape of the figure's torso.

Negative shapes also play a part in the organizing of our images. In Figure 4.97 the triangular

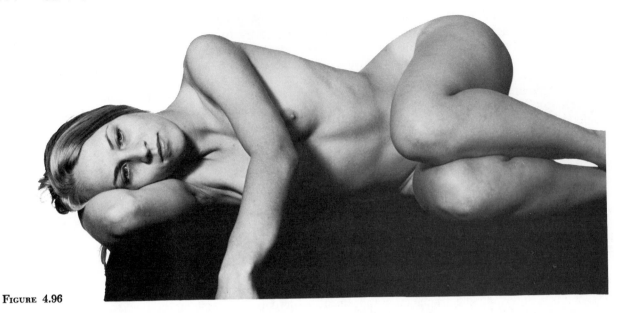

Figure 4.96

nature of the negative shape enclosed by the contours of the figure's back and arm is similar to the triangular shape of the right upper leg. And the smaller triangular shape separating the legs echoes the shapes of the right breast and the neck.

Direction—the straight or curved course of an edge or an axis—is one of the strongest visual forces that synthesize an image. Note, for example, the similarity between the horizontally oriented arcs of the left upper leg, the left forearm, and the left clavicle. Note, too, that the left thigh's arc continues to sweep upward to the neck, generating a strong action that is countered by the downward thrust of the right thigh, right lower arm, and left upper arm. Such moving rhythms, when noted at the outset of a drawing, help us understand both the design and the orientation of the masses of the subject before us.

In the back view shown in Figure 4.98, the long, pointed negative shape between the left arm and the torso is related to the downward-pointing shard of light on the left scapula, and finds its opposite in the dark and downward-pointing left arm. Note that the shape of the foreshortened right upper arm is nearly the twin of the negative shape alongside it. Directionally, the right thigh, the contour of the waist on the right side, the spinal furrow, and the left upper arm all lean somewhat toward the right, countered by the turn of the head, the left-leaning scapulas, and the similar direction of the light-toned area of the sacrum and right buttock.

Here the earlier noted large plane of the female's lower torso is clearly evident. Note the gentle mound of the sacral triangle, the disappearance of the iliac crests beneath the fatty tissue at the hips,

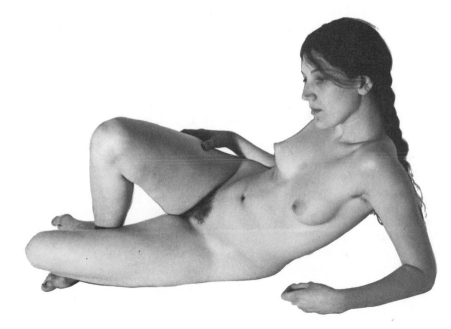

Figure 4.97

and the gluteus medius extending farther out at the side than the gluteus maximus. Note further that the lower tendonous plateau is more crowded by surface forms than it is in the male. In the extended arm, the hollow on the outer side of the elbow is formed by the supinators' taking a different course from that of the extensors. The relaxed hand is aligned with the long axis of the lower arm, and the differing positions of the arms show the range of the scapulas' movements on the back.

Lillie's interpretation of a similar back view pose (Figure 4.99) shows the surface anatomy discussed in the previous illustration transformed into engaging graphic ideas. Lillie, especially sensitive to the design possibilities of anatomy, exaggerates some forms and seems to call to the surface others that were probably only weakly discernible in the model. Here structural and dynamic discoveries fuse, amplified by the artist's knowledge of anatomy and his instinct for dynamic order—an expression of certain truths about the nature of human form *and* spirit.

FIGURE 4.98

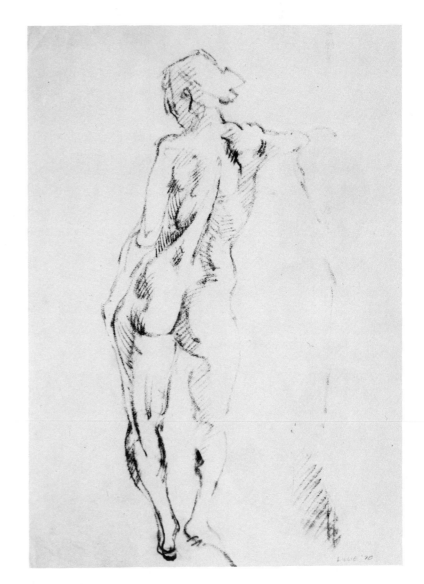

FIGURE 4.99
LLOYD LILLIE (1932–   )
*Standing Figure, Back View*
Black chalk. 12 x 17 1/2 in.
*Courtesy of the artist.*

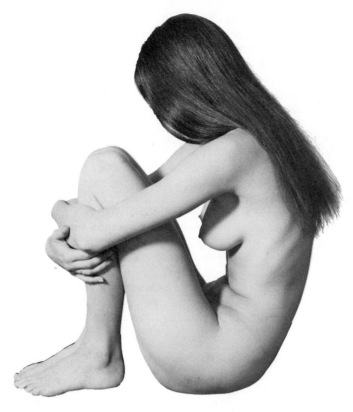

FIGURE 4.100

FIGURE 4.101

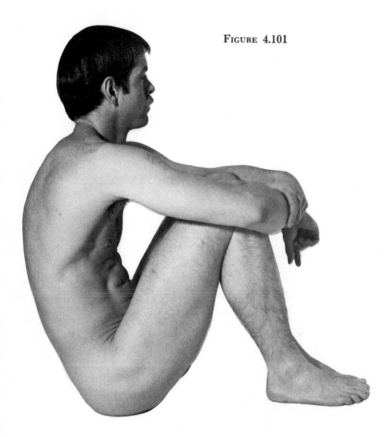

Note that the negative shape that separates the legs bears a striking resemblance to the several light and dark shapes that construct the figure's back. The head and neck, the left hand, the lower left leg, and the indicated support on the right side of the sheet all share a common direction that counteracts the figure's overall tilt to the right, thus balancing the image on the page.

In the female, the greater distance between the rib cage and the pelvis accounts for the longer, more flexible waist area that keeps the upper torso from being pressed against the lower torso in a compressed, seated pose, such as shown in Figure 4.100. The rib cage and pelvis approach a right angle arrangement, yet the upper torso appears free of compression against the forms below it. In the male, the larger rib cage and the taller pelvis bring these bony masses almost together, resulting in a more compressed arrangement of forms (Figure 4.101). Note, in Figure 4.100, that there are two folds in the torso: The upper one represents the lower boundary of the rib cage; the lower fold, the upper boundary of the pelvis. Note also that in this pose more of the abdomen is visible than is the case in the male figure, while in the male figure the rectus abdominal muscles and the latissimus dorsi are far more prominent.

In a standing pose the patella is quite visible (Figure 4.94), but when the legs are bent to the extreme degree shown in Figure 4.100, the patella all but disappears between the broad protuberances of the femur and tibia. In this view of the upper leg, the gentle curve of the femur is reflected in the curve of the fleshed form. The foreshortened view of the left upper arm clearly shows the rounded form of the upper part and the squarish form of the lower one. Notice the ball-like mass of the bones of the wrist and the graceful rhythm of the hand.

Comparing Rembrandt's drawing of a heavy-set woman (Figure 4.102) with the woman in Figure 4.100, we notice the effects of substantial deposits of fat on surface forms. But because fat is stored mainly on the lower torso and upper parts of the limbs, the skeleton and muscles still play an important role in shaping the surfaces of even obese figures, if only in the lower parts of the limbs and at the joints (Figure 4.82). Moreover, bone and muscle continue to influence, if only weakly, the *general* structural character of the rest of the body, however much overlaid by fat.

In Rembrandt's drawing, the shape of the cranium, the angularity of the jaw, and the bony passages and projections at the joints all show the skeleton at the surface. And, except for the abdomen, firm inner masses and shafts of support are sensed throughout the figure. Rembrandt subtly suggests the rib cage, the scapular muscles, the latissimus

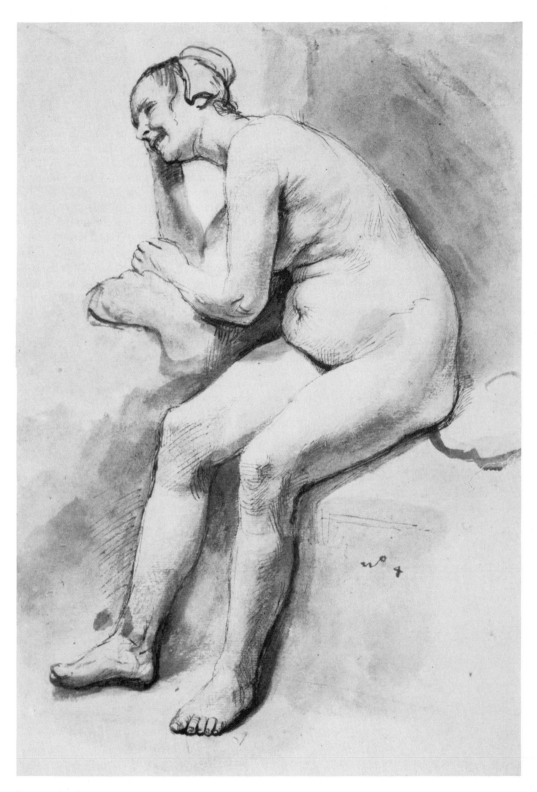

**FIGURE 4.102**
REMBRANDT VAN RIJN (1606–1669)
*Seated Nude Woman*
Pen and ink, some washes.
10 1/4 x 7 1/4 in.
*Cabinet des Dessins, Musée du Louvre, Paris.*

dorsi, and on the figure's left hip, the heavily over-laid wing of the pelvis.

A major theme in this drawing appears to be the figure's weighty substantiality. To convey this, Rembrandt simplifies the forms by grouping many small planes into the major and secondary ones they conform to. For example, he interprets the legs as blocklike and even treats the knees as squared off. Likewise, the lower torso hints at its spherical basis, the head and upper torso suggest ovoids, and the neck and upper limbs, cylinders. In discreetly hinting at the geometric essence of the forms, Rembrandt achieves a strong sense of solidity.

But nowhere is this move toward monumentality allowed to override important characteristics of surface anatomy that heighten the drawing's humanistic theme: a woman relaxed, lost in some pleasant reverie. Rembrandt always avoids dehumanizing solutions. Here, structural and anatomical factors interact in a way that allows each to contribute to the sense of weighty human form. Rembrandt's grasp of *any* form's structural essential helps him to convincingly and economically convey anatomical observa-

tions such as the complex structure of the knee, or the arrangement of the flexors and extensors of the arms. Conversely, his knowledge of anatomy assists his structural theme of summarizing the figure's forms. For example, the blocky plane in the left upper leg is only a modest exaggeration of the flattening effect of the ilio-tibial band. And, in the lower leg, where many artists might use the pronounced line of the tibia's sharp edge to explain a change in planes, Rembrandt draws the tibialis muscle as the dividing line between the front and side planes to continue the blocky L shape of the entire leg. The tibia's influence on the surface of the lower leg is always visible, but Rembrandt wisely omits it here, gaining structural and organizational clarity.

Here, as in most of Rembrandt's drawings (and paintings), the formula is to resist simplifying structure when it would intrude on the humanistic aspects of his image, and to omit surface niceties when they would diminish its structural and dynamic strength. Rembrandt recognizes that indiscriminate denotations of surface conditions usually obscure a subject's main structural character, and that drastic

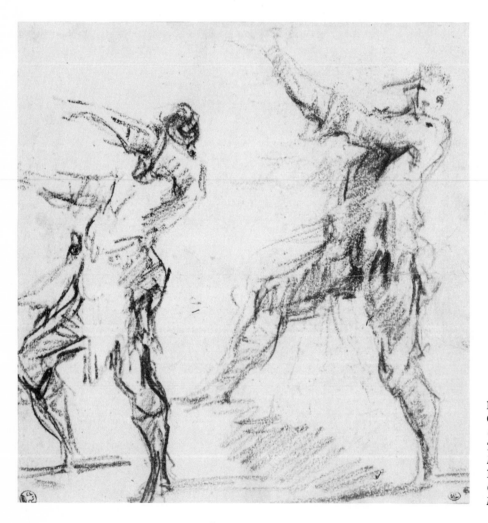

FIGURE 4.103
GIOVANNI BATTISTA PIRANESI
(1720–1778)
*Two Studies of a Man Standing,
His Arms Outstretched to the Left*
Black and red chalk. 7 3/4 x 7 5/8 in.
*Cabinet des Dessins, Musée du Louvre,
Paris.*

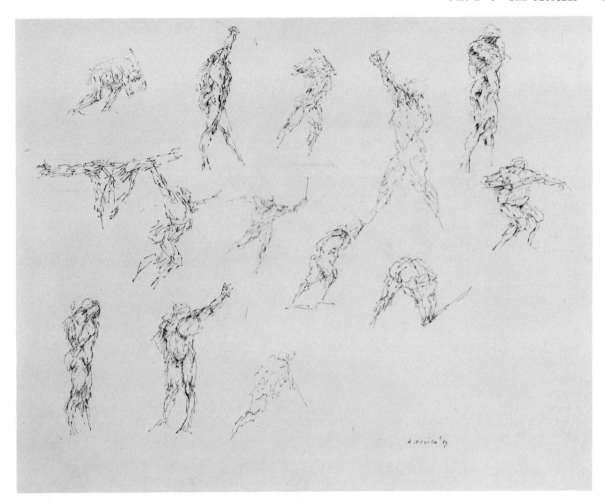

**FIGURE 4.104**
**HAROLD TOVISH (1921–    )**
*Study for Man with Sword II*
Pen and ink.
*Worcester Art Museum, Massachusetts.*

structural summaries may weaken its evocative, figurative impact. Further, he knows that the figure's structure and anatomy must congenially interplay with its design and expression too, that the subject's substantiality of form and significance of spirit must be felt as well as seen.

A sound understanding of structure and anatomy is evident in master drawings, even when the subject is the draped figure. In Piranesi's studies of an action pose (Figure 4.103), the underdrawing of the nude figure helps him to establish the gesture and basic masses of the forms to be draped, and to drape them more convincingly. In the figure on the left the clothing, stretched taut upon the upper right leg, forms sharp folds that turn and radiate in a way that describes the form and action of the leg, and suggests that further raising of the leg must meet even more resistance from the restraining pant leg.

Despite the drapery, we know the tilt and mass of the upper torso and the differing direction and mass of the hips. The arms and legs are still more fully revealed. In the legs Piranesi even suggests the upper leg's overlapping of the lower one at the knee, and the contours of the tibialis and gastrocnemius muscles.

In Tovish's *Study for Man with Sword II* (Figure 4.104), expressive design interests strongly modify structural and anatomical ones, yet a close examination reveals the artist's sophisticated control of both of these constructive factors. In these first searching probes for forms to be finally realized as sculpture, the artist extracts gestural energies and relationships between the figure's parts in various positions, testing their emotive and plastic possibilities. In exploring the substance and spirit of these figures, masses and meanings are interacting matters.

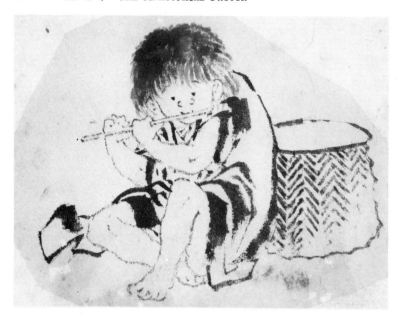

FIGURE 4.105
KATSUSHIKA HOKUSAI (1760–1849)
*Boy with Flute*
Ink and brush. 11.5 x 15.9 cm.
*The Freer Gallery of Art, Washington, D.C.*

FIGURE 4.106
RICO LEBRUN (1900–1964)
*Running Figure* (1948)
Ink. 18 3/4 x 24 3/8 in.
*Collection, Whitney Museum of American Art, New York.*

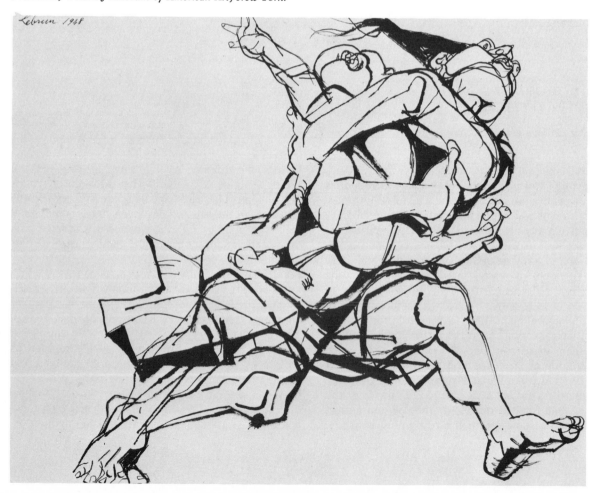

This being so, the essential forms and dynamics of these quick sketches is usually clear. But, in passages of a few of these figures, certain inquiries into gesture, rhythm, or energy overtake structural and anatomical ones—and rightly so. If a hierarchy exists among the factors, clearly the search for a subject's visual and expressive essentials should precede the analysis of the masses that are to convey these essential states. For it is the subject's *total* visual expressive condition that we first respond to, that suggests its creative potential, and not the measurements, however important, of the subject's parts.

Tovish's knowledge of anatomy, as noted above, is apparent in the clarity of his shorthand graphic solutions to the anatomical complexities of torsos, arms, and legs. This is especially clear in the second figure on the left, in the top row, the first, second, and fifth figures in the middle row, and the first and second figures in the bottom row.

Even when masters of figure drawing do not emphasize anatomical matters, the certainty of their understanding is evident in their work. In Hokusai's *Boy with Flute* (Figure 4.105), the seemingly casual contour drawing of the limbs is rich in anatomical detail, discriminating between bone and muscle and showing their effect on surface forms. The bony joints of the limbs are suggested by short lines at the knees and elbow, and we sense the continuance of the limbs beneath the drapery. Although the drawing of the head conforms more to convention than observation, the rest of the figure reveals Hokusai's ability to utilize anatomical fact for expressive purpose.

While the skeleton and muscles may be thought of as the substances that shape the figure's structure, anatomy need not always be wedded to the realization of volumes in space. In Lebrun's *Running Figure* (Figure 4.106), the artist is more concerned with the shapes than with the surface terrain that anatomy provides. By exaggerating the ins and outs of the figure's contours, and emphasizing enclosed linear units, Lebrun creates violent clashes of strong shapes that add to the drawing's forceful expression of terror. Lebrun's mastery of anatomy enables him to create powerful interpretations of human forms, whatever their positions, as the inventive drawing of each of the arms and legs demonstrates.

While Lebrun distorts the figure's forms, he never ignores or violates fundamental anatomical facts. These distortions are not changes invoked without regard for the figure's essential form-character. On the contrary, they are intensifications of the way bone and muscle really do shape human surfaces. Even the strained-looking placement of the child's legs is only a slight exaggeration of an anatomically possible situation. In the study of anatomy it is useful to hold in mind drawings such as these,

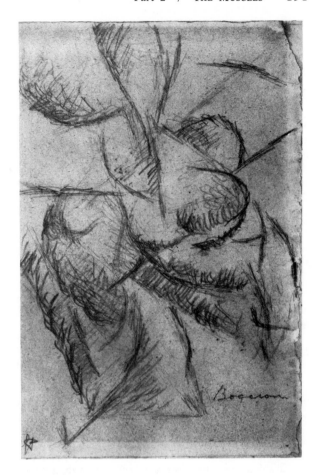

FIGURE 4.107
UMBERTO BOCCIONI (1882–1916)
*Male Figure in Motion towards the Left* (1913)
Pencil. 6 x 4 1/8 in.
*The Lydia and Harry Lewis Winston Collection.*

to realize how important a knowledge of the figure's substructure is to the expansion of our options of response.

An example of just how far such knowledge may carry us into the realm of abstract and two-dimensional drawing solutions to the figure's limitless challenges is Boccioni's *Male Figure in Motion toward the Left* (Figure 4.107). Here, despite the strong insistence on the two-dimensional activity of line, value, texture, and open-ended shapes, bone and muscle still stimulate dynamic activities, still help express human forms and movements.

In this chapter we have seen that the purpose of a knowledge of anatomy, whether we simplify, embellish, or objectively record the figure's forms, is to increase the structural, relational, and emotive quality of our figure drawings. Anatomy's contributions to the factors of structure, design, and expression are many, then, but among the most important is its imparting to our drawings the ring of truth without which figure drawings cannot come alive.

## SUGGESTED EXERCISES

These exercises approach the study of anatomy taking into account its participation as a factor in creative figure drawing. You may expand on them in any way that is compatible with your approach to drawing, for any examination of anatomical facts will stimulate more inventive responses. Although the anatomical illustrations in this chapter should suffice, these exercises may be done with the help of other anatomical texts (see bibliography). As in the previous chapters, vary the size and media of these drawings, but favor large rather than small drawings, and use erasable rather than permanent media. Unless otherwise indicated, work from the model. If none are available to you, work from the photographs provided here or in other books. Unless otherwise noted, there are no time limits on any of these drawings.

1. Draw two more or less simplified skulls: one front, one side view. Then place a sheet of tracing paper over these and draw the muscles of the head as they would appear in each view. Next, place a sheet of tracing paper over the muscle drawing and draw schematic, planar versions of the two heads. Try to reduce the planes of the head to the fewest necessary to convey the essential form-character of every segment of the heads, taking into account the forms of the muscles and the bones already drawn. These schematic heads should look somewhat like unfinished marble sculptures—strong planar judgments, but no fussy modeling. Lastly, reverse the planar drawing and, by vigorously rubbing with a spoon or any broad instrument, transfer the pencil or chalk drawing to an illustration board or sheet of bristol or vellum paper and check for errors in proportion, location, etc. Using this transferred drawing as a guide, draw the surface forms of the two heads, making one female, the other male. These heads should be developed tonally, the idea being to draw convincing, volume-informing representations of two heads.

   Of course, this process of developing a part of the figure from the bones up to the surface is an excellent way of studying *every* part of the figure, and is suggested for segments that you find especially difficult to understand.

2. Draw a three-quarter front view and a three-quarter back view of the flayed torso. Refer to the Houdon flayed figure reproduced in this chapter, but avoid choosing views that closely match these illustrations. Instead, select a view and pose that involves some small bend or twist in the torso. If your first attempt becomes overworked and confused, make a second draft on a sheet of tracing paper overlaid upon the first. In this way you can salvage those areas that are successful. If you wish, these two views may be begun by working from the model. Once the pose has been established, develop the muscular forms on the same sheet or on a tracing paper overlay.

3. Using the flayed torso drawings of the previous exercise, place tracing paper over them and freely follow the undulating pathways of the contours and edges of muscles. Allow your lines to move along the rhythmic routes. Start by following the strongest movements, and later in the drawing shift to less evident or smaller curves and rhythms. Try not to lift your pencil or chalk at all. Instead, travel over earlier drawn lines to reach other areas, to strengthen the rhythmic energy of an area, or to leave off following edges to draw the muscle bundles of a part, or to describe the straight, curved, or radiating flow of muscle fibers. Keep the line moving, but should you stop, simply refrain from lifting your pencil until you begin again. This exercise is intended to familiarize you with the graceful movements that course through the torso's musculature. There is no need to be concerned with structure or even unyielding accuracy. The more scribbled and busy these drawings are, the more rhythmic harmonies you have probably uncovered.

4. From any standing pose of the male figure, reduce the surface forms to simple, planar masses that do not ignore or distort major anatomical facts. Next, from the same or a similar pose of the female figure, make another drawing in the same manner. Here, the results should show rather broadly carved figures, somewhat similar to Giacometti's or Cambiaso's drawings (Figures 1.41 and 4.90). When you have completed both drawings, try to superimpose upon them (or draw on a tracing paper overlay) the position of the bones of the skeleton, as in Figures 3.5, 3.43, and 4.79.

5. Working either from the model or by using a mirror and your own free arm, draw the following:

   a. Any supinated view of the extended arm.

   b. Any pronated view of the extended arm.

   c. Any view of the arm in a bent position, with the hand either prone or supine. This drawing may show a quite foreshortened view.

   Next, on a tracing paper overlay, draw the muscles as they would appear in these differing views. On another sheet of tracing paper make a study of the rhythms of the arm muscles, in the manner described in Exercise 3. Finally, returning to your original three views of the arm, rework or even redraw them, suggesting lean, muscular arms that strongly suggest the bones at those places where they come to the surface. Here you should stress the clarity of the muscles as they might appear if the skin were translucent.

6. In the same manner described in the previous exercise, draw the following:

   a. A front view of the legs, the weight on one leg, the other relaxed, but straight.

   b. A side view of the legs, the weight on one leg, the other relaxed, but slightly bent.

   c. A three-quarter back view of the legs, the weight on one leg, the other slightly raised by being placed on a small block or stool.

**d.** A front view of the legs as they would appear in a seated pose with the legs crossed at the knees.

7. Using your own hands and feet as models, draw as many lifesize views of them as you can conveniently fit onto a sheet of paper about 20″ × 30″. Some of these drawings may go off the page; some may be partially hidden behind others. Use a mirror to increase the variety of poses and views. Begin each drawing with a light gray chalk, or any comparably light-toned chalk, using it to establish the general masses and proportions. Next, using a slightly darker tone of chalk, draw in a sparing and simplified way the general masses of the bones and major muscles and tendons of the hands and feet. Finally, using black chalk, and allowing some erasures of the underdrawing wherever you wish to simplify or soften it, draw the surface forms as convincingly as you can, concentrating on the impression of solid, weighty volumes.

8. Using a light gray or comparably light-toned chalk, draw one male and one female figure in action poses. Make each figure about thirty inches tall, and suggest their muscles as strongly as might be the case if their skin were translucent. That is, draw these figures in a way that suggests the muscles and tendons below, but in a generalized, suggestive manner. You may want to generalize some of the smaller muscles, establishing their collective mass instead. Here, too, favor emphasizing the rhythms and flow of the muscles. Suggest bony passages where they come to the surface. Next, lightly rub the drawings to further generalize and soften them, and continue the drawing with black chalk, establishing the surface forms, but allowing the underdrawing to influence the amount of muscular detail to be shown. The completed drawing should be of rather lean but muscular figures, their skin still "thin" enough to permit us to see many of the forms and harmonies of the anatomy below the surface, as is often the case in Michelangelo's drawings (Figures 3.20, 4.89, and 4.92).

9. Using Figure 4.108 as your subject, draw the figure from any other view. Imagine being able to step around to his left or right side. What would the forms look like from these views? It is best to develop these invented views by stages, working first with structural summaries on tracing paper, until you work out the arrangement of the basic forms of these imagined views.

10. Using Figure 4.109 as your subject, make a free interpretation of these figures, allowing some modest exaggerations and distortions to express your impression of these two struggling figures. You can stress or subordinate volume; you can, within reasonable limits, relocate parts of these figures, and even make anatomical matters play a minor role.

11. Using Figure 4.104 as an example, fill a page with small, action poses that show the interactions of structure, anatomy, and your feelings and ideas about the mood and energies of each pose. Although we have not yet discussed the factors of design and expression in depth, every pose suggests a mood,

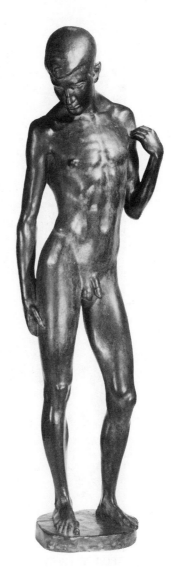

FIGURE 4.108
ARISTIDE MAILLOL (1861–1944)
*Young Cyclist* (1908)
Bronze. Height 38 in.
*Courtesy The Fogg Art Museum, Harvard University.*
*Purchase, Friends of the Fogg and Alpheus Hyatt Fund.*

temperament, or emotive action; all possess harmonies and contrasts of direction, shape, value, and mass. Try to convey something about these visual and expressive states in each pose. Each of these small figures should be drawn in less than seven or eight minutes; even five minutes allows for some comment on each of the four factors. These poses may be of both male and female figures, or may show consecutive stages of a particular action. For example, you can show the various stages of a dancer completing a leap or spin, a boxer falling down, an acrobat performing a stunt, etc.

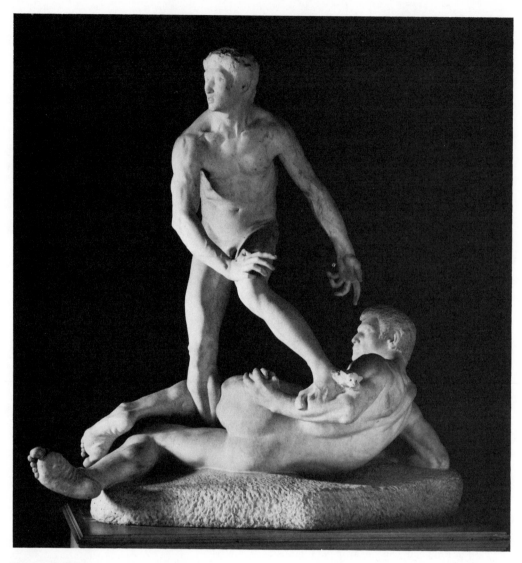

Figure 4.109
GEORGE GREY BARNARD (1863–1938)
*Struggle of Two Natures in Man*
Marble. Height 101 1/2 in.
*The Metropolitan Museum of Art, New York.*
*Gift of Alfred Corning Clark, 1896.*

12. Make two or three copies of drawings by artists whose approach to figure drawing strongly attracts your interest. Next, try to draw several figures (from the model) in the manner of these artists. Study and copy their drawings in order to sense the artist's intentions and interests, but not to adopt their "handwriting." Select artists who draw very differently from each other. For example, Michelangelo, Degas, and Pascin provide an informative collection of themes, attitudes, and approaches to the figure's anatomy.

13. Cover a small-size sculpture armature, manikin, plastic skeleton, or plastic skull with muscles you have shaped out of plasticine clay. If such supports are not available, make an armature out of simple wooden, metal, or even cardboard forms, wrapping a thin-gauge wire around them to better hold the clay. If you make this a reclining figure, the problems of a homemade armature are far easier to cope with.

14. Make a drawing of the model (or figure in a photograph) as she or he would look after gaining fifty pounds. Remember that fatty deposits vary throughout the figure.

15. Draw a flayed figure that represents your guess at what the "missing link" in human evolution looked like. Start by drawing a generalized skeleton that shows some differences in proportion. Then develop

the forms as described in Exercise 8, taking into account the differences in the musculature that this skeleton may require.

16. Make a drawing of a draped male figure. Suggest as much as you can about the surface forms below. Make a similar drawing of a female figure. Think of the drapery as being wet, clinging to the forms in some places, its folds explaining the general masses in other places.

17. Rework or redraw some of your earlier life draw-ings, indicating important bony and muscular land-marks. In some of these drawings try to show the figures as emaciated, their bones and muscles strongly evident.

18. Place a sheet of tracing paper over each of the Albinus drawings (Figures 4.75, 4.76, and 4.77) and draw the figures as they would look in the living state. Working tonally, allow some of the important anatomical landmarks to be quite evident in the completed drawings.

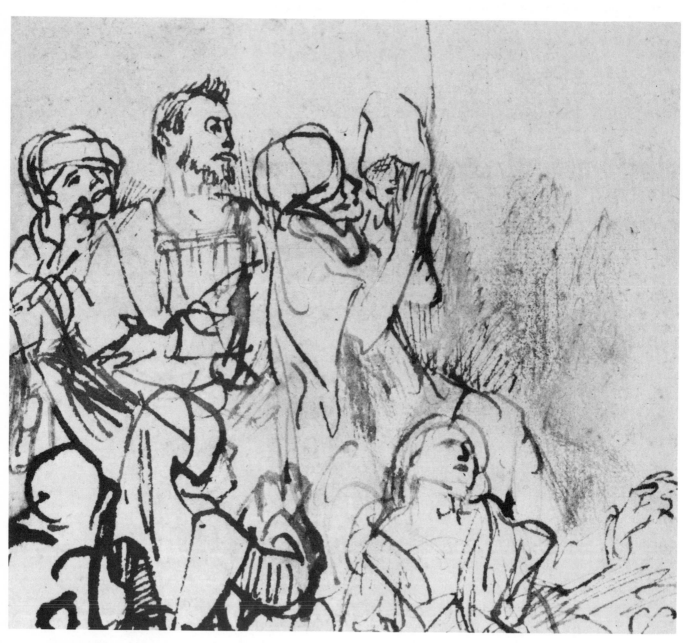

FIGURE 5.1
REMBRANDT VAN RIJN (1606–1669)
*Study for the Group of the Sick
in "The Hundred Guilder Print"* (detail)
Pen and ink.
*Staatliche Museen Preussischer Kulturbesitz.
Kupferstichkabinett. West Berlin.*

# FIVE

# THE

# DESIGN FACTOR

*The Relational Content of Figure Drawing*

## SOME GENERAL OBSERVATIONS

In the three preceding chapters we concentrated on what can be thought of as the "semantics" of figure drawing—the structural and functional meanings of the figure's forms. In this chapter and the following one we will examine the "syntax" of figure drawing—the ordering of the relational and emotive meanings of the figure's forms. Throughout our discussion we should bear in mind that separating design considerations from those of expression, insofar as it can be done at all, unnaturally divides interacting aspects of what we perceive as *one* phenomenon in a drawing. For example, the design strategy of Lillie's *Running Figure* (Figure 5.2) is based on the rhythmic harmonies of an airy web of thick-thin and light-dark curvilinear lines. But the urgent speed of these lines, their furious calligraphy, and their allusions to supple, straining human forms are powerfully expressive messages. All these lines are engaged in both syntactical functions simultaneously.

Nevertheless, separating these two dynamic factors for the time being will help us to explore more fully the essential nature of each. For, while always

deeply interlaced, each factor has its own discernible effects. A drawing's design is the state of its relational life and order—its plastic condition; a drawing's expression is its emotional content—both its psychological mood as conveyed by the design *and* (in figure drawing) by the emotive nature of its human theme. A drawing's design, then, is the consequence of its abstract and figural occurrences—the visual nature of the tensions, movements, and relationships that exist among the drawing's marks and meanings. A drawing's expression is the felt effects of these occurrences on the viewer. In this chapter we will concentrate on the visual relationships at work in well-designed drawings.

Simply stated, a good design is one in which all the seemingly differing parts relate visually to form a balanced unity. But don't we naturally associate the things we see? After all, isn't it almost impossible to keep from seeing that a finger belongs to the greater unit of the hand, that a small fold in the brow is similar in shape to one in the cheek, or that arms are shorter than legs? Of course we see these and countless other relationships, and try in our drawings to state as many of these relational bonds as we can. But where we fail, all too often, is in showing these relationships only within a part; that is, only in small clusters *that do not relate to each other*. Thus, the finger is seen as part of the hand, but its similarity or contrast with the fold in the brow or cheek may be missed; the arms and legs are drawn in proportion, but their various shapes and directions might not be related to other shapes and directions in the torso or elsewhere in the drawing. In the best drawings, however, every line and value, every shape, every inference of movement is interrelated with others on the page in some kind of visual activity that aims at a particular scheme of design throughout the drawing. These schemes, sometimes intended and sometimes intuitive, involve the visual elements in various kinds of *visual themes*.

A visual theme can be any sequence or configuration among the visual elements that reappears in

FIGURE 5.2
LLOYD LILLIE (1932–    )
*Running Figure*
Pencil. 15 x 18 in.
*Courtesy of the artist.*

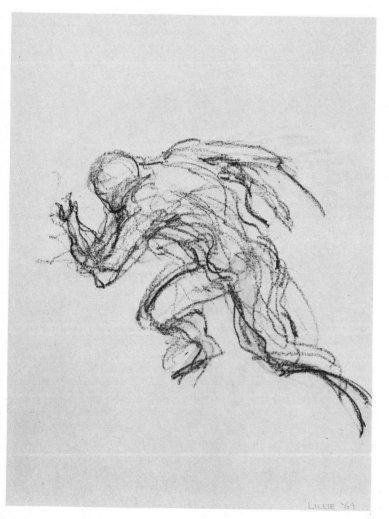

a drawing, always in variations on itself. Variations may include an inversion of order; the symmetrical composition, for example, is based on a reversal of material along a vertical midline. Or a visual theme that repeatedly appears among the shapes and forms of a drawing may be developed into a large unit of compositional significance. A visual theme may be gradually transformed into or fused with another theme. Rembrandt's *Study for the Group of the Sick in "The Hundred Guilder Print"* (Figures 5.1 and 5.3) provides an excellent example of the interrelation of the elements, and of several visual themes at work. Here *all* the marks and the shapes and masses they suggest, every value, direction, and rhythm cooperate in building the drawing's dominant organizational idea: a large pyramidal configuration. In doing so, Rembrandt shows a roughly symmetrical arrangement of the figures—the inversion of the order. This great triangular shape is the culmination of the many smaller triangular shapes in the work. Each of the figures, to varying degrees, suggests the triangular shape of the group; each carries the seed of the dominant design strategy.

A second design theme, the rich curvilinear rhythms that coil through the group, animates and further unites the figures. Note that some of these curvilinear lines participate in forming the smaller triangles, as in the headdress of the boldly drawn kneeling figure in the foreground—the fusing of themes. A third system of circular shapes and forms provides still another visual theme that takes our eye into and around the group, giving us the sense of these figures as forms in space. Note how firmly Rembrandt builds this pyramid, the boldest lines and tones at its base. Note too that he creates a path between the left and right side of the group. The path is illuminated, as if some force is about to come among them. The figures, looking up, add to the sense of an impending activity moving leftward.

A visual theme can be a certain mode in the treatment of an element, a way of using, say, line or value. The rippling action of the lines in Figure 5.2 is such a theme; the lines, enacting many variations of the idea of an undulating movement, impart to the figure a strong sense of motion.

Not unlike a musical theme, a visual thematic idea appropriate to the subject matter occurs to the artist, is stated, and its essential character repeated in variations that serve to weave the work together and to magnify its expressive point. Each theme, through its subtle variants, and in contending with counter-themes, creates tensions and energies in the drawing of a *formal* kind, that is, of a purely abstract nature. And, as we shall see in the following chapter, a drawing's expressive character emerges as much from these abstract activities as from its representational meanings.

Although sensitive to a figure's placement on the page, the design of many figure drawings does not reach out to engage the entire surface of the sheet. Usually it is concentrated in the figure itself. In Rembrandt's drawing, however, the shape surrounding the group actively contributes to the drawing's ordered, visual condition (and consequently to its expression). The background tones and the suggestion of a column help establish the sense of space, its two triangular wings echo the pyramidal theme, and its small scale adds strength to the group's forms and actions by making them appear almost too energetic to be contained in so small a format. Had the background been smaller, the drawing would have been too crowded, the forms choked by the tight enclosure; had the background area been larger, much of the drawing's power would have been dissipated.

Villon's *Study for a Washerwoman* (Figure 5.4) is a clear example of visual themes that are held to the figure itself. Again, a dominant theme envelops the entire image. It is a system of intersecting diagonals that cascade down the figure. We feel these diagonal thrusts move downward for two reasons: First, each of the bold diagonal marks appears to have been begun at its top and drawn downward, the lines and tones growing darker as they descend; and second, as Denman Ross points out, our eyes tend to move in the direction of diminishing intervals,* and here, the crisscross of diagonals occurs

* Denman Ross, *On Drawing and Painting* (Boston: Houghton Mifflin Co., 1940), pp. 75–79.

FIGURE 5.3
**REMBRANDT VAN RIJN** (1606–1669)
*Study for the Group of the Sick
in "The Hundred Guilder Print"*
Pen and ink. 11.7 x 11.4 cm.
*Staatliche Museen Preussischer Kulturbesitz.
Kupferstichkabinett. West Berlin.*

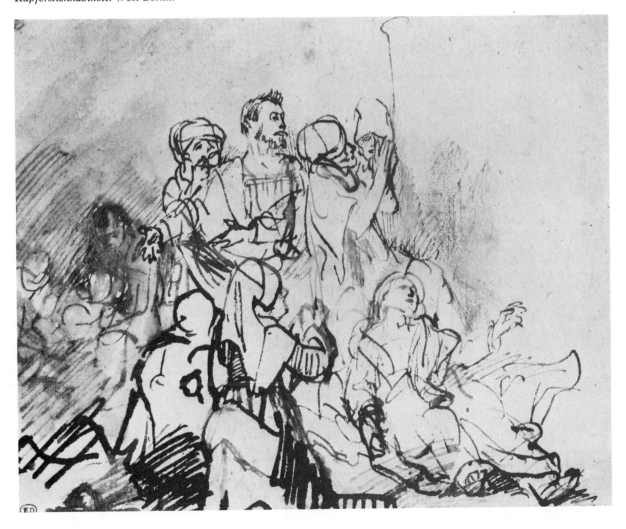

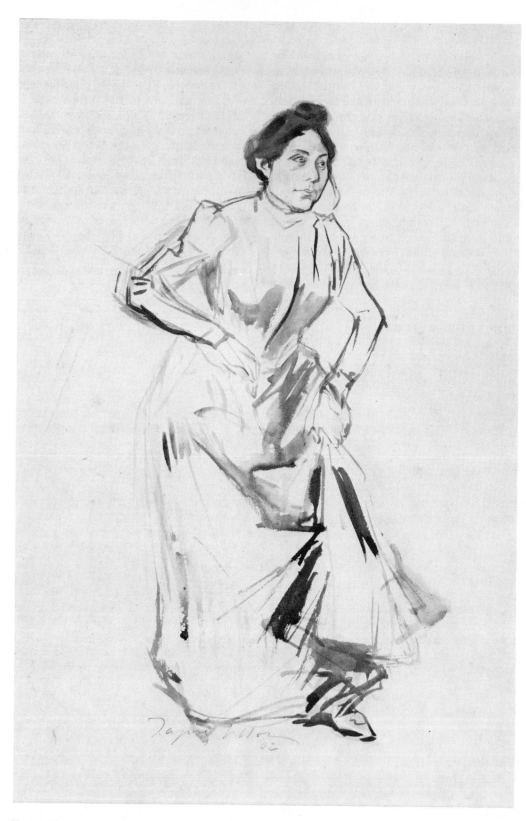

Figure 5.4
JACQUES VILLON (1875–1963)
*Study for a Washerwoman*
Pencil and wash. 49.5 x 32.1 cm.
*Courtesy Museum of Fine Arts, Boston.*
*Gift of Louis Carre.*

more frequently in the drawing's lower section. This intensifying zigzag activates the figure's gesture and, by its reoccurring role, unifies the image. A second theme that treats shapes in a harsher triangular manner than in Figure 5.3 is also at work, lending a crisp angularity to the woman's movements while it conveys something of the texture of her attire.

As these drawings show, in a good design all parts interrelate through various visual kinships and contrasts, every mark participating in the drawing's particular systems of ordered, thematic actions. And, as we saw in Rembrandt's and Villon's drawings, there is usually more than one visual theme at work. The kinds of visual themes possible are, of course, limitless. We have been examining some rather evident ones. Others can be very subtle. Consider, for example, in Villon's drawing, the inversion of the shape of the hair in the tones that define the breasts and several folds in the dress.

Further, a good design reveals an order of visual importance, a hierarchy of its visual themes. Without such a hierarchy, Rembrandt's pyramid and Villon's cascading diagonals would be lost amid the confusion of competing systems; we would be unable to decide, or even to see, what organizational and expressive meanings the artist intended. In Chapter One we saw that an important common denominator of the best figure drawings is the artist's insistence on stating a necessary point of view. But drawings made without regard for an ordering of their parts, or where a hierarchy of visual themes is absent, do not convey a point of view, but only ambiguities and indecision. Such works do not make a felt and lucid statement; they merely emit confusing utterances about their various parts.

Still another necessary condition for a good design is the balanced resolution of its parts on the page. Balance occurs when a drawing's measurable components of scale, shape, mass, value, position, etc., and its abstract forces—that is, its expressions of weight, movement, tension, and rhythm—achieve a distribution of elements and energies that convey a state of stability. This stability is based on visual activities that check and regulate each other—a system of compensations that suggest mutual restraint rather than immobility. In a balanced drawing we sense equilibrium in both the physical and visual weight of the forms and in the behavior of the visual forces. Drawings without a balanced resolution of parts and energies cannot hold together. With weight and movement unchecked, forms and forces break loose; isolated, floating, or falling parts and movements in conflict overwhelm any other aspects of order in the image. In the confusion and disorder of imbalance, abstract and figurative meanings are also lost, the chaos of conflicting and ambiguous visual clues making it impossible to sort these meanings out. In figure drawing the repose and tranquility of a reclining figure can be shattered by a hovering dark tone, so placed as to appear about to fall; by unchecked diagonals that slide the figure down toward a corner of the page; or by any other element or energy that remains unstabilized in either its depictive or dynamic function. The balanced governing of forms and forces is necessary not only because we instinctively react with unease to a state of disequilibrium, but because the clarity of a drawing's total expressive content depends upon its balance.

Implicit in the foregoing is that all good design is *unified*. In a well-ordered drawing, the harmony and cohesion of the parts and thematic actions, the artist's consistency of intent, and the manner of execution—his or her style of handling—all work together in a unity of visual (and expressive) purpose. All good drawings appear to be of a piece, having an ultimate oneness. Despite the often powerful visual exchanges between their contrasting parts, they convey a sense of necessity and belonging, qualities vital in making an expressively sensible image.

But the artist must be mindful of a danger inherent in the search for unity. In art the opposite of the chaos of visual anarchy is the monotony of visual rigidity and sameness. When the desire to organize an image leads to its overstabilization, when it is too rigidly interlocked by similarities, the results—being obvious in their sameness—are dull. A chessboard is certainly a unified design, but it is a boring one. In a good design, unity is achieved by the harnessing of contrasts: utilizing their contrapuntal behavior to emphasize certain passages, enriching the visual interplay of the marks, and balancing the image, as well as by the congenial merger of similarities. A good design always depends on variety, on the presence of stabilized differences, to keep from being excessively harmonized.

In drawing, then, to design is to clarify our meanings, to compose content in a visual syntax that communicates clearly. And the requirements of a good design—the interplay, hierarchy, balance, and unity of a drawing's parts and dynamics—are met by our ability to perceive relationships. As Delacroix put it, "What does it mean to compose? It is the power to associate. . . ."

For artists, all things in nature have line, shape, scale, value, volume, color, texture, position, and direction *in relation to other things*. They know that these measurable, physical properties have no visual meanings until they are related to other like or unlike properties. They know, too, that these relationships needn't be recorded only as seen; that by selecting those which support their goals and subordinating all others, they can make visual associations that form a complete statement of intent.

Henry James once observed that, "universally, relations stop nowhere, and the exquisite problem of the artist is eternally but to draw, by a geometry of his own, the circle within which they shall happily appear to do so."* In a good design, then, the "circle," the field of energy within which relationships work, exhibits a sense of self-contained order, one in which we don't want to add or remove anything.

A sensitive design begins, as Delacroix observed, with the ability to make estimates, comparisons, and judgments about the similarities and differences in a subject's physical and dynamic actualities. The artist translates these perceptions into objective or highly interpretive visual terms by means of the visual elements—the six basic tools of graphic communication. (Color, an occasional participant in drawing, is omitted here because it is incidental to the essentials of this book.) Although a thorough exploration of the visual elements, more appropriate to a basic drawing book,† is not at-

* Henry James, *Prefaces* (1907–1909), Roderick Hudson.

† See Nathan Goldstein, *The Art of Responsive Drawing,* 2nd ed. (Englewood Cliffs, N.J.: Prentice-Hall, Inc. 1977), chap. 8.

**Figure 5.5**
**GERBRAND VAN DEN EECKHOUT (1621–1674)**
*A Boy Lying Down*
*Rijksprentenkabinet, Amsterdam.*

tempted here, it is necessary to discuss these tools in more than a passing way to see some of their limitless relational possibilities.

## THE VISUAL ELEMENTS

The six elements we will examine are *line, value, shape, volume, space,* and *texture.* Of these, line and value enjoy a special importance inasmuch as all the other elements are made by one or the other, or by their combined use. Of these two elements, line is the more universally used in drawing, the more direct and versatile, the element most at the heart of drawing. Indeed, the completely tonal drawing, photograph-like in its absence of line, is relatively rare. Nevertheless, value used alone can produce powerfully effective images, as can be seen in the conté crayon drawings of Seurat (see Figure 6.18). Van den Eeckhout's *A Boy Lying Down* (Figure 5.5) is a fine example of a drawing developed almost exclusively with tone; in this case, applied by brush. More typically, though, whether in dry or fluid media, values in drawing are made by hatched strokes that collectively create the various tones we

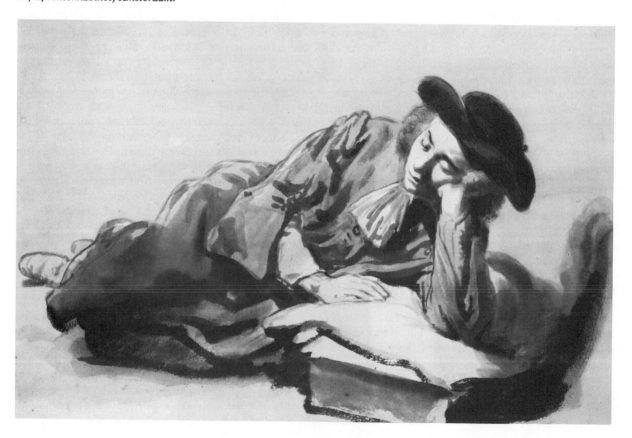

see, even when the use of value in a work exceeds that of line. The function of space will receive further attention when we turn to examine the energies of the elements in action. This elusive element, which gives visual meaning to the location of all the other elements, cannot be directly examined, for space has no meaning outside the context of the elements that create and interrupt it.

## Line

As an element, line refers to more than drawn lines. Boundaries of shapes and forms, even when established by rough washes of ink tones, function as lines of separation from adjacent shapes, values, forms, or spaces. The long axis of a shape or form is also seen as a line phenomenon. Not only is this true for the figure's more slender forms, but for all of its forms and form-units, large and small. The curve in a bending torso or an eyelid is, essentially, a linear action. The long axis of the head may lie on a different line from that of the neck. Line runs through groups of shapes and forms that may differ in scale, value, texture, and substance; it may do so even when shapes and forms are separated from each other by considerable amounts of space. Indeed, the shape of a space separating solids can also participate in their linear arrangement. People "line up" for tickets to the theatre, furniture may be "aligned" in straight or curved arrangements, and a model's extended arm may be "in a line with" the top (line) of a bureau across the room.

Matisse's *Girl with Tulips* (Figure 5.6) demonstrates all of these types of invisible line. In addition to the behavior of the artist's drawn lines, some of which course through forms or state the main visual theme (a large triangular arrangement similar to that of Figure 5.3), there is the linear effect of the dark shape of the hair, important to the drawing's design strategy. Note how the shape's projection on the figure's right side is restated by the action of the lines that constitute the figure's right arm. Note, too, how similar the shape of the hair is to the shape of the light gray turtle-neck blouse and to the shapes of the upper body, the leaves, and the flower pot. All these edges, and the forceful way in which they are drawn, produce a bold, rhythmic line play that envelops the entire configuration. Additionally, we sense lines not actually drawn, as in the large curved sweep of the two arms and the shoulders. By repeating lines that define the location of the arms and torso, Matisse causes line to suggest movement in the figure.

Although lines do not exist in nature—do not surround forms and spaces—they are the most direct and visually logical means for conveying descriptive, plastic, and expressive matters, which makes line the basic drawing element for searching out a subject's gestural behavior. This is shown in Creti's *Studies for Jacob Wrestling with the Angel* (Figure 5.7). Here the artist uses line to feel out the essential character of the action of the four groups of figures. In so doing, he extracts the linear design of these interacting figures to reveal that these images wrestle at the abstract as well as the representational level; these animated swirls of interlacing lines not only describe, they also enact the figures' energetic activities.

Line is capable of suggesting differing moods and even speeds. In contrast to Creti's spirited calligraphy, the line in Kuhn's *Seated Woman* (Figure 5.8) is, for the most part, slow, easy-going, and largely restricted to defining edges. Likewise, the unseen lines of rhythms and directions are also slow-paced. Instead of using lines to act out strong rhythmic movements, Kuhn restrains their speed and assigns them the task of suggesting the figure's graceful, resting forms. But the artist's interest in using line to accent the subject's shape-state—the two-dimensional arrangement and nature of its forms—makes him hold back from suggesting heavy, limpid forms; the figure and the legless chair seem almost weightless. To underline the drawing's dominant line quality, Kuhn alters the character of some of the lines of the chair, speeding them up in a series of bold scallops. He also reinforces his two-dimensional theme by a pattern of dots and one of broad ink strokes. Both of these systems rise to the surface of the page, making the design function on the picture plane as well as in space. In this way the artist calls our attention to the element of space as simultaneously existing in two-dimensional and three-dimensional terms—as interspace and field of space.

Kuhn's knowledge of structure and anatomy is evident in the line's volume-informing delineations. Although an impression of weighty mass is intentionally subdued, the few lines used to define the figure tell a good deal about its essential structure and its anatomy. Indeed, one of the more appealing qualities of this drawing is the large amount of abstract and representational content conveyed with such an economy of line. There are no unnecessary embellishments and no "unemployed" lines—each mark has a function in the drawing's depictive and dynamic states.

Parker's *Sheet of Studies of the Female Figure* (Figure 5.9) demonstrates an integration of several attitudes toward line. Hatched lines drawn in the direction of a plane's tilt in space serve structural purposes; other lines, especially those defining contours, take on a more animated, playful quality. Some lines, mainly in the drawing of the hair, suggest texture, and still others, running at right angles to the hatched lines of some shaded planes, serve as

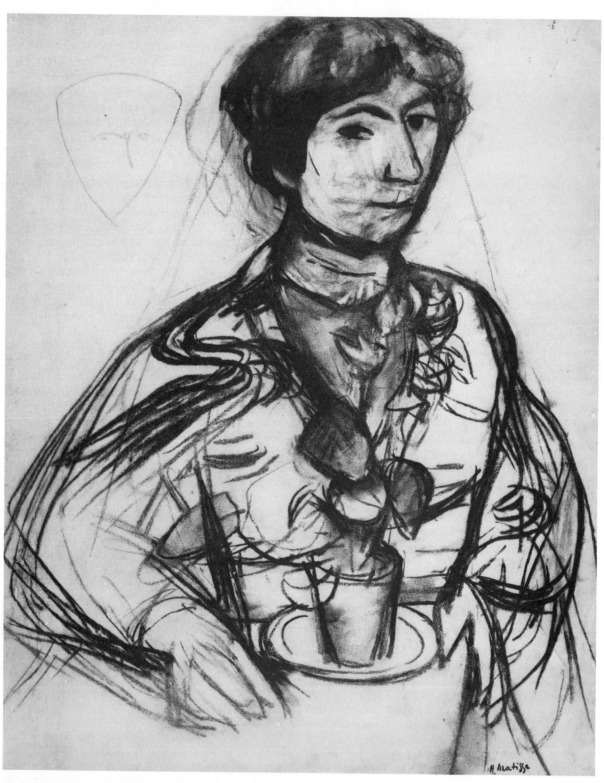

**FIGURE 5.6**
**HENRI MATISSE (1869–1954)**
*Girl with Tulips*
Charcoal on buff paper. 23 3/4 x 23 in.
*Collection, The Museum of Modern Art, New York.*
*Acquired through the Lillie P. Bliss Bequest.*

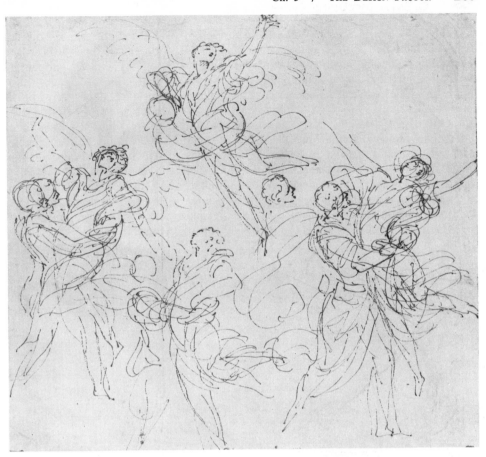

FIGURE 5.7
DONATO CRETI (1671–1749)
*Studies for Jacob Wrestling
with the Angel*
Pen and brown ink. 21.6 x 24.3 cm.
*The Art Museum,
Princeton University.*

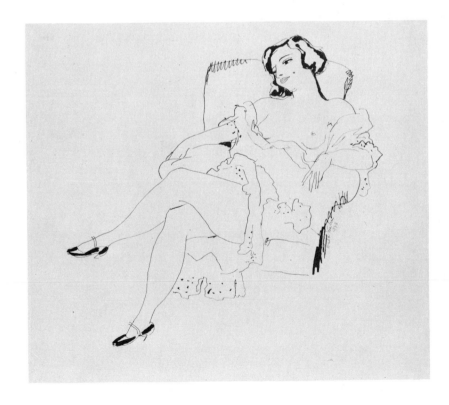

FIGURE 5.8
WALT KUHN (1880–1949)
*Seated Woman*
Pen, brush and ink.
13 13/16 x 16 1/16 in.
*The Metropolitan Museum of Art,
New York.
Rogers Fund, 1955.*

the long axis of various forms and establish a design theme of light and shaded shapes. Parker successfully unites these differing interests in the lines' structural, dynamic, and shape-making functions by intermingling the varying kinds of line throughout each figure.

As Parker's drawing shows, lines can take on different functions simultaneously. Lines in the hair are both textural and structural, shape-making lines define planes and direction, and so on. Lines can be sorted into several broad categories, but all lines either function in more than one way, or can alter their role and character along their course. A line begun as a gentle caress may end up as a vehement slash.

Structural lines, discussed in Chapter Two, diagrammatic lines—those loose, schematic lines that roughly indicate direction, shape, dimension, and generalities of mass—and delineating or *contour* lines can impart a wide range of dynamic qualities. Each of these types of line may be primarily investigative, descriptive, or declarative in function, but will always convey other qualities. Diagrammatic, structural, and contour line functions can be seen in Michelangelo's *Studies of Nude and Draped Figures* (Figure 5.10). Diagrammatic lines, such as those in the right arm and drapery of the female figure (back view), underlie most of the structural lines that more fully model the forms. Instead of employing a pronounced, independent contour line, Michelangelo

FIGURE 5.9
**ROBERT ANDREW PARKER** (1925–    )
*Sheet of Studies of the Female Figure*
Pen and ink. 17 x 21 in.
*Courtesy of the artist.*

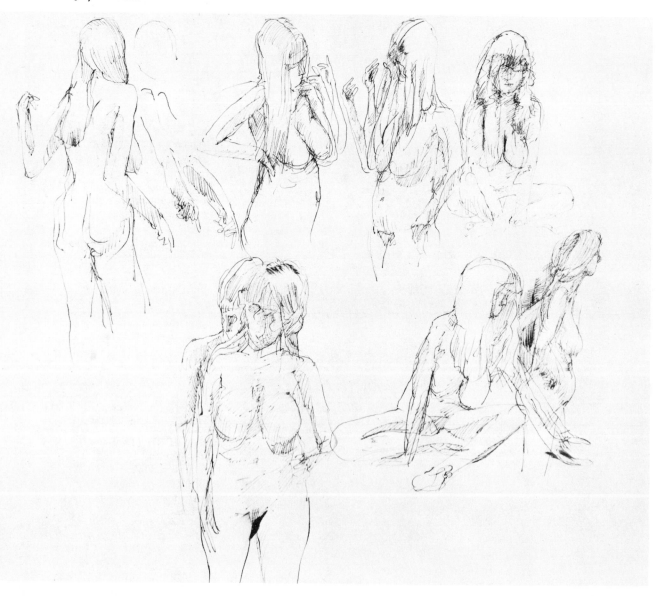

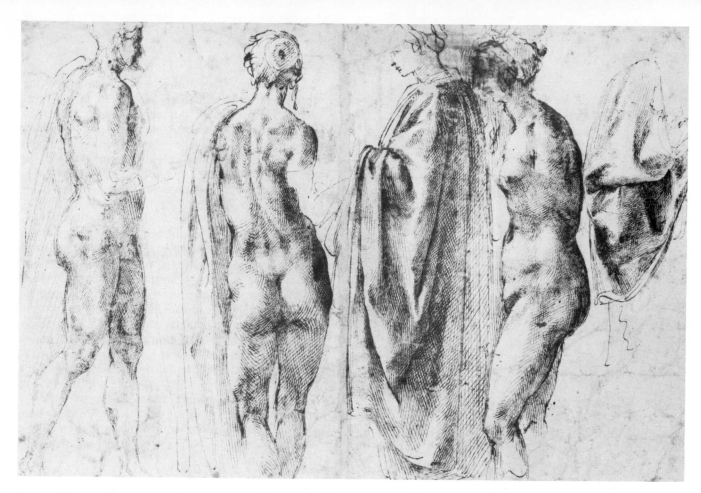

FIGURE 5.10
MICHELANGELO BUONARROTI (1475–1564)
*Studies of Nude and Draped Figures*
Pen and ink. 18 3/8 x 15 1/4 in.
*Musée Condé, Chantilly, Photo Giraudon.*

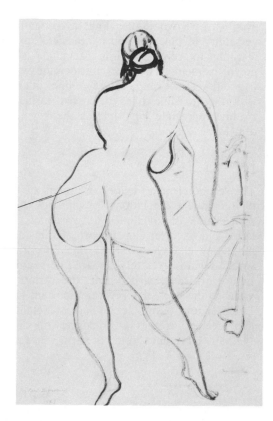

delineates forms by massing or darkening structural lines as they approach edges, only occasionally reinforcing an edge by a short segment of contour line. These especially dark, declarative segments are sometimes used to emphasize the weight of a part, to show the effect on the figure's surface of inner, anatomical forms, or to amplify a visual theme of periodic, rhythmic curves.

Some lines, although they may function in various descriptive ways, are often of an animated and curvilinear, or *calligraphic,* nature. They more strongly call attention to their own abstract activity, as well as to their representational roles. Such lines are often bold and emotive, as can be seen in Lachaise's *Back of a Nude Woman* (Figure 5.11), where the calligraphy takes on an oriental elegance.

FIGURE 5.11
GASTON LACHAISE (1882–1935)
*Back of a Nude Woman* (1929)
Pencil, quill pen, and India ink. 45.5 x 30.9 cm.
*The Brooklyn Museum.*
*Gift of Carl Zigrosser.*

207

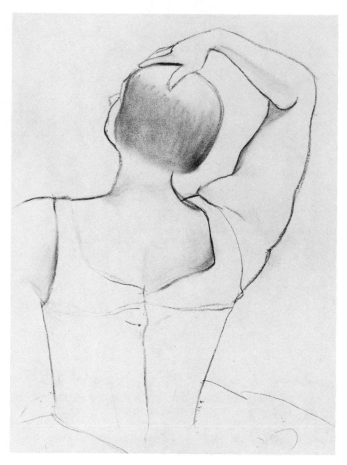

**Figure 5.12**
ANDRÉ DERAIN (1880–1954)
*Ballerina with Raised Arm*
Charcoal on cream-white paper. 624 x 484 mm.
*Gift of Wrights, Ludington, 1944.*
*Santa Barbara Museum of Art.*

But calligraphic lines—lines *inherently* active and seemingly aware of each other in their abstract interplay—can be less flamboyant and more fixed on objective depiction, as in Derain's *Ballerina with Raised Arm* (Figure 5.12). Here, despite Derain's insistence on defining the figure's forms and volumes in more realistic terms, the calligraphic behavior of the lines themselves, their autonomous life as line acting on line, comes through.

Hence, in figure drawing, as Lachaise's and Derain's drawings demonstrate, the calligraphic line, even the most expressively ornate kind, has its depictive duties to perform, just as the most descriptively motivated lines have plastic and expressive obligations to the drawing's dynamic state. In the best figure drawings every kind of line is, to one degree or another, engaged in depicting and enacting, and thus in expressing.

A calligraphic attitude to line animates the forms in Rembrandt's *Esau Selling His Birthright to Jacob* (Figure 5.13). Although we can discern diagrammatic, structural, and contour lines, all are activated by an energetic play of movements and rhythms between the often diagonally situated planes, forms, and tones that have calligraphic overtones. Every line serves several needs at once. For example, the bold hatched lines of the tablecloth, while essentially diagrammatic and structural in function, are, in the context of the other lines of the drawing, strenuously calligraphic as well. Rembrandt strengthens some contours, such as those defining the arms of the two figures, to gain both dynamic and representational clarity. The bridge formed by these arms spans the two halves of the drawing, a link that bolsters both the drawing's design and its dramatic impact. Note how structurally informing are the calligraphic lines of Esau's turban and boots. In this drawing, despite the rich variety of line—the range in their value, width, texture, and length—all lines interrelate strongly. They call to each other by rhythms, tensions, directions, and textures, whose interactions offset their contrasts, together creating a cohesive order at both the abstract and figurative levels.

As Rembrandt's drawing demonstrates, descriptive lines can sometimes be so emotive in their calligraphy, and expressive lines can be so descriptive, that they cannot be defined as being predominantly one or the other. But as we see in the drawings of Michelangelo, Lachaise, Derain, and Kuhn, many artists prefer lines that plainly disclose a dominant attitude, whether structural or calligraphic. In whatever way we would use line, a recognition of its versatility of function and character is important in learning to command this seemingly simple but potent element. When we consider the wide figurative and abstract range of drawn lines in conjunction with the invisible lines discussed earlier, we can readily appreciate why line is the key element in drawing.

*Value*

The second element, *value,* also offers a broad range of functions and relational possibilities. As we have seen, value is sometimes a byproduct of hatched lines and is often an important consideration in modifying the character of lines in drawings we would regard as purely linear. For example, while Figure 5.11 is clearly linear, the variations in the value of the lines play several important visual roles. Lachaise uses pure black to suggest weight, as in the shoulder and breast, and to suggest the dark tone of the hair. Gray lines, some of them very faint, permit

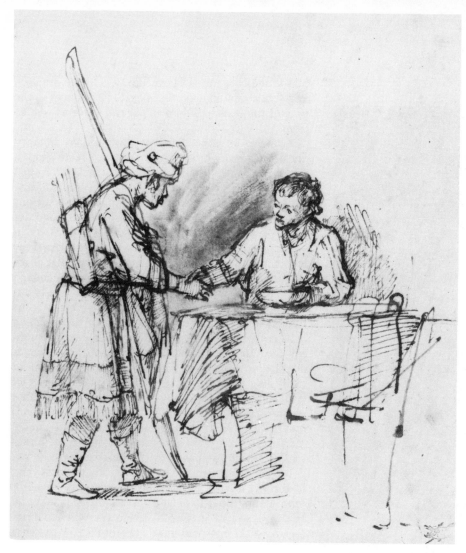

FIGURE 5.13
REMBRANDT VAN RIJN (1606–1669)
*Esau Selling His Birthright to Jacob*
Reed and quill pen, and wash. 20 x 17.3 cm.
*Trustees of the British Museum, London.*

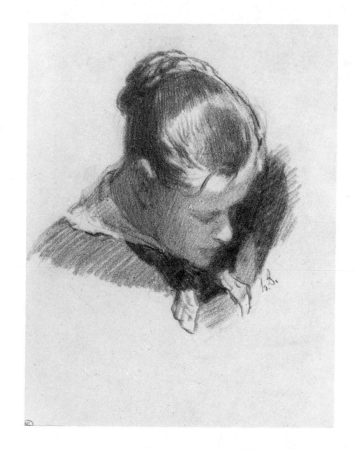

FIGURE 5.14
HONORÉ DAUMIER (1808–1879)
*Head of a Woman*
Black conté crayon. 15.2 x 18.7 cm.
*Cabinet des Dessins, Musée du Louvre, Paris.*

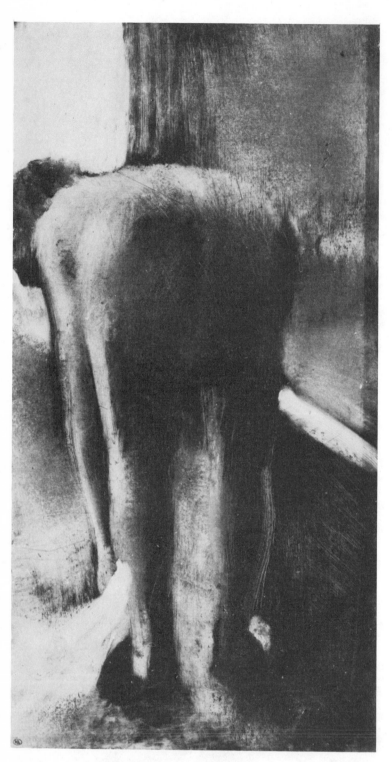

**Figure 5.15**
**EDGAR DEGAS** (1834–1917)
*Woman Wiping Her Feet near a Bathtub*
Monotype. 17 3/4 x 9 3/8 in.
*Cabinet des Dessins, Musée du Louvre, Paris.*

him to indicate forms farther away, delicate drapery, and subtle anatomical notations. Such changes in the tone of the lines help him to suggest space as well as form.

Patches of tone, whether produced by hatched lines, washes, or broad chalk strokes, create shapes. These shapes, by their proximity to each other, can produce volumes; and, by the surface state of the tones—the character of their application—various textures can be suggested. Such shapes of tone are often so fused, overlaid, or subtly graduated in value that their essential shape state is obscured, as in Figure 4.82. But in Daumier's *Head of a Woman* (Figure 5.14), the shapes of tone are distinct enough to serve as a useful example of their volume-creating ability. By grouping all of the many values of his subject into three tones—the white of the paper, a light gray, and a dark gray—Daumier also strengthens the sense of an ordered arrangement of values on the picture plane. These values, in addition to their descriptive function, enact a playful abstract visual theme of variously toned, curved shapes that seem to revolve on the page. Note the differing tones and textures, and the clarity of the planes that model the form of the hair and forehead, the most structurally developed passages in the drawing.

Value, then, can exist in line, shape, mass, and texture. It is also an efficient and forceful means of representing both two- and three-dimensional space, as demonstrated in Degas' monotype *Woman Wiping Her Feet near a Bathtub* (Figure 5.15). A sense of atmosphere envelops the figure. This is suggested by gently modulated gray tones and by the contrasting flash of white at the upper left corner. This contrasting value holds its place in space because it suggests daylight streaming in through a far window and because it is strongly overlapped by the bending figure. Two-dimensionally, the values, again limited to some three or four tones, are arranged into a design that consists of three interrelated visual themes. By squinting at Degas' drawing you may be better able to see the following tonal activities.

The first consists of the blocky shapes surrounding the figure, whose widely differing values serve to call attention to themselves as tones upon a flat surface. But they are related by a rough sameness in scale, by their encircling action, and by a subtle tendency to aim toward the center of the page—like dulled arrowheads. Some touch the figure, some are overlapped by it. A second tonal theme forms a large, dark, inverted U shape composed of the figure's legs and buttocks, and repeated by a thinner, light gray shape fitted over the first, formed by the woman's arm and back. At the open end of the dark shape are flashes of light tone at either ankle that associate with the longer, oblique light tones to either side of the legs and with the large, white shape at the upper left corner. A third tonal system forms an inverted Y shape that reaches across the entire page, incorporating the oblique light tones of the towel and the bathtub rim as the arms of the inverted Y, its central stem being the vertical, dark, draperylike shape that extends to the figure's back. These three tonal themes are interdependent and complementary. As we look at the drawing, first one, then another of these themes emerges, each graciously subsiding to allow the next its turn at our attention—yet all working together to form a unified, pulsating tonal design.

Degas' drawing shows us that values can make unlike things relate. Tonally, the white towel and the bathtub rim, despite being far apart spatially and as substances, are visual first cousins. Although their oblique orientation and shape are roughly similar, it is their intense white tone that seals the visual bond. Similarly, the woman's hair and slippers associate through value. Again, in Goldstein's *Crouching Figure* (Figure 5.16), the figure's right upper arm and leg and her chest are all affiliated by their common value. Value can also make like things contrast. In Figure 5.16 the shoulders and lower arms are almost symmetrical, but their contrasting values subdue their physical kinship. Likewise, the two legs differ in value, and while the raised leg is only subtly different from its tonal surroundings, the lower leg contrasts sharply with the values encircling it.

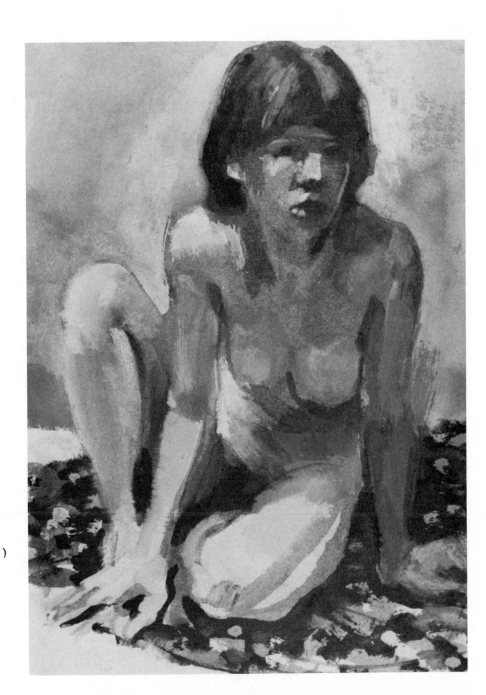

FIGURE 5.16
NATHAN GOLDSTEIN (1927–   )
*Crouching Figure*
Sepia ink and watercolor washes.
5 3/4 x 8 in.
*Collection of the author.*

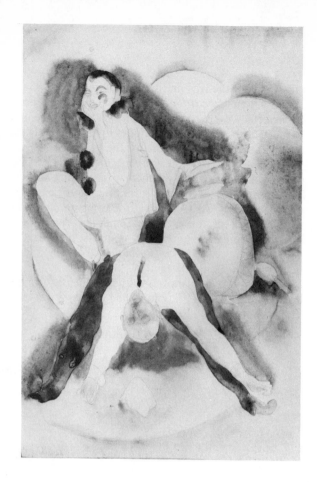

FIGURE 5.17
CHARLES DEMUTH (1883–1953)
*Clowns*
Watercolor and pencil. 7 1/2 x 11 in.
*The Metropolitan Museum of Art, New York.*
*Bequest of Charles F. Iklé, 1963.*

FIGURE 5.18
PABLO PICASSO (1881–1973)
*The Painter and His Model*
Etching and aquatint. 32.5 x 47.5 cm.
*Courtesy Museum of Fine Arts, Boston.*
*Lee M. Friedman Fund.*

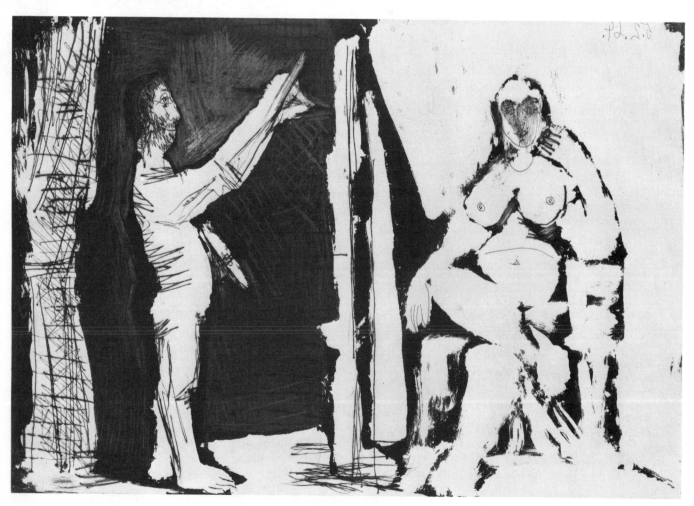

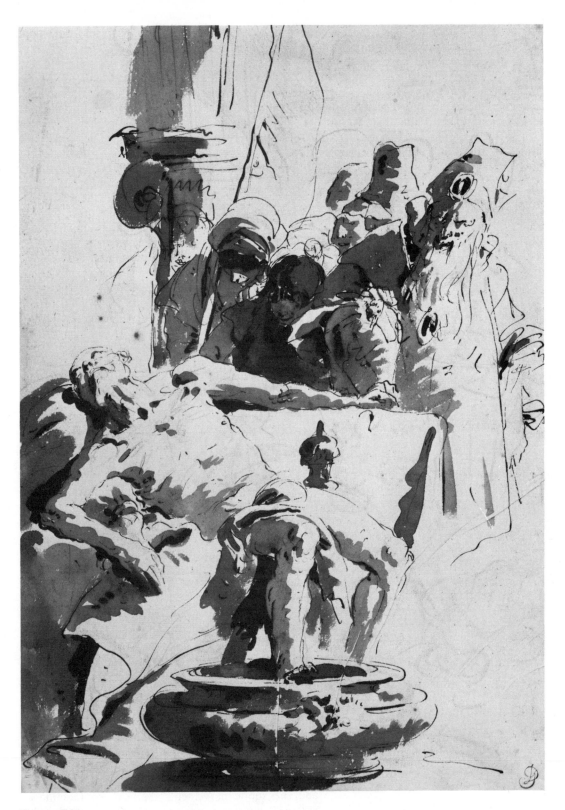

FIGURE 5.19
GIOVANNI BATTISTA TIEPOLO (1696–1770)
*The Death of Seneca*
Pen, brown ink, and wash. 34 x 24 cm.
*Courtesy of the Art Institute of Chicago.*
*Joseph and Helen Regenstein Collection.*

Value's ability to make dissimilar parts relate and similar ones contrast is an important compositional device. It is a means by which to guide the viewer's visual tour of the image, and to balance and unify the work. In Demuth's *Clowns* (Figure 5.17), the dark legs of the lower figure are more easily associated with the dark tones above him than with the lightly toned legs of the standing figure. A similar visual bond is formed by the standing clown's head and the two pompons of his coat, while the relationship of the two heads is reduced by their visual contrast.

Picasso relies heavily on value to establish the design in his etching *The Painter and His Model* (Figure 5.18). Reading from left to right, large, vertically oriented shapes of light and dark tones alternate until they come together and "fragment" in the drawing of the seated figure. Picasso intentionally makes the figure-ground relationship between the nude and her surroundings a complex and ambiguous one; it acts as an engaging visual coun-

FIGURE 5.20
REMBRANDT VAN RIJN (1606–1669)
*Self-Portrait*
Red chalk. 5 1/8 x 4 11/16 in.
*National Gallery of Art, Washington, D.C.*
*Rosenwald Collection.*

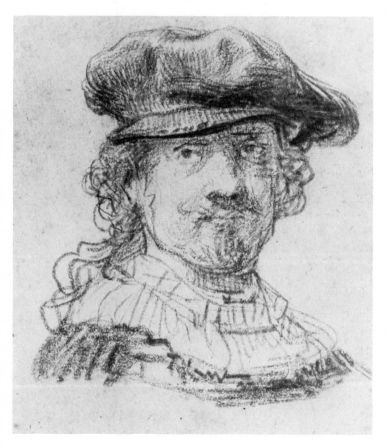

terpoint to the steady beat of the black and white vertical shapes that precede it.

Picasso uses the same value to associate the painter's upraised arm to the easel and to the diagonal edge of the background beyond the easel, and further relates arm and easel by aiming them at the upper center of the page. Note that the shape on the far left and that of the painter's figure are similar in shape, direction, value, and texture, but that both shapes are related to the background surrounding the painter by the dark-toned shape behind the painter and by the texture of the rest of the dark background. Thus Picasso relies here on texture to overcome the tonal polarity among these shapes. To associate opposing elements in some way, whether by a similarity in texture, shape, scale, direction, or value, is a sound practice of design. When some element or some segment of a drawing finds no visual relationship with other elements or segments in the work, it becomes isolated from, and destructive to, the drawing's order.

In addition to its potency as a relational force, value is an important structural tool (as we saw in Chapter Two) and is the necessary means of establishing both the local tone and illumination of forms. As a structural tool, value is capable of carving the boldest masses or the gentlest nuances of terrain, as demonstrated by Tiepolo's *The Death of Seneca* (Figure 5.19). Here, broad washes of tone, guided by the artist's sensitive structural and anatomical understanding, forcefully construct major masses, while smaller mounds and hollows are suggested by the undulating edges of these broad washes and by small, incisive daubs of tone.

The impression of an intense light bathing this scene is strengthened by the artist's consistency in darkening all planes turned away from the light source. Except for a few passages, such as the black mask or the dark-haired boy, Tiepolo doesn't identify the local tones of the figures and objects depicted; the impression of brilliant light would have been lessened had he done so. Strong light and the dark shadows it produces make local tones difficult to see.

But the gentle light in Rembrandt's *Self-Portrait* (Figure 5.20) permits both local tones and subtle modeling to be easily seen. In this brief sketch, Rembrandt manages to utilize value's organizational, structural, and textural abilities, and to describe both the inherent tone of a part and the effects of light falling on it. Note that all of the drawing's tones, and the subtle movements that enliven the image, are made by lines massed in various densities. The beret, the collar, and the thin band of tone representing the jacket, in creating graceful variations on a horizontally oriented, lazy S shape, move gently across the top and bottom of the page, rippling brackets to frame the stilled head. Rembrandt's consummate skill in modeling forms is amply displayed in the economical and incisive tonal modeling, especially telling in the beret.

That values can imply visual action is further demonstrated by Katzman's *Byron Goto* (Figure 5.21), where dark, sometimes curved wedges of tone, as in the chair back, trouser folds, head, and shadowed regions of the figure move in a forceful way. There is movement, too, in light wedges, such as the large ones of the trousers and the smaller ones of the arms and hands (as well as in the several light-toned wedges of negative space). Katzman's vigorous handling of the chalk strokes adds to the energy of these actions; even the gray tone on the right side of the background is activated by its shape and "scribbled" treatment.

### Shape

In examining line and value we have of course been discussing the other elements as well. After line and value, *shape* is one of the most omnipresent elements in drawing. Indeed, when we begin a drawing, the size and shape of the surface chosen represents our first shape judgment—and that choice will influence all our subsequent decisions.

The use of line for shape-making purposes is universal. Children and adults alike, whether primitive or civilized, naturally form images by denoting, and at the same time separating, their constituent parts by line boundaries. A circle represents a head; ovals, the eyes and ears; and so on. What is generally unrecognized by the beginner is that drawn shapes simultaneously produce other shapes, namely, the shapes of the remainder of the page and those which result from subdividing existing ones. The head's shape, when other shapes denoting eyes, mouth, shadows, planes, and so on, are placed within it, and more shapes representing ears, hair, or hat are placed adjacent to it, is dynamically affected by these new shapes, just as it is affected by its relation to the enveloping shape of the page.

Such effects on the relational nature of a drawing's *figure and ground* state, that is, the shape-state of its parts and of the spaces between them, have important organizational meanings. To understand the overall shape organization of a drawing it is important to recognize these two distinct types of shape. *Figure,* or positive shapes, are those formed or enclosed by line or tone, and which represent either tangible things or segments of things, or the presence of substance—of "somethingness." *Ground,* or negative shapes, denote the areas which separate or surround figure shapes. The ability to objectively perceive the visual properties in our subjects of these two types of shape enables us to make better depic-

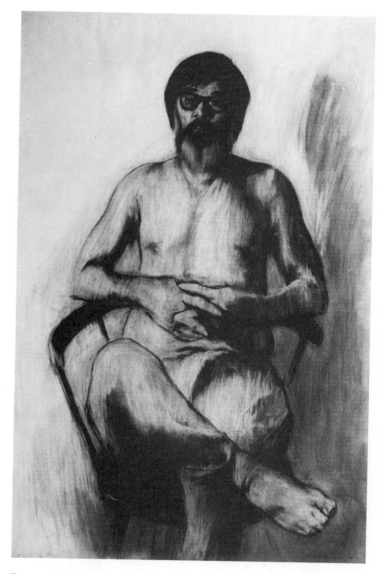

FIGURE 5.21
HERBERT KATZMAN (1923–    )
*Byron Goto*
Sepia chalk. 72 x 48 in.
*Courtesy of Terry Dintenfass, Inc., New York.*

tive and design judgments about *all* the shapes that subdivide our page.

As an aid to more objective measurement, whether of the location, direction, scale, or contour of shapes, most artists find it helpful to reverse their figure-ground impressions as a means of "proving" the accuracy of their observations. For example, if, in Figure 5.22, we concentrate on seeing the shape actualities of the spaces that separate the arms from the torso and the large wedgelike shape created by the location of the legs, and actually try to draw those shapes, we discover important facts about the location, direction, scale, and contour of the arms,

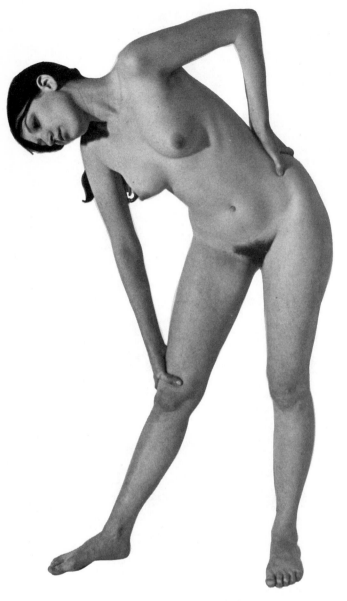

space between the ankle, arm, and upper leg, seems to function as ground; but by actively inserting itself in that location it appears figural. This dark oval shape, the result of a single stroke, simultaneously draws the contours of the parts that surround it.

These drawings show that figure-ground relationships may sometimes be reversed to good advantage. They also suggest some of the characteristics by which figure and ground are determined: small shapes and overlapping ones usually appear to be figural; large, or overlapped ones, ground. In virtually every instance, figure shapes are active—they assert themselves and demand our attention; ground shapes are passive—they occupy those places on the page that figure shapes "permit." By reversing the characteristics of figure and ground shapes, the sense of three-dimensional space is lessened and the two-dimensional spatial relations of the drawing's elements are increased.

Desnoyer's *Getting Dressed* (Figure 5.23) demonstrates some other ways by which intentionally subduing figure-ground cues can heighten a drawing's two-dimensional impact. The artist makes the shape of the checkered floor less negative by stressing its convex edges where it meets the bureau. Convex edges are a characteristic we tend to associate with figural parts. In some places, as in the bureau on the left, the shaded modeling suggests concave drawers, while the lines dividing the drawers show them to be convex. In other places, as in the light gray wedge shape that touches the shoe of the seated figure, the artist avoids overlapping, thereby making it uncertain which shape is nearer. Then, too, by making that wedge shape light, instead of dark, he further denies us a three-dimensional effect, for the shape is of course a cast shadow created by the pitcher. Some parts are shown as transparent or interpenetrating, another effective way of lessening the impression of volumes in space. The artist resists modeling some forms, sometimes neglecting even to explain their shape boundaries, or he aligns various edges to suggest that shapes in near and far positions in the room are on the same plane in space. This occurs with the line that marks the midline of the standing figure's legs, continues along the pitcher, and becomes the upper edge of the aforementioned wedge shape.

All of these interruptions of figure-ground cues, and the artist's emphasis on sharply defined edges throughout, work to amplify the condition of the drawing's two-dimensional design. Although the sense of masses in space is restrained to permit the shape-oriented design to assert itself, here both considerations are compatibly integrated.

All shapes, of course, are produced by line or value, or by a combination of both. They can, as we have seen, stand for "thing," denote "empty" inter-

**Figure 5.22**

torso, and legs. Furthermore, such occasional reversals of figure-ground impressions help us to see the two-dimensional nature of our subject's parts and of the spaces among them, enhancing our appreciation of the dynamic possibilities inherent in the subject's shape-state.

Responses influenced by this kind of "reverse seeing" are evident in Figures 5.15 and 5.16. In the Degas drawing, as we have seen, intentional shape ambiguities endow most of the shapes with both positive and negative functions. In Figure 5.16, a light-toned, wedge-shaped segment of the background takes on figural characteristics by actively forming the edges of the knee and shoulder. Again, at the ankle, a dark oval shape, by appearing as an open

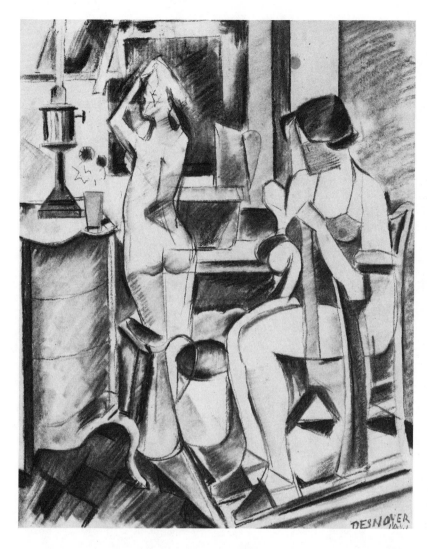

FIGURE 5.23
FRANÇOIS DESNOYER (1894– )
*Getting Dressed ("La Toilette")* (1941)
Pencil and chalk. 6 3/4 x 8 1/4 in.
*Musée National d'Art Moderne, Paris.*

spaces, or possess an ambiguity that suggests both figure and ground at the same time. As Figure 5.18 shows, they can be textured, change value within their boundaries, or be plain and unvarying. Shapes can be hard-edged, as we saw in Figure 5.23, but they can also be so unfocused as to appear cloud-like (Figure 5.32). Shapes can be geometric or organic in character; in complex forms they can show both traits. Shapes can be closed or open. Closed shapes are those entirely encircled by line, composed of tone, or by linear and tonal shapes arranged to form an enclosure. Open shapes are those showing breaks in the linear or tonal enclosure. For example, in Figure 5.18, the shapes denoting the seated woman and her immediate surroundings all show avenues of access to neighboring shapes.

Except for circles, squares, pentagons, and other shapes whose boundaries are more or less equidistant from their centers, all shapes suggest movement in the direction of their long axis. Even those few shapes that do not inherently imply move-

ment will take on the directions and movements of the shapes they relate to. For example, one or more circular shapes aligned with various other shapes will be oriented in whatever direction the group of shapes takes.

As noted in Chapter Two, all masses have shape. Even the most complex pose imaginable, no matter how foreshortened and interlaced the forms may be, shows its particular shape when silhouetted. In figure drawing, a sensitivity to shape's informing presence is an important aid in making foreshortened forms more manageable. For Cesari to draw the foreshortened torso in his *Studies for a Flagellation of Christ* (Figure 5.24), he had to do more than piece together its form-units; he had to see (or envision) its general shape-state. Although his drawing does not dwell on "shapeness," underlying these forms are the artist's shape judgments. A confirmation of the search for shape early in the drawing's development can be seen in the unfinished sketch in the lower right. Here, Cesari relies on shapes to

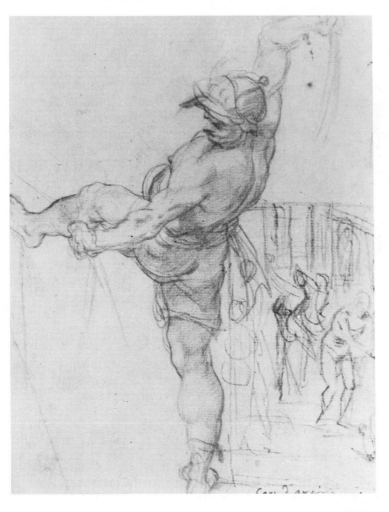

FIGURE 5.24
GIUSEPPE CESARI, Cavaliere d'Arpino
(1568–1640)
*Studies for a Flagellation of Christ*
Red and black chalk. 20.1 x 15.5 cm.
*Cooper-Hewitt Museum of Decorative Arts and
Design, Smithsonian Institution, New York.*

FIGURE 5.25
NICOLAS POUSSIN (1594–1665)
*Drawing for the Rape of the Sabines*
Pen and wash over black chalk. 11 x 8 cm.
*Windsor Castle, Royal Library.*
*By gracious permission of Her Majesty
the Queen.*

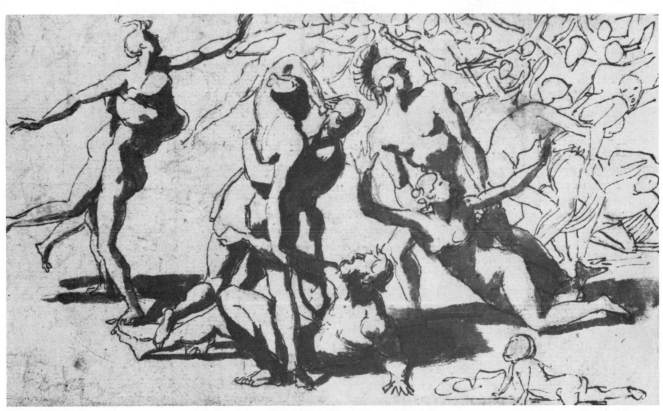

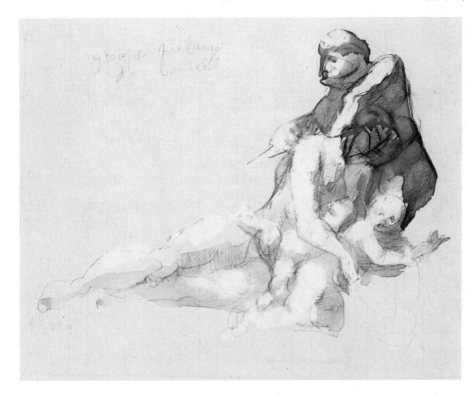

FIGURE 5.26
AUGUSTE RODIN
(1840–1917)
*Study for a Bas Relief*
Pen, heightened with
white on ruled paper.
5 1/2 x 7 9/16 in.
*Courtesy The Fogg
Art Museum,
Harvard University.
Bequest of
Grenville L. Winthrop.*

establish the basic design and disposition of the drawing's forms.

Many artists, recognizing shape as a potent agent of design, emphasize it in preparatory sketches for works in other media. Poussin's *Drawing for the Rape of the Sabines* (Figure 5.25) illustrates shape's importance in the artist's organizational conception in this preparatory sketch for a major painting. By imagining a strong light source, the artist creates a pattern of dark shapes that sometimes envelops more than one figure. Establishing these inherently animated light and dark shapes enables Poussin to examine and further plan the role of shape's contribution of energy to the dramatic action scene he envisions for the painting. Again, in Rodin's *Study for a Bas Relief* (Figure 5.26), the design of his subject's shapes is clearly an important basic aspect of the artist's explorations.

The Poussin and Rodin drawings demonstrate, as our earlier examination of the structural factor disclosed, that a strong sense of shape can be highly compatible with boldly structured images. After all, planes, the basic building unit of masses, are shapes at various angles in space.

### Volume

A drawing's shapes, then, like its lines and values (and textures, as we shall see) all function both two- and three-dimensionally. In doing so, they give two-dimensional design meanings to volumes in three-dimensional space. In Chapter Two we discussed volume as the goal of the structural factor, and examined the means by which its impression on a flat surface is achieved. Here we will consider the design functions of volume, noting in particular what effects a volume's scale, value, weight, and position in space (and in the drawing's picture plane) have upon a drawing's design. And just as the two-dimensional aspects of the element of space were necessarily touched on in discussing line, shape, and value, so will its three-dimensional aspects emerge in examining volume.

In drawing, all volumes suggest two kinds of weight: real weight, the sense of gravitational pull on a solid mass; and visual weight, the sense of forces acting within and upon a mass for the purpose of stabilizing it or relating it to other forms or shapes in the pictorial field. A single diagonal line drawn on a blank page produces a sense of tension, imbalance, and a striving for a more stable position. Similarly, the drawing of a tilted volume will also produce tension and imbalance that we feel as visual rather than actual weight. Unlike physical weight, the visual weight of volumes in a drawing can pull in any direction, depending on their shape and location and on their relation to each other and to other elements in the work. Visual weight has to do, as much as anything else, with eye-appeal—with the importance of a volume's visual behavior in the de-

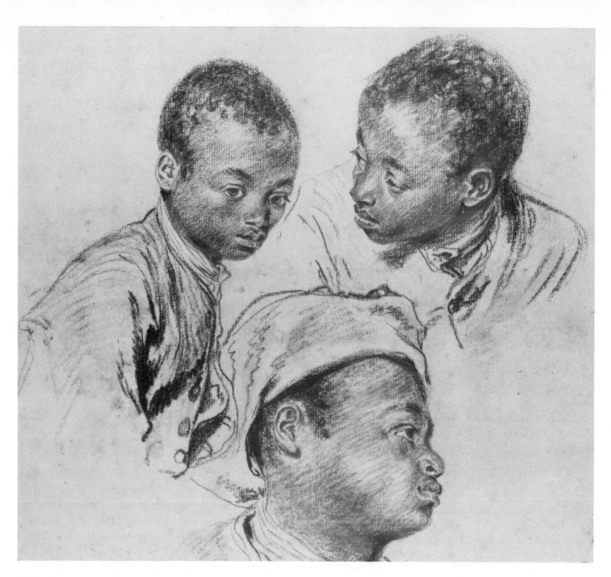

FIGURE 5.27
ANTOINE WATTEAU (1684–1721)
*Three Studies of a Young Negro*
Red, black, and white chalk,
gray ink washes.
9 5/8 x 10 5/8 in.
*Cabinet des Dessins,*
*Musée du Louvre, Paris.*

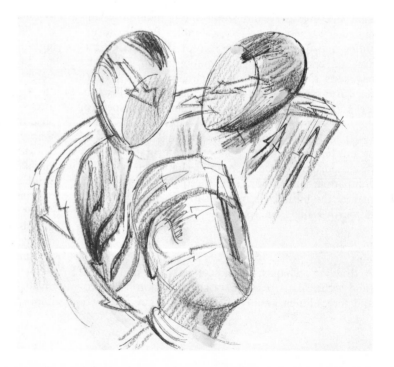

FIGURE 5.28

sign. In Figure 5.23, some of the forms, such as the standing figure and the bureau and lamp to the left, pull upward. Furthermore, visual weight is felt to be as much a two-dimensional phenomenon as a three-dimensional one.

Visual weight (which will be more fully examined later, when its effect on all the elements can be discussed together) always influences our understanding of a volume's design function. Although it is a more evident force in drawings that suggest little physical weight (Figure 5.18), visual weight is an inherent property of even realistically conceived drawings.

For example, in *Three Studies of a Young Negro* (Figure 5.27), Watteau creates both a two- and three-dimensional balance by the location, movement, scale, and value of his subject's volumes. The three heads are arranged to form a triangle that exists both two- and three-dimensionally, as does

the larger, curved triangular wedge composed of the figures' shoulders and torsos.

Two-dimensionally, the placement of the figures creates an inverted Y-shaped space between the heads, whose symmetry and centrality impart a stable pivot point around which the configuration seems to rotate in a counterclockwise direction. Partly for representational reasons (the heads face counterclockwise), the direction of the rotating action is strongly influenced by the "swing" of the large wedge and by the rhythmic actions illustrated in Figure 5.28.

Three-dimensionally, Watteau's design strategy depends just as much on this enveloping, circular action. In the same way as a rotating disk will remain balanced but tilt to one side when stationary, these forms achieve balance by their revolving action. If we were to disregard their dynamic behavior and try to see these volumes as static, we would

**FIGURE 5.29**
**REMBRANDT VAN RIJN** (1606–1669)
*Head of an Oriental with a Dead Bird of Paradise*
Pen and bistre washes, some gouache. 11.7 x 11.4 cm.
*Cabinet des Dessins, Musée du Louvre, Paris.*

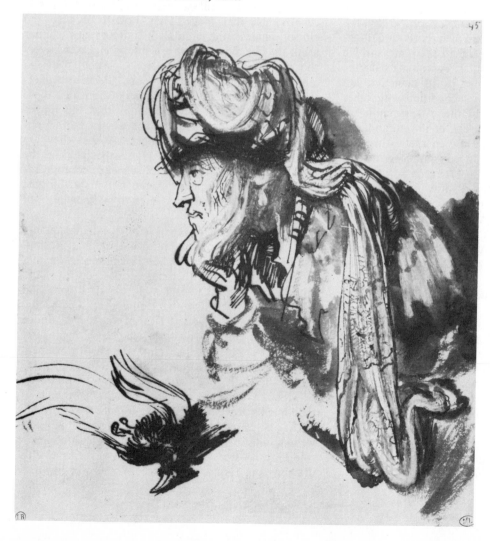

notice that their collective disk is fixed at an un-stable angle. Seen this way, the figure on the left leans precariously toward the other two, and the po-sition of the heads seems arbitrary—the drawing seems fragmented and unstable. It is their common motion that creates a stable three-dimensional bal-ance. The three heads "need" each other to achieve this. Individually they fall in different directions, but collectively they compensate each other's diagonal thrust and achieve equilibrium. Note how subtly Watteau resolves the problem of the structurally ex-plicit weighty heads upon the more generalized and fading bodies. By gradually decreasing the clarity and value of the draped forms, he avoids disem-bodying the heads. At the same time, he takes ad-vantage of the looser handling in the drapery to reinforce the overall rotation and to impart a sense of open space between the figures.

The sense of deep space, made more convincing by the "road" formed by the shoulders, accommo-dates the three figures in a way that further bolsters the drawing's two-dimensional design. Seen this way, the large wedge stops just short of the sheet's left and right boundaries, avoiding isolated triangles of space at each of the four corners.

As this analysis illustrates, masses, like all other elements, suggest movement. They do so by the physical and visual nature of their parts and func-tions, that is, by the nature of all their measurable qualities and dynamic activities. A volume's degree of action is largely determined by its depictive and visual weight, by its relational condition with other elements in the design, and by the artist's manner of expressing it. A form securely balanced and pa-tiently rendered will appear less energetic than the same form tenuously balanced and aggressively drawn.

The volumes in Watteau's drawing move at a moderate pace, slowed somewhat by the easy pace of the handling and by the thorough modeling of the heads that makes them at once independent from, and united with, the main design theme of rotation. We *can* enjoy the drawing of each figure separately, but we are always aware of their interdependence.

In contrast, the volumes in Rembrandt's *Head of an Oriental with a Dead Bird of Paradise* (Figure 5.29) undulate and whirl with furious energy. The strong downward pull of the head's physical and visual weight is increased by the lively climbing ac-tion of the scarf, which coils and "springs" upon the turban, adding its mass and weight to the head. Furthermore, by making the scarf intensely ener-getic, Rembrandt suggests that its crescendo of ac-tion in the turban—its wild swirls—cannot be con-tained there. So he provides an avenue of release through the head, beard, and arm by repeating the scarf's swirling actions in these forms.

Rembrandt's placement of the figure on the page also tends to heighten the downward pull upon the turbaned head, but for other reasons. The down-ward movement is necessary to establish balance in a configuration otherwise too tilted and located too far down in the lower right corner of the page. And the means for this counterbalance, in addition to the scarf's contribution, are present in the downward-aiming arrowhead shape formed by the turban, the bearded head, and the hand. Also, Rembrandt fur-ther emphasizes the physical weight of the scarf-laden turban by placing a deep shadow on its under-side. To give the downward-moving thrust a visual anchor and goal, he places the dead bird enticingly close to the arm, thus extending the downward movement into it by providing a dynamic, if not an actual connection. Whenever a small space separates any two or more parts, we see them as connected. This phenomenon is referred to as *closure*.

In Chapter Two we saw that drawing convincing volumes is a demanding perceptual skill, but in the hands of a knowledgeable artist the impression of volume can survive strong attempts at its suppres-sion. In Parker's *Reclining Nude* (Figure 5.30), the volumes, almost overwhelmed by the artist's insis-tence on shape, still suggest broad structural and even anatomical facts. They do so because the blocky planes and simplified contours are neither arbitrary nor naive. They are intentional, sensitively chosen responses that amplify a particular design theme that concentrates on shape. Parker's under-standing of structure and anatomy makes these changes count. Note in the limbs that the planes conform to anatomical fact. The planes are simpli-fied and strive toward rectangularity, but they are not willful distortions. Likewise, especially in the legs, breasts, and head, the artist makes contour ad-justments that emphasize shape, not mass, but the form of these summaries comes from knowing, not caprice.

Because physical weight is an incidental quality here, Parker relies more on visual weight to estab-lish balance. Although the hair, being more convinc-ingly modeled than other parts, does suggest a de-gree of real weight, it is mainly the dark tone and bold shape of the hair that counterbalance the fig-ure's location on the left side of the page. Notice that the artist further decreases the sense of physical weight by suggesting the figure's upward movement by the principle of closure. In being thus held to the top of the sheet, the figure seems almost weightless.

At the opposite extreme, the design theme of Goodman's *Reclining Nude at Window #1* (Figure 5.31) is based mainly on the figure's physical weight, although visual weight plays an important role here, as we shall see. Because we bring to this drawing our prior knowledge of the weight of a

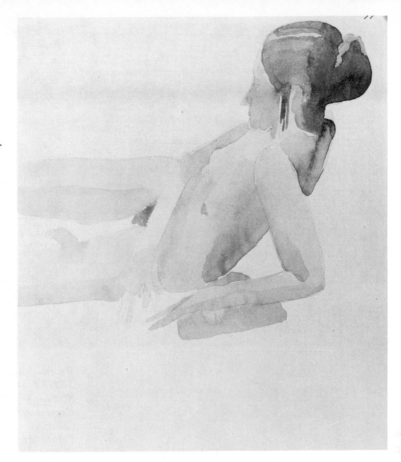

FIGURE 5.30
ROBERT ANDREW PARKER
(1925–   )
*Reclining Nude*
Ink and watercolor washes. 8 x 9 in.
*Collection of Christopher Parker.*

FIGURE 5.31
SIDNEY GOODMAN (1936–   )
*Reclining Nude at Window #1*
Ink. 8 1/2 x 12 in.
*Courtesy, Terry Dintenfass, Inc.,*
*New York.*

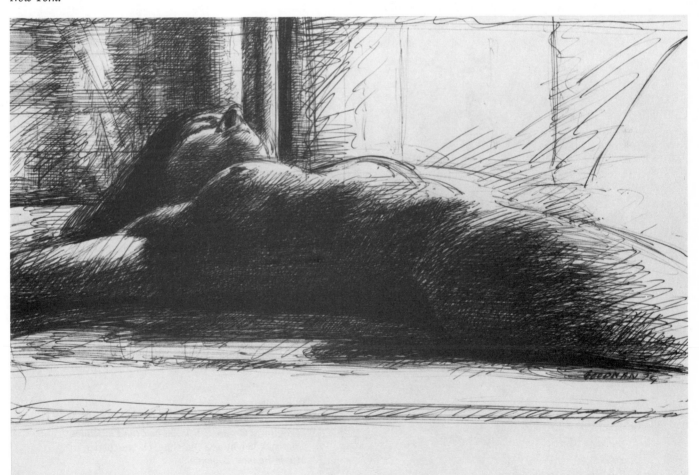

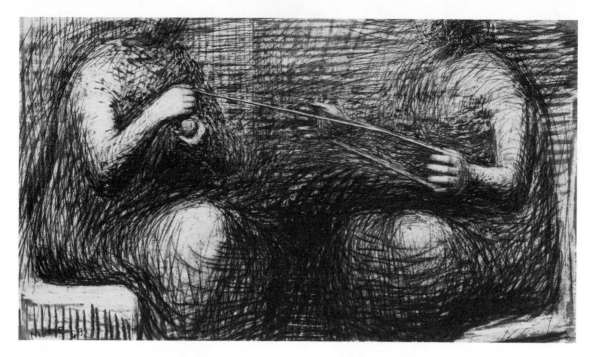

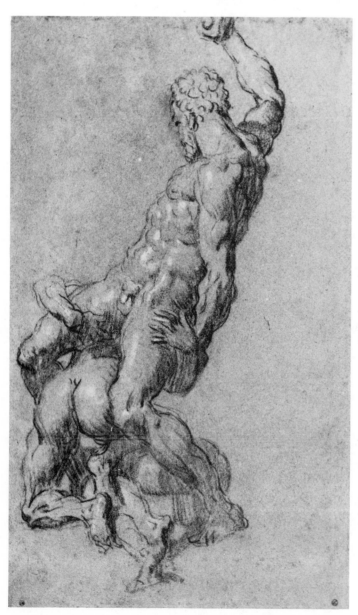

FIGURE 5.32
HENRY MOORE (1898–    )
*Women Winding Wool* (1949)
Crayon and watercolor. 13 3/4 x 25 in.
*Collection, The Museum of Modern Art, New York.*
*Gift of Mr. and Mrs. John Pope in honor*
*of Paul J. Sachs.*

human figure, we know that the great weight of the figure's unseen legs (increased by the figure's slightly downward tilt toward the lower right corner, where forms are felt to be heaviest) demands the compensating physical weight the artist emphasizes in the figure's upper body. He does this by several means: by the downward flow of the mass of black hair, by the more fully modeled masses of the head and upper body, by the downward flow of these masses as expressed by the breasts and the straight lower contours of the arm, back, and thigh, and by the bold value contrasts and large expanse of dark tone on the drawing's left side. All these devices signify physical weight. But, to more emphatically give the required weight to the drawing's left side, Goodman places the fast-moving vertical lines that define the window frame at just the right place to add visual weight where it will do the most good.

Volumes, then, can vary greatly in the impression of solidity—from the sculptural clarity of forms by Goodman to the teasing ambiguity of those by Parker. Some artists, however, utilize volume's ability (usually in tonal drawings) to be "lost and found" as a design device. In Moore's *Women*

FIGURE 5.33
JACOPO TINTORETTO (1518–1594)
*Study for a Group of Samson and the Philistines*
Charcoal, heightened by white, on blue paper.
*Musée Bonnat, Bayonne.*

*Winding Wool* (Figure 5.32), volumes vary widely in the clarity of their mass and edge, creating some passages of monumentality and some of mystery. By regulating clarity, Moore dramatically accentuates the subject's essential design: the action of the large, horizontal figure eight enveloping the two upper halves of the figures, and the pulsations of the light tones in the two lower halves.

### Texture

The term *texture* designates several visual phenomena. Generally, it is used to describe the tactile nature of a material; we speak of the texture of hair, skin, cement, or silk. In drawing, the term also applies to the visual characteristics of the drawn marks. The texture of charcoal lines differs greatly from pen and ink lines. Additionally, the texture of the surface drawn upon influences the textural character of the image. For example, a pen or pencil drawing made on a glossy paper will show a different surface texture than when these materials are used on a rough-grained paper.

We can also distinguish textural differences among marks made with the same medium. The texture of the ink lines in Figures 5.7, 5.8, 5.9, and 5.10—their density on the page and the nature of their calligraphy—differ strongly from each other. In a similar way, texture also refers to the density of other elements on the page. The shape-textures of Figures 5.23 and 5.25 are quite different. Texture also defines the visual repetitions of patterns such as plaids or stripes, and is often extended to include the massing of any group of forms that are similar in nature. Fingers intertwined, a cluster of folds or creases, or a pileup of ball players or boulders all exhibit different visual textures. The figure's textures include more than those of hair and skin; some artists interpret human forms in a way that emphasizes the texture of their hills and valleys, as Tintoretto does in his *Study for a Group of Samson and the Philistines* (Figure 5.33). In this drawing we can even discern textures within textures. For example, the recurrent, rhythmic beat of all the ovoid forms on the page creates one texture, while within the figure of Samson the ripple of the abdominal muscles, the thoracic arch, and other forms protruding on the torso create another more active texture of small, highlighted ovoids than is present in other parts of the figure.

Millet's *Man with a Wheelbarrow* (Figure 5.34) demonstrates several of the aforementioned aspects of texture in drawing. Additionally, it shows how texture can serve to regulate the similarities of like and unlike things.

By describing the texture of the leaves, Millet unites all of the leaf clusters, whatever their dif-

ferences in value, shape, scale, and position. In using diagonal lines to suggest the texture of the contents of the barrow, he strengthens the contrast between the shaded portion of the hay and the shaded, wooden sides of the barrow. Those diagonal lines serve more than textural interests. By their tilt, they "reach" for the point of the large, curving mass of leaves, creating a visual tension that carries their common arc through the figure. The direction also restrains the unity of the collective dark tone of the doorway and the loaded wheelbarrow, which would otherwise have been isolated in their similarity. Note that nowhere does a material's texture overtake its volume. How often, in student drawings, is the mass of, say, the head lost in the concentration on the texture of the hair and skin! In such drawings, textures seem to rise to the surface of the page,

**FIGURE 5.34**
**JEAN-FRANÇOIS MILLET (1814–1875)**
*Man with a Wheelbarrow*
Black conté crayon. 6 x 4 3/8 in.
*Courtesy Museum of Fine Arts, Boston.*
*Gift of Martin Brimmer.*

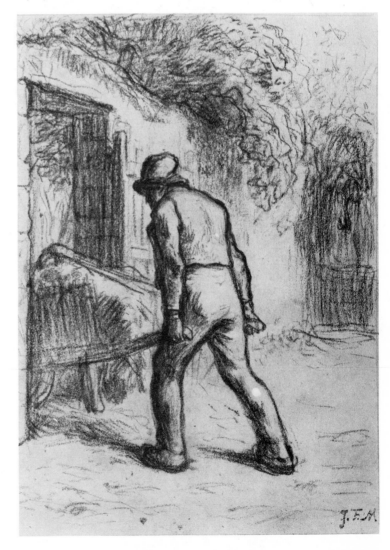

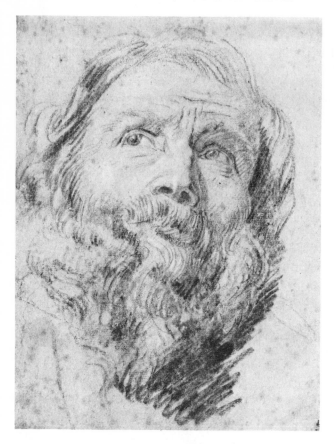

FIGURE 5.35
**ANTHONY VAN DYCK** (1559–1641)
*Head of an Apostle*
Black and white chalk. 10 1/2 x 8 1/16 in.
*The Metropolitan Museum of Art, New York.*
*Gift of Mr. and Mrs. Janos Scholtz.*

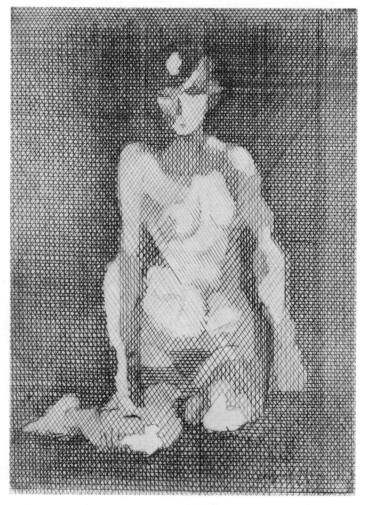

FIGURE 5.37
**JACQUES VILLON** (1875–1963)
*Kneeling Nude* (1930)
Etching. 8 1/16 x 11 1/4 in.
*Print Department, Boston Public Library.*

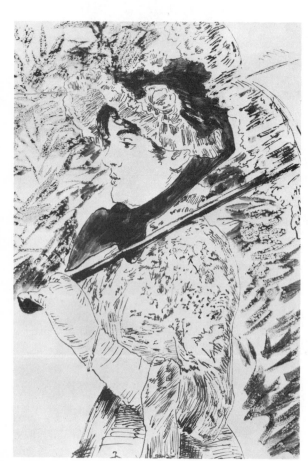

FIGURE 5.36
**EDOUARD MANET** (1832–1883)
*Springtime*
Pen, brush, and ink, on white, glazed paper.
12 15/16 x 8 3/8 in.
*Courtesy The Fogg Art Museum, Harvard University.*
*Bequest of Grenville L. Winthrop.*

FIGURE 5.38
RICHARD DIEBENKORN (1922–   )
*Seated Woman No. 44* (1966)
Watercolor, gouache, crayon. 30 1/4 x 23 1/2 in.
*Gift to the University at Albany Student Art Council*
*by President Evan Collins.*

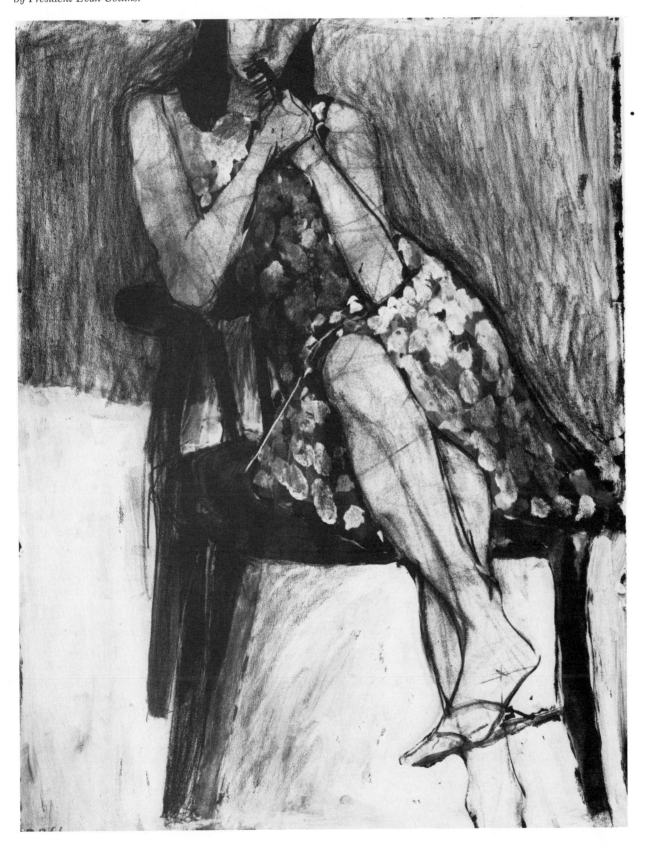

conflicting with the sense of structural masses in space. That this need not occur is amply illustrated in van Dyck's *Head of an Apostle* (Figure 5.35).

But when a two-dimensional design is to be emphasized, it may be desirable to permit textures to come to the surface. Manet's *Springtime* (Figure 5.36) communicates the airy, active feel of his subject by a profusion of differing textures. All alike in their energetic and lacelike nature, they unite in forming an almost page-filling design. Their unity is reinforced by the visual counterpoint of the drawing's few black and white shapes. Manet makes the forms of the figure and those of her surroundings less structurally insistent, and amplifies the textures, creating a design that functions well in either its two- or three-dimensional sense.

Manet's attitude toward the textural effects of his medium differs markedly from that of Millet or van Dyck. The latter are less concerned with the virtuosity of their media than Manet, who delights in making the pen and brush produce a sparkling surface "fabric." Villon, in his etching *Kneeling Nude* (Figure 5.37), is even more unswerving in his concentration on the texture of the etched lines. He produces a system of mechanical, crosshatched lines whose shapes and textures are as pronounced as their values. Villon's persistent texture suggests that the lines do not actively express forms, but rather that they obligingly halt to permit an edge or a value to occur. Here the mechanical texture behaves mechanically. But, to avoid a too rigid result, Villon takes care to provide some line and texture variety. A secondary system of seemingly curved edges resulting from straight line hatchings (there are no curved lines in the drawing) creates gentle, even sensual, forms and at the same time establishes a texture composed of undulating shapes and edges.

Differing textures intensify each other. Whether it is the texture of a medium itself, of a material, or of a decorative pattern, textures, in opposing and enhancing each other, produce visual contrasts that can play important organizational and expressive roles. In Diebenkorn's *Seated Woman, No. 44* (Figure 5.38), the texture of the crayon lines in the background not only continues the upward-directed motion of the figure and chair but intensifies the impact of the stark, white shapes of the floor. Likewise, the floral design of the dress, an oasis of rich organic activity in the drawing's otherwise more austere pattern of shapes, gives meaning to those shapes. We sense the artist's involvement with the play of these unadorned shards that make up the figure's forms, and those of the chair, wall, and floor. The floral pattern, in its contrast to them, both clarifies and relieves this play among the shapes.

In discussing the elements, we have already seen some of the visual energies at work: Direction, tension, and weight are all powerful relational forces. Although we concentrated on the various manifestations of each element and some of the ways each element might relate to others of its kind, we also observed some relational actions among different elements. To better understand how such energies issue from, and act on, elements, we turn now to examine the various ways in which elements form the visual bonds that consolidate a drawing's figurative and dynamic content.

## THE ELEMENTS IN ACTION

In every drawing each of the elements participates in several relationships at the same time. Indeed, lines and values being what the other elements are made of, they are always active in the visual behavior of those elements. And because the shapes, masses, textures, and spaces they give rise to are engaged in visual activities with one another, a single line or tone may be shunted onto several tracks of visual association that will carry its kinships with other elements far across the pictorial field.

All visual relationships generate energies that suggest movement, or a striving for movement.* And a sensitivity to movement, to any kind of motion, weight, or change, is not only at the heart of what stimulates the artist toward organizational balance and unity, it is a matter of vital concern to each of us as we function on a daily basis. We instinctively react to real motion or change because such activity may spell danger or opportunity. Such a stimulus in our field of vision automatically attracts our attention. Like the kitten or the housefly, we find movement demands heed. So deeply engrained is this response that, in humans, even the illusion of motion or change attracts our attention. We respond to the visual forces in a work of art with interests that have deep roots in our psyche.

Some kinds of energy are discernible even within a single element. For example, some lines, according to their character and route in a drawing, move quickly, as in Figures 5.7 and 5.11. Other lines move slowly, as in Figures 5.8 and 5.9. The same is true for shape; the oval, for example, suggests leisurely movement; a narrow rectangle or triangle implies faster motion. And an even gradation of value or size seems to change faster than a modulation that occurs by abrupt differences of degree.

* Rudolf Arnheim, *Toward a Psychology of Art* (Berkeley and Los Angeles: University of California Press, 1972), pp. 75–89.

FIGURE 5.39
HENRI MATISSE (1869–1954)
*Dancer Resting in an Armchair* (1939)
Charcoal. 25 1/4 x 18 13/16 in.
*National Gallery of Canada, Ottawa.*
*Copyright S.P.A.D.E.M.*

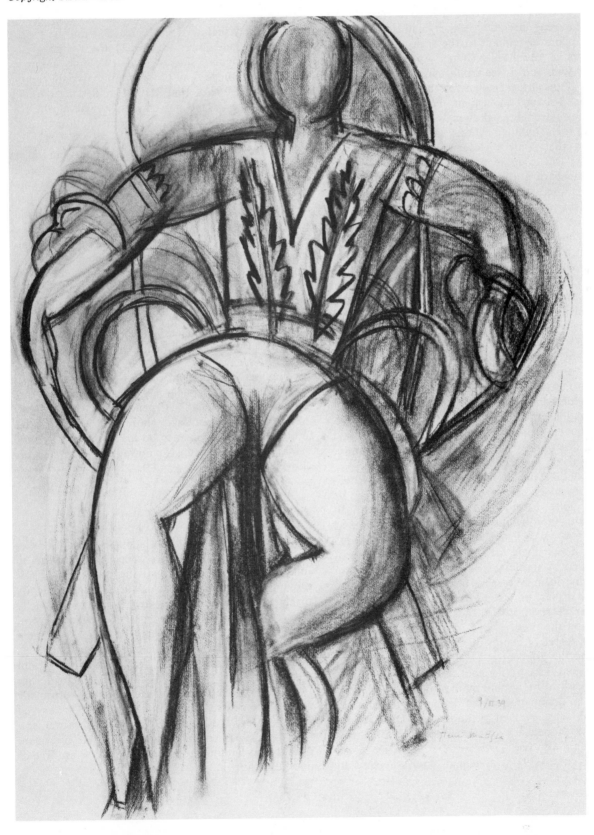

But other energies are generated only between like elements: The visual impact and action of a large shape's size and movement depends for its meaning on its relation to the scale and behavior of other, smaller shapes, and even on its relation to the page. A shape will appear larger on a small format, as in Figure 5.35, where the rugged head seems all the more imposing because of the small scale of the picture plane in relation to the scale and animated character of the head's shape. An arm, a leg, a drapery fold, and a tree trunk may all be related in a work if the artist emphasizes the rhythm of their common S-shaped movement. Figures 5.3 and 5.7 show how strongly a drawing's shapes may relate through such rhythmic actions. Here we should bear in mind that some or even all of the relational forces we will examine may simultaneously act upon the elements of a drawing.

Relational energies can be grouped in several ways. This presentation is arranged to take into account the important influences that the representational actions of the figure and its surroundings have on a drawing's abstract order. Because of the simultaneity of the various energies interacting in most relationships—the relational "chords" that strike our senses—any attempt at classifying such interdependent activities invariably fails to account for some phenomena too elusive and ineffable to be snared in print. All such classifications are really more convenient than defensible. They attempt to identify broad types of visual energy in order to heighten our awareness of the rich dynamic life possible in drawing. And, though some actions, tensions, and energies elude any system of grouping, comprehending the nature of the many forces that *can* be described is the necessary route to apprehending those that cannot.

To understand the nature of these visual forces we must understand the term *movement* in its broader sense, as *any kind of action or change.* In addition to the obvious movements of direction, as when we draw a figure standing *up* with its arms hanging *down,* there are other motions that are not determined by the long axis of an element or of an identifiable form. We sense movement when groups of lines, shapes, or volumes relate by a gradual increase or decrease in their scale, value, texture, or spacing on the page.

The degree of energy of such movements is suggested by the gradient of change within or between relating elements: by the collective shape and directional thrust of the group, by the force with which it ascends to domination in the design, by the number of visual steps involved in the change, and even by the vigor or delicacy of the artist's handling. For example, in Matisse's *Dancer Resting in an Armchair* (Figure 5.39), a system of circles appears to radiate upward from the center of the page. Their similar shape and behavior and their gradually increasing scale and spread provide a strong common movement. A bold contrasting movement is seen in the downward rush of straight lines and shapes that gradually diverge from the center of the figure. We sense all these to be moving down, not up, because of (1) the visual need for "release" from the weight of the legs and lower torso, (2) the weight of the tilted rectangular shapes, and (3) not unimportantly, the suggestion of gravitational pull on the skirtlike folds. Note that Matisse unifies these totally opposing shapes and movements by making the collective behavior of their antagonistic thrusts form one radiating burst of energy.

These two strong actions, the billowing up of circular elements and the rushing down of straight ones, gain energy by the number of participants and the simplicity of their action. However, they are held in check by even stronger forces, namely, the bold, forward thrust of the figure and the curved movements of the arms and legs. By placing the figure on top of the system of overlapped shapes that surrounds it, Matisse creates a series of forward-moving shapes that push the figure toward us; and by their bold and simple contours, the limbs swing around in strong arcs.

Some kinds of relational energy, such as visual weight, physical weight, or tension (to be discussed), suggest that movement is either necessary or imminent rather than occurring. Others, such as location or those concerning various types of similarity or contrast, will, depending on their context in the drawing, produce motion or a striving for motion. But the dynamics of *direction, rhythm,* and *handling* are those most endowed with the sense of movement.

### Direction

The discernible continuity of a single element or elements moving on straight or varied paths toward an intended point on or beyond the picture plane, or moving forward or backward in a field of depth, produces directed action. Such movements usually suggest visual or physical weight. The figure's forms, being for the most part tapered (whether a segment is as large as the head or torso or as small as a deltoid or finger), can be shown as moving with vigorous speed toward specific points (Figure 5.15). Long lines, edges, shapes, and volumes, especially when their course follows simple straight or curved paths (Figure 5.39), make for stronger movement. Only shapes or volumes such as circular or square ones, forms without a dominant long axis, are free of directed energy.

When changes in value or texture agree with the direction of a shape or volume, the speed of those elements is increased. For example, in Figure 5.34, the downward-curving movement of the great mass of leaves above the wall gains energy by changes in the value's gradation and the texture's increased animation. Both changes occur along the same direction as that of the shape of the leaves. Again, in Figure 5.20, the force of the beret's movement to our right is heightened by the texture's loss of clarity and the value's lowered tone.

Thus, textures, values, and even interspaces (Figure 5.17) have directional motion. Blurred elements move faster than sharply focused ones, and the movement of any element can be slowed or checked altogether by other elements that overlap or intersect it.

### Rhythm

Most clearly observed in the repetition of similarly directed movements among lines, shapes, or volumes, rhythm can be produced by a reoccurrence of similar characteristics of any kind among the elements. A certain pace in the grouping or density of the elements, a reoccurring texture or degree of tonal change, or a discernible pattern or treatment among like elements, all produce rhythm. It can be sensed among unlike elements when their sameness in direction, formation, or handling is strong enough to withstand their contrasting identities and functions. For example, in Figure 5.17, round or half-round lines, shapes, and volumes, whether large or small, light or dark, near or far, all suggest rhythm by their curved basis. The more often a rhythm is reinforced, the stronger is its movement (see Figures 5.2, 5.29, 5.35, and 5.39). While generally directional, rhythms can suggest a sense of beat, as does the reoccurrence in Figure 5.16 of a system of ovoids emerging from the figure's right knee, the shoulders, and the breasts. One aspect of this relational energy—the rhythmic accents in lines, as in Figures 5.2, 5.4, and 5.7, or in shapes, as in Figures 5.17 and 5.18—overlaps the next category.

### Handling or Character

The stylistic or idiosyncratic accents and cadences of lines, tones, and shapes are a powerful source of moving energy. The artist's "handwriting"—the deliberate, playful, delicate, or vigorous treatment of the elements—can make unlike elements relate, as in Figure 5.13, where diverse parts exhibit the unifying stamp of the artist's particular manner of presentation. Like things can be made to contrast when, for purposes of variety, design, or expression,

the style is varied, as in the legs of Figure 5.16 or in the figures of Figure 5.18. Partly a matter of neuromuscular coordination and partly the result of one's temperamental and creative attitude toward the subject, the artist's handling creates a kind of visual meter that sets a certain speed among the elements and the forms they constitute. For example, there is, in McKibbin's *Female Figure, Back View* (Figure 5.40), a brisk animation that contrasts with Kuhn's more deliberate pace in Figure 5.8. One factor in the energetic fluency of McKibbin's use of line is the periodic emphasis of the darker segments. Not only do these bolder passages clarify structural facts, they create a visual meter that relates various parts of the figure. These darker segments heighten the lines' energy, some of which is sensed as a quality of the figure itself.

FIGURE 5.40
ALEX McKIBBIN (1940–    )
*Female Figure, Back View*
Black chalk.
*Collection of Ms. Lindy Walser, Hagerstown, Maryland.*

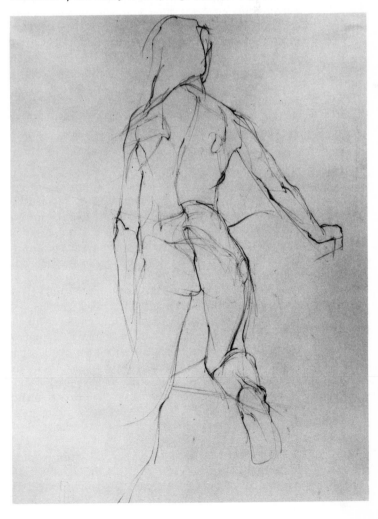

Handling is to some degree always influenced by the nature of the medium and the tools employed in drawing. These materials not only affect the range and character of the marks but, because of their various traits and limits, even influence the kinds of observations the artist makes. Had Kuhn used chalk, and McKibbin, ink, each drawing would have been changed in more than surface texture. The different options that these two media offer would have influenced what the artist looked for and what he did about it.

### Location and Proximity

The relational energies of location and proximity are produced by the association of like or unlike elements according to their position on the picture plane or in a field of depth. Elements equally distant from the horizontal or vertical center of the page may relate in their sameness of location. For example, in Figure 5.18 the dark and light halves of the background relate in part because they evenly surround the figures and roughly divide the page. Clusters of elements may relate by their density if surrounding elements differ markedly in scale, value, texture, or direction, as in Figure 5.19. Here, the entire group of shapes, forms, lines, etc., above the outstretched arm of Seneca, in addition to the many other relational activities within it, is related by the density of its components. Affinities based on location and proximity are strong visual forces. Symmetrically located parts form the strongest bonds.

### Subdivision

In a related group of elements, subgroups may form because of similarities in shape, value, texture, or any other properties that distinguish them from the parent group. For example, in Figure 5.3, the darker lines in the lower left side of the page pull away from the lighter ones surrounding them; they still belong to the larger group of lines, but form a discernible subgroup. Again, in Figure 5.39 the large circle behind the figure and the circles below each arm, while maintaining their visual union with all the other circular lines, shapes, and interspaces, form a subdivision. They do so by virtue of their more complete roundness, and because they are symmetrically arranged. Often, such subdivisions gain enough independence to relate to elements quite far away. In Figure 5.4, the three or four darkest strokes on the dress call to the similarly dark ones of the hair.

All elements, as noted earlier, can form several links simultaneously. For example, in Figures 5.19 and 5.26, strong values create large light and dark shapes—"super shapes"—from the many smaller shapes. These large shapes exist independently of any ties to one particular volume; they form their own abstract relationships. But the smaller shapes, although "recruited" into these super shapes, continue to function in forming volumes, disclosing directions, rhythms, and so on.

Elements, then, relate to each other in various combinations based on their similarities and contrasts with other elemental properties. The texture and value of lines, the shape and value of volumes, the texture and value of shapes, are all characteristics that determine how elements will associate with one another. Additionally, they will relate according to visual functions such as direction, rhythm, weight, or tension, and according to scale, handling, and proximity.

### Visual Weight

As mentioned earlier, all elements possess visual weight on the picture plane. Thick lines and dark values weigh more than thin lines and light values, large shapes and interspaces weigh more than small ones, and pronounced textures are visually heavier than subtle ones. Although, as noted earlier, such weights can press in any direction, in many drawings visual weight, like physical weight, is resolved by being balanced seesaw fashion on either side of an imaginary fulcrum in the drawing's center (Figures 5.3, 5.13, 5.15, and 5.18).

Even Figure 5.14, which consists of a single, compact, centrally located configuration, shows its elements balanced around a central point. However, additional visual weights keep the image from appearing to fall through space. The tone, shape, and location of the figure's right shoulder seem to push toward the left side of the page where they are (by the phenomenon of closure) visually anchored.

Directional energies are often the driving force behind visual weight. In Figure 5.14 the wedge composed of the neck, neckerchief, and shoulder throws its weight to the side instead of downward. Similarly, the left shoulder and the dark cast shadow swing upward, their weight aimed for the upper right corner of the page. The shapes and tones of the hair provide a third group of elements whose visual weight goes toward the top of the page. These forces modify the physical weight and seem to keep the image secure in its location. Again, in Figure 5.11, the visual weight of the thick lines in the head makes for its stronger upward thrust.

Although directional forces usually accompany the actions of visual weight, the latter, being in part a matter of eye-appeal—of visual attraction in the drawing—is present even when elements convey little or no direction. In Figure 5.18 the large, dark shape of the background has a strong sense of visual weight, but not of direction. More often, however, these two relational forces are seen working together, each intensifying the visual impact of the other. Whether we see a single element or a large segment of a drawing as *primarily* suggesting direction or visual weight largely depends on its context in the design.

### Tension

A frequent characteristic of other energies such as direction, location, handling, and both visual and physical weight, tension as used here describes a sense of elements threatening change, striving to meet or repel each other, or to alter their shape or location. When two or more elements or parts of the same element are so arranged as to almost touch, we feel their striving to complete the union. Likewise, when elements or whole parts of a drawing are directed away from each other, we sense their desire to move farther apart. Arrangements in which the directional forces are ambiguous or in conflict also produce tension between the components—a sense of standoff between antagonistic energies. Thus, the two ends of a C shape, if not too far apart, strive to complete the interrupted circle we feel the shape intends to be. Similarly, the five or six wedges of a star shape strive to pull away from their common base, each moving in the direction it points to, while their common base strives to hold them to itself. And lines formed into an H arrangement suggest that whether we see the two vertical bars as attacking or retreating, the horizontal bar prevents their doing either, and creates a pulsating tension of forces pulling and pushing.

In our need to understand the visual condition of whatever we see, we feel tension in any arrangement that only weakly hints at its essential form-state, or that contains ambiguous visual cues; instinctively, we want to more firmly resolve our perceptions into some comprehensible order. Just as our anxiety subsides when we see a parachutist touch down safely, so does our unease at viewing a drawing of a falling figure subside when we find a basis for its stability within the design. This stability neither completes nor neutralizes the act of falling. Indeed, it underscores the drama of the event by showing it against the backdrop of the drawing's total order. But it also prevents the *act* from causing the design itself to fall. When what fills our field of vision is *itself* in collapse, particular falling parts within it have little meaning. The figurative action in well-designed drawings never overwhelms their abstract order.

In Figure 5.25, the three groups of fighting figures in the foreground suggest a tenuous but balanced tripod. The artist makes the action of each group more powerful by joining their visual forces, and, by showing their various falling states within the context of a stabilized design, gives them greater expressive impact. Here, strong tensions work to bring the groups together. Diagonal directions, in departing from the inherent stability of vertical and horizontal ones, produce tensions. There is in this drawing a high degree of motion and tension in the attraction and repulsion among the diagonally placed elements and in the groupings they make. Note the absence of a single vertical or horizontal movement among the figures, but an insistent horizontal "pedestal" of tone beneath them, helping to stabilize the design. In Figure 5.24 tension is experienced in the large figure's limbs. They strive (as do the arms of the star shape) to pull away from each other, but are checked by their collective balance on the page, and by the roughly equal tensions in all directions that cancel each other's thrusts. Ambiguous tensional forces are felt in Figure 5.32. The wedges formed by the bent arms, the directional thrust of the figures' weighty hips, and the downward slope of the laps all produce tensions—a striving to pull away from each other. At the same time, the link of the wool thread, the dark tone enveloping both figures, and the design's pronounced symmetry all produce tensions that pull the two halves of the drawing together. The result is a tension-filled confrontation—a balance based on mutual restraint.

The participants in a tensional conflict of any kind suggest a charged field of energy between them; they seem aware of each other. It is as if such lines, textures, masses, directions, or values do battle with each other for supremacy. For example, in Figure 3.26 the large white drape and the large black tone vibrate with tension as they contend for dominance. It is mainly the figure's leg "invading" both of these contrasting areas that keeps them from tearing the composition apart.

A single element may also contain tension within it, as the C, H, and star shapes, or as exists in any element that takes more than one direction. Volumes, especially those of the figure, suggest tension when inner parts press against their container of skin, as in Figure 5.33, or pull against each other, as in Figure 5.24, or when their structures show strong interjoinings and multiple directions. The artist's handling can increase or decrease the force of a tension by emphasizing its aggressive or gentle nature.

A drawing's tensions, then, arise largely from the activities of the elements, and from the artist's temperament and handling. They exist in both the most tender and turbulent works. In a broader sense, a drawing's tensions are clues to its expressive nature. Tensions can be of a warring or a playful sort, but, being a natural phenomenon of the effect that elements have on each other, they make their appearance early in a work and must be considered a given factor in drawing. Whether they support or weaken a drawing's purpose is determined by how well the artist governs their behavior.

### Figurative Influences

The physical requirements of representational forms in a given context act as a strong modifier of the relational bonds discussed above. For example, a drawing of a figure leaning upon a fern will not appear balanced because of what we know about the structure and weight of both forms, though in formal visual terms such an image may be faultless. Replacing the fern with a cane will balance the figure in its representational sense, but may cause the design to collapse. To prevent this, the artist must compensate for the cane's weak two-dimensional properties—its slight visual impact—in the design. He may choose to increase its directional energy; he may join it in various strong rhythms or tensions; he may place larger objects around it; he may strengthen its contrasts of value or texture with other parts of the design; or he may combine several of these steps or turn to still others. For while the cane has the physical strength to support the figure, the artist must give it the visual strength to support the design.

As this example suggests, a drawing's two- and three-dimensional design must make visual sense at both the abstract and representational levels. The more convincingly forms suggest recognizable objects and activities, the more do their various identities, locations, and directions in space influence a drawing's balance. Representational subject matter, unless drawn with a regard for its two-dimensional condition, always weakens more than the order of the picture plane; it also diminishes its own expressive function.

In Figure 5.13, a sensitive interplay exists between figurative and abstract needs, and between two- and three-dimensional ones. Rembrandt avoids splitting the design in half by softly fusing Esau's draped figure with the tablecloth and by aligning the tablecloth's top and bottom edges with those of Esau's belt and coat fringe. This horizontal band creates a broad and subtle introduction—a visual prelude—to the dynamic action of the two arms. The scene's dramatic import would have been far weaker if the link between the two figures had been only their clasped hands. Note how many lines and values are directed to those hands. Note too that

Rembrandt relies more on visual weight than on physical weight in his drawing of the table. Its presence is necessary to counter the weight of the standing figure, but to have made so large a form physically heavy would have weighted the drawing too much on the right.

Again, the design of Figure 5.19 discloses a knowing interplay of abstract and figurative order. Tiepolo's drawing, like Rembrandt's, relates two separate groupings of forms. A system of diagonal motions zigzags through the figure of Seneca and the nearby group. Tiepolo places a drape's dark shadow in alignment with Seneca's left lower leg, and creates a large trapezoid out of his arms and the same dark shadow. Here, our appreciation of the weight and direction of Seneca's limp figure is essential to the drawing's design. Seneca's visual weight alone is too slight to provide the counterthrust necessary to balance the visual and physical weight of the nearby figures, as we see if we turn the drawing upside down. Tiepolo reinforces the sagging figure's weight by introducing the drape on the left, the direction and modeling of which add visual weight toward the lower left corner of the page, but it is our sense of gravity's downward pull on the figure that completes the drawing's equilibrium. Note that Tiepolo emphasizes abstract actions to underscore physical inaction. The furled drape, the insistent swirls of the cornice, and the curves of the drapery and the pottery all serve to accentuate the stillness of death.

### EXAMPLES OF RELATIONAL ACTIVITIES IN THE FIGURE

In examining the elements and energies of drawing, we may seem to have drifted far from our earlier considerations of structure and anatomy. In fact, we have only been discussing another kind of structure and anatomy: that of the figure's dynamics. Like its physical counterpart, the dynamic anatomy of the figure is a given aspect of figure drawing and is present in any observed or invented pose. How these two anatomies will interact is, of course, determined by our perceptual understanding and our intent, but neither can be disregarded if our figure drawings are to have both dynamic and representational life.

Although the relational activities in drawings that concentrate on the figure are active mainly within the boundaries of the image, such activities are still understood in relation to the page. Therefore, the location of a single figure on the page still requires sensitive compositional judgment.

The way Degas has placed the figure in his *Sketch for a Ballet Dancer* (Figure 5.41) reveals a fine balance of two- and three-dimensional consid-

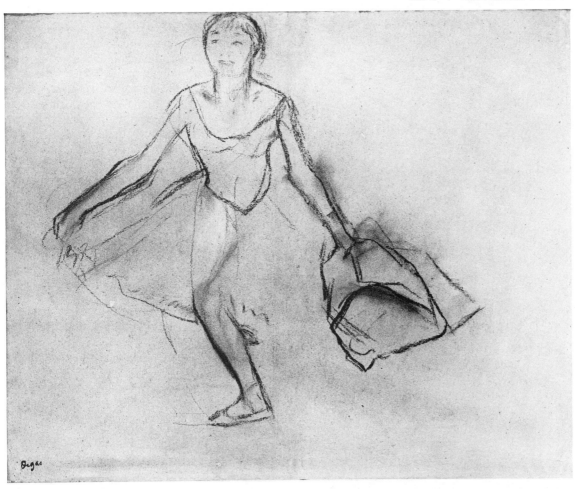

FIGURE 5.41
EDGAR DEGAS (1834–1917)
*Sketch for a Ballet Dancer*
Charcoal. 18 1/8 x 23 5/8 in.
*Courtesy Museum of Fine Arts, Boston.*
*Gift of H. Walter Child.*

erations. Although we might question the visual necessity of the head touching the edge of the page, the integration of two- and three-dimensional weight throughout the drawing establishes a balance within the image and between the image and the page. Degas, anticipating the visual and physical weight of the large bouquet, places the figure well to the left of center. To have located the dancer farther to the right would have tilted the scale to the right side and would have cramped the bouquet in the lower right corner of the page. To further lighten the load on the right side, Degas barely suggests the dancer's left leg and simply omits the skirt covering it. Sensing the need for still more weight on the left side of the page, Degas strengthens the edges of the limbs and the costume on that side, giving them more visual weight. Even so, when we turn the drawing upside down, the bouquet retains its visual dom-

inance. But, rightside up, our response to the figure's physical weight adds just enough force on the left to balance the drawing on the page. Of course, Degas could have easily balanced the bouquet by making the figure more structurally solid and thus heavier, but that might have lessened the sense of the subject's graceful agility. Then, too, this is one of a number of quick, preparatory sketches. Partly notation, partly exploration, such drawings are complete when the simplest expressive order of a particular arrangement of forms yields promising ideas. Note some other forces working to convey the dancer's physical balance: a fanlike rhythm relates the arms, skirt, and bouquet in a way that poises the figure's right arm and the bouquet in a tension for balance. These energies, and the animated handling, make us experience the dancer adjusting to keep her balance.

In Villon's drypoint *Standing Nude, Arms Up-*

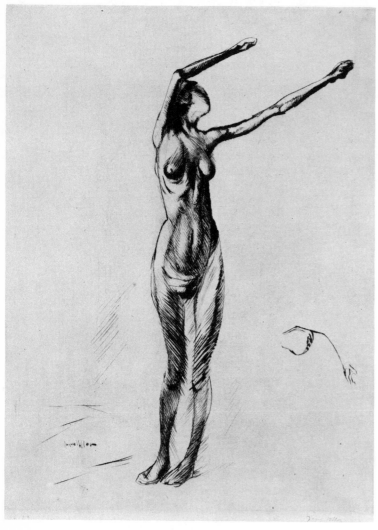

FIGURE 5.42
JACQUES VILLON (1875–1963)
*Standing Nude, Arms Upraised*
Drypoint. 54.9 x 42.4 cm.
*Courtesy Museum of Fine Arts, Boston.*
*Lee M. Friedman Fund.*

*raised* (Figure 5.42), an even stronger tension exists in the placement of the figure's arms. We feel their imminent movement downward, and even that they will swing back up on the other side of the page. Villon suggests this in several ways. First, the arms themselves carry a heavy burden of visual as well as physical weight. Notice that Villon models their form with solid black areas instead of the lighter hatching used throughout most of the rest of the figure. In the context of an otherwise nearly symmetrical design, we sense that diagonally placed forms of much weight are striving for a location more consistent with the rest of the design. Second, what we know about human forms helps us recog-

nize that the arms are swinging, not reaching. A reaching action engages the entire body, but here the figure is almost at attention and turned *away* from the direction of the arms' motion. Without the assistance of the rest of the figure, such a movement is understood as a single "frame" in a sequence of positions that make up the swinging motion. Third, the figure's location in the center of the page, in making the counterswing possible, makes it more necessary. Last, Villon's modeling of the figure strongly hints at movement—teases us with diagonally drawn structural lines that suggest the back and forth swing. Even some lines on the left side of the page beckon the arms downward.

Villon's knowledge of anatomy provides him with a basis for establishing visual relationships that support his design theme without violating essential structural truths. For example, the directions of the lines modeling the legs, in their diagonal rush toward each other, not only reinforce the theme of motion but also accurately describe the angle of the major curved planes of those forms. In fact, throughout the drawing, the modeling simultaneously conveys the artist's design theme and the figure's structural and anatomical generalities. Strong visual bonds of direction, rhythm, tension, and figurative behavior weave these forms into a single, animated human statement.

But appealing visual activity doesn't always require such visible evidence among the elements. Sometimes, as in Anderson's *Variant on Ingres' Figure Odyssey* (Figure 5.43), forces work in a more concealed way. Here the artist calls our attention to a circular motion enveloping the figure by making fine adjustments in the clarity and visual dominance of various forms. The shadow cast by the figure's right upper arm, the contour of the back, and the plane of the underside of the right upper leg, in being subtly darker than surrounding lines and tones, unite to form a half-circle. The directions of the left upper leg and left forearm complete the circle. Anderson continues the rotating movement by aligning the thumb of the upraised arm with the edge of the figure's right trapezius muscle. Note that he subdues the impression of volume in the right lower arm and the lower legs; he even makes their shapes more open and draws them more lightly. Emphasizing these forms would have impeded the rotating motion. A second visual theme is based on a "family feeling" among the drawing's shapes. The artist discreetly refines the contours to accentuate a system of S curves, and sharpens the tips of shapes to emphasize their pointed endings. The resulting pattern of delicately fashioned arrowhead shapes creates graceful darting motions between parts of the figure and the interspaces formed by the torso, arms, and legs. Note the reversed but similar shapes of the space enclosed by the figure's left arm, breast, abdomen, and leg, and the one bordered by the drape and legs. In the figure, sharp-pointed shapes, such as those of the right breast and left leg, relate to the surrounding interspaces, unifying and enlivening this seemingly straightforward drawing. Thus, the associations made by subgroups of line and shape lend graceful abstract meanings to graceful representational ones.

Anderson is sensitive to the three-dimensional design of forms in a field of space. While he takes care to preserve the design of the picture plane, he also organizes the forms in space, varying the weight and focus of lines and values to call our attention to various points in space. For example, in subduing the clarity of the head and in stressing the curve of the shoulder girdle he gives the rotating action a three-dimensional basis as well as a two-dimensional one. And, in strengthening the values in places such as the armpits and waist and in darkening the lines along certain segments of the contour, he not only heightens our understanding of the location of the forms in space, but also creates a spatial beat of such points of emphasis.

Here, as in all good representational drawings, figurative energies influence abstract ones and vice versa. We tend to regard the drape as having less visual impact, not only because it is lightly indicated but because in the context of the design it has little physical weight. Likewise, the rotating motion gains force where the torso adds its own weight to the action.

FIGURE 5.43
**LENNART ANDERSON (1930–    )**
*Variant on Ingres' Figure Odyssey*
Pencil. 10 3/8 x 15 1/2 in.
*The Graham Gallery, New York. Photo Geoffrey Clements.*

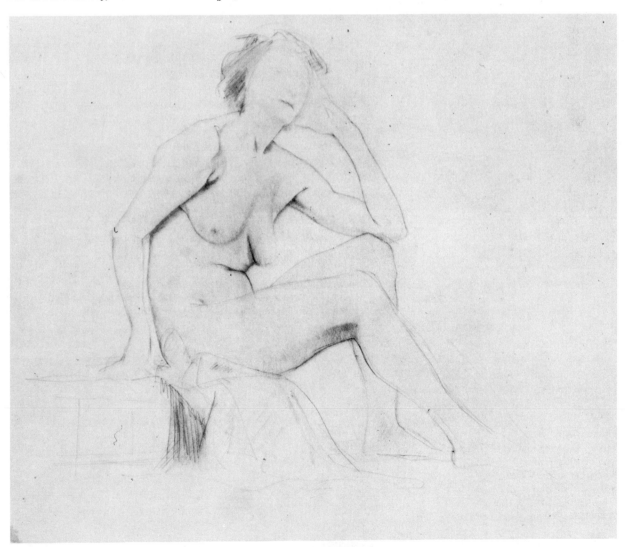

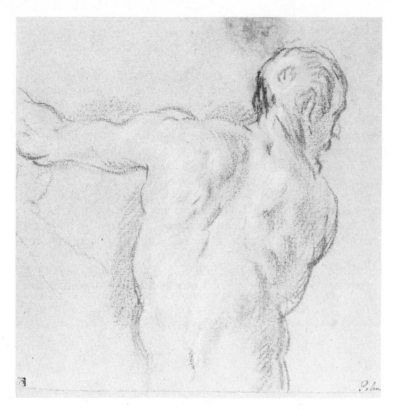

**Figure 5.44**
**JACOPO PALMA,** called
**GIOVANE PALMA** (1544–1628)
*Back View of a Nude Male Figure*
Black chalk, heightened with white,
on blue paper.
19.8 x 18.9 cm.
*The Art Museum, Princeton University.*

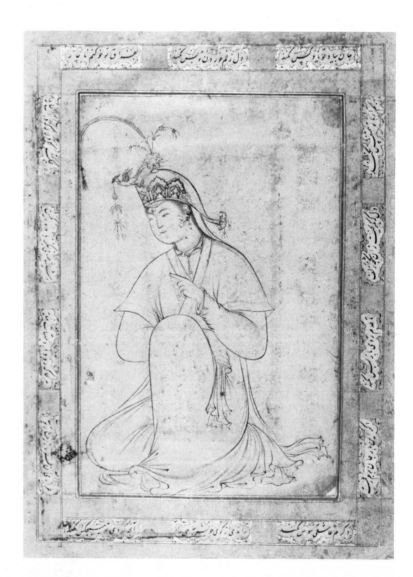

**Figure 5.45**
Persian Drawing, Safavid Period
(end of 16th Century)
*Portrait of a Noble Lady
with an Elaborate Headgear*
Brush and ink. 19.7 x 13 cm.
*Cabinet des Dessins, Musée du Louvre, Paris.*

238

Just how influential the known properties of the figure can be is demonstrated in Palma's *Back View of a Nude Male Figure* (Figure 5.44). Here some of the answering thrust to the direction of the extended arm is effectively carried by the direction of the man's gaze to the right. Palma's drawing also shows how useful a knowledge of anatomy is in providing and sustaining inventive responses to the figure's actions, responses that order and express as well as describe. Knowing the skeleton and muscles of the back enables Palma to accentuate those inner forms which enhance the force of the figure's twisting action. For example, to emphasize the torsion in the neck and head, Palma produces a system of reversed C curves throughout the figure which, in contrasting with the turn of the head, amplify the force of its twist. Note that the artist stresses the curves of the scapula and the muscles on and around it to begin the arm's leftward movement well inside the torso. The wavelike undulations of the arm's contours suggest the leftward force of the "storm" gathered at the scapula and, even beyond, in the curves of the ribs and contour of the right side.

In addition to the aforementioned gaze to the right, the only other major force that counterbalances the image's powerful leftward motion is the slight rightward arc of the torso itself. One enormous C curve, its physical weight neutralizes the visual weight of the rest of the design. All the categories of relational energy are present even in this "simple" preparatory sketch. And, although the energies provided by direction, rhythm, visual weight, and figurative influences dominate, those of handling, location, subdivision, and tension play important supporting roles.

In the sixteenth-century Persian drawing *Portrait of a Noble Lady with an Elaborate Headgear* (Figure 5.45), a different system of relational energies gives prominence to rhythms, handling, and location. Lines and shapes produce gracefully flowing rhythms whose elegance is reflected in the sure and fluid handling. Some lines, such as those of the shoulders, elbows, and knees, form a subgroup of large, simple curves; others relate by their smaller scale and by the action of the line clusters they are a part of, as do the lines of the radiating folds. The shapes achieve equilibrium by congenially answering each other's gentle movements. Nowhere do lines and shapes move unaware of the actions of their neighbors.

Three-dimensionally, too, there is a deliberate elegance among the volumes. Note the downward force of the two arms in contrast to the monumental rise of the figure's left leg; these moves and countermoves among the volumes occur leisurely, almost in slow motion; they contrast with the faster movements in the drapery and headdress. By its location

in the image, the figure's left arm takes on the necessary visual and physical weight to balance the drawing's heaviness on the left. It does so by gaining force from the downward flow of the headdress and by overhanging the empty area of the lower right corner of the page.

Note how well these forms, despite the simplicity of their structure and the absence of tonal modeling, suggest convincing volumes. Such an economical statement of solid, graceful masses conveys the artist's sound grasp of structural and anatomical essentials as well as a penetrating sensitivity to dynamic order. Although these forms are insistently stylized—as much the result of convention as of personal response—they reveal a conviction and eloquence that no convention of figure drawing can provide (or suppress).

**Figure 5.46**
**JEAN-BAPTISTE GREUZE (1725–1805)**
*A Young Man Standing*
Black, red chalk with gray and brown wash,
heightened with white. 50.7 x 29 cm.
*Courtesy of the Art Institute of Chicago.*

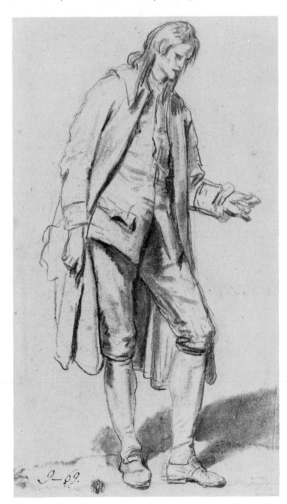

Greuze's *A Young Man Standing* (Figure 5.46) differs in many ways from the previous drawing, but in both works forms are simplified, enhancing the sense of motion. Although the Persian artist employs a fixed system of curvilinear form-solutions and Greuze summarizes forms according to their inherent geometric nature (an attitude that anticipates Cézanne's approach to form), both artists make us conscious of the directed motion of the shapes and volumes, and of the lines and tones that produce them. At the heart of any form is its particular orientation in space. The more we strip away its surface embellishments, the more we reveal its directional (and structural) nature. In doing so, subdivisions of lines, shapes, values, and masses emerge, grouped according to direction and scale. Here, as in Figure 5.45, we find such groups of related elements. The shapes of the neck, collar, cuffs, hands, and shoes are all related by their scale; lines denoting edges of forms and shadows relate by the common wedgelike shapes they produce.

For some artists, the abstract visual forces take on the fury of a storm. For them, creating a figure's living presence has little to do with surface niceties or refined adjustments of value or proportion. In their drawings, vigorous graphic energies become the visual equivalents of those which animate the living figure. But their drawings, while more intuitional than deliberate, are never unreasoned or arbitrary. There is, in fact, as compelling a necessity in the ordering of the marks as there is in the most deliberately arranged image. Naturally enough, their

**FIGURE 5.47**
**OSKAR KOKOSCHKA (1886–   )**
*Bust of a Girl*
Red crayon. 17 3/4 x 21 7/8 in.
*Courtesy of the Art Institute of Chicago.*
*Gift of Tiffany and Margaret Blake.*

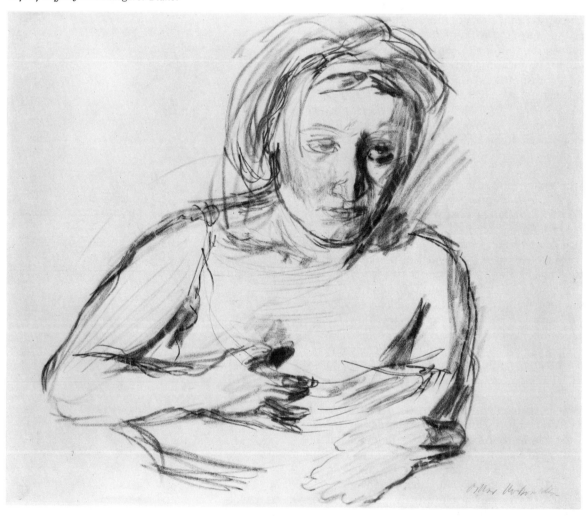

drawings tend to show strong direction and handling energies.

This is clearly the case in Kokoschka's *Bust of a Girl* (Figure 5.47). Unlike the drawings already examined in this section, where to varying degrees forms suggest energies, here we feel that energies "consent" to imply forms—that is, the real subject matter is the *behavior* of visual forces of the image, and not the physical behavior or character of the model. Although the best exponents of figure drawing always contend with the interacting factors of structure, anatomy, design, and expression, each artist evolves a personal formulation of these considerations. Kokoschka's solution places structure and anatomy in subordinate roles, making them the servants of an expressive design. He does this not out of indifference to the figure's fixed, measurable aspects, but because his main interest is in evoking its dynamic ones.

Here, urgently racing lines and values seem only partially concerned with depictive tasks. In sweeping across forms, in leaping from one edge to another, they reveal how forcefully the artist responds to the subject's clues for such actions. In addition to the almost frenzied pace of the handling, Kokoschka makes effective use of various other devices that speed up visual motion.

He avoids sharply focused shapes and forms, simplifies their contours, omits surface details, and gives the entire configuration a tension-producing tilt to the right side. Only in the head, the focal point of many of the drawing's moving forces, do these devices abate somewhat, permitting a more structured and figuratively demanding treatment. Strong rhythmic actions heightened by blurred edges and by the furious manner of drawing the hair, the various hatchings, and the folds in the dress further add to the expression of energy.

Although we can hardly select two artists more opposite in temperament for comparison, note that Kokoschka, like the anonymous Persian artist, uses the device of the overhanging arm to balance the figure on the page. Had Kokoschka drawn the figure's left arm and hand with the clarity and visual weight of the right one, the image would have remained too heavy on the right side. Because the elements are all strongly engaged in motion, we sense tensions throughout the drawing. Each line and value strives for change or continuance, each form only tenuously occupies its space on the page; the woman's hair and hands never really settle into any one position. Yet Kokoschka gives us a stabilized design. Despite the drawing's violent calligraphy and action, no directional thrust remains unchecked. In fact, the image suggests an arrangement approaching symmetry. There is a near symmetry of plastic forces as well. Circular motions predominate, but are regulated or

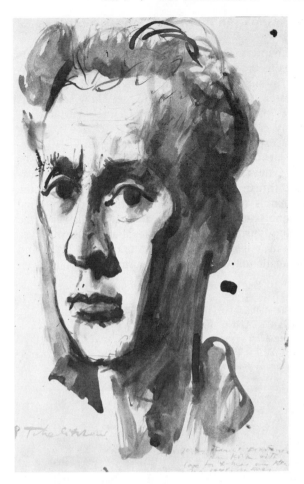

FIGURE 5.48
PAVEL TCHELITCHEW (1898–1957)
*Self-Portrait*
Sepia, wash and brush. 11 3/4 x 7 1/2 in.
*The Metropolitan Museum of Art, New York.*
*Gift of Mr. and Mrs. R. Kirk Askew, Jr., 1968.*

checked by various diagonal movements. Only the overall tilt to the right side threatens to unbalance the image, and this, as noted above, is answered by the overhanging arm's wedgelike thrust to the left; a giant tension, it summarizes all the drawing's smaller ones.

In Tchelitchew's stormy *Self-Portrait* (Figure 5.48), everything suggests motion. There is movement in the forceful undulations of the light tone of the hair and in its darkening as it turns downward to define the side of the head. Similar movements animate the drawing's smaller values. The artist intensifies the energies that strong directions and rugged handling generate by making the image fill the sheet. There is a tensional strain on the boundaries of the page by the strong force of vertical movements. The same drawing in a larger pictorial field would lose some of its visual and expressive impact.

## ANATOMY AS AN AGENT OF DESIGN

In Chapters Three and Four some references were made to the role that anatomical considerations may play in stimulating dynamic activities. Here we will examine several drawings to see how relational forces may be generated by a figure's surface anatomy.

Cézanne, in his *Rowing Man* (Figure 5.49), establishes a rhythm composed of long, diagonal hills and valleys that accentuate the figure's straining, forward thrust. Especially clear in the center figure, the rhythm is formed by the teres major, the external oblique, the pectorals, the thoracic arch, and the midline furrow of the rectus abdominus muscles. Cézanne's lively treatment, the undulating lines, and the angle of these swelling forms (which is even

more extreme than the angle of the torso) all combine to produce a strong sense of physical and abstract action. To achieve this rhythm Cézanne not only stresses the volume and rhythmic action of these surface forms but also subdues or omits others.

By contrast, in Michelangelo's *Studies for "The Punishment of Aman"* for the Sistine Chapel (Figure 5.50), we find every surface change that bone, cartilage, and muscle can provide, with some forms additionally exaggerated or even invented. In the torso, Michelangelo enlarges or exaggerates the clarity of the flank pads and surrounding forms, the serratus muscles, the thoracic arch, the ribs, and the muscle bundles of the pectoralis major. In fact, one of the interesting characteristics of Michelangelo's figure drawings is that he almost always shows each muscle in a state of contraction, when it would re-

FIGURE 5.49
PAUL CÉZANNE (1839–1906)
*Rowing Man*
Pencil. 22.7 x 29.9 cm.
*Museum Boymans-van Beuningen, Rotterdam.*

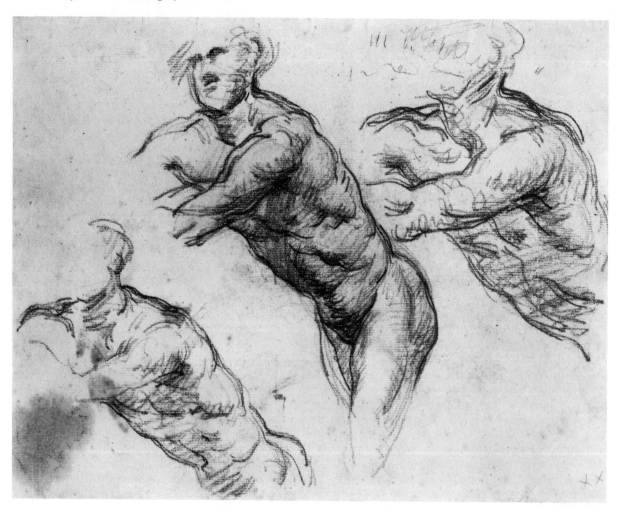

242

veal its swelled form. In the legs he elaborates on the form of the rectus femoris, even suggesting different constructions for this muscle in each leg; in the left leg he shows the adductor group with the clarity it would have only in the flayed figure.

By these anatomical changes Michelangelo creates a different kind of rhythm from the fast-moving one in Cézanne's drawing. We sense a pulsating beat in the Michelangelo, both visual and physical—a constant rise and fall of ovoid forms. Instead of enhancing directional movement, this rhythm slows down the figure's vertical thrust. This occurs because the human eye hunts for and feeds on change of any kind. The eye is a rover, constantly searching for visual problems to solve. Simple structures, rhythms, and textures are quickly understood and as quickly dismissed. But when the eye encounters complexities it slows down to explore and experience them. We might be quickly bored by the easy structure and pattern of a new picket fence, but would dwell on an old, battered, and irregular one, finding its deviations of form, value, and direction more visually engaging. So does the figure of Aman make us pause to study the always interesting changes in its surfaces and contours.

The contrast between the figure's energetic movement and the braking action of its surface activity creates tension throughout the image; the forms do not so much seem to move as to strive for movement. This tension is in harmony with the contrast between the bold pressure and straining of inner forms against each other and upon the figure's surface, and the delicacy of the handling. Notice that Michelangelo unifies the figure by making some of the smaller form-units echo much larger forms. For example, the complex form of the figure's right knee, in addition to relating with other form-units in the torso, also repeats something of the contours that describe the limbs and even the large shape of the torso.

That the same anatomical forms can initiate and serve an endless variety of relational activities is seen in Boccioni's *Reclining Male Nude* (Figure 5.51). He utilizes the torso's anatomy for visual functions as different from those of Figures 5.49 and 5.50 as the Cézanne and the Michelangelo differ from each other. Boccioni subordinates the sense of volume to concentrate instead on the shapes of the torso's surface forms. A pattern of shapes formed by groups of large and small muscles engage in movements against each other, creating two-dimensional tensions that parallel those produced by the pressure, strain, and weight of the muscles themselves. The artist, in simplifying these contending knots of shape, stresses straight and curved lines that reinforce the drawing's two-dimensional design as well as the rigid and supple condition of the forms. Thus,

FIGURE 5.50
**MICHELANGELO BUONARROTI (1475–1564)**
*Studies for "The Punishment of Aman"*
*for the Sistine Chapel*
Chalk. 16 x 8 1/4 in.
*Trustees of the*
*British Museum.*

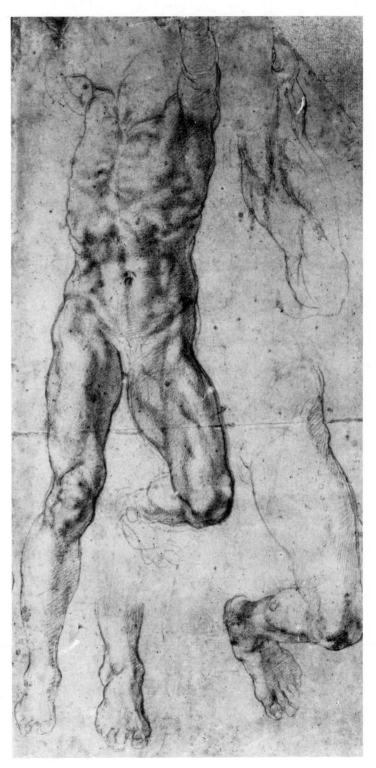

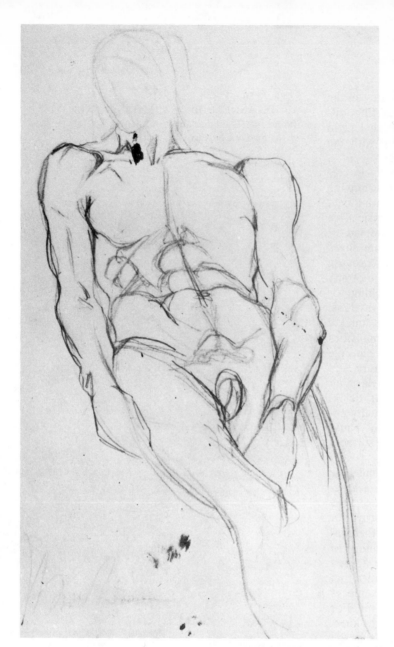

FIGURE 5.51
UMBERTO BOCCIONI (1882–1916)
*Reclining Male Nude* (ca. 1909)
Pencil. 11 7/8 x 7 1/2 in.
*The Lydia and Harry Lewis Winston
Collection.*

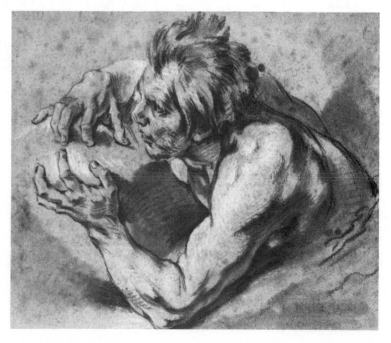

FIGURE 5.52
FRANCOIS BOUCHER (1703–1770)
*Triton* (study for the Triton in
the painting *"Sunrise"*)
Black, white, and red chalk, on gray paper.
22 x 27 cm.
*Courtesy of the Art Institute of Chicago.
Joseph and Helen Regenstein Collection*

Boccioni, in responding to the figure's anatomical *and* plastic condition, gains insights that enhance the drawing's representational and dynamic force. A subject's particular form arrangement always contains the seeds of its dynamic solution. Naturally, each artist will nurture these seeds in his or her necessary way to bring about the subject's realization in visual terms that reflect the artist's interests. But it is the subject's form-character that largely stimulates the nurturing process.

Boucher suggests the vitality and power of the sea god in his *Triton* (Figure 5.52) by a large diamond shape composed of the figure's arms, and by a system of diagonals and wedges—shapes and directions well-suited to evince energy and motion. Strong rhythms emerge from the repetition of these angular shapes and counteracting directions, urged on by Boucher's aggressive treatment. But it is Boucher's sound grasp of structure and anatomy that provides tangible justifications for many of these powerful abstract actions. Throughout the figure, bones and muscles and the form-units they make furnish the artist with plenty of visual ammunition for these dynamic exchanges. For example, in the left arm, the wedgelike shape of the deltoid digs hard into the biceps and triceps below, while they counter with a pincerlike swing under the deltoid and, at their opposite end, mount their own assault upon the supinators at the elbow.

Again, among the forms of the chest and back, muscles overlap and interlace aggressively, and, in the arrangement of the hands, the blocklike fingers provide a variation of the explosive force of the hair. As in Kokoschka's similarly energetic drawing (Figure 5.47), Boucher stabilizes the visual energies among the parts, and in the figure's overall surge to the left, by using an essentially symmetrical design and by investing great visual and physical weight in an overhanging arm. Here too a rotating action envelops the forms. This action, along with Boucher's use of swelling curves, keeps the drawing's angularities from appearing too brittle or harsh.

Surface anatomy, even if only of the most general kind, can continue to guide associational bonds, as Hiroshige's *Two Women Playing* (Figure 5.53) indicates. The contours of the robes that describe the backs of the two women, in addition to providing visual parentheses that unite these figures, take some of their graceful flow from the nature of the forms they cover. These contours, especially the one on the left, supply us with a surprising amount of information about the figure's anatomy. In that contour we can locate the beginning of the gluteal muscles, sense the absence of any obstruction to the robe's fall until the gastrocnemius muscle, and follow the edge of the lower leg to the ankle. Additionally, it describes the oblique and tapering nature

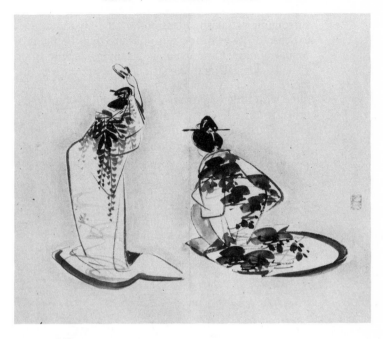

**FIGURE 5.53**
ANDO HIROSHIGE (1797–1858)
*Two Women Playing*
Ink and watercolor. 27.9 x 16.9 cm.
*Freer Gallery of Art, Washington, D.C.*

of the supporting right leg. Hiroshige's sensitive summary of the figure's larger masses enables him to more effectively convey their congenial arrangement in the spatial field.

## THE FIGURE AND THE ENVIRONMENT

In the best drawings showing the figure in an environment, the figure is always an integrated component of the design. Whether it is dominant in the drawing or represents only a small part of it, the figure, at least in its formal, visual sense, fully relates with other segments of the drawing and is part of a consistent visual syntax. It can be thought of as part of a large still life, interior, or landscape design—a form among other forms. To do so is not to disregard the figure's singular nature and importance; on the contrary, by integrating the figure and its surroundings to create a greater unity, we enlist the environment's differing character as a visual foil against which the figure's unique qualities and meanings can have greater visual and expressive impact.

Treating the figure in a distinctly special way only isolates it from its surroundings, destroys the drawing's unity, and obscures the very meanings that such special attention endeavors to express. Too often, beginners who include the model's surroundings lavish attention on the figure at the expense of its environment, unaware that the figure's representational and dynamic meanings depend on a visually logical and consistent integration of the *entire* subject. As we have seen, the figure can come alive with little or no surrounding support, but when other forms are part of the design, no matter how abbreviated and vague their treatment is, they must relate to the figure's forms.

Such an attitude is evident in Brandt's *Seated Nude* (Figure 5.54), where there is as much sensitive caring about the easy flow of the drape or the graceful swelling of the vase as there is about the figure's classical fluency. Further, the U-shaped segment of the drape, in addition to "receiving" the three-dimensionally oriented and inverted U shape of the figure's legs, is answered by the inverted U-shaped

action of her arms. Throughout the drawing, such movements and countering movements integrate the figure and her environment.

Hopper, in his preparatory *Drawing for Etching "East Side Interior"* (Figure 5.55), builds a classical design of vertical and horizontal units. Shapes and values, lines and volumes, all conform to a checkerboard alignment in which the seated figure participates. She does not, at first glance, attract our attention. That is commanded by the strong, bright shape of the window, made even more visually attracting by its dark frame and by its alignment with the chair below it, adding to the window's vertical motion. To the left, the dark picture on the wall echoes the window's shape, while throughout the drawing, other vertical directions and light-toned shapes relate with the window, further strengthening its visually com-

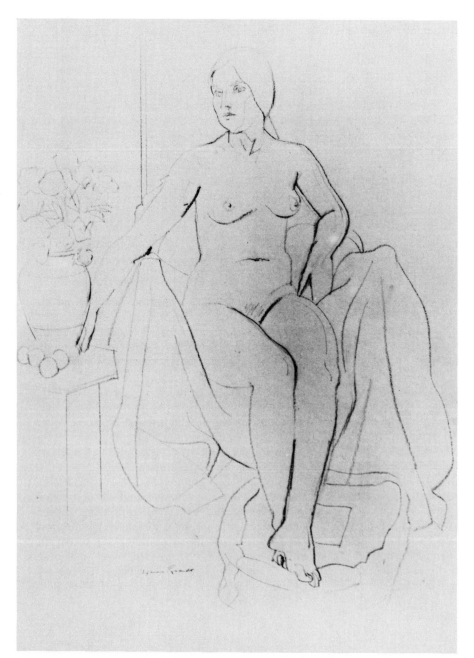

FIGURE 5.54
WARREN BRANDT (1918–    )
*Seated Nude*
Pencil on buff paper. 24 x 18 in.
*Courtesy, the Fischbach Gallery,
New York.*

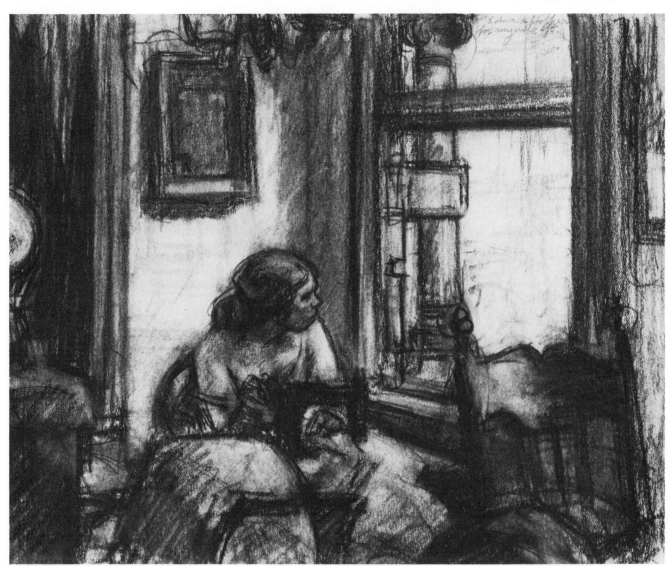

FIGURE 5.55
EDWARD HOPPER (1882–1967)
*Drawing for Etching "East Side Interior"*
Conté and charcoal. 8 15/16 x 11 1/2 in.
*Collection, Whitney Museum of American Art, New York.*
*Bequest of Josephine N. Hopper.*

pelling power. The window attracts these shapes; even the sewing machine strives to move to the right.

Only a few areas that contrast with the drawing's hard geometry seem to resist the window's magnetism. The globe on the far left, the curved chair, the woman's head, and a few dark shapes in the lower left corner emerge as a secondary visual theme of organic shapes and forms that begin to command attention. Once this system is recognized, we also sense that the figure's central location, added to the curvilinear units encircling it, give the figure a unique visual power. Additionally, her sharp glance

toward the window and the slight leftward tilt of the torso, in revealing both physical and visual resistance to the window's attracting force, heighten her importance in the design. Hopper, by firmly integrating the figure in the design, establishes a visual unity that can bear the gradually accumulating attention and importance that her location, form-character, and human gesture command. To have given her more prominence in scale, value, or "finish" might have destroyed the drawing's unity and the visual activities that support the artist's *human statement*. Our appreciation of her precious alive-

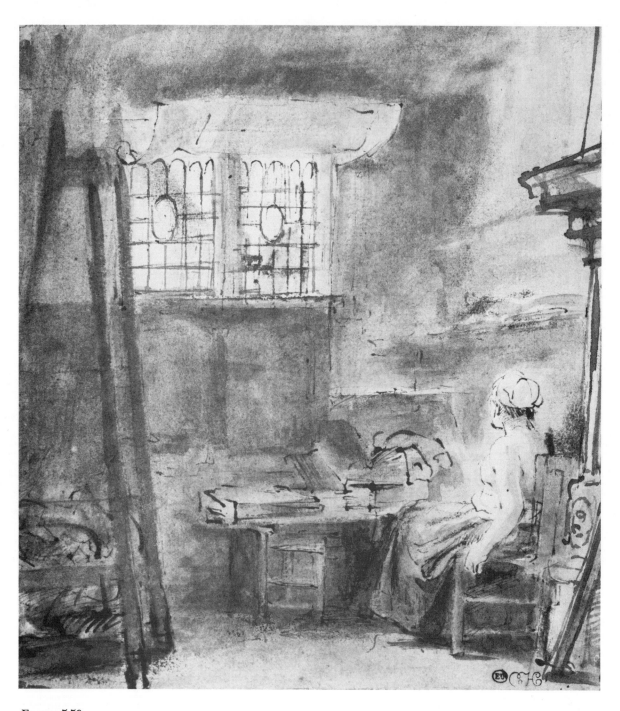

**FIGURE 5.56**
**REMBRANDT VAN RIJN (1606–1669)**
*The Artist's Studio*
Pen and ink with wash, touched with body color.
20.5 x 19 cm.
*Ashmolean Museum, Oxford.*

ness, of the sudden gesture that suggests an unseen interruption, depends on the abstract and representational context in which we find her.

In a similar vein, the seated figure in Rembrandt's *The Artist's Studio* (Figure 5.56) is *found* to be unique and important, rather than announced as such. She occupies an even smaller portion of the design than does the figure in Hopper's drawing and, in strictly visual terms, seems even more relentlessly regarded as an object. Far from stressing the figure's visual impact, Rembrandt almost camouflages her forms. He does this by matching the light tone of her torso with that of the nearby wall, and the darker tone of her skirt with the shadowed areas surrounding it. Additionally, he makes the forms surrounding the figure more structurally assertive, draws them in a more rugged manner than he does the figure, and further restrains her visual impact by having the chair overlap her back, while minimizing the effects of the figure's forms overlapping her surroundings. The overall effect makes the figure something of a visual rest area between the more vigorously handled segments on either side. As in Figure 5.55, Rembrandt's design strategy is also based on a pattern of vertical and horizontal lines and shapes. An overall light tone muffles the beat of rectangular shapes that appear throughout the drawing; even the woman's torso and the direction of her bent legs suggest conformity to this grill-like pattern. But, although completely integrated in the design, she is not a minor component in its order. In fact, despite her small scale and quiet visual behavior, she is the keystone of the design. Rembrandt reveals her dynamic role as subtly as he defines her figurative one.

The long diagonals of the easel at the far left, by contrasting with the drawing's system of vertical and horizontal movements, create the need for some answering diagonal. This is provided by the figure's lower arm and leg, and by the long lines of the fireplace behind her. By making the seated figure take part in both the grid movements and the diagonal ones, Rembrandt makes her location and form necessary.

Another diagonal links the windows to the figure. This results from the alignment of the circle in the window on the right, the staggered corners of the two dark shapes on the wall, and the woman's head. Rembrandt further strengthens the figure's relational play with the windows by giving them a common value and vertical-horizontal orientation on the page. And, in reserving the drawing's strongest value contrast for the figure and the nearby dark tone below the table, Rembrandt furnishes still another means of *indirectly* calling attention to the seated figure. In creating this gentle interior scene, Rembrandt does more than describe the small, light-bathed figure resting in a corner of the large studio. By abstractly conveying the importance of this small and subtle segment of the design, he deepens our comprehension of her human significance in a large, inanimate setting.

When the figure *is* dominant in the design, its stronger dynamic condition must be regulated by equally strong relational bonds with the environment. In Degas' monotype *The Wash Basin* (Figure 5.57), the leaning figure is kept from upsetting the balance of the design by counterthrusts to its strong diagonal location. These answering diagonals include the white shelf, the overall shape of the basin and tabletop, the top edge of the figure's robe, and the black shapes of the mirror and the area below the tabletop. Additionally, long, dark- and light-toned vertical shapes and the folds of the woman's drapery also help to modify the figure's tilt while further integrating her in the design.

In Cretara's *Seated Male Figure, Arms Outstretched* (Figure 5.58), the figure's dominant scale and location is further amplified by its symmetry, but is integrated by the similarity of the figure's values to all those below the top edge of the drapery. By matching the figure's values so closely to these dark tones, the contrast between the drawing's lower three-fourths and its lighter upper fourth makes a visual impact as strong as the figure's contrast with the environment. Note that the figure's slight rightward location and the head's glance to the lower right corner are balanced on the left by the intensity of the large dark shape of the arm and drape, and the large light shape of the wall. The artist also diminishes the weight on the right side by placing the man's left leg back and by adding a dark shape at the lower left corner.

The observant reader may already have noted that in earlier discussions of balance, as here, the problem often comes down to the impression that elements to the right of center seem to weigh more than comparable elements to the left of center. That we do judge parts to have more weight on the right can be easily proven if we examine Cretara's drawing (or any of the others in this book) by holding it up to a mirror. While the reasons for this phenomenon are obscure, it is nevertheless universal, a given condition of perception that we must take into account in establishing a balanced resolution of forces.*

* Another strange phenomenon is that we regard a part located high on the picture plane as weighing more than if it were located lower. For a useful discussion of the experiencing of visual weight, see Rudolf Arnheim, *Art and Visual Perception* (Berkeley and Los Angeles: University of California Press, 1969), chap. 1.

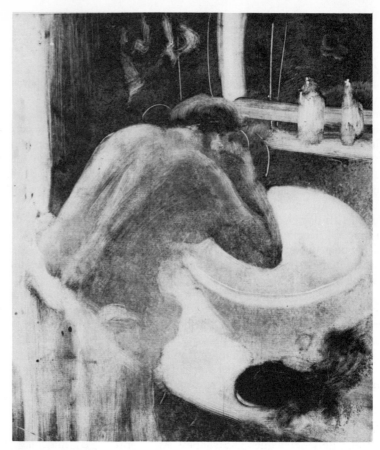

FIGURE 5.57
EDGAR DEGAS (1834–1917)
*The Wash Basin*
Monotype, black ink. 12 5/16 x 10 3/4 in.
(plate)
*Sterling and Francine Clark Art Institute.*
*Williamstown, Massachusetts.*

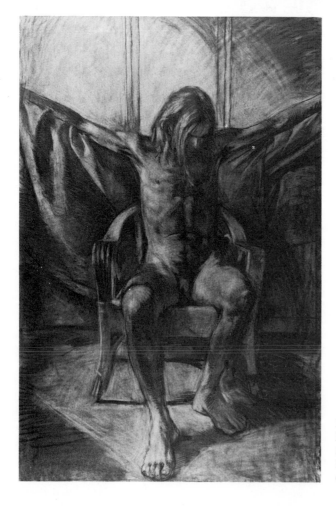

FIGURE 5.58
DOMENIC CRETARA (1946–    )
*Seated Male Figure, Arms Outstretched*
Raw umber chalk. 69 x 46 in.
*Courtesy of the artist.*

The beginning art student, struggling to make his or her figure drawings come alive, may sense some of the figure's underlying structure. He or she will sooner or later come to see the need to gain an understanding of anatomy, and will always have known, even as a child, that the human figure can convey a limitless range of expressive meanings. Yet most beginners have never seriously considered the importance of examining the abstract forces released by the elements which, in paralleling the order, vitality, and motion of living organisms, fertilize the image and give it life. Developing an awareness of the dynamic cues in the subject and of the means of translating them into ordered, expressive graphic terms is essential to creating figure drawings that *enact* and *evoke* as well as define.

## SUGGESTED EXERCISES

Unless otherwise indicated, the following exercises are not restricted to any particular medium or size and have no time limits. But because they vary widely in purpose, give some thought to choosing a medium and size suitable to the nature of each exercise. In each, establish a design strategy based on visual ideas that originate in the subject. That is, let the pose and the character of the forms suggest the placement on the page, the size of the image, and the major visual activities and themes. Once you have formed an attitude about the nature of the subject's visual condition, stick to it. Our first impressions are usually guided by our temperamental interests, the ones most likely to produce original results. They are usually the right ones to base our interpretation on. In each of the following drawings, whatever the particular goals, remember that you are always trying for a balanced and unified resolution of the elements and energies.

1. Working from a model, make the following drawings *of the same pose:*
   a. A gestural line drawing, somewhat in the calligraphic and rhythmic nature of Figures 5.2, 5.3, and 5.7. Emphasize directions and a strong sense of animation.
   b. A deliberate, continuous line drawing, somewhat in the manner of the contour line used in Figure 5.8. Rely on shapes rather than on a profusion of lines, and stress the subject's two-dimensional aspects.
   c. A structurally insistent, volume-informing line drawing which may include a moderate amount of hatching. Intentionally emphasize physical weight in establishing balance.

2. Working from a model, and using an erasable medium such as vine charcoal or soft graphite, restrict your drawings to values only. The values may be formed by groups of lines, but avoid explaining edges or folds by lines only. Include the model's immediate surroundings. If you wish, apply a moderately dark tone to your paper before you begin to draw, and use an eraser as well as your charcoal or graphite to establish the tonalities. Now your goal is to suggest movement within values, and through their shape and handling. This drawing need not include the entire figure, and should not exceed forty-five minutes. In general, promote a bold, aggressive handling, as in Figure 5.21.

3. Working from a model, make the following drawings *of the same pose:*
   a. Using Figures 5.17 and 5.18 as rough guides, draw the model in a manner that intentionally makes for figure-ground ambiguity.
   b. Using Figure 5.19 as a rough guide, draw the model in a manner that makes for strong light and dark tones. Be sparing in your use of line; try instead to make values establish the forms. For this drawing you may wish to use artificial light to produce strong value contrasts.

4. Working from a model, make the following drawings *of the same pose:*
   a. A drawing that subdues the sense of volume and relies mainly on visual weight for balance.
   b. A drawing that emphasizes a strong sense of volume and relies mainly on physical weight for balance.

5. Working from the draped model in an environment, and using Figure 5.36 as a rough guide, make a pen, brush, and ink drawing that relies heavily on texture as a major means of organizing the design.

6. Using Figure 5.59 as your model, make a free adaptation of these forms as they might look in the living model. Although your drawing will not show the figure in the flayed state, emphasize the textural character of the muscles, as in Figure 5.33.

7. Using either Figure 5.60 or 5.61 as your model, make the following two drawings:
   a. With Figure 5.39 as a rough guide, and by inventing any environment necessary, interpret the model for its design possibilities in similarly energetic terms.
   b. With Figure 5.47 as a rough guide, and by inventing any environment necessary, use pen, brush, and ink to establish a drawing that conveys a similarly powerful sense of motion among the elements.

8. Using Figure 5.42 as a rough guide, *invent* a pose that suggests the figure's imminent movement. Do

this through the pose, the modeling, and the handling.

9. Using Figure 5.23 as a rough guide, invent a two-figure composition in an interior or exterior setting, that emphasizes shape, texture, and value, and that aims at a strongly two-dimensional image.

10. Using either Figure 5.60 or 5.61 as your model, make the following two drawings:

   a. Using Figure 5.21 as a rough guide, make a chalk drawing in which the medium's texture plays an active role in the drawing's movement and energy.

   b. Using Figure 5.32 as a rough guide, make a drawing in which the figure's forms are "lost and found" in a dark background.

11. Make the following two self-portraits:

   a. With chalk or graphite on a sheet no larger than 10″ × 14″, and using Figure 5.35 as a rough guide, make a drawing that fills the page. Here, the structural lines that model the forms should also function to balance the design on the page.

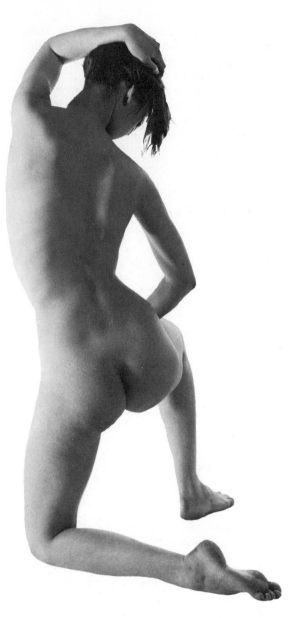

FIGURE 5.60

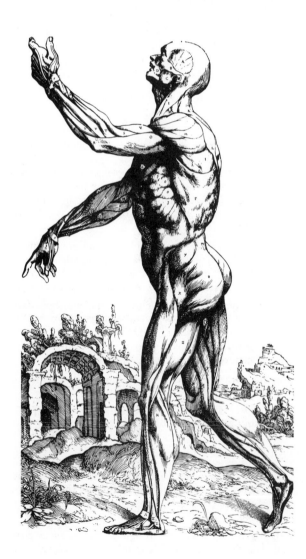

FIGURE 5.59
ANDREAS VESALIUS (1514–1564)
Plate 25 from *De humani corporis fabrica*, Book II
Engraving.
*Courtesy of the New York Academy of Medicine.*

**b.** Using Figure 4.22 (Villon's *Head of a Young Girl*) as a rough guide, and working actual size, make a "drawing" using small cut and torn shapes of white, gray, and black paper to represent the planes. Don't use more than three degrees of gray for this collage, and think of it as a kind of mosaic process. Try to convey a sense of volume, shape, and value order.

**12.** Rework or redraw two or three of the exercises done for Chapter Four, freely interpreting the forms to emphasize strong rhythms among the muscles.

**13.** Working from the model, arranged in an interior or exterior environment, make the following three drawings:

    **a.** A drawing in which the figure is almost camouflaged by value, shape, and placement among the surrounding objects, as in Figures 5.55 and 5.56.

    **b.** A drawing in which the figure is dominant, but strongly integrated in the design, as in Figures 5.57 and 5.58.

    **c.** A drawing that may stress or subdue the importance of the figure in the design, but which is strongly animated, relying on strong actions and directions, as in Figures 5.31 and 5.52.

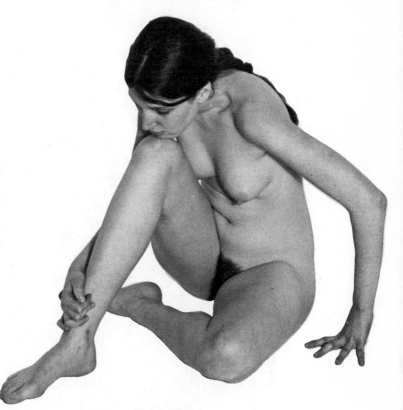

FIGURE 5.61

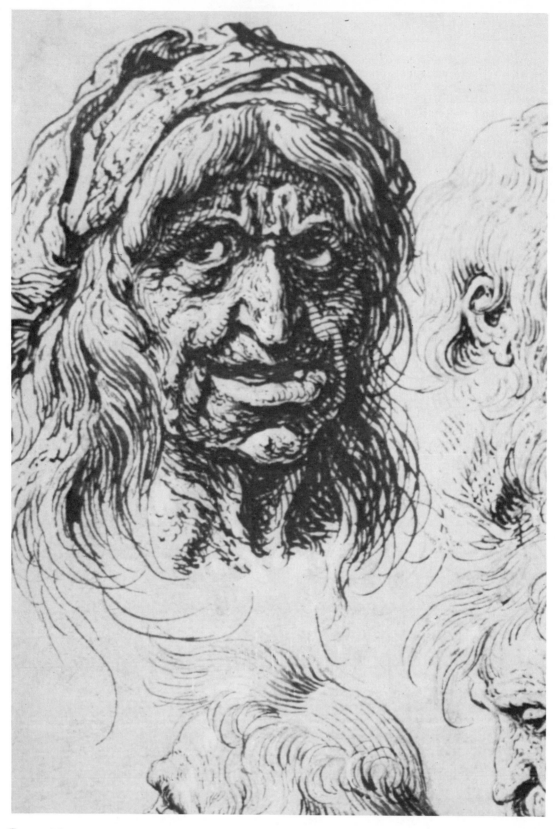

**Figure 6.1**
**JACOB DE GHEYN II** (1565–1629)
*Study of Four Heads* (detail)
Pen and ink over charcoal, white chalk highlights.
*Teylers Museum, Haarlem.*

# SIX

# THE

# EXPRESSIVE FACTOR

*The Emotive Content of Figure Drawing*

## SOME GENERAL OBSERVATIONS

In Chapter Five it was observed that design and expression are really aspects of the same phenomenon: the dynamics of the elements that form the drawing. That these factors are deeply interwoven is evident in the expressive nature of the very terms that describe most of the relational categories. Direction, rhythm, handling, weight, and tension suggest types and degrees of moving, attracting, and pulsating energies, and of strivings for change among the parts of a drawing. In responding to these visual activities we do more than recognize their presence—we *experience* their differing kinds of behavior. We cannot help but empathize with these abstract and representational thrusts, stresses, weights, and tensions, for their expression is inherent in the character of the marks that shape the drawing's parts and in the design of the parts themselves.

A drawing's design scheme reflects more than conscious plan. Artists rely on intuition and feelings as much as on intellect to shape their images. If the design is the mind's strategy, that strategy is influenced by subconscious as well as conscious feelings that the mind initiates, and by emotive qualities in the subject *and* in the emerging drawing. Thus, the resulting energies within and among a drawing's marks do more than function in their visual, or formal and depictive roles. They allude to psychological and spiritual states we can apprehend, and that enable a drawing to express, instead of only describe, human and visual events and attitudes. The artist's feelings, his or her psychological state during the act of drawing, are, of course, important in the forming of the image. Our reality is shaped by our moods. The same pose can strike happy and melancholy artists differently. In a lighthearted mood, artists may see in the figure's pose an affirmation of life's beauty and a reflection of their own good feelings, and this identification is bound to be mirrored in their drawings. The unhappy artist feels the bitter contrast between the figure's vitality and his or her own inner sadness, and this too is echoed in the drawing. Thus a figure drawing's expression reveals something about the artist as well as the model.

In the best drawings we can sense a prevailing mood: daring or delicacy, rage or repose, sorrow or sensuality pervade these drawings because such feelings loomed large within the artist, influencing his or her response to the subject. And these moods are conveyed by the form as well as the content. The lines and tones that express playfulness are not the lines and tones of pathos, and the energies of anger are unlike those of love. It is through these emotive marks and forces that figure drawings take on universal importance. Such qualities raise a drawing out of its time and culture and make the image a symbol that holds meanings for any society, at any time.

We can all apprehend Rembrandt's love (Figure 5.3), Kokoschka's excitement (Figure 5.47), Picasso's humor (Figure 5.18), Hopper's melancholy (Figure 5.55), and de Kooning's rage (Figure 1.35).

We also experience emotive meanings in drawings that seem to focus more on formal visual issues, that seem less expressively motivated. Cambiaso's enthusiasm for structure (Figures 2.5 and 2.34), Desnoyer's thoughtful explorations of two- and three-dimensional space (Figure 5.23), Manet's spirited play with texture (Figure 5.36), and Moore's engrossment with monumental form (Figure 5.32) are all discernible expressions, each conveyed by elements, actions, and handling that imply these attitudes.

Expression, then, should be understood as issuing from more than the emotional or psychological state of the figure's representational situation; it is a quality inherent in the drawing's dynamics too. Because both meanings of the term are important in figure drawing, they must not only complement but reinforce each other. In drawings where they conflict we sense an aimlessness of purpose, a confusing ambiguity of expressive cues. A drawing of a fist can express power, threat, avarice, confidence, or fury. Without some emotive clues beyond the depiction, the fist is only described; it can be identified, but not clearly experienced.

If drawings are to convey some expressive meaning, the artist must first experience it in what is observed or envisioned. As the poet Horace observed, "If you wish me to weep, first you must grieve." But, in contemplating the expression of a model, the artist searches for more than outward physical manifestations of a mood or event. He or she also searches for the figure's essential plastic and structural characteristics, not as ends in themselves, but because they reveal those dynamic properties by which the artist can evoke the figure's expression in ways that mere description cannot. The crux of a figure's expressive content is conveyed by the *overall* condition of its forms.

This is why so many artists begin their drawings by establishing the figure's gestural aspects. By temporarily disregarding the figure's smaller surface-effects and details, and by seeing its arrangement of forms as *one expressive system* and not a collection of separate parts, the artist perceives the figure's essential masses, plastic activities, *and* mood.

The best figure drawings begin with a grasp of generalities that excite the artist's interest and end with those necessary specifics demanded by the original excitement. The artist's adherence to his original theme tells him when the drawing is complete—when his interpretation of the subject's important physical and dynamic (and hence expressive) conditions are present in the work. And this must be done by deduction, not induction—by proceeding from the general to the specific. To reverse this process and draw each segment sequentially, bit by separate bit, does not allow for perceptions that uncover the general structural and dynamic conditions of the figure *as a whole*—perceptions vital to its figurative as well as evocative state.

Among the most common results of such a piecemeal approach are unintentional distortions in proportions and in the location of parts, and the loss of the relational activities necessary to a drawing's balance and unity. To begin with details is to end with a tiresome collection of them, for details greedily devour essentials and strongly resist an integration of the figure's forms into a system of expressive order. Bypassing a felt analysis of the subject's dynamic and structural armature invites dead, frozen imagery; no unified energies or expressions emerge.

But if expression is largely conveyed by the character and mood of the drawing's abstract and structural condition and by the artist's handling, it is also, and importantly, a product of the subject's recognizable state. Facial expressions, physical actions, the event in which the figure takes part, that is, the story-telling aspects of the subject matter, strongly affect the drawing's expression. However, as noted earlier, these two sources of expression must be mutually supportive. A precise and delicate rendering of a figure drowning would suggest a conflict between form and content. We don't shout our whispers or scream quietly.

A compatible rapport between the dynamic and representational aspects of expression is demonstrated in the detail from de Gheyn's *Study of Four Heads* (Figure 6.1). The artist does more than skillfully denote the physical expression of an old woman's grimace. Her fearful disquiet is carried in the rapid lines of the hair and in the gnarled and nervous lines of the face, in the abrupt changes of value, and in the tortuous shapes and forms of the head and bonnet. The intensity of her gaze is heightened by the circular movements around the eyes and throughout the head. By rhythmically repeating

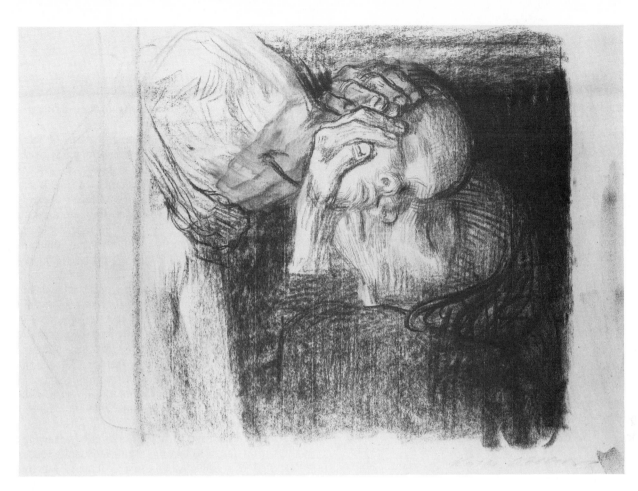

FIGURE 6.2
KÄTHE KOLLWITZ (1867–1945)
*Mother and Child*
Charcoal. 18 7/8 x 24 3/4 in.
*National Gallery of Art, Washington, D.C.*
*Rosenwald Collection.*

FIGURE 6.3
SIGMUND ABELES (1934–    )
*Black Camasol, Black Evening*
Charcoal pencil. 23 x 30 in.
*Collection of Terry Shaneyfelt, Newton, Mass.*

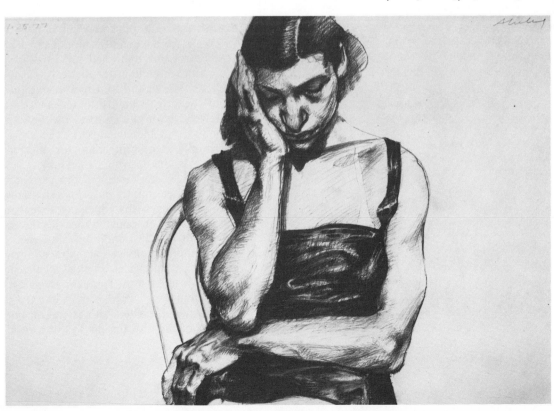

lines in the hair, bonnet, face, and neck, de Gheyn endows the image with a nervous vibrancy. Visual tensions abound, reinforcing the anatomical ones in the strained features. The unusual contrast of the fixed gaze and the animated abstract movements, the latter due in part to the forceful handling, adds to her expression of anxious displeasure.

Kollwitz's *Mother and Child* (Figure 6.2) is a moving evocation of love and death. The hands that embrace the child's head hug with a tender intensity born in the abstract nature of ruggedly carved arcs enveloping gently rounded forms. The intimacy between the mother and child is revealed in the subtle fusion of their faces and in the tender sensuality of the modeling that continues across them. Kollwitz bathes the forms in tone; only the child's cheek and the mother's hand are in light. The drawing's strong horizontal and vertical directions are given contrast

**FIGURE 6.4**
**AUGUSTUS JOHN** (1879–1961)
*Nude Study*
Red chalk. 9 x 11 5/8 in.
*The Metropolitan Museum of Art, New York.*
*Rogers Fund, 1908.*

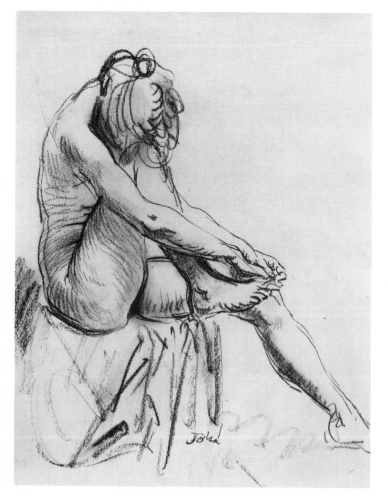

only by the diagonal movements of the ghostlike arms that grip the child. Note how visual and physical weight carry on the same struggle that the figurative image depicts.

Form and content work together in Abeles' *Black Camasol, Black Evening* (Figure 6.3), evoking a bleak mood. The woman's lonely isolation is amplified by the stark white shapes of the background and by their contrast with her ruggedly modeled forms. As in the Kollwitz drawing, a major visual theme is the system of mainly vertical and horizontal directions; but the weighty head, the supporting arm, and the figure's drooping left hand depart from the drawing's design grid, calling attention to the figure's body language. A second visual theme creates a large circular movement that begins with the curving chair, arcs across the shoulders, and sweeps down the figure's left arm to begin again. This, too, brings our attention to the head and supporting hand, and, in adding to the forceful actions of the image, further magnifies the woman's isolation and mood through the contrast of the image's inner tensions and movements with the relentless emptiness of its surroundings.

As the foregoing examples make clear, drawings made with a desire to feelingly realize an observed or envisioned expressive state must call on those dynamic forces that can evoke that state. Without some empathic involvement we lack a basis for selecting and organizing those abstract and figurative clues essential to expression. Drawings developed without some expressive goal, whether that expression is to be found only in the character of the drawing's relational life or in the interplay between the expressive forces in the subject and in the elements, are like rudderless boats; they move in no certain direction, but drift according to the winds of chance.

What we have stated should not be understood as a license for unbridled self-expression. Creative expression communicates the artist's experience of a subject's visual and spiritual condition. We learn about the artist's ability to feel and intuit by how effectively he or she conveys *the figure's* expressive meanings, not merely those of the artist. Using the figure only as a springboard for an emotional high dive makes the drawing's real subject the artist, not the model. A conscious concern with self-expression too often deteriorates into an essentially nonvisual emotional binge—that does not reveal responses to certain truths or potentialities in the subject's abstract and human condition. However, highly subjective interpretations that extract important dynamic and psychological qualities in the figure or the situation can be most eloquent (Figures 1.36, 6.12, and 6.14).

As noted earlier, expressive meanings are revealed not only by the figure's structural nature, as

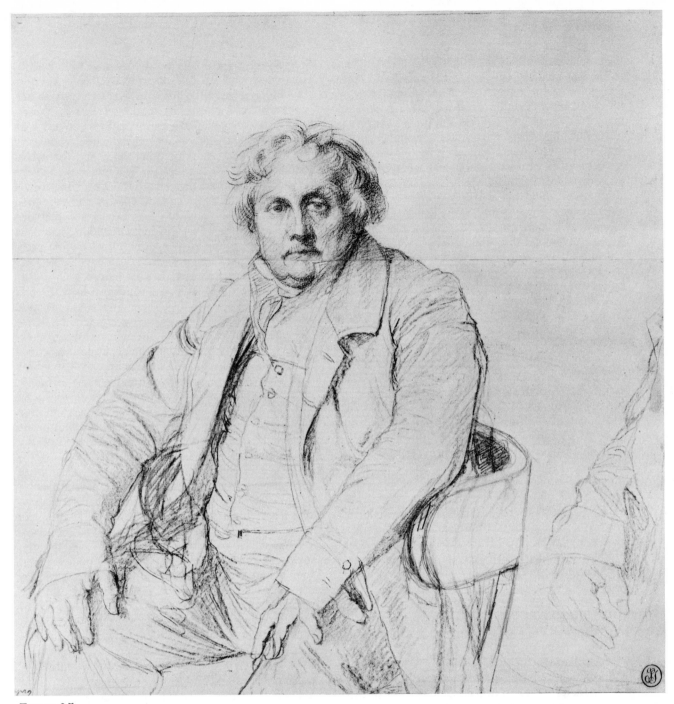

**FIGURE 6.5**
**DOMINIQUE INGRES** (1780–1867)
*Study for the Portrait of Louis-François Bertin*
Chalk and pencil on pieced papier. 13 3/4 x 13 1/2 in.
*The Metropolitan Museum of Art, New York.*
*Bequest of Grace Rainey Rogers, 1943.*

can be seen by comparing Picasso's simplified and granitelike figures (Figure 2.8) with the animated and supple figure by Tintoretto (Figure 2.20), but also by the means used to model the forms. De Gheyn's spirited calligraphy, Kollwitz's gentler strokes, and Abeles' rugged fluency disclose something of the drawing's psychological tone. Even in drawings that do not convey strong human emotions, the artist's interpretation and treatment of the subject will convey a particular expressive attitude. The nonchalant pose in John's *Nude Study* (Figure 6.4) could as easily have suggested melancholy, monumentality, or furious motion. Imagine what Michelangelo, Degas, Kollwitz, or Matisse might

259

have done with this pose. John's responses lead him to the harmonious cadence of the curvilinear edges and volumes; he extracts their easygoing, rhythmic lilt. Hair and limbs, lines and tones, all move along in playful accord, all support the artist's interpretation of the figure as imbued with graceful form and motion. But the visual and expressive potentialities of most poses are great enough to support a wide range of interpretations. Michelangelo would probably have found monumentality here; Degas, a unique blend of sensuality and classicism; Kollwitz, a poignant sentiment; and Matisse, a vigorous play between two- and three-dimensional matters.

Impressive physical weight can be a strong agent of expression, as in Figures 4.82 and 4.84, or as in Ingres' preparatory sketch, *Study for the Portrait of Louis-François Bertin* (Figure 6.5). Ingres bolsters the figure's implacable and assertive stance by a pose that stresses both the sitter's considerable bulk and a stable arrangement of his forms. There is strength and resolution in the large U-shaped curve of the two arms, reinforced by the similarly curved chair back and the figure's legs. These grand curves, by the large spaces and forms they envelop, also suggest bigness, substantiality, and stability. Such abstract expressions of staunchness and solidity amplify the sitter's determined stance and gaze. Too often the beginner relies on the model's facial expression to convey the mood, but as Ingres demonstrates, the mood is best imparted through the entire image. Notice that Ingres, in drawing the small active forms of the tousled hair and clawlike fingers, adds subtle psychological insights and visual counterpoints of scale that further emphasize the sitter's imposing bulk and personality.

## THE INHERENT EXPRESSION OF THE ELEMENTS

We have said that in addition to the emotive content of the subject's figurative situation there is the emotive character of the drawing's elements. Such characteristics evoke recollections and insights about movements and energies that we feel as expressions of various kinds. In Chapter Five we discussed the inherent visual nature of the elements and saw how each mark either adds to or detracts from a drawing's balance and unity. We were interested in the differing functions and energies of the elements for order-forming purposes. We saw how an indifference to the relational life of the elements, in failing to clarify both a drawing's abstract and figurative conditions, seriously alters and weakens its meanings. Now it only remains to point out that these differing abstract activities also carry emotive content which, if overlooked, also diminish meaning.

Every mark is felt as well as seen by the sensitive viewer. A boldly drawn arc representing a downturned mouth, lips pressed tightly together, contains the force of the mouth's frowning expression to a far greater degree than the same arc hesitantly drawn. Additionally, the bold arc, in relating to the inherent traits of other lines and tones, becomes part of a larger system of expressive elements that further support the emotive force of the frown. But if the arc is to express discontent, the artist must, as Horace advised, first experience that discontent. It must be part of his perception. The most careful description of a figure's forms cannot communicate what felt lines and tones can evoke. Accuracy without ardor is mere imitation.

In neglecting to support what is seen with what is there to be felt, the beginner's lines and tones still continue to express; they convey indifference or inhibition in the presence of the figure's dynamic expression. Such drawings may be accurate inventories of forms, but the forms fail to come alive, for they lack an expressive incentive. Lebrun had this failure to feel in mind when he observed that all too often "in teaching, we neglect to sponsor passion as a discipline. The only discipline we teach is that of the deadly diagram supposedly to be fertilized later by personal experience. Later is too late."*

Each of the elements can enact a broad range of expressive actions. Lines, tones, and shapes can suggest fast or slow movements; they can seem playful, threatening, nervous, sensual, stately; they can relate with other elements to form reassuring or uneasy states of balance in a drawing. Even the elements we use to make a diagram or a doodle suggest their inherent and distinctly different expressive personalities. Just how great a range of expression the elements can convey is demonstrated by the drawings throughout this book, each reflecting the artist's excitement, curiosity, and identity with the emotive nature of his subject *and* of the emerging drawing. In Figure 1.20 the sensually rhythmic lines, the rugged shapes and forms, and the vigorously drawn tones and textures all amplify Rubens's expressive message. A more mechanically oriented use of elements would have violated the artist's intent. But Villon's interpretation of a figure (Figure 5.42) depends on just such an orientation; a more vigorous treatment would have hampered *his* intent. And John's interest in an easygoing image (Figure 6.4) could not have been served by the types of expression in the elements in either Rubens's or Villon's drawings.

By calling on powerfully active elements, Rembrandt enlivens what might otherwise have been a

* *Rico Lebrun Drawings* (Berkeley and Los Angeles: University of California Press, 1961), p. 25.

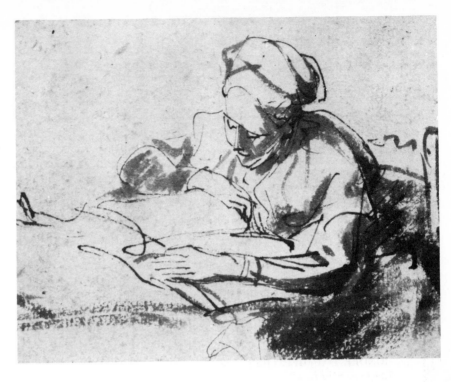

FIGURE 6.6
REMBRANDT VAN RIJN (1606–1669)
*Woman Reading*
Pen and brown ink, brown wash.
2 5/8 x 3 7/16 in.
*The Metropolitan Museum of Art, New York.*
*Rogers Fund, 1926.*

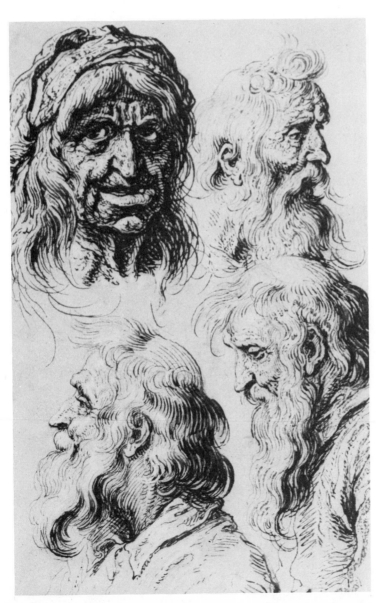

FIGURE 6.7
JACOB DE GHEYN II (1565–1629)
*Study of Four Heads*
Pen and ink over charcoal,
white chalk highlights.
14.8 x 9.6 cm.
*Teylers Museum, Haarlem.*

261

rather ordinary domestic scene (Figure 6.6). Rembrandt suggests the woman's excited absorption in the book by fast-moving calligraphic lines, nervously active shapes and forms, and roughly stated tonalities. These furiously active energies abstractly fuse the figure and the book (probably the Bible), their bold motion providing an intensity and strong sense of light that elevates the simple act of reading to an engaging expression of dedication and wonder that has universal meaning.

When de Gheyn changes his expressive goal, his use of the elements changes also. In Figure 6.7 the expressive behavior of the elements in the three views of an old man's head are more rhythmic, gentler, and the illumination less harsh; the tonal changes are more gradual; the shapes friendlier and less gnarled than those of the woman's head.

An important consequence of using the emotive power of the elements to reinforce their figurative themes is that the best artists make the elements perform as metaphors that deepen or transcend these themes, as the foregoing examples have shown. Sometimes the event represented is enigmatic and can only be understood by experiencing the behavior of the elements. For instance, the faint, quavering lines in Daumier's *The Imaginary Invalid* (Figure 6.8) suggest the tremulous unease of the patient and of the two strange attendants. Symmetrical and delicate at first glance, the drawing's agitated lines and the single shock of dark tone surrounding the patient's head begin to alert us to the scene's quiet nightmare, which grows in terror while we watch.

By way of an interesting contrast to Daumier's deceptively light and gentle treatment, Aronson's

**FIGURE 6.8**
**HONORÉ DAUMIER (1810–1879)**
*The Imaginary Invalid*
Pen and black and gray ink, and gray wash over black chalk. 12 8/16 x 13 7/8 in.
*Yale University Art Gallery, New Haven.*
*Bequest of Edith Malvina K. Wetmore.*

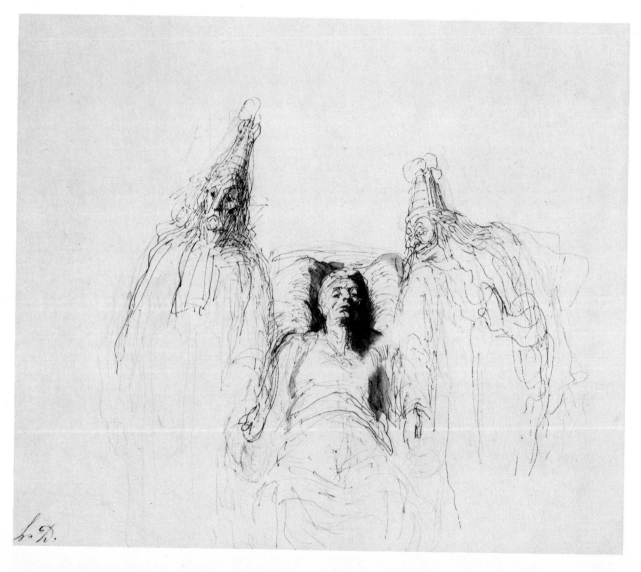

FIGURE 6.9
DAVID ARONSON (1923–    )
*Rabbi III*
Brown pastel. 40 x 26 in.
*Courtesy Museum of Fine Arts, Boston.*
*Gift of Arthur E. Vershbow, Benjamin A. Trustman,*
*Samuel Glazer and Dr. Earl Stone.*

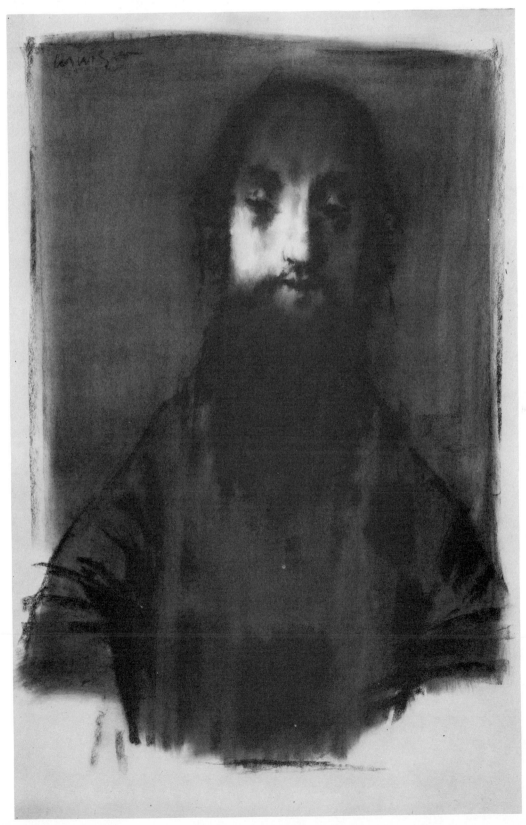

*Rabbi III* (Figure 6.9), dark and seemingly brooding, is a statement of tranquil introspection, and the dominant behavior of the elements supports that theme. The stable monumentality of the shapes and forms, the unchanging tone of the background, the gentle transitions of tone in the head, the figure's centrality, and its union of physical and visual weight all attest to an enduring serenity. The sudden bursts of black strokes, harshly carving planes and hollows intrude like blows while they strengthen the forms.

The dynamic power of the elements in Kuhn's *Study for "Roberto"* (Figure 6.10) abstractly augments the power described in the hefty forms of the resting acrobat. Similar to Aronson's drawing in its stability and implications of perseverance, Kuhn suggests a sense of raw strength and confidence by the rugged nature of the elements. There is nothing facile about the man or the handling; both are straightforward expressions of inherent vigor. That expressive intent can dramatically alter form and handling is evident in comparing Kuhn's drawing of a seated woman (Figure 5.8) with this powerful work.

FIGURE 6.10
WALT KUHN (1880–1949)
*Study for "Roberto"*
Brush and india ink, heightened with white.
8 1/4 x 13 7/8 in.
*Courtesy Museum of Fine Arts, Boston.*
*Charles Henry Hayden Fund.*

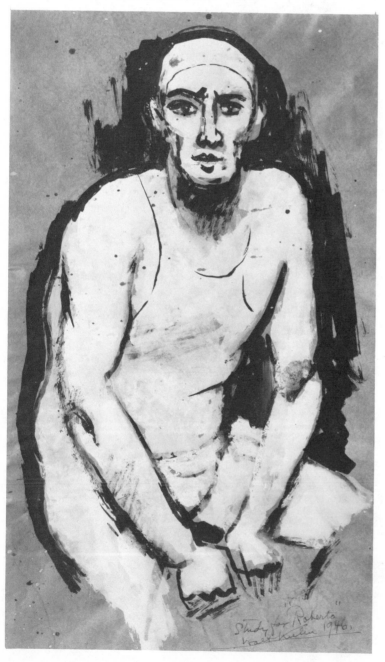

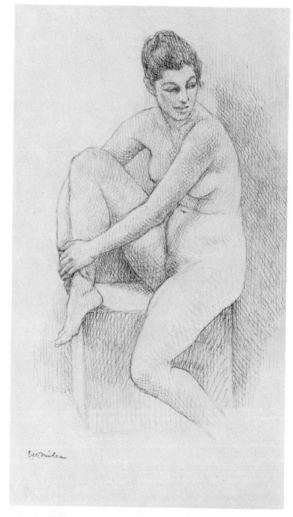

FIGURE 6.11
EMILY WINTHROP MILES (1893–1962)
*Seated Nude*
Pencil. 14 1/2 x 11 3/4 in.
*The Metropolitan Museum of Art, New York.*
*Gift of Mrs. Darwin Morse, 1965.*

What can happen when we disregard the figure's suggestions for dynamic activities that make the act of figure drawing an exciting encounter with life, and not a dutiful interrogation, is indicated in Figure 6.11. While the artist is skillful in measuring and analyzing a part's essential mass (although the forms of the legs and the general area of the shoulders seem uncertain), there is little relevance between the nature of the forms or the pose and the nature of the elements. Nowhere do the lines that model the forms suggest an awareness of the rhythmic arrangement of those forms. The figure's shapes and edges seem spiritless; they seem not to have been regarded as sources for evoking something of the figure's rhythms and energies. As a result, the forms themselves do not convince. Hands that do not grip at the abstract, feeling level do not do so at the representational level. In the absence of an empathic involvement, the sternomastoid muscle doesn't strain in its action, the lower right leg doesn't press against the upper leg, and the figure itself fails to sit upon the block.

Even the artist's preoccupation with a mechanical style of crosshatching is nowhere made visually or expressively *necessary*. Instead, the lines appear to be only the product of a manner, a method; they have a sameness throughout which causes them to be seen as a texture that rises to the surface, weakening the forms they are meant to define.

As noted earlier, in avoiding an encounter with a subject's plastic and emotive qualities, we reveal a timidity about encountering these vital sensibilities in ourselves, and our drawings will disclose this fact. This is not to suggest that figure drawings must be stridently dynamic. We have seen excellent examples of drawings in which the dynamics are subtle and delicate (Figures 1.17 and 5.43). But delicacy is not timidity. It is a special kind of caring about nuance and inflection, a style of expression, and, as such, an affirmation of intent. Timidity is only a style of evasion.

## DISTORTION

Since figure drawings are the results of analysis, selection, emphasis, and intent, strictly speaking they are all distortions of human forms. All carry the stamp of our impressions, our imagination, our idiosyncrasies. But sometimes an artist's interpretation demands changes that drastically alter human proportions, forms, or textures. In the best figure drawings these more obvious changes are never the product of impulsive fancy or private symbolism; rather, they are attempts at philosophical or psychological assertions that cannot be expressed in more objective figurative modes.

Often such drawings use the figure metaphorically. De Chirico, in his *The Condottiere* (Figure 6.12), creates an image that may be a man becoming a still life or a still life becoming a man. Either way, the drawing offers intriguing considerations. Of particular interest is the artist's insistence on a considerable amount of specific anatomical fact. Note the highly altered but still discernible clavicles, pectoralis muscles, abdominal muscles, and flank pads. In the figure's left leg there are even suggestions of the adductor group and of the rectus femoris and vastus muscles.

The term *still life* takes on a grim meaning in Peterdi's engraving *Still Life in Germany* (Figure 6.13). The artist's emphasis on the intricate system of muscles, tendons, and veins in these brutalized and withered extremities implies his disgust with those who would destroy such magnificence. Peterdi distorts these broken forms to magnify the suffering and evil that are his theme, but he draws them with the care and precision of a medical illustrator. This deliberate emphasis on details and textures—on a

FIGURE 6.12
**GIORGIO DE CHIRICO** (1888–1978)
*The Condottiere*
Pencil. 31.8 x 21.9 cm.
*Staatliche Graphische Sammlung, Munich.*

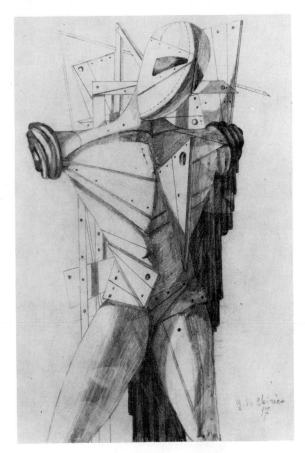

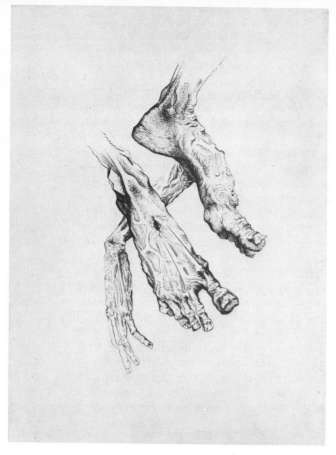

FIGURE 6.13
GABOR PETERDI (1915–   )
*Still Life in Germany* (1946)
Engraving. 12 x 8 7/8 in. (plate)
*The Brooklyn Museum.*
*Gift of Gabor Peterdi.*

FIGURE 6.14
RICO LEBRUN (1900–1964)
*Lone Great Mutilated Figure*
Ink on paper. 39 11/16 x 28 in.
*Worcester Art Museum, Worcester, Mass.*

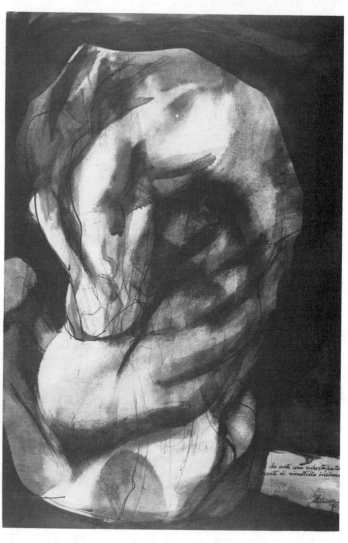

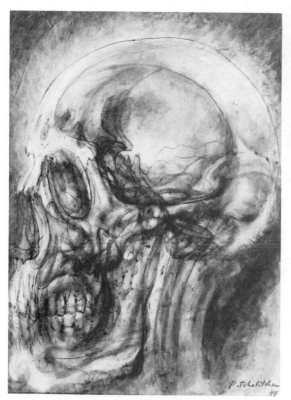

FIGURE 6.15
PAVEL TCHELITCHEW (1898–1957)
*Study for "The Crystal Grotto"* (1943)
Ink wash. 14 x 11 in.
*Collection, The Museum of Modern Art, New York.*
*Gift of Mr. and Mrs. Sam A. Lewisohn.*

relentlessly sharp focus—beckons us to consider the causes of such destruction with the same patient concern.

The forms in Lebrun's *Lone Great Mutilated Figure* (Figure 6.14), though largely unidentifiable, not only evoke the character of human forms but convey a sense of anguish and tragedy through their struggling interactions, and because of their rough-hewn structure and the harsh light that strikes them. The background's brooding tone, the cast shadows, the medium's texture, and the impassioned handling all intensify the expressive mood. Comparing Lebrun's drawing with Figure 6.11 reveals how steadfastly the sense of aliveness may evade forms that denote facts, and how intensely it can pervade forms that evoke feelings.

In Tchelitchew's *Study for "The Crystal Grotto"* (Figure 6.15), the forms of the skull undergo a metamorphosis that suggests landscape and cave formations. The double-exposure effect, especially evident in the facial bones, creates a strong vibrating motion, strengthening the sense of a change in subject matter. But even such a subjective interpretation of the cranial forms reveals the artist's authoritative understanding of anatomy.

Walkowitz, in his *From Life to Life, No. 1* (Figure 6.16), fuses figures in a way that hints at cloudlike formations while at the same time stressing the two-dimensional pattern of the elements. Either reading of the image evinces the sensual pliancy and rhythms of human form. Note the delicate nature and handling of the lines and tones, and the resulting delicate movements.

Sometimes, though, distortions mainly involve changes in contour and scale relationships, as in Evergood's *Pensive Nude* (Figure 6.17). Here the artist exaggerates the undulations of edges and of size differences between parts. Despite the absence of extensively modeled forms, these knowing contours are able to imply a great deal about the figure's volumes. The resulting expression is one of sensuality, weightiness, and patient introspection.

## THE EXPRESSIVE ROLE OF THE MEDIUM

The intrinsic character and range of the materials used in drawing have a decided influence on a drawing's emotive nature. By their range of textural effects, their erasable or permanent nature, and their adaptability to different uses, they always affect the artist's handling and even the kinds of judgments he or she will make. For example, because the reed pen cannot easily produce the gradual tonal changes that are natural to the sable brush, an artist working with the pen will avoid such gradations of tone, but may

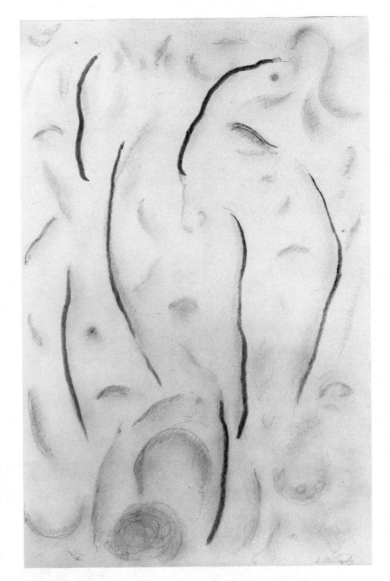

FIGURE 6.16
ABRAHAM WALKOWITZ (1880–1965)
*From Life to Life, No. 1*
Pencil. 12 9/16 x 8 1/2 in.
*The Metropolitan Museum of Art, New York.*
*Alfred Stieglitz Collection, 1949.*

search out reasons for including them when using the brush.

The effect of different media is evident when we compare Degas' treatment of the figure drawn with chalk (Figure 1.32) with a similar figure done in an ink monotype (Figure 5.57). Degas takes advantage of chalk's dry, abrasive character to create masses and light effects with blunt strokes and subtle blendings; using ink, which in the monotype technique can be removed as easily as applied, he models the forms by broad swipes of a brush or cloth, stressing their shapes and directional speed rather than their structure, as in Figure 1.32.

FIGURE 6.17
PHILIP EVERGOOD (1901–    )
*Pensive Nude*
Pen and ink. 24 x 18 3/4 in.
*Courtesy of Terry Dintenfass, Inc., New York.*

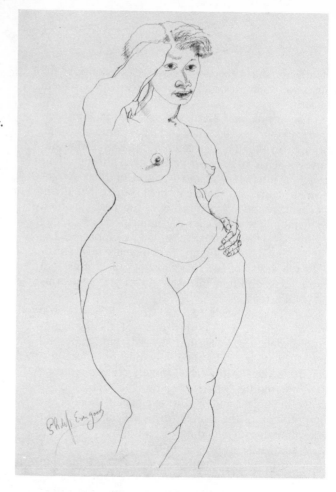

FIGURE 6.18
GEORGES SEURAT (1859–1891)
*Seated Boy with Straw Hat*
Black conté crayon. 9 1/2 x 12 3/8 in.
*Yale University Art Gallery, New Haven.*

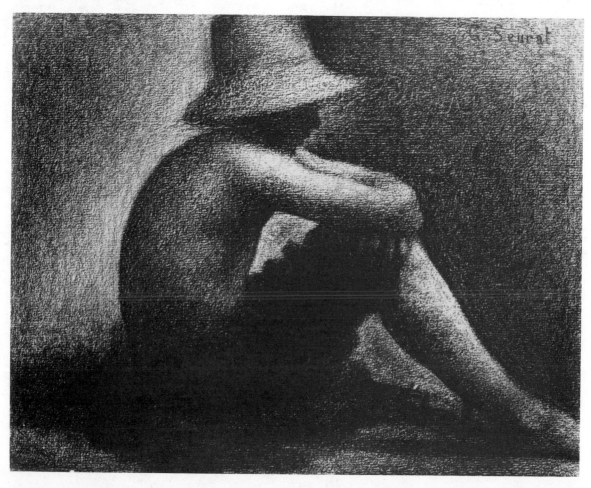

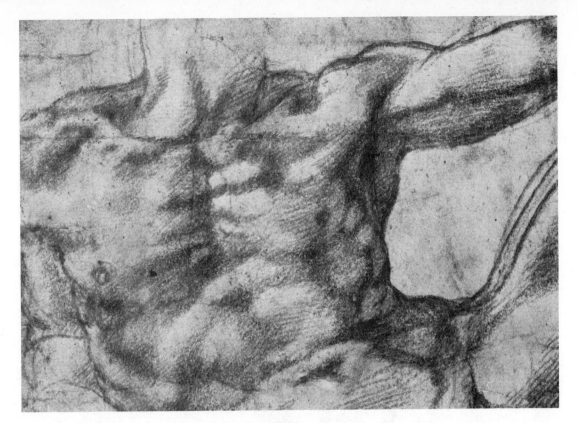

FIGURE 6.19
MICHELANGELO BUONARROTI (1475–1564)
*Study of Adam for "The Creation of Adam" in*
*the Sistine Chapel* (detail)
Chalk on tan paper.
*Trustees of the British Museum, London.*

FIGURE 6.20
EGON SCHIELE (1890–1918)
*Mother and Child* (detail)
Black crayon, watercolor, gouache.
*Courtesy Museum of Fine Arts, Boston.*
*Edwin E. Jack Fund.*

Had Tchelitchew used a soft graphite pencil and Wolkowitz a brush and ink, each would have been restricted by their medium from making many of the linear and tonal judgments we see in their drawings. But each would no doubt have gone on to utilize what their medium *could* produce. Their meanings might have been as successfully conveyed, but not often by the same graphic maneuvers.

The mood of some drawings seems to depend heavily on the particular medium employed. When this is the case, considerations concerning its use rate close in importance to the factors of structure, anatomy, design, and expression. The stately solemnity of Seurat's *Seated Boy with Straw Hat* (Figure 6.18) owes something to the medium's compatibility with the artist's interest in monumental forms. Seurat, in selecting a paper with a pronounced grain, and by using the side of a stick of conté crayon, utilizes the textural properties of both to create the gentle play of broad tones that express their quiet grandeur.

It would be far more difficult to obtain these results with a sharpened, harder chalk on less grainy paper. But such materials are exactly suited to Michelangelo's fascination with the drama inherent in the powerful inner tensions and pressures among the bones and muscles pressing against the figure's surface (Figure 6.19). And Schiele's need for a more sensual and spontaneous expression of rhythmic shapes, lines, and tones leads him to a use of mixed media: black crayon, watercolor, and gouache (Figure 6.20).

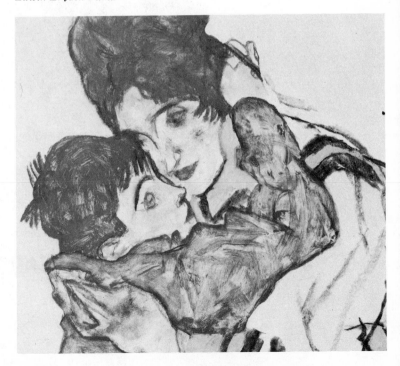

FIGURE 6.21
SALVATOR ROSA (1615–1673)
*St. George Slaying the Dragon*
Pen and ink, watercolor. 9 x 5 7/8 in.

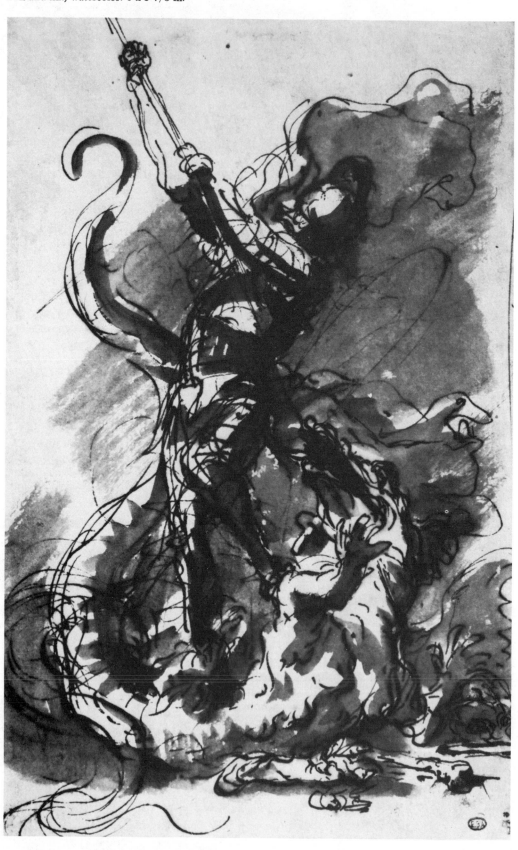

All good drawings exhibit a congenial rapport between meanings and media, but an overdependence on the powers of a medium to convey our intent may cause the medium to dictate the results instead of enhancing them. Such drawings often provide a showy display of facility that makes the drawing's dominant expression an exhibition of technical cleverness, not a statement of felt responses based on something encountered or imagined.

## EXAMPLES OF EXPRESSION IN FIGURE DRAWING

Here we will examine further ways in which the expressive meanings of a drawing's figurative state are amplified by the expressive character of its abstract behavior. Although the range of possibilities of the elements and energies to augment figurative meanings is limitless, these few examples may serve to suggest something of the inventive freedom possible, and to encourage us to trust our intuitive responses more. Our gut reactions to a subject's essential character, in the first moments of our seeing or imagining it, usually carry the key to how we should draw it. Editing and censoring our *original* impression makes us lose sight of (or surrender) our initial interest in the subject. This occurs when structural, anatomical, textural, or other demands divert us from our initial motivation and purpose, or when our second thoughts force us to resist or even withdraw our personal responses in favor of a more realistically "correct" image, or in order to bring our attitude into conformity with some admired manner or style.

Had Rosa, in his envisioned image (Figure 6.21), or Rodin, in his quick sketch of an observed event (Figure 6.22), backed off from the fervor that is at the heart of both drawings (in favor of a more accurate accounting), neither work would move us as it does. Rosa magnifies the force of St. George's lance by avoiding any other straight direction. In the context of the scene's roiling turmoil, the lance's diagonal movement strikes with fatal force. The artist goes after the violent action of man and beast, and the furious whorls, slashing lines, and splashing tones express this. Observe, though, that despite this furious treatment and the figure's suit of armor, important physical landmarks are still noted, as in the arms, abdomen, and legs. Note too that our eye moves along the serpent's body toward the tail, where we partake in the swift descent of the lance to its target.

Rodin's drawing, because it expresses a different kind of fervor, shows a different kind of treatment. Again, curvilinear shapes, and forms predominate, but unlike the Rosa drawing, where the

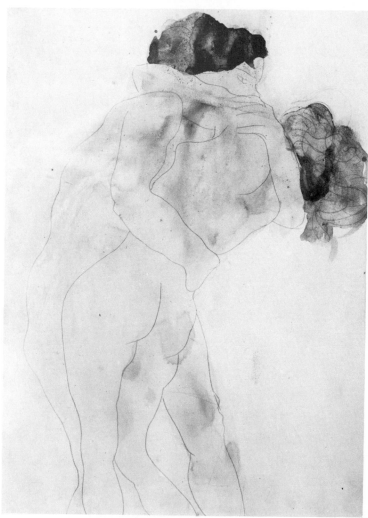

FIGURE 6.22
AUGUSTE RODIN (1840–1917)
*The Embrace*
Pencil, with brownish and black watercolor washes.
12 15/16 x 9 7/16 in.
*Ashmolean Museum, Oxford, England.*

elements as well as the figures engage in vehement battle, here the elements, like the figures, express pliancy as well as compliance. As in Figure 6.17, contour lines carry the main responsibility of conveying the sense of volume and do so most convincingly. A careful study of these figures will show just how much anatomical fact Rodin includes in these seemingly carefree contours.

The emotive power of Lebrun's *Figure in a Dust Storm* (Figure 6.23) benefits from the rhythmic lines, the vague and lost edges, the delicate and light-toned values that model the forms, and the substantiality of the forms above and below the fast-moving tone that obscures part of the figure. The strong movement energies of these subtly stated

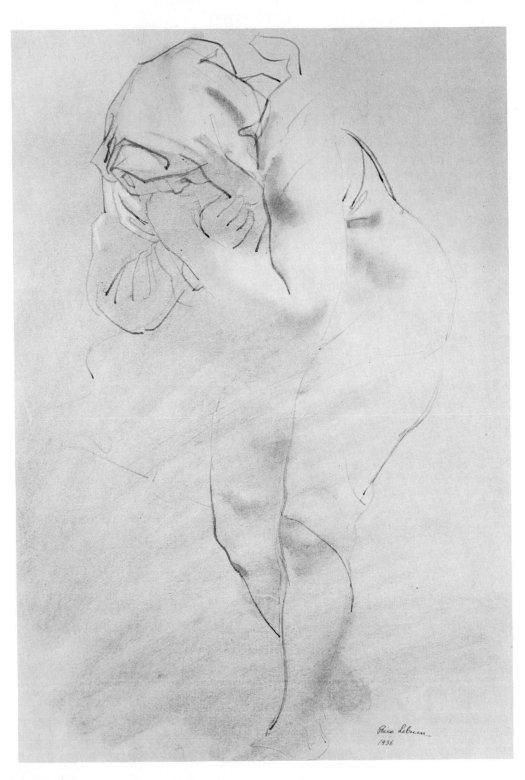

**FIGURE 6.23**
RICO LEBRUN (1900–1964)
*Figure in a Dust Storm*
Ink and conté crayon. 24 1/2 x 18 in.
*Courtesy The Santa Barbara Museum of Art.*
*Artist in Residence Fund.*

elements and the overall diagonal movement of the forms give the drawing's representational theme the added force to make us feel the figure's struggle against the wind and dust. Notice how the contrast of the harsher, linear treatment of the head and arms bolsters the impression of the force of the windswept dust.

In Pascin's *Reclining Woman* (Figure 6.24), sensuality is evoked in the frank tactile nature of the contours and in the rhythms and pliancy of the shapes, tones, and textures. The very few straight lines (in the upraised arm and the eyebrows), by differing from the others, reinforce their flirtation with eroticism. But it is flirtation only. In the subdued sense of volume, in the decorative air of the open shapes and some of the large curved lines surrounding the figure, and in the floating quality of the figure and the bedding, the drawing's sensuality is more dreamlike than purposeful, more playful than pornographic.

A very different mood pervades Despiau's treatment of this kind of subject. In *Reclining Nude* (Figure 6.25), the artist imparts a feeling of tranquil

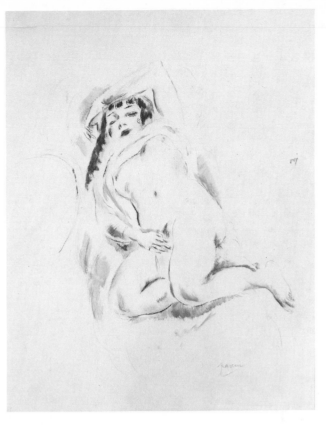

FIGURE 6.24
JULES PASCIN (1885–1930)
*Reclining Woman*
Watercolor, pencil, and ink. 17 7/8 x 14 9/16 in.
*The Metropolitan Museum of Art, New York.*
*Alfred Stieglitz Collection, 1949.*

FIGURE 6.25
CHARLES DESPIAU (1874–1946)
*Reclining Nude*
Red chalk on buff paper. 23.2 x 36.2 cm.
*National Gallery of Prague.*

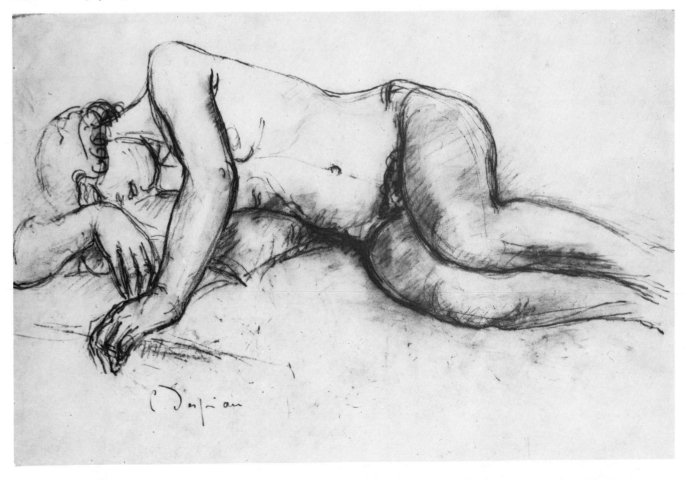

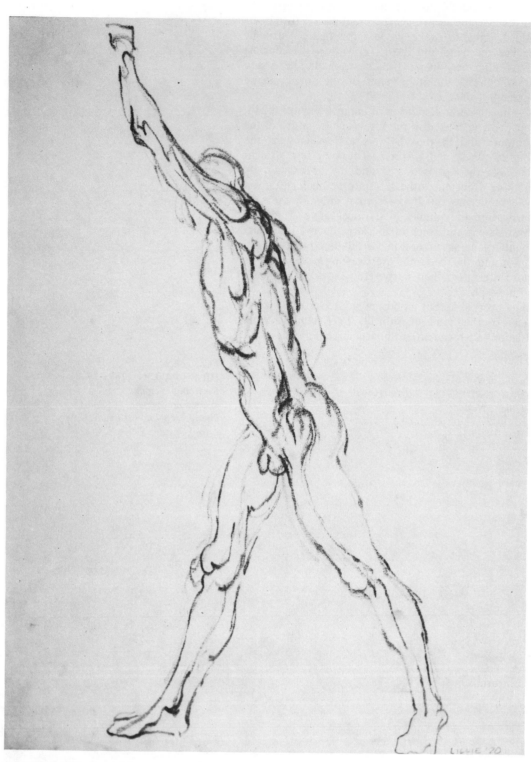

FIGURE 6.26
LLOYD LILLIE (1932–    )
*Male Figure, Side View*
Pencil. 9 3/8 x 14 in.
*Courtesy of the artist.*

permanence by emphasizing the columnar character of the forms. But here all is not monumental and stilled. The stable shapes and volumes and the sense of great weight give the figure the serenity of a Greek sculpture, but the spirited treatment that produces the forms emerges from an authoritative and searching attitude that carves and shapes the forms with vigorous directness. In contrasting the quiet mood of these shapes and forms with the vibrant spirit with which they are drawn, Despiau suggests the feel of restrained power, of a striving to change, to awaken.

The power of the anatomical factor as an agent of expression is well illustrated in Lillie's vigorous *Male Figure, Side View* (Figure 6.26). Here the artist's gestural attack is pressed beyond the point where it might serve as an underdrawing to guide and enliven more fully realized forms. Instead, the figure's gestural action and the powerful relational energies that express that action are the drawing's chief purpose. Each of the four factors is intensely active and interacting with the others. The lines that develop the structure simultaneously clarify the anatomy and, by their animated but ordered calligraphic behavior, convey an expressive design that supports the representation of a rugged but graceful figure. Lillie's penetrating sensitivity to the dynamic potentials of the figure's structure and anatomy, and the attractive spirit of his responses, should alert the beginner to the inventive and liberating possibilities of a sound grasp of the figure's architecture and machinery.

Even when the figure is draped, anatomical considerations can continue to play an important expressive role, as we see in Zuccaro's *Study of a Man Seen from Behind* (Figure 6.27). The artist's interest in the figure's powerful action is strengthened by the straining action of the lower half of the body, revealed beneath the drapery. Zuccaro also reinforces the figure's action by establishing folds in some areas and stretching the cloth taut elsewhere. But it is the lively system of lines, shapes, and forms that, in being equally active at the abstract level, gives us the *feel* of the action. Here, everything curls and spirals, evoking a sense of the figure's turning action.

But when a stationary pose is to be shown, more than the figure should be stilled. In Watteau's *The Savoyard* (Figure 6.28), the figure has paused, balanced between the case on his back and the container suspended from his neck. The stable nature of the elements—the tenuous but balanced standoff between their various movements—matches the checked action of the figure. Watteau has drawn the figure in a position that suggests the man has just stopped walking or is about to start. At the abstract level, the physical and visual weights, the cancelling

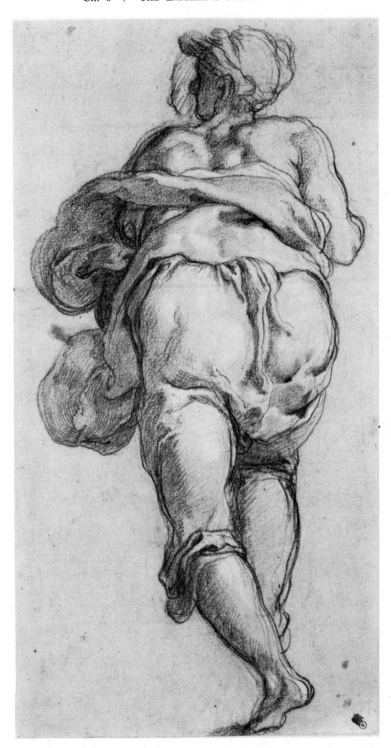

**FIGURE 6.27**
**TADDEO ZUCCARO (1529–1566)**
*Study of a Man Seen from Behind*
Red chalk, heightened with white.
34.2 x 18.2 cm.
*National Gallery of Art, Washington, D.C.*
*Ailsa Mellon Bruce Fund.*

out of diagonal lines, the stable and unstable shapes, the alternately vigorous and gentle handling, and the fluctuation between bold and subtle tonalities, all suggest a barely maintained truce between energies. They also suggest an ambiguity between actions just ended or about to begin. By the tensions among these balanced but contradictory forces, Watteau supports a psychological tension in the figure that is summarized in his facial expression: a blend of cynicism and uncertainty, of resolution and introspection.

Because all visual relationships suggest move-

ment, it is natural enough that the expressive meanings of many figure drawings are principally rooted in the figure's physical actions. For example, Tiepolo's *Psyche Transported to Olympus* (Figure 6.29) is, aside from its mythological comment, an expression of figures in flight. Movement is at the very core of this drawing and each free-flowing line and tone expresses action. Fast-moving shapes and rhythms, the sparse but volume-informing modeling, and the drawing's diagonal rush across the page help us experience these figures as being in flight, rather than falling. Note how the configuration's main

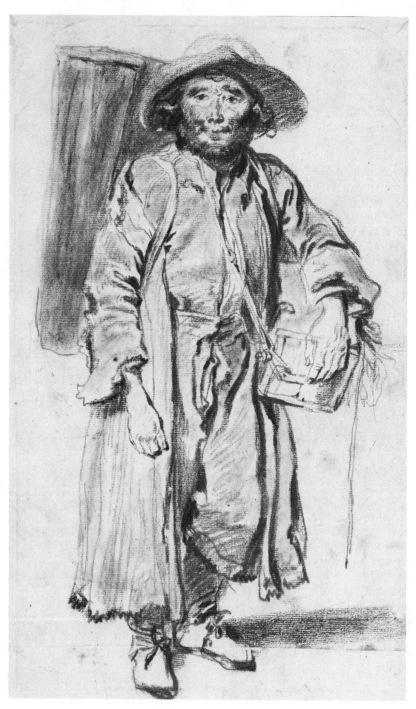

**FIGURE 6.28**
ANTOINE WATTEAU (1684–1721)
*The Savoyard*
Red and black chalk.
*Courtesy The Art Institute of Chicago.*
*Joseph and Helen Regenstein*
*Foundation.*

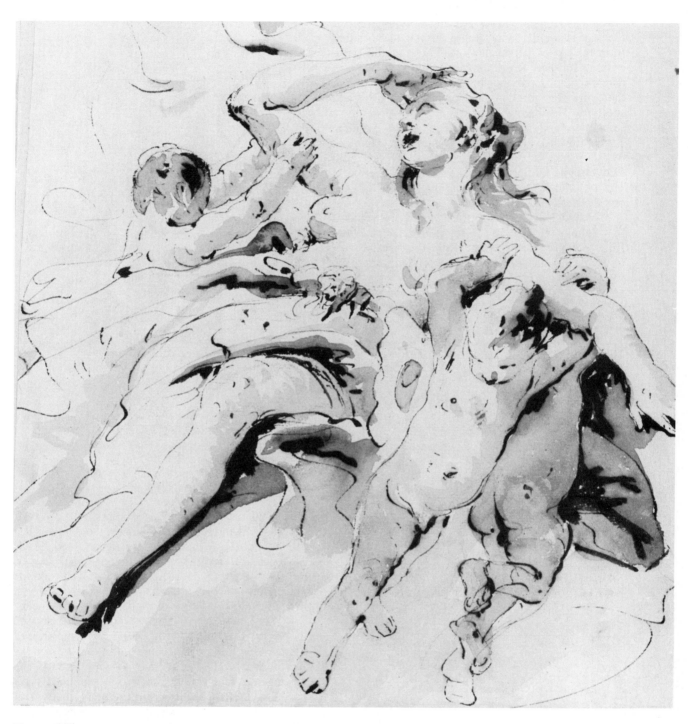

**Figure 6.29**
**GIOVANNI BATTISTA TIEPOLO** (1696–1770)
*Psyche Transported to Olympus*
Pen and brown ink, brown wash, over black chalk.
8 3/4 x 8 11/16 in.
*The Metropolitan Museum of Art, New York.*
*Rogers Fund, 1937.*

movement from the lower left to the upper right of the page is countered by an implied diagonal running from the upper left to the lower right of the page.

In another Rosa drawing, *Witches' Sabbath* (Figure 6.30), the moving action sweeps through the entire configuration, enveloping both figures and specters. The nightmarish scene is conveyed by a serpentine coil of skeletons and beasts winding slowly upward in a mutually reinforcing blend of frenzied lines and fearful apparitions. Rosa skillfully designs the large rib cage to "urge" the spiral upward, and relates it to the curling smoke throughout the drawing.

Although less evident, the dynamic movements that animate the figures in Goya's *Provincial Dance* (Figure 6.31) are of a piece with the sprightly actions of the dancers. Goya supports the energetic

**FIGURE 6.30**
**SALVATOR ROSA (1615–1673)**
*Witches' Sabbath*
Pen and brown ink, gray wash. 10 11/16 x 7 1/4 in.
*The Metropolitan Museum of Art, New York.*
*Rogers Fund, 1912.*

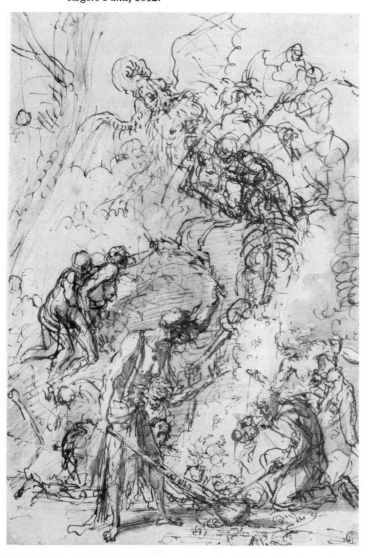

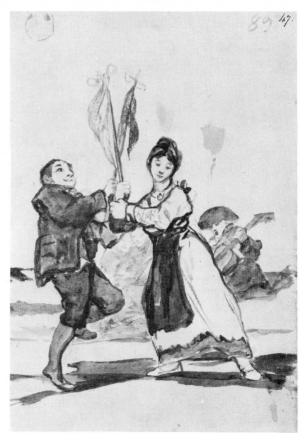

**FIGURE 6.31**
**FRANCISCO DE GOYA (1746–1832)**
*Provincial Dance*
Wash drawing in sepia. 8 1/8 x 5 5/8 in.
*The Metropolitan Museum of Art, New York.*
*Harris Brisbane Dick Fund, 1935.*

movements of the dancers and the flutter of their clothing and the flags they hold by avoiding vertical and horizontal directions in the figures, and by his use of loose brushwork and ragged-edged shapes. Further, by using abrupt contrasts of value in the shapes of the background, Goya enlists them in strengthening the lively movements of the dancers.

The sense of movement among compressed forms can produce a strong feeling of constrained energy. In Picasso's etching *Minotaur, Drinking Sculptor, and Three Models* (Figure 6.32), the moving rhythms among the figures, confined arms and legs, and the artist's suggestion of their great weight impart a feeling of accumulated energy, capable of an explosive change. A similar feeling of pent-up force exists in the crowding of the five heads, in the large, bent leg, coiled as if about to spring free, and in the hatched tones that seem too vibrant for the shapes they are confined in. These conditions create strong visual tensions throughout the work, intensified still more by the forceful nature of the lines. The tactile sensuality evident in many of the contours and in the emphasis on physical weight, as well as the intimacy of the poses, suggests a clue to the psychological nature of the heightened tensions.

Because of its emphasis on motion, Duchamp's famous painting *Nude Descending a Staircase* (Figure 6.33) serves here as a final example of the expressive power of movements that can emerge from the relational interaction of the elements. The intensity of movements is due largely to the high degree of similarity among the directions, shapes, sizes, and locations of the figure's severely abstracted but still identifiable parts. Even in this highly subjective interpretation of human forms a sound knowledge of anatomy underlies the image: Clav-

icles, pectoral and gluteal muscles, pelvic forms, and even a faithful set of human proportions help us to identify with the figure's energetic descent.

We have seen that a drawing's expression is revealed not only by the depictive matter but by the intrinsic character of the elements, in the pace and temperament of their interplay, in the artist's "handwriting," and even in the uses of the medium. Expression is as much a part of the drawing's design as the design is a key to the drawing's expression.

But some intangible quality remains that eludes analysis: some spirit or state—a presence—that we

FIGURE 6.32
PABLO PICASSO (1881–1973)
*Minotaur, Drinking Sculptor, and Three Models* (1933)
Etching and aquatint. 29.8 x 36.5 cm.
*Courtesy Museum of Fine Arts, Boston.*
*Lee M. Friedman Fund.*

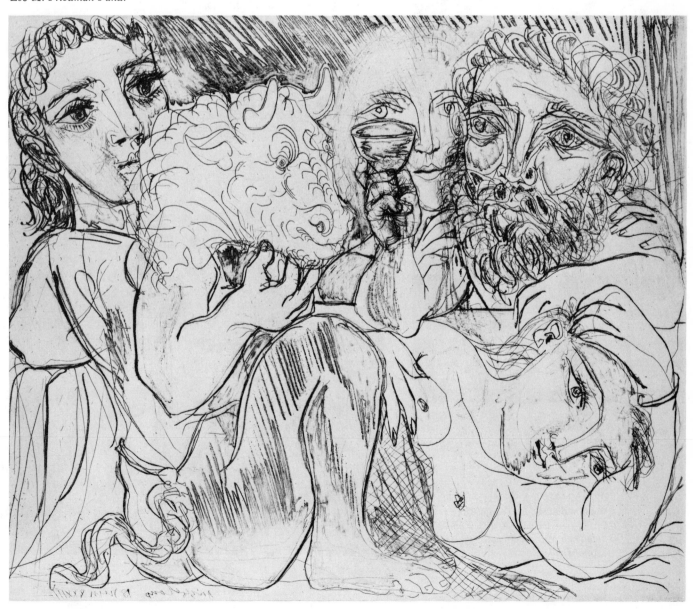

sense giving life and universality to the best figure drawings, remains as mysterious as those forces that give life to the figures themselves. Perhaps it is the result of a critical degree or pitch of dynamic activity, or of a crucial blend of the artist's intellectual, intuitive, and subconscious responses and intentions; certainly it demands the interaction of the four factors we have been examining, and, though indefinable, its absence in a drawing leaves the image somehow unrealized. But if this quality cannot be isolated, one fact about it is certain: No matter how faintly or obliquely sensed, an honest acceptance of our own responses and of our intent, although no guarantee of its presence, is an essential condition for achieving it.

The shadowy and moving expression of Rembrandt's *Woman Seated, in Oriental Costume* (Figure 6.34), emerging from the harmony between the depiction and the dynamics, seems imbued with this impalpable quality of "rightness" and life. The drawing's unselfconscious nature, in revealing that Rembrandt's paramount concerns were to inquire, experience, and respond, suggests that approaching figure drawing with a desire to know, instead of to show, may lead to that mysterious presence that transforms knowledge and skill into art.

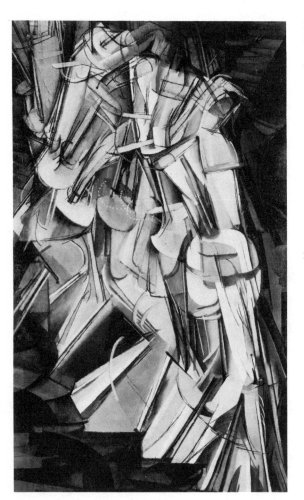

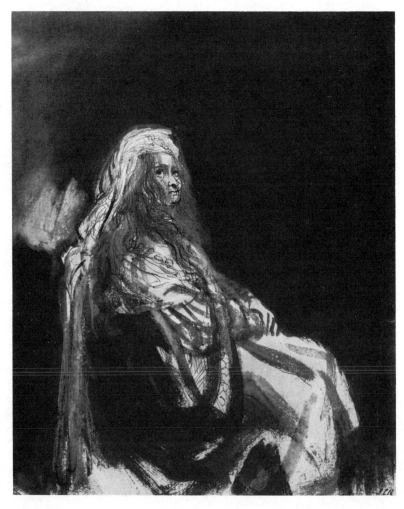

FIGURE 6.33
MARCEL DUCHAMP (1887–1968)
*Nude Descending a Staircase*
Oil on canvas. 37 3/4 x 23 1/2 in.
*Courtesy Philadelphia Museum of Fine Art.*
*Louise and Walter Arensberg Collection.*

FIGURE 6.34
REMBRANDT VAN RIJN (1606–1669)
*Woman Seated, in Oriental Costume*
Brush, pen and ink. 20 x 16.2 cm.
*Staatliche Museen Preussischer Kulturbesitz.*
*Kupferstichkabinett. West Berlin.*

# SUGGESTED EXERCISES

Unless otherwise indicated, there are no time limits on the following exercises, and they may be drawn to whatever scale and with whatever medium you require. Where necessary, you may combine media.

The nature of these drawings will demand your entire commitment to the depictive and abstract emotive theme concerned in each. Although summoning up feelings on demand is difficult, perceiving the structural and dynamic possibilities in each of the observed or imagined figures is fundamental to good drawing. Being aware of these possibilities will help you to gain insights about the subject's expressive condition and about the means to convey it. Indeed, one of the main challenges in these exercises is to have the drawing's expression come through the elements as well as the figural depiction.

1. Working from the model and using a large sheet of paper, draw some fifteen to eighteen small-sized, one-minute action poses. Using Figures 4.104, 5.7, and 6.26 as rough guides, emphasize the rhythms of inner forms as well as edges, and suggest the general structural nature of the forms. Next, using these sketches as models, make the following two drawings:

   a. Select any three or four of these action poses and combine them in a drawing that suggests battle, or some other aggressive state, adjusting the poses to conform to this theme. Your treatment of the figures, and the choice and use of the medium selected, should advance the idea of combat or struggle (see also Figure 5.25).

   b. Select any three or four of these action poses and combine them in a drawing that suggests flight, or any rhythmic and dancelike actions, as in Figures 6.29 and 6.31. Again, handling and medium should be compatible with your theme.

2. Working from one or more models, or using a mirror, make the following three drawings of heads, in which the facial expressions are reinforced by the character and behavior of the elements:

   a. Someone shouting happily or excitedly.
   b. Someone scowling or frowning.
   c. Someone sleeping.

3. Working from the model, make two drawings *of the same pose* that could serve as illustrations for:

   a. A mystery story.
   b. A love story.

4. Working from the model, make two drawings *of the same pose*, using a different medium for each. For example, the first drawing might be done in pen and ink, the second, with the side of a stick of conté

crayon. Extract those abstract and figurative qualities in the model that the medium can more easily produce. That is, allow the medium to influence what you say about the model in each drawing.

5. Working from the model or your own earlier drawings, make four drawings that suggest the figure's metamorphosis into:

   a. A cloud.
   b. A tree.
   c. A machine.
   d. A rock formation.

6. Working from the model, and using Figure 6.14 as a rough guide, make three comparably abstracted drawings to suggest:

   a. Melancholy.
   b. Joy.
   c. Anger.

7. Using Figures 6.2, 6.9, and 6.18 as rough guides, make the following, largely tonal drawings based on your imagination:

   a. One figure carrying another.
   b. Two or three figures dancing.
   c. A sleeping or dead figure.

8. Using Figure 6.27 as a rough guide, invent a drawing of a comparably draped figure performing some strenuous physical act.

9. Referring to the muscle illustrations in Chapter Four (or to any other source), invent a drawing of a flayed figure lifting a heavy object, such as a rock.

10. Using Figure 6.33 as a rough guide, invent the following two drawings:

   a. A ballet dancer in motion.
   b. Two wrestlers in action.

11. Using Figure 6.13 as a rough guide, make your own "still life" of human forms, not necessarily as a horror show, but to suggest Peterdi's general theme or any other expressive idea.

12. Using Figure 6.32 as a rough guide, invent a drawing of several figures in some comparably compacted arrangement which suggests constrained energies.

13. Using Figure 6.30 as a rough guide, and referring to the anatomical illustrations in Chapters Three and Four (or any other source), invent a drawing that conveys your version of a "Witches' Sabbath."

14. Working from the model, and using Figure 6.6 as a rough guide, make several drawings in which the elements and the handling activate passive, resting poses.

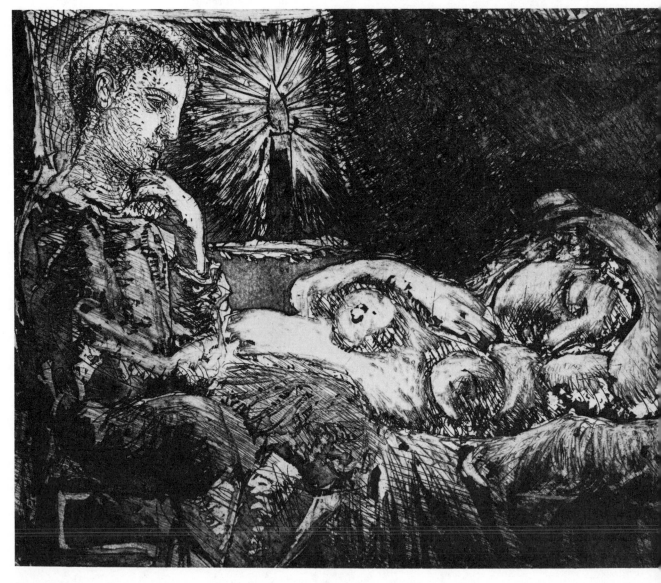

FIGURE 7.1
PABLO PICASSO (1881–1973)
*Boy Watching over Sleeping Woman* (1935) (detail)
Etching and aquatint.
*Courtesy Museum of Fine Arts, Boston.*
*Lee M. Friedman Fund.*

# SEVEN

# THE

# FACTORS

# INTERACTING

## *Some Examples*

## DIFFERING FORMULAS

Throughout this book the central theme has been the high degree of interdependence and mutual support among the factors of structure, anatomy, design, and expression. We have seen that the measurable factors of structure and anatomy are as deeply interlaced with the dynamic ones of design and expression as they are with each other, and that each factor has both figurative and abstract functions to perform. As we examined each of these factors we saw some examples of how they function in their own sphere and how they assist the function of the other factors.

Many of the lines used to establish the structure of, say, a head, might additionally convey some salient anatomical facts which add to both the drawing's representational and design needs and to its expressive meanings. Conversely, expressive-design considerations concerning the treatment of the head might require that these lines be either plentiful or sparse in number, and curvilinear or mechanical in

character, and such considerations will influence the degree of structural and anatomical clarity of the head.

Earlier, too, we saw that all artists, according to their perceptual, temperamental, and aesthetic needs, formulate some personally necessary hierarchy of importance for the roles these factors will play in their drawings. In this section we will examine some of these "prescriptions" for their usage. For we understand a drawing not only by the ways in which the factors interact but by their order of importance in the image.

In Ricci's *Man between Time and Death, Evoking Hope* (Figure 7.2), forms emerge from the swarm of spirited lines, the excited calligraphy "permitting" the depiction, rather than the demands of the depiction permitting some calligraphic play, as in Dürer's *An Oriental Ruler on a Throne* (Figure 7.3). Dürer insists on a precise articulation of each plane and volume, of each tassel and jewel. Further, he constructs a more formal and stilled design than does Ricci. In emphasizing the subject's volumetrics,

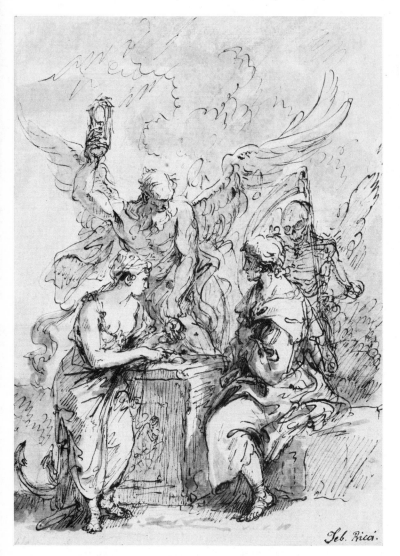

**FIGURE 7.2**
SEBASTIANO RICCI (1659–1734)
*Man between Time and Death, Evoking Hope*
Pen and brown ink, gray wash, over black and red
chalk. 10 3/4 x 7 3/4 in.
*The Metropolitan Museum of Art, New York.*
*Rogers Fund, 1967.*

Dürer makes the structural factor dominant; in arranging them symmetrically, he calls our attention to the two-dimensional aspects of the drawing's design. This stress on structure and symmetry, however, is not developed without an appealing calligraphy of its own. Indeed, the lines are both graceful and incisive, qualities difficult to combine. But it is clear that Dürer's intentions demand steady ranks of structurally oriented lines, while Ricci counts on the flutter of numerous agitated hatchings to reinforce the drama of the life or death discourse.

Although very little of the surface anatomy is directly visible in Dürer's drawing, it too is more

fully explored (and more inventively stated) than it is in Ricci's drawing. But Ricci's use of anatomy, it somewhat less convincingly knowledgeable than Dürer's, is expressively compatible with the rest of the emotionally charged drawing. Hope's classical simplicity, Time's heroic ruggedness, the man's idealized head and entreating stance, and Death's "incorrect" but expressively effective "body" are well cast in their parts and feelingly drawn to impart the character and role of each of the participants in the event.

The contrasting goals of these two drawings are reinforced by their very different design strategies. Ricci calls on powerful rhythms and diagonal movements, on animated figurative motion, and on a loose and urgent handling. Dürer's method depends on a careful cancelling out of movements, the stability of vertical and horizontal axes, a motionless figure, and a more deliberate handling. Each relies on a contrapuntal device to intensify the main emotive character of his image: The stable block in the center of Ricci's swirling forces and the swirling sash in the center of Dürer's stabilized forces both serve to reinforce (and provide some visual relief from) the drawing's dominant expressive attitude.

Although Ricci emphasizes dynamic matters and Dürer measurable ones, each drawing reveals a sensitivity to qualities in the other. We are all the more delighted in the amount of quiet but playful rhythmic activity at work throughout the Dürer because we see it in the context of the drawing's rigid symmetry. Likewise, we are all the more relieved to find the stabilizing forces within the Ricci because they keep the forceful energies from running wild. Note in the Dürer the unsymmetrical but balancing results of the long sword on the left against the dark tones on the right, and, in the Ricci, the steadying function of the rough symmetry between the two figures in the foreground.

In a more daring abstract invention, Cambiaso's *Male Nude on Horseback* (Figure 7.4) departs from his more structured and geometric approach to forms (previously seen in Figures 2.1, 2.5, 2.34, and 4.90) to create a whirlwind of action. Responding to the oval format as well as to the forms of his subject in this action-filled scene, Cambiaso relies heavily on curvilinear lines and animated, interweaving shapes. Here, everything is in a state of turbulent motion. The drawing's equilibrium is tenuous: We no sooner react to the visual and physical weight pulling the man downward to the left than we realize he is being wrenched toward the right by the downward action of the horse. Led down to the meeting of the horse's legs and head, our eyes are drawn upward by the fanlike burst of directions in that area; we can then follow any of several routes back onto the mainstreams of directional energy.

FIGURE 7.3
ALBRECHT DÜRER (1471–1528)
*An Oriental Ruler on a Throne*
Pen and black ink. 30.6 x 19.7 cm.
*National Gallery of Art, Washington, D.C.*
*Ailsa Mellon Bruce Fund.*

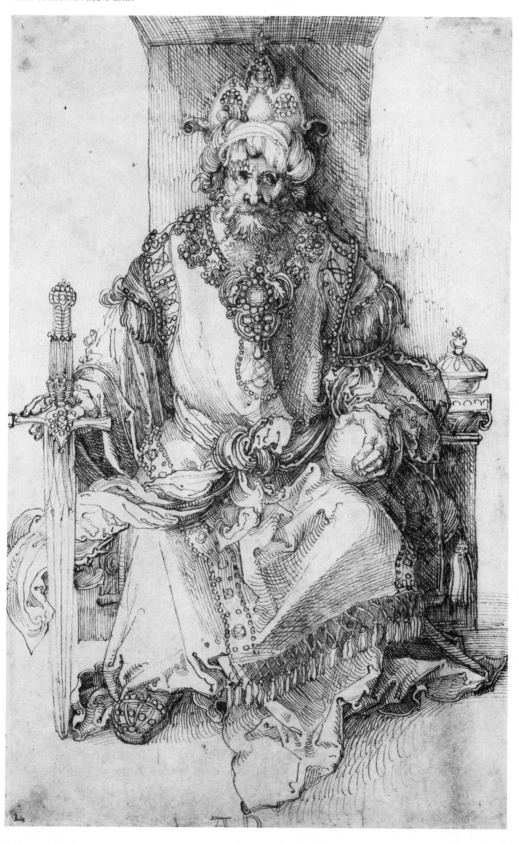

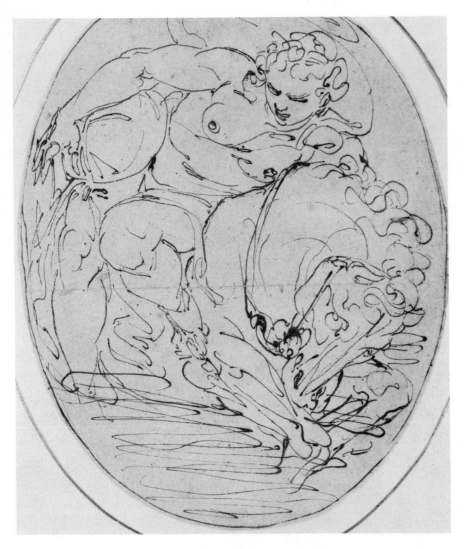

Figure 7.4
LUCA CAMBIASO (1527–1585)
*Male Nude on Horseback*
Pen and ink. 29 x 25 cm.
*Courtesy The Fogg Art Museum,*
*Harvard University.*
*Austin A. Mitchell Bequest.*

The longer we examine this drawing, the greater our sense of being hurled about in a whirlpool.

The contour lines, although forceful in their actions, are delicately stated and almost weightless. Further, the gracefully energetic rhythms that course through the drawing act as modifiers of the impression of solid masses in space. These effects, in calling our attention to the drawing's two-dimensional life, reveal the artist's fascination with the drawing's dynamics on the picture plane. These felt and sophisticated extractions from the raw material of man and horse, by their insistence on energetic line and shape patterns, show the factors of design and expression to be dominant in the artist's strategy for conveying the event.

But structure and anatomy, although secondary, participate vigorously in the drawing's lively animation. To appreciate the importance of their contribution, we have only to turn the drawing upside down. Now its movements, while not appreci-

ably slowed, are more delicate than driving, for they have lost the dramatic substantiality that abstract forces have when moving through known volumes and spaces. Seen this way, the fine-tuned balance between the graceful and the rugged is gone.

Notice how economically Cambiaso conveys structural conditions. His ability to summarize complex forms to reveal their more nearly geometric state helps us to better understand the basically ovoid form of the head, the cylindrical basis of the extremities, and the construction and interjoining of smaller form-units in both the man and the horse. These interjoinings are especially clear in the figure's arm and legs and in the horse's head. Cambiaso's incisive treatment of structural matters adds to the drawing's energies and thus to its expression. To have thoroughly explored these forms would have entailed a multitude of lines and tones and a careful crafting of the image, a treatment that would have lessened the drawing's vibrancy and would certainly have intruded on the airy weave of animated actions on the picture plane, a condition central to Cambiaso's visual-expressive theme.

Cambiaso balances anatomical considerations with the drawing's dynamic nature. He screens these as selectively as he does the structural clues, accepting only those necessary to establish a convincing figure and to emphasize its action. The artist's profound grasp of anatomy is evident in how much is conveyed about bone and muscle in the few lines given to these details. For example, the nine or ten lines of the figure's upper arm suggest the deltoid and its insertion point, the contour of the lateral head of the triceps as well as some of that muscle's tendonous lower portion, the olecranon process, a bit of the supinators, and the body and insertion of the biceps. Note the equally economical and informing drawing of the knees, and how clearly the anatomical differences of their differing positions are explained. Despite their anatomical function, these lines never "forget" to take part in the spirited nature of the handling and of the design. Nor does the figure's powerful musculature fail to benefit from the strong energies that course through it, contributing to the drawing's expressive character.

By comparison, de Gheyn's *Boy Seated at a Table with a Candle and Writing Tools* (Figure 7.5) is immediately more structurally oriented. Not unlike Dürer's "recipe" for using the four factors, de Gheyn's greater stress on a warmer, more vigorous use of line and his lesser concern with details give his drawing a stronger sense of spontaneity and movement. But if de Gheyn is less precise than Dürer, he carves more insistently than Cambiaso, and does so in an appealing, tactile way also seen in the head of the Oriental in Dürer's drawing. But, while Dürer reserves this more sensually tactile attitude for the head and some few other passages, de Gheyn models all the forms by lines that feelingly ride upon the surfaces. De Gheyn's relentless desire to experience even the figure's unseen forms is what makes him draw the figure's clothed forms in a way that convincingly suggests the presence of the torso and arms. In the Dürer drawing, however, the artist's fascination with details of the drapery makes him occasionally lose the figure beneath it. Indeed, it is only Dürer's emphasis on a decorative formality—on an image as much symbolic as alive—that keeps the figure's occasional disappearance from becoming an inconsistency in the drawing. De Gheyn is more concerned with the spirit than with the letter of a form. This is apparent when we compare the hands in both drawings. In Dürer's the hands are structurally lucid but without the enveloping rhythm and animation of the hand in de Gheyn's.

A subtle visual theme organizes de Gheyn's drawing. In addition to the diagonal of the table cancelling out the opposing diagonal of the boy's upper arm, a system of small units forms an encircling beat that moves around the page. The extended hand, the objects below it, the bowl in the lower left corner, the objects nearby, the collar overhanging the cloak, and the hat all take part in this revolving beat. Of these, the bowl in the lower left corner is an especially important component in the design. Its visual and physical weight provide that extra bit of leverage necessary to keep the design from being too heavy on the right. Note too how the vertical fold of the cloak joins the bent arm and the gesturing hand in forming an extended M shape whose direction moves to the left, additionally weighting the drawing on that side.

FIGURE 7.5
JACOB DE GHEYN II (1565–1629)
*Boy Seated at a Table with a Candle and Writing Tools*
Pen and iron-gall ink on brownish paper.
5 5/16 x 4 1/16 in.
*The Yale University Art Gallery, New Haven.*

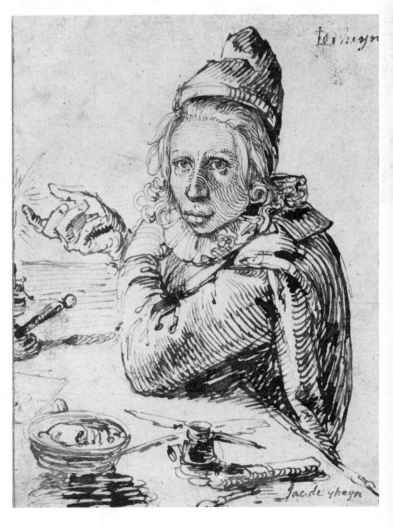

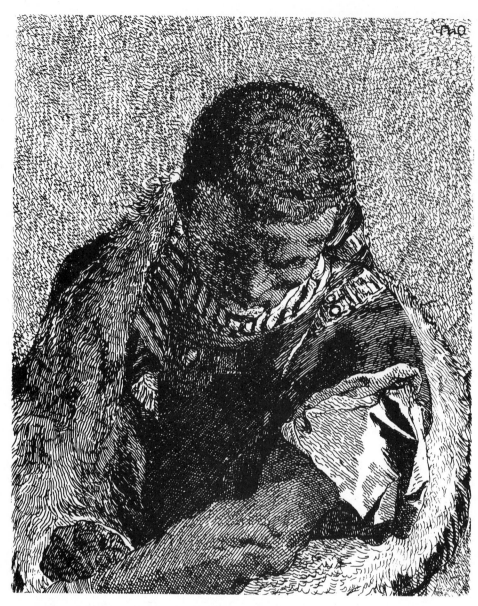

**FIGURE 7.6**
**GIOVANNI DOMENICO TIEPOLO**
**(1727–1804)**
*A Negro*
Etching, 2nd state. 5 3/4 x 4 9/16 in.
*Courtesy Museum of Fine Arts, Boston.*
*George R. Nutter Fund.*

Although the drawing's emotive force is not a dominant matter for de Gheyn, the artist shows obvious pleasure in modeling the forms. The boy's gentle but energetic spirit is harmoniously interwoven with the mood that issues from the drawing. These moods do not seem imposed by the artist's desire to stress either state; we feel them because he did, and his empathy with the subject comes across to us through the functioning of the factors.

An even stronger mood imbues Tiepolo's etching *A Negro* (Figure 7.6). Like Dürer and de Gheyn, Tiepolo relies heavily on the structural factor, but here structural lines do more than feel out the changing terrain. An overall texture of generally wavy lines, in addition to explaining the subject's topography, creates a soft, almost Impressionist-like atmosphere. These lines produce tones that bathe the forms in a gentle light, intensified by the flash of sunlight on the sleeve of the figure's left arm.

By gently graduating values and avoiding strong contrasts between them, Tiepolo evokes an atmosphere of hushed restraint that supports the figure's introspective mood. The overall feeling of quiet contemplation is reinforced by the circular movements of the design. These make the figure appear to withdraw inward, even as he is actually withdrawn from the forms surrounding him. Tiepolo locates the figure at the far end of what we sense to be a cone of motion. By making the shapes, textures, and value contrasts of the cloak and arms more visually active in their overall impact and in their revolving action than the forms farther back, the artist makes us aware of the distance separating us from the young man's head and torso. Tiepolo further bolsters both the conical swirl and the mood by reducing the value contrasts and the clarity between the forms farther back. Both the tone of the background, in approaching that of the light side of the head and of the cape on the figure's right side, and the tone of the tunic, in approaching the tones of the scarf and the dark side of the head, help to strengthen the figure's physical *and* psychological retreat.

The pronounced textures, which tend to muffle the structural clarity of the forms and of the surface anatomy, and the structural clarity, which tends to force its way through the textural web, are not conflicting ideas but mutually supportive ones. The etching's texture depends on these precise structural explanations simply because it needs something to be textured *for*—some reason for changing value and pattern. And, were the forms less fully realized, they would be buried under such conspicuous textural activity. Likewise, these strongly carved forms, while needing to be visible through the texture, would, if stripped of this softening atmosphere, lose their emotive character.

As Tiepolo's etching indicates, structural considerations can lead the way to quite subtle and moving dynamic states. And, as all the drawings thus far examined in this book illustrate, an understanding of anatomy is necessary for more than the ability to make economical and convincing statements about human forms; it provides a rich source of stimulating plastic responses that serve other factors. Even in Dürer's drawing, where anatomy has such a small role to play, the design of the facial forms is consistent with the design of the surrounding segments, and may even have stimulated his solution to the design of the beard and the headdress. In fact, except for Figure 7.4, all the examples thus far in this chapter show little of the figure itself. But in each (except for Dürer's necessary lapses) the drawing of the drapery makes it clear that the artist is well aware of the nature of the forms below; they continue to influence the drawing's design and expression as well as the forms we do see.

This is again evident in a contemporary drawing similar in arrangement to Tiepolo's. Abeles' *New Year's Eve, 1978* (Figure 7.7) utilizes a number of the same tactics we find in Tiepolo's etching, such as the circular orientation of the forms, the averted glance, and the use of textured passages (especially in the background) to create the psychological tone of the work. Again, introspection and withdrawal are expressed by the curved arms, one hand resting upon the other, and the head is the focal point in the design. As in our earlier examples, we are convinced of the figure's presence beneath the heavy layers of drapery. We can tell that the figure's left leg is

crossed upon the right one, we can locate the woman's left elbow, can discern the form of the breasts and shoulders, and can even note that despite the heavy clothing the figure is lithe.

Further, there is in Abeles' drawing an emphasis on shape similar to the emphatic role of shape in the Tiepolo. Here too the structural factor is an important theme in its own right, yet it also lends to the drawing's design an engaging system of triangular shards. These result from the planar nature of the coat, but the artist continues to expand this triangular theme throughout the work. The large shapes of the coat, collar, and chair all hint at their triangular basis; even the darkened background is composed of two large triangles.

Again, in Vespignani's *Girl in Bed—Graziella* (Figure 7.8), little shows of the figure itself. But the artist's understanding of its masses beneath even these thick layers of bedding assures us of their presence. Where we do see the forms themselves Vespignani reveals his mastery of anatomy in suggesting so much of their structure by volume-informing contours and a very economical selection of lines within those contours. In the hand the only lines inside the contours are those few that describe the metacarpal heads and some folds in the fingers and mark off important planar junctions. Even in the head, where the artist restricts his observations to the features, the contour of the face and the drawing of those features trigger strong clues about the planes of the rest of the head.

Although Vespignani's gentle drawing is expressively the opposite of Cambiaso's (Figure 7.4), they both show a similar concern with contours that sets them apart from the more structurally insistent artists discussed above. The absence of swarms of structural lines carving masses in space clears the picture plane for other visually expressive events.

In this drawing the emotive theme is the tranquillity of the resting figure. Almost everything shown is in a state of surrender to gravity. The girl's limp forms accommodated to the pliant bedding suggest their unseen substantiality by the mattress bending under her weight and by the folds radiating from beneath her head and arm. The folds of the sheet and the patterned blanket "give in" to their own weight, or, where they are supported by the figure, adhere to her forms with little resistance. Only a few folds in the bedding try to hold themselves up, a half-hearted attempt that only underscores the easy yielding of the rest of the drawing's forms.

Tranquillity is also implied by the pearly tone and soft texture of the wall, by the emphasis on the horizontal (which includes the shape of the page), and by the majestic undulations of the bedding. By giving the figure and her immediate surroundings the same white tone, Vespignani further stresses her visual harmony with the surroundings. Only the dark tone of the girl's hair breaks the visual silence of the drawing's peaceful character, and in so doing calls attention to her quality of gentle introspection— the psychological as well as the visual center of attraction.

Another design theme directly employs the structural considerations of the forms. If we cover all but the lower fourth of the drawing, the pat-

terned coverlet appears to lie flat on the picture plane. When we expose only the lower half of the drawing, the arm and the mound of the legs are clearly volumetric, but are minor masses when compared to the more formidable volumes in the upper part of the drawing. By this ordered increase of forms in scale and substance Vespignani creates a uniting pattern of growth that gives each mass a necessary part to play in expressing it.

FIGURE 7.7
SIGMUND ABELES (1934–   )
*New Year's Eve, 1978*
Charcoal.
*Courtesy of the artist.*

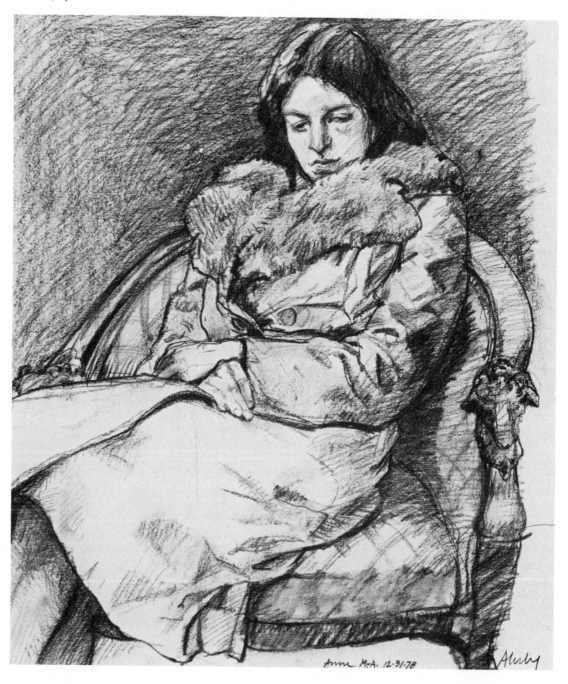

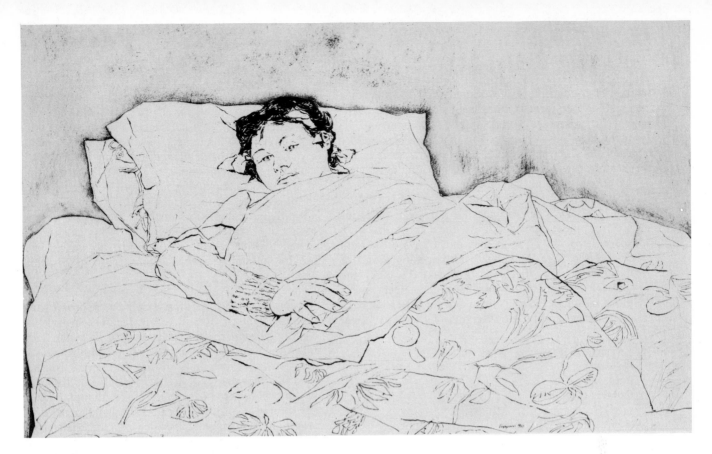

**FIGURE 7.8**
**RENZO VESPIGNANI** (1924–  )
*Girl in Bed—Graziella* (1953)
Pen and ink, washes. 20 3/4 x 35 1/4 in.
*Courtesy The Fogg Art Museum, Harvard University.*
*Bequest of Meta and Paul J. Sachs.*

**FIGURE 7.9**
**ARTHUR POLONSKY** (1925–  )
*In Sleep*
Brush and ink. 22 x 28 in.
*Courtesy of the artist.*

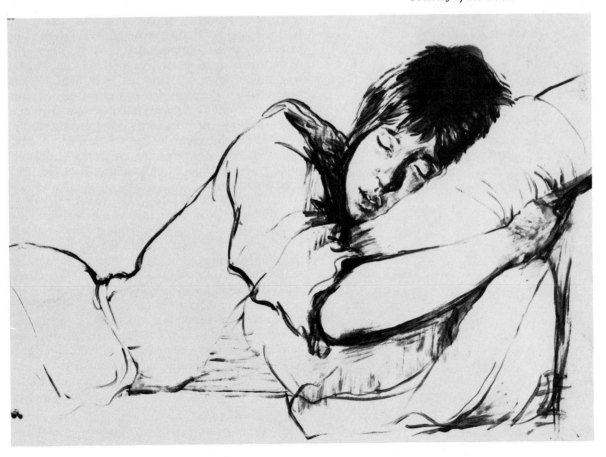

This concept of a work growing toward some crescendo of form is more frequently seen in drawing than we might at first suppose, as a glance at the many drawings reproduced in this book shows. Figures 1.6, 2.39, 4.14, 5.26, and 6.9 are some examples of drawings that culminate in strong mass clarity at one place in the configuration.

Something like the same strategy guides Polonsky in his *In Sleep* (Figure 7.9). Instead of forms growing more substantial as they move back in space, here they do so as they move toward the right side of the page, building to an imposing group of heavy forms on that side. Polonsky balances the drawing by the counterweights of the upper torso's blocklike mass bearing down on the lower left side of the page, and by the direction of the head, lower

**FIGURE 7.10**
**ARTHUR POLONSKY** (1925–    )
*Portrait of J. G.*
Brush and ink. 28 x 22 in.
*Courtesy of the artist.*

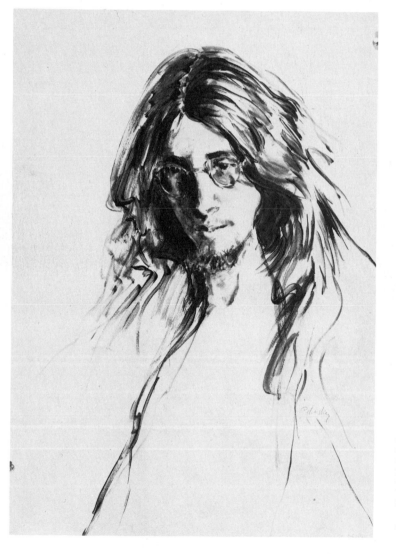

arm, and pillows, which also aim for the lower left corner. Additionally, the figure's arm, drawn to imply ample weight, echoes the bend in the torso, adding emphasis to the torso's downward pull to the left.

The artist, in subtly emphasizing the subject's shapes, calls our attention to the dynamic condition of the picture plane. Here the soft, rounded wedges of the shapes of the arm and the pillows, moving with the force inherent in long wedgelike shapes, assist the expression of pliancy. This creates an image that is relaxed in surrender to weight and gravity, yet imparts an engaging sense of rhythmic action.

Note that Polonsky, like Vespignani, is led by his emotive theme of limp weight to the use of undulating contour lines that convincingly suggest the essential nature of the masses. Structure and anatomy too are enlisted in serving the drawing's expression. Because the lower arm must suggest weight, Polonsky gives it a cylindrical simplicity and weights its lower end by bold strokes that emphasize the olecranon process; because the hand must work at gripping the pillow, he suggests the metacarpal heads and a generally more bony mass. Again, in the head, the girl's relaxed right side is simplified, but the compressed left side is more structurally stated.

As we have seen, artists who are sensitive to the total behavior of a subject's forms extract dynamic qualities in order to clarify the subject's representational condition. What they select, omit, and alter, and the manner in which they handle the work—the character of the marks—is determined by their largely intuitive sense of what is necessary to convey their interpretation. Thus the artist's interpretive purpose determines the importance of the role each of the four factors will play. When Polonsky draws a sleeping girl, expressive design considerations only slightly overtake those of structure and anatomy; the drawing's movements and its mood are both temperate, and the handling is moderately paced. But when he confronts a different subject, his perceptions and feelings lead him to a different formula.

In Polonsky's *Portrait of J.G.* (Figure 7.10), an explosive design is more expressively insistent, and structure and anatomy, although they play important roles, are more subordinated to the plastic needs of this spirited image. The handling is far bolder, the shapes more animated, and the values more aggressively stated and active. Polonsky's response to the powerful force inherent in the subject's forms leaves little time (or need) for structural or anatomical nuances. Instead, it demands (logically enough) that he convey these cascading forms with an immediacy and vigor that match the subject's character.

Rothbein's *Seated Woman, Leaning* (Figure 7.11) depicts little physical action yet evokes a sense

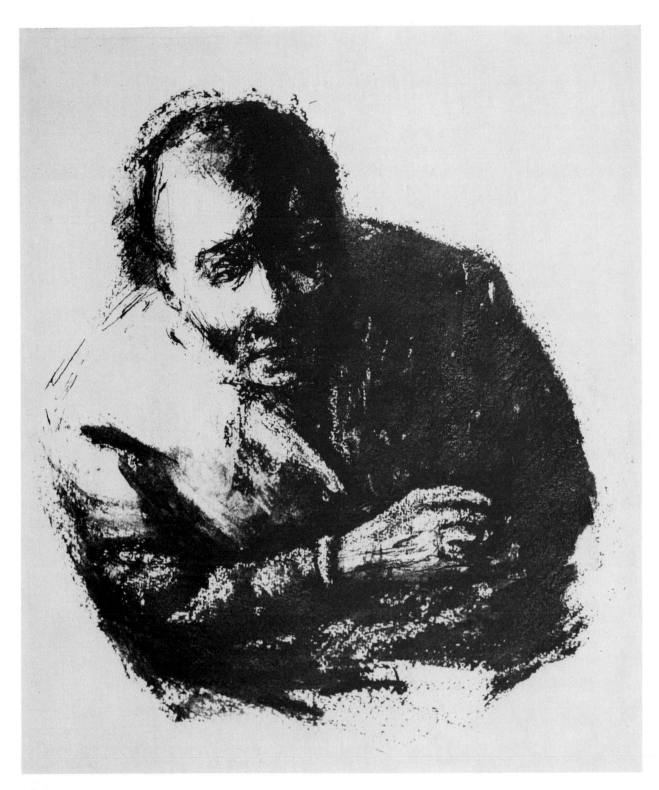

**FIGURE 7.11**
**RENEE ROTHBEIN** (1924–    )
*Seated Woman, Leaning*
Pen, brush and ink.
9 x 11 1/4 in.
*Courtesy of the artist.*

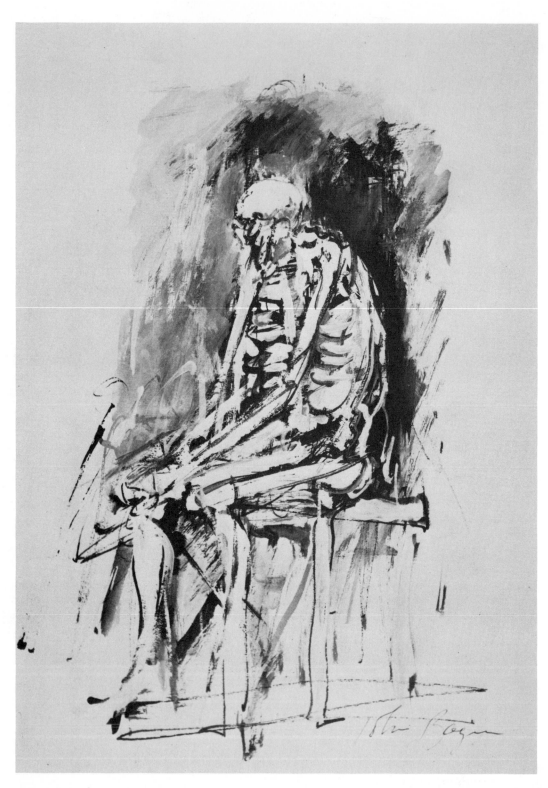

FIGURE 7.12
**JOHN BAGERIS** (1924–    )
*Seated Skeleton II*
Sepia and black ink, white gouache. 13 x 17 in.
*Collection of Mrs. Lucy Stone, Cambridge, Mass.*

294

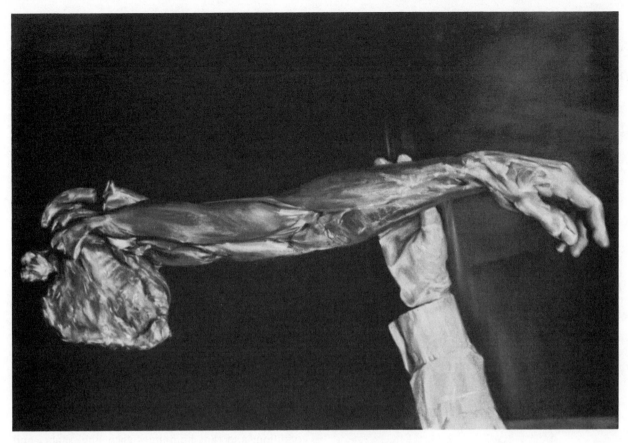

**FIGURE 7.13**
**ARTHUR HAHN** (1923–    )
*Cadaver's Arm*
Chalk pastel. 30 x 40 in.
*Courtesy of the artist.*

**FIGURE 7.14**
**JAMES GILL** (1934–    )
*Laughing Woman—Closeup* (1964)
Wax crayon. 28 5/8 x 45 1/8 in.
*Collection, The Museum of Modern Art, New York.*
*Eugene and Clare Thaw Fund.*

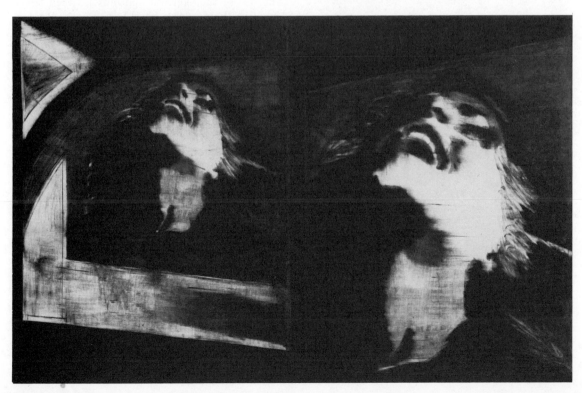

of turbulent dynamic and emotive force. There is an intangible but intense quality in the design and handling that suggests both repose and disquiet. The forceful relational energies hovering on the brink of balance produce tensions which, in their uneasy equilibrium, impart the same unsettled mood that we sense in the figure's gesture and expression.

There is tension between the figure's tilt to the left side of the page and the counterthrust to the right side by the massive dark tone on the arm and torso, between the harshly contrasting values and the gently revolving movements, and between the alternating passages of broad and precise handling. These tensions create abstract visual sensations that

FIGURE 7.15
LENNART ANDERSON (1930–    )
*Portrait of Mrs. Susan Peterson*
Charcoal.
*Present location unknown.*

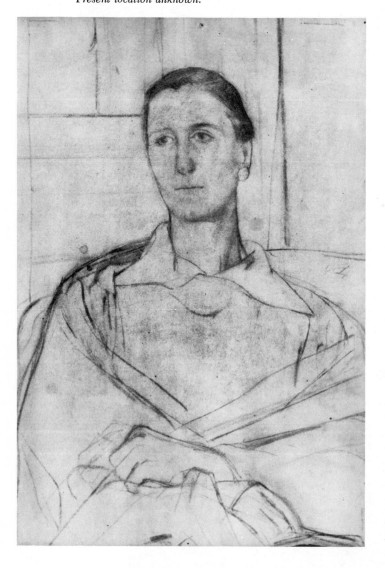

reinforce the figurative ones. Both are assertive *and* tentative—the woman's enigmatic gesture hovers between reaching out and withdrawing.

These broadly conceived forms, carved by a strong light source, impart a weighty monumentality that adds force to the struggle between the physical weight on the left side and the visual weight on the right. And, in the weathered terrain of the head and hand, as well as in the knowing shapes and structure of the figure's draped parts, the artist reveals her knowledgeable control of anatomy. Although the dominant property of Rothbein's drawing is its expressive impact, it is clear that this expression emerges from the interaction of all the factors.

Bageris's *Seated Skeleton II* (Figure 7.12) is a variation of the theme we saw in Figure 3.59. Here again the artist creates a frenzied but ordered swarm of dark and light strokes whose movements animate the background and chair as well as the skeleton. These powerful spasms and strivings for change are all the more provocative because they issue from a seated and supposedly lifeless subject. Indeed, an important part of the drawing's expressive theme is the ominous energy of the subject, which threatens to explode the image despite the several stabilizing vertical and horizontal directions and its "still life" nature. Note that Bageris wisely subdues structural considerations to intensify the subject's abstract condition, and that he imbues each line, shape, and tone with an almost unbearable urgency. Such a bold utilization of the skeleton as an agent of expressive design requires more than a passing familiarity with its design and construction; we are not likely to see or intensify the energies and rhythms of forms we know little about.

The use of the skeleton and muscles themselves as a creative theme dates back to the early Renaissance. An interesting example of this ongoing tradition is Hahn's *Cadaver's Arm* (Figure 7.13). With the anatomical factor a given in this drawing and the structural factor an equally important consideration in the image, the drawing's design and expression are hardly less strongly stated. Note how delicately Hahn balances the few forms and shapes that make up the image, and what a respectful rather than clinical attitude is expressed.

Gill's *Laughing Woman—Closeup* (Figure 7.14) uses an unusual kind of rhythm idea. In addition to the shapes and values that, by their active and spontaneous character, support the expression of laughter, the artist repeats and enlarges the woman's head, further reinforcing the beat of laughter. But in the brooding nature of the surrounding tones, in the allusions to strange apertures and movements, and even in the figure's advancing toward us, Gill implies an ominous undertone. Note that the throat is drawn in conformity with anatomical fact, but is illuminated in a way that produces a particularly animated shape, thus enacting the vibrating movements of laughter. Note, too, how the design strategy has the heads and their gray, windowlike "containers" moving to our right, while the overall, bulletlike shape of the entire configuration rushes to our left. Gill's contrasting of the organic form of the head with the more mechanical, angular forms and spaces surrounding it further emphasizes the animation of the laughing woman.

But contrasting the figure with more angular forms can serve other purposes. In Anderson's *Portrait of Mrs. Susan Peterson* (Figure 7.15), the blocky divisions of the background only directly state what is hinted at in the figure, where rectangular and triangular shapes underlie every part. Here, a major visual theme is the sensitive adjusting of overt and covert pure forms. The artist integrates the strongly modeled form of the head with the rest of the design by its location, direction, and under-

lying blocklike shape. Note how the winglike character of the woman's collar is echoed in the hands and in the grand spread of her shawl. These passages of fluttering action, contrasting with the generally more stately character of the drawing's expressive mode, keep the image from seeming either brittle or stilled.

This is yet another example of a drawing that gathers itself together to culminate in a strongly modeled form—in this case, the head. This idea is carried through in part by the changing role of structure and anatomy, which grow more explicit in the drawing's upper half.

Picasso's etching *Boy Watching over Sleeping Woman* (Figure 7.16) shows a complex interweaving of the four factors that shifts in emphasis from a strong use of structure on the left side of the page to a more two-dimensional ordering of the forms on the right side. But Picasso takes care to make this a subtle transition, and further unifies the design by the enveloping dark tones and by rhythms, such as

FIGURE 7.16
PABLO PICASSO (1881–1973)
*Boy Watching over Sleeping Woman* (1935)
Etching and aquatint. 23.7 x 30 cm.
*Courtesy Museum of Fine Arts, Boston.*
*Lee M. Friedman Fund.*

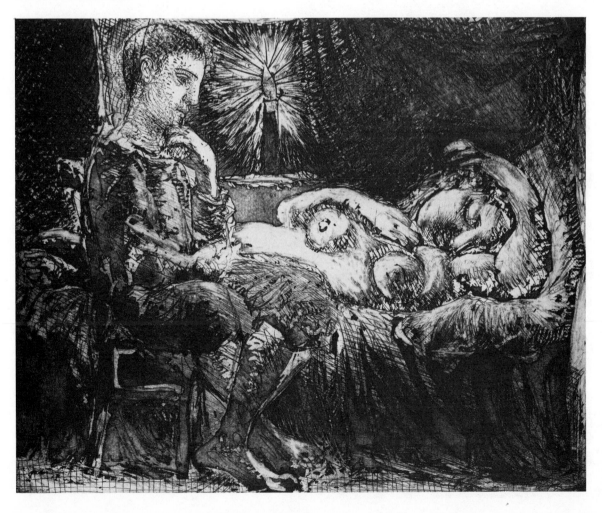

the C-shaped curves that relate all the arms and hands. In addition, he knits the image together by arranging shapes and forms that call to each other across the page. This occurs with the shape of the boy's head and that of the window behind him, and in their association with the spherical and blocky forms of the woman and the pillow. Picasso establishes an expressive need for this shift in emphasis from more structured forms on the left to more shape-oriented ones on the right. The boy's enigmatic but protective character is strengthened by the substantiality of his forms, just as the woman's state of deep sleep is enhanced by the rhythm of her more abstracted and shape-oriented forms.

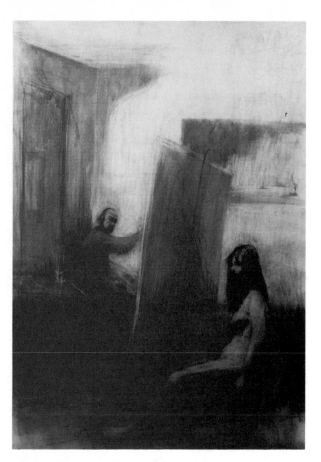

FIGURE 7.18
HERBERT KATZMAN (1923–    )
*The Studio* (1976)
Sepia chalk. 67 1/2 x 48 in.
*Courtesy of Terry Dintenfass, Inc., New York.*

FIGURE 7.17
Bolognese School, 17th Century
**Burial Scene**
Pen and bistre wash over black crayon.
8 7/8 x 5 7/8 in.
*Courtesy The Fogg Art Museum, Harvard University.*
*Bequest of Charles Alexander Loeser.*

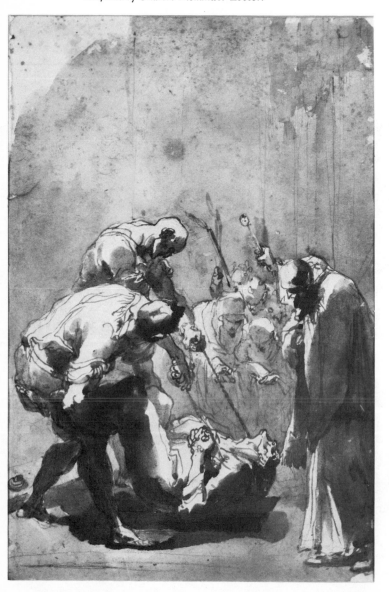

The etching's mood is both hushed and troubled. The harsh light of the candle, the sly shifts from three- to two-dimensional stresses, and the overall level of reality all suggest a strange, dreamlike state. The very active role of textures also adds to this mood. In their rich abstract play, the textures call our attention to a degree of dynamic activity that belies the innocence of the depiction. Picasso's formula results in an image that pulsates between representational and abstract readings. We cannot disregard the unusual life in either the depiction or in the dynamic means used to establish it.

The anonymous Bolognese artist who created *Burial Scene* (Figure 7.17) reveals a similar sensitivity to the visually expressive forces that, in activating a representation, intensify its psychological meanings. He utilizes several important strategies that amplify the mood of this mysterious and fearsome event. By placing all the figures and the darkest tones low on the page, and by clarifying the structure of the lower-placed forms more than those higher up on the page, he strengthens the dramatic impact of the scene by focusing our attention on the corpse's interment. The artist emphasizes the sagging body's weight (and destination) by blending the cast shadows of the corpse and the nearby figures with the dark tone of the tomb opening, thereby adding a strong visual weight to the lowering action.

Some of the more discreet touches that add to the drawing's disquieting mood are the taut ropes that serve as a visual foil for the curvilinear and animated forms; the extended hands of the figures in the background that seem to urge the body downward; and the upthrust of the corpse's head, mouth, and chin—a last visual and human "protest" to the downward actions. Note how effectively the artist uses the overhead light source to emphasize some parts and hide others so as to control the design and our reading of it. The artist further stimulates the

figurative and abstract actions and mood by exaggerating the curvilinear rhythms of the surface anatomy and the drapery, giving them a nervous vibrancy.

The tactic of giving great visual and physical weight to a drawing's lower portion serves a different purpose in Katzman's *The Studio* (Figure 7.18). A large, slightly curved and downward-flowing movement envelops the entire page. Here, everything gains force and weight as we proceed downward. Values darken, masses grow bolder in modeling, contrasts of tone and direction increase, and handling grows more forceful as our eye moves down the page. Only the model's counter-turning arc and light tone prevent these forces from running off the page. In fact, her forward-thrusting lower leg and foot lead us to move upward to start the action over

**FIGURE 7.19**
**GIOVANNI BATTISTA TIEPOLO** (1696–1770)
*Error and Falsehood*
Pen and brown ink, brown wash over black chalk.
7 5/8 x 10 1/8 in.
*The Pierpont Morgan Library, New York.*

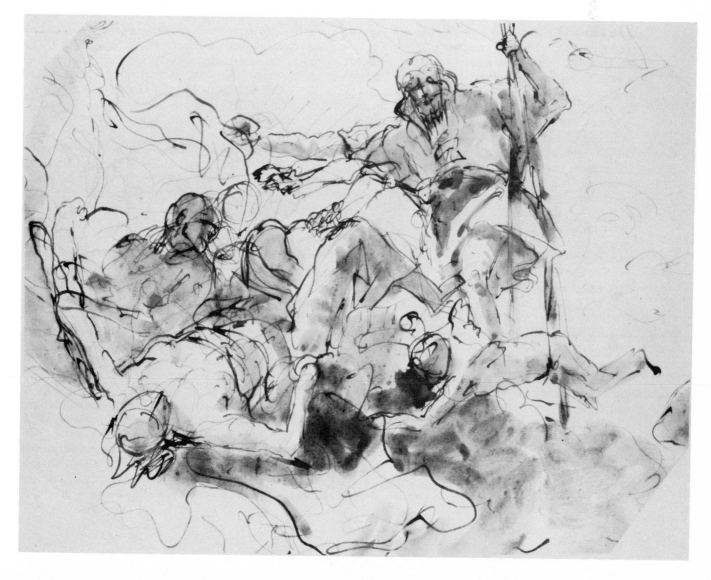

again. This image-filling strategy calls our attention to the seated model, thus matching the attention shown by the artist in the drawing. Here, the four factors interact, as they do in Picasso's etching, by a shifting from shape-oriented design considerations in one place to more structurally realized masses in another. Again, the transition is gradual and the expression grows from these large, rushing changes. Note Katzman's knowing control of anatomical matters, and the untypical (but handsome) reliance on value rather than line as the major graphic means of expression.

Tiepolo's arrangement of the four factors in his *Error and Falsehood* (Figure 7.19) places the bold moving actions of strong directions and rhythms ahead of even figurative energies. Not unlike Cambiaso (Figure 7.4), Tiepolo relies on a stormy two-dimensional design to activate the image. As this exploratory sketch for a painting shows, most artists approach a visual challenge with a concern not for its representational specifics but for its dynamic essentials. And, although this is a preparatory work, it is a complete graphic statement. Expressive design considerations are dominant, but structure and anatomy, their broad masses and bold surface undulations adding fuel to the drawing's powerful actions, are inventively interacting concepts.

Here all the elements are in a state of strong agitation, but they compensate each other's actions to produce an orderly pattern of forces. Despite all the visual commotion, an encircling system of arms embraces the configuration and, on its periphery, encircling clouds reinforce this containing device. On the right, the vertical thrusts of the standing figure and the staff he holds produce a needed visual weight to balance the drawing's overall movement toward the lower left corner. Thus, for all the excitement of the elements and the handling in this spontaneous sketch, the artist is in control of the image, and communicates the figures' troubled ferment.

The use of the elements in such an agitated way is an effective means of suggesting the physical action of figures. In Daumier's *A Clown* (Figure 7.20), we cannot resist seeing the arms of the clown as energetically flailing, just as we know the bent figure to be drumming. Daumier, a master of designing with strong shapes of tone, here arranges the pale tone on the left, the clown's deeper tone, and the strong dark tone of the drummer in a manner that creates space, variety, and balance. Nor are the white shapes merely places that are "left." Notice that the large white segment of the background on the left echoes the general wedgelike shape of the clown, while at the same time leading us into the configuration; and that the white area that separates the two figures is shaped almost into an imitation of

the clown's left arm and lower body, only exaggerated and enlarged. Both of these background shapes, in aiming toward the clown's feet (as does the drummer's right arm), bring us to the necessary starting point for viewing the clown and feeling his impassioned movements; our eyes rise up the figure to the waving arms in just the same way that we sense the arms' thrashing action to have begun in the clown's feet; that is, the wildly active gesturing involves his entire body. Such expressive eloquence would hardly be possible in a carefully rendered drawing of the subject. And while here, as in Tiepolo's drawing, design and expression are the dominant factors, structural clues clarify and strengthen the configuration (note the strong dark-toned plane that explains the clown's left side), and even anatomical information is provided to help find our way along the clown's figure. The essential form of the clown's feet and legs, the general heft and arched state of the torso, and the expressive drawing of his head all reveal a sure grasp of anatomical facts.

McGarrell's lithograph *Elephant Bathers I* (Figure 7.21), even busier in design than Tiepolo's or Daumier's drawings, creates almost the opposite emotive effect. In contrast to their furious calligraphy, McGarrell's lines are more deliberate and structural. Likewise, his tones are less shifting and fluid, his shapes more sharply defined. Instead of serpentine or diagonal movements of great force, McGarrell stresses horizontal motion and, by an almost Cubist-like criss-crossing of directions, keeps all other directions from generating any strong-moving force.

McGarrell's surrealistic theme requires these less turbulent forces and feelings. This troubled and equivocal scene, half snapshot, half dream, needs the fragmented shapes and passages of ambiguity between figure and ground to impart a sense of anxiety and even of quiet terror. The artist achieves this by carefully integrating changes in perspective and scale, by concealing figures among matching values and shapes, by using subtle metamorphic occurrences, as in the animal-like head of the figure at the lower left corner, and by camouflaging interspaces separating groups with veils of tone or overlapping and undefinable forms. The artist further merges vision with reality by teasing suggestions of figures and animals forming in unexpected places: White shapes on the table at the right suggest a small, upright animal upon a figurelike group of shapes; behind the basketball player (whose ball suggests a skull) a reclining figure appears in a textured area, which, because of the shifts in perspective, may be read as clouds or waves. Structural lines sometimes clarify and sometimes obscure forms; similarly, surface anatomy occasionally denoted objectively is sometimes distorted or obscured.

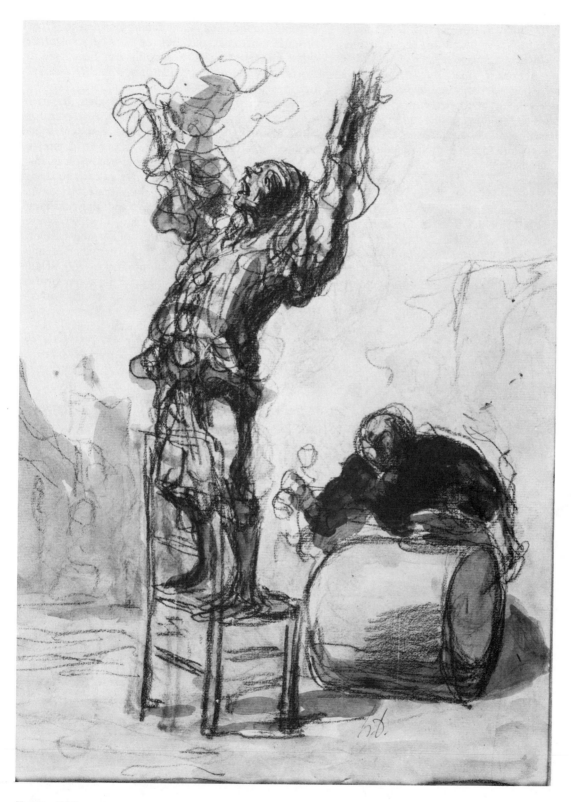

Figure 7.20
HONORÉ DAUMIER (1808–1879)
*A Clown*
Charcoal and watercolor. 14 3/8 x 10 in.
*The Metropolitan Museum of Art, New York,*
*Rogers Fund, 1927.*

The resulting mood of this densely filled image in which forms are lost and found, lucid and dream-like, finds support at the abstract level of its order. The interjoining shards of small shapes and tones cancelling out strong movements; the often carefully stated textures and patterns returning us to the picture plane; the ambiguities of figure-ground associations; the overall windblown nature of the drawing; and the temperate pace of the handling all evince the same ineffable feeling of anxious expectancy.

As the foregoing examples indicate, the differing degrees of importance of the roles of the four factors in figure drawing are virtually limitless. Although the drawings we examined are hardly an extensive sampling of such combinations of usage, they show that in every master drawing no factor is left unregarded, nor is any factor elevated to a level of importance that excludes the consideration of the other factors. No figure drawing can bear such an isolating attention to any factor and survive as a system of expressive order.

Without the governing influences that the interacting factors impose on each other, any or all of them can be disengaged from the rest and made foreign to the image they were meant to dominate. An overconcern with structure can become a tedious fixation on measurement and mass as ends in themselves. Although an acute analytic sensitivity to the structural nature of *any* form is nothing less than crucial—we simply cannot draw anything whose essential construction we don't understand—an obsessive fascination with structural matters not only excludes important aspects of form that belong within the purview of the other factors, but reveals

FIGURE 7.21
JAMES McGARRELL (1930–    )
*Elephant Bathers I*
Lithograph. 28 x 36 in.
*Courtesy Museum of Fine Arts, Boston.*
*Gift of the International Graphic Arts Society.*

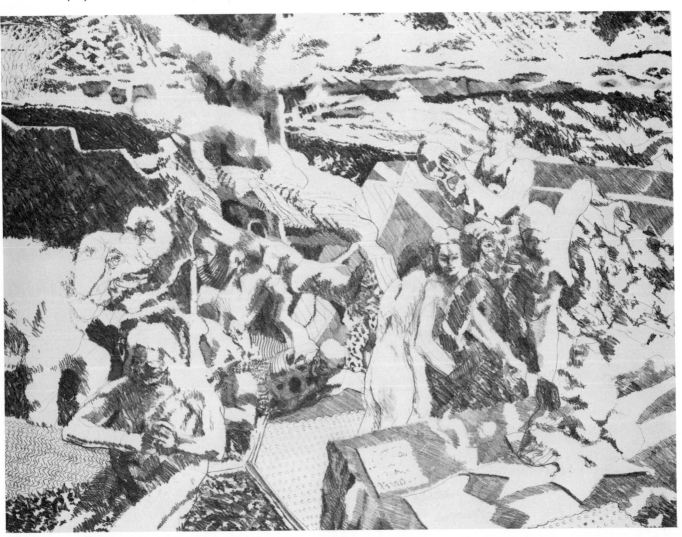

an attitude that holds drawing to be no more than a kind of pretend sculpture. At best, a figure constructed without the contributions *and* demands that all four factors make remains only a report on the container the living figure comes in.

An obsession with anatomy quickly deteriorates into a slavish faithfulness to physiology. While a knowledge of anatomy is essential for a keen understanding of a figure's structural and dynamic possibilities, a compulsive concentration on the figure as merely a machine produces only a thorough inventory of its parts. Generally, the more successful such drawings are as records of anatomical fact, unrelieved by engaging, provocative dynamic considerations, the more cadaverlike and artless are the results. More than scrutiny and exactitude are needed to create the graphic equivalent of life.

An exclusive interest in design soon becomes an intellectual exercise, a kind of visual chess game. Instead of the birth of a graphic organism which, like the real organism, has an equivalent structure, order, and temperament, the results of runaway design considerations—with design as an end in itself—are, at most, clever sensory entertainment. More frequently, such works seem self-consciously novel and contrived.

As noted in the previous chapter, a concentration on expression as an end in itself instead of as a necessary state of receptivity to what is actual or inferred in the subject quickly becomes an essentially nonvisual and self-indulgent emotional fling. Such drawings do not really tell about the artist's interpretive responses to an observed or envisioned figure, but only record a kind of vague, free-association statement stimulated by some general aspect of the figure. The real subject remains the artist's psyche. But creative expression is not a retreat from reason or order. It is an attitude that, while directing what the eye should search for, is still open to receiving stimulation from the subject's objective state. Thus it is the force that both generates perceptions and, in containing much of what constitutes the artist's "screen" of intent, largely directs the filtering of all his or her perceptions. The best exponents of figure drawing always transmit the subject's message as well as their own.

## IN CONCLUSION

In the last chapter we observed that when the expressive order of a drawing depends heavily on the nature of the medium, the medium rates closely in importance with the four factors as a consideration in perceiving and responding. So we must now extend our examination of the interacting factors to include some observations and examples concerning the role of the materials, especially when they strongly affect the image. We will also briefly consider the needs of the emerging drawing. For in addition to the skills and interests we bring to the act of figure drawing, and besides the subject's supply of measurable and dynamic data, the drawing as it forms makes suggestions of its own. And, finally, because we want our drawings to say what we mean them to, we will examine some drawings to see why the intent to arrive at a particular goal is the necessary point of entry into figure drawing, even though our perceptions, materials, and the needs of the emerging drawing always influence our intent.

As noted earlier, all good figure drawings show a congenial alliance between the artist's intentions

FIGURE 7.22
**REMBRANDT VAN RIJN** (1606–1669)
*Three Heads of Women, One Asleep*
Etching, 2nd state. 14.2 x 9.7 cm.
*Courtesy Museum of Fine Arts, Boston.*
*Gift of the Estate of Lee M. Friedman.*

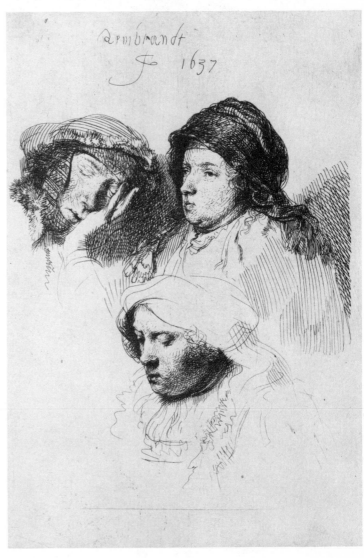

and the medium's character. When we find that a medium exerts a strong influence on our handling and judgments, its value for us is determined by our ability to adapt the medium to our purposes or adjust our goals to take advantage of the medium's properties.

When Rembrandt uses the etching needle he accepts the restrictions it imposes on the broad, calligraphic manner of his drawing style with other

**FIGURE 7.23**
**GIOVANNI BATTISTA TIEPOLO** (1696–1770)
*Standing Man*
Pen and wash. 22.5 x 13.7 cm.
*The Art Museum, Princeton University.*

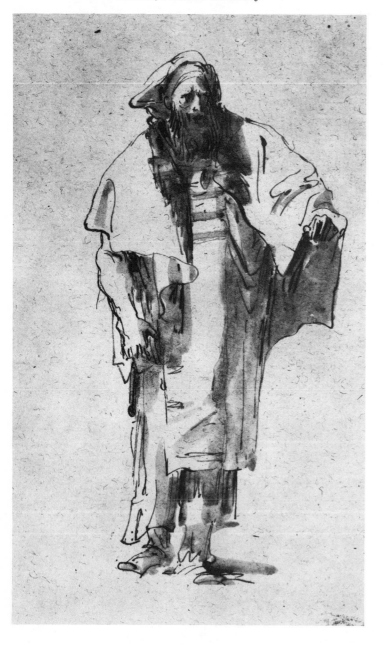

media (Figures 5.1, 5.13, and 5.20). But because he responds to the needle's linear precision and delicacy, the fine weave and textural range of its tonalities, and even its restrictions on a more aggressive handling, he adjusts his goals away from the more painterly manner of his drawings in ink, wash, or chalk and accepts etching's challenge to be especially resolute and direct. In his etching *Three Heads of Women, One Asleep* (Figure 7.22), although he does little to relate these three studies beyond their tasteful arrangement, there is a sensitive controlling of the pace of the values among the heads and in conveying the gentle rhythms among the forms. Instead of the vigorously animated play between the broad strokes and bold tones of his ink and chalk drawings, Rembrandt chooses to tell about subtle surface changes, textures, and light effects. He does so not as an end in itself, but as clues to the moods of the three women. For example, the sleeping head is securely held, not only by the dependably sturdy hand, but by the "cushion" of crosshatched lines which, in completing the circle begun by the woman's hat, adds to our appreciation of the weight of the head, relaxed in sleep.

Though an etched line is difficult to alter or remove, Rembrandt still begins to draw each figure with free lines that search out movements, rhythms, shapes, and major planes and masses. Note that in drawing heads, Rembrandt doesn't concentrate on the eyes, nose, and mouth, but is equally attentive to *all* the form-units.

In Tiepolo's pen and wash *Standing Man* (Figure 7.23), the materials assist the artist in grasping the passing gesture of the model. Although such a pose might be as successfully captured in several other media, none can move with the speed and vitality of the quill or steel pen, or produce the range of tones from near white to pure black as easily as can washes of ink and watercolor. The speed of execution that Tiepolo's pen lines make possible not only reinforces the expression of the old man's sudden gesture, but conveys the trembling inflections of his momentary stance and of the drapery's fluttering action. Likewise, the immediacy of the broad washes suggests the moving nature of the figure's gesture.

But these lines and tones do more. They deftly establish important structural and anatomical conditions, note textures and local-tones, and illuminate the forms in a strong light. Notice how well the line of the hat's brim explains the force of the head, how the corrugator muscles affect the structure of the forehead, and how the sinewy muscles of the lowered arm expend effort. Tiepolo convinces us of the presence of the figure's forms beneath the heavy drapery—he even manages to tell us about the deltoids, the man's left knee, and that at the ankle the medial malleolus is higher than the lateral one.

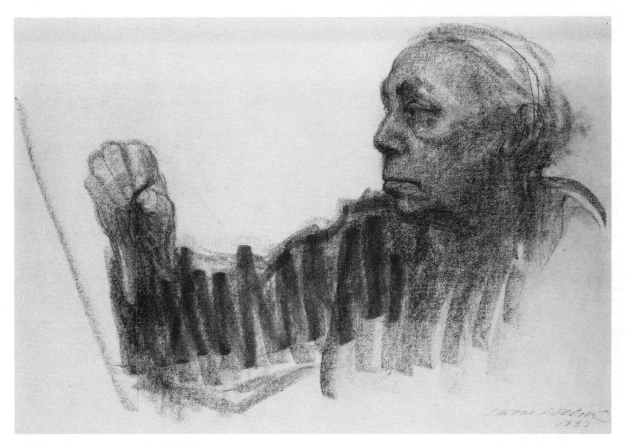

FIGURE 7.24
KÄTHE KOLLWITZ (1867–1945)
*Self-Portrait*
Charcoal. 18 3/4 x 25 in.
*National Gallery of Art, Washington, D.C.*
*Rosenwald Collection.*

And all this is stated with a simultaneous vigilance to the dynamic nature of the forms and to their collective action, strengthened by the fast-moving cadence of the medium. In stressing the upward expansion and growing substantiality of the figure, from its tremulous beginning at the feet to the monumental finale of the upper body, Tiepolo adds even greater force and spirit to the expressive gesture of the old man's head and arm.

The especially harmonious interplay between the artist's needs and the medium's character earns our immediate appreciation in Kollwitz's charcoal drawing *Self-Portrait* (Figure 7.24). Unlike Tiepolo's drawing, this image is difficult to imagine being formed by any other medium. Charcoal, which is simply carbonized wood, has the sooty, velvetlike texture so necessary to Kollwitz's suggestions of atmosphere; it makes us see the figure as through a veil of tone. The artist's interest in a delicate modeling of powerful forms is aided by the ease with which charcoal can change in value from whispered light tones to mellow, dark ones. Few other media will as readily respond to such demands.

Like Tiepolo's drawing, Kollwitz's depicts a figure in action. Because the hazy nature of charcoal enables even the darkest tones to fuse with surrounding ones, Kollwitz is able to express the vigorous movements of the extended arm with vigorous movements in the broad strokes that rush up and down along it. This sudden flurry of intense activity is so expressively necessary and so well integrated in the design that we accept it as an inventively effective strategy.

Kollwitz securely anchors this furious departure from the drawing's otherwise delicate tonal activity in several ways. At the sleeve, the vertical strokes enacting the arm's movements are blended with the tone and direction of the lower arm. All along the arm the strokes roughly suggest the sleeve's folds, and one stroke falls exactly at the bend of the arm, further integrating itself with the arm. Another dark stroke corresponds to the contour of the torso, and

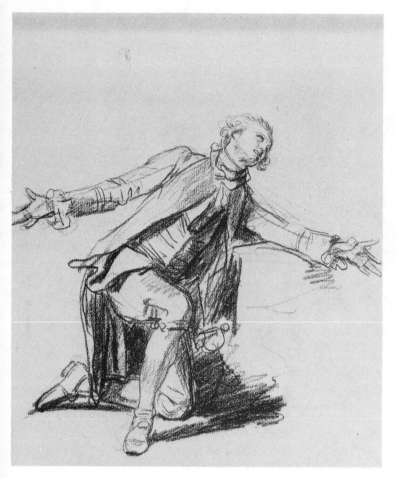

**FIGURE 7.25**
**JEAN-BAPTISTE GREUZE** (1725–1805)
*A Kneeling Youth with Outstretched Arms*
Red chalk. 14 1/4 x 11 3/4 in.
*Courtesy The Fogg Art Museum, Harvard University.*
*Gift of Paul J. Sachs.*

the few bold strokes on the torso relate in direction to the lighter ones all across the chest. Further, by beginning a fanlike spread of directions with the foreshortened drawing board (convincingly suggested by a single line!) that extends across the page, the broad strokes on the arm form a necessary part of that dynamic action. As insurance, the artist defines the arm's shape in the lighter underdrawing, and even allows it to stand free of the broad strokes in the area below the elbow.

Kollwitz moves easily from structural to dynamic matters. In the hand the fingers are deftly summarized, the artist's knowledge of anatomy guiding the solution; but in the darkened palm, structure gives way to lines and tones that evoke, rather than delineate, the squeezing together of the muscle and skin—we feel the force of the grip on the charcoal stump.

This drawing, too, reveals the characteristic earlier noted and so often seen in master drawings: the avoidance of an all-over sameness of structural or dynamic emphasis. Note how this drawing seems to begin faintly, reach an intense pitch of activity, and then subside. Had Kollwitz continued to develop the forms of the back of the head and of the torso, not only would the drawing's present balance have been sacrificed, but its emotive force would have been dissipated. Here, the grand U-shaped sweep of the entire configuration and the developed forms of the face and hand unite to heighten the drawing's dramatic impact.

It is of course virtually impossible to point to those places in a completed drawing where lines and tones exist (or are absent) because the drawing, as it formed, demanded these conditions. The sensitive artist responds to three considerations which participate in the act of drawing: (1) his or her temperamental and creative interests in general and the intentions for the drawing under way; (2) the subject's measurable and dynamic actualities and potential for stimulating creative ideas; and (3) the emerging drawing's needs for further development and integration of the four factors, and *its* creative potentialities—the hints and ideas the still malleable image suggests.

Did Kollwitz add the broad strokes along the arm because she intellectually or intuitively planned to? or because the folds in the observed sleeve suggested them? or because the drawing needed something bold to enliven it and pull it together? Perhaps these strokes exist for all three reasons. Again, did she refrain from further developing the back of the head by prior intent? or because the gray tone of the hair blended with the tone of the wall? or because the drawing's expressive order advised against it? All we can say with any certainty is that some and perhaps much of the drawing was determined by its own visual and expressive requirements.

Greuze, in his *A Kneeling Youth with Outstretched Arms* (Figure 7.25), accepts the general state of the model's pose and proportions, but "essays" the forms; that is, he edits out all but the essential movements and masses. No doubt the forms moved with something of the force shown, offering clues to some of the clarifying summaries of mass we see, and the clothing had more folds and wrinkles than are drawn. In making his selections and adjustments, Greuze means to convey his chief interest in the model: the graceful flow of this impassioned gesture. But, in addition to the subject's state and the artist's goal, the emerging drawing seems to have made demands of its own.

Surely the figure is posed in an indoor or outdoor setting that contains some forms and tones, some textures and planes; but, except for the cast shadow extending from the legs, the surrounding environment is absent. This may well have been the artist's intention—to show the pose unencumbered by surrounding forms. But if that is the case, how do we explain the cast shadow? It seems to be asking too much of the artist's ability to foresee the problems of an as yet nonexistent drawing to assume he had anticipated its overall weakness of tone without the cast shadow—or even that its shape and directional thrust would so harmoniously accord with that of the man's left arm. No, it is extremely doubtful that the cast shadow was part of the original visual theme. It is far more likely that this dark tone, in strengthening the drawing's tonal design, in echoing the arm above it, and in imitating the thrust of the lower left leg (thereby creating a delightful pattern composed of the arms above and the lower left leg and cast shadow below) was Greuze's judgment of what the drawing needed at that point in its development. The problem arose in the drawing, not in the subject, and the solution was determined by the state of the drawing, not of the model.

That drawings are the result of a three-way conversation between artist, subject, and drawing is of course more immediately apparent in more subjective works, or when the subject is envisioned, not observed. Figures 7.2, 7.14, and 7.16 did not appear in the mind's eye of the artists, complete in every detail and needing only to be transferred to paper, line by line. A general vision and intent were there, unfocused and tentative—something far less than the realized drawing yet more than an impulse; but these drawings were resolved by negotiations between the artist, the subject, and the emerging drawing. And, as in the Greuze drawing, such negotiations occur in objectively observed drawings made in the presence of the model. The model's expressive needs, too, help shape the final result, as many of the drawings in this book show (Figures 1.23, 2.10, 5.42, and 7.20).

Bloom's *Autopsy* (Figure 7.26), done in his studio after having attended a number of autopsies, bridges the categories of subjects observed and those envisioned. Here too we feel the drawing was formed partly by the artist's response to *its* visual and expressive dynamic needs, as well as to his own remembered observations and intent. Indeed, the harmonies, contrasts, balance, and unity of any drawing, if they are to avoid looking arbitrarily imposed or only weakly managed, must form from an ongoing awareness of the drawing's strengths, weaknesses, and possibilities at every stage of its development.

The Bloom drawing also demonstrates how powerfully the nature of the abstract activities can influence our reaction to a depiction. The drawing of the cadaver, despite its dissected state, is strangely lyrical, its forms seemingly windblown. Its graceful rhythms impart a transcendental air to the forms and compete with the disagreeable nature of the event itself. But there is something instantly unpleasant in the outstretched arms placed upon the cadaver. The furious rush of those arms, their clawlike fingers, and, because they end within the page, their ghostly quality, are conveyed by their directional speed, shape, and treatment, all of which are *inherently* aggressive (compare with the more "benign" arm holding the cadaver's limb in Figure 7.13). Likewise inherently, the forms of the dissected corpse, by virtue of their graceful flutter, gentle tonal changes, and delicate treatment, seem far less forbidding than would a straightforward depiction of the subject (again, see Figure 7.13, where the expressive roles of the living and dead forms are reversed).

In the best figure drawings, the artist's intent— a blend of excitement and curiosity about the visual and expressive actualities and possibilities issuing from a particular subject—is what determines the overall character of the drawing. Although the subject and the emerging drawing provide important information and counsel, and create demands and opportunities that must be considered, their influence should serve to regulate and strengthen intent, but not divert or overrule it.

Once a drawing is under way, the temptations to "alter course" are often great, especially when we attempt something just beyond our reach. Sometimes we don't perceive certain possibilities until the drawing is well advanced, possibilities that might be interesting (or promise a less demanding conclusion), but are far from our intended goal. Sometimes the drawing takes on unintended characteristics that beckon us to some other (often commonplace) conclusion. And sometimes the medium itself begins to dictate to us. The artist must have both discipline and faith in his or her original theme to steer clear of such diversions. This does not mean that one cannot pursue an interesting creative possibility which may lead to a more inventive result. Indeed, ideas that germinate in one drawing should be nurtured in subsequent ones, as Bageris does in his seated skeleton drawings (Figures 3.59 and 7.12). But allowing the drawing or the medium to take command is a serious surrender of control and intent, certain to produce poor results.

Bloom is faithful to his theme. The consistency of the drawing's traits and mood, the character and harmonious interplay of its elements, and its balance and unity attest to the artist's unvarying faith (and enthusiasm) in his theme, a theme conceived in an especially engaging formulation of the four factors.

As we observed in Chapter One, the frank declaration of a particular point of view is central to

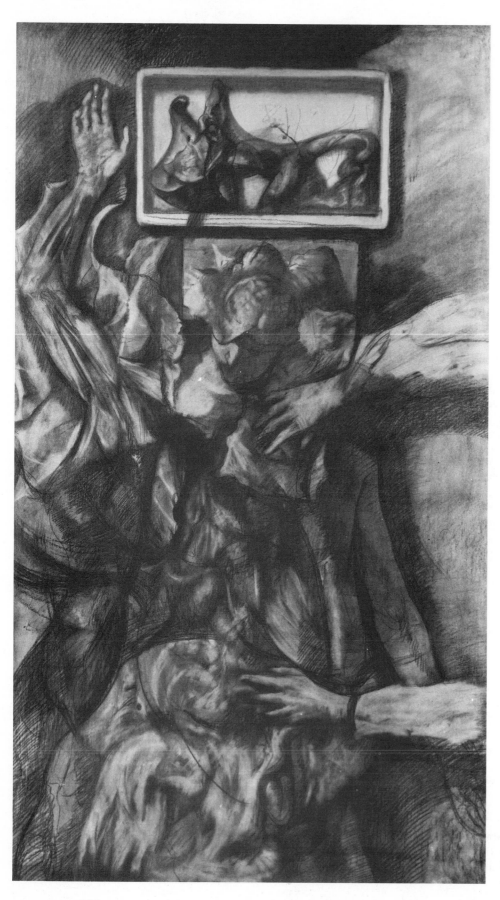

FIGURE 7.26
HYMAN BLOOM (1913–    )
*Autopsy* (1953)
Crayon. 54 1/2 x 37 1/2 in.
*Whitney Museum of American Art,*
*New York.*

the art of figure drawing (and of course to any work of art). It is also central to originality. Too often, the beginner in search of a point of view confuses novelty with originality. Novelty *may* result from originality, but should never be pursued for its own sake. Genuine originality, the kind that makes images come alive, begins with the effort to respond honestly to our interests and our perceptions. And each perception increases our emotional, intellectual, and intuitive involvement with the subject, with our emerging work, and with our theme, thereby creating a state of receptivity in ourselves that enables our responses to become *increasingly* more personal, more insistently *ours,* and thus original. Genuine originality is the natural result of genuine caring. As Sir Kenneth Clark has observed, "Facts become art through love, which unifies them and lifts them to a higher plane of reality. . . ."*

Schiele's intent and his perceptual acuity are both apparent in his *Seated Nude Girl Clasping Her Knee* (Figure 7.27). His candid satisfaction in the tactile experiencing of the forms *and* in the calligraphic play of the lines is revealed in the nature of the lines. And not only do these interacting directional thrusts, textures, speeds, and tensions among the lines fail to conflict with Schiele's sensual theme, they support it—their abstract expressive nature amplifies the psychological tone of the artist's search of the forms.

For Matisse, in his *Nude* (Figure 7.28), expressive interests are more structurally than sensually motivated, and the dynamic nature of the elements is more forcefully active in both volumetric and directional than in tactile behavior. In contrast to Schiele's varied and lively, but leisurely, contours, these are almost entirely comprised of C-shaped segments that race boldly on counterchecking, volume-informing, and shape-enclosing functions. As in Schiele's drawing, the elements' figurative and abstract roles complement rather than compete with each other. Although these two drawings are roughly similar in their figurative sense, they are very different in temperament and theme. Both were begun and sustained by the artists' deeply felt responses to perceptions "programmed" and guided by intent, and in both, conditions in the forming image and those set by the medium played important roles in determining their final resolution.

Likewise, Rembrandt's *Study of a Female Nude Reclining on a Couch* (Figure 7.29) shows a complemental play of figurative and abstract activities among the elements. Less calligraphically active than Schiele's drawing, and less structurally insistent than Matisse's, Rembrandt's drawing nevertheless con-

* Kenneth Clark, *Landscape into Art* (New York: Transatlantic Arts, Inc., 1961), p. 16.

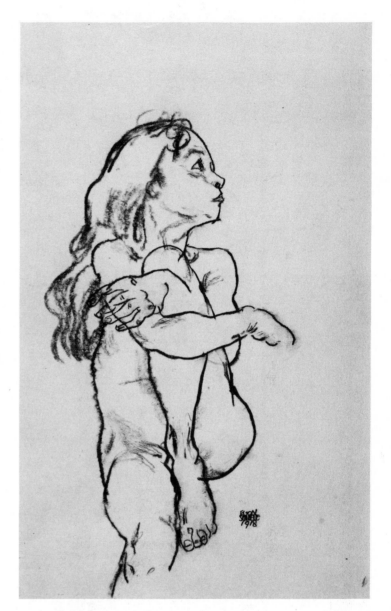

**Figure 7.27**
EGON SCHIELE (1890–1918)
*Seated Nude Girl Clasping Her Knee*
Charcoal. 18 1/8 x 11 5/8 in.
*Worcester Art Museum, Worcester, Mass.*
*The Dial Collection.*

veys qualities of calligraphic play and structural clarity that go beyond the others in economy, conviction, and the level of dynamic life. Furthermore, in embracing both of these challenges, he succeeds in an interweaving of the four factors that shows each equally active. This is not to suggest that such a formula is intrinsically superior (though it is perhaps more demanding), but to point out that all four factors can be abundantly active at the same time.

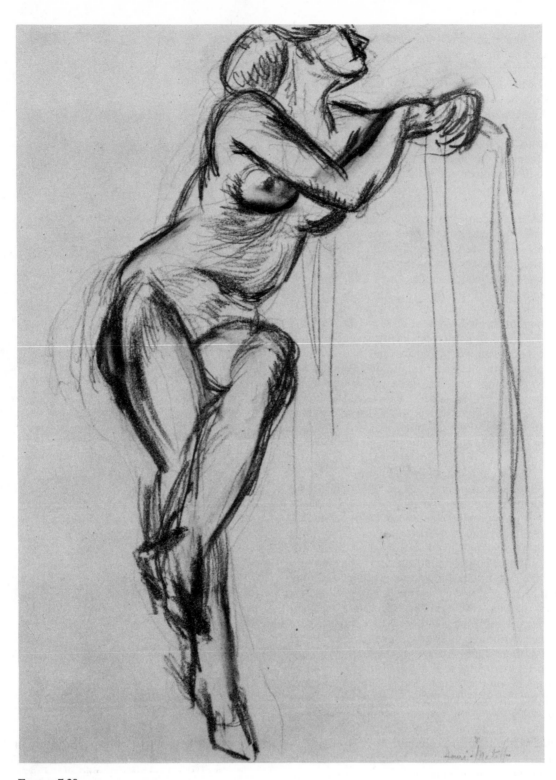

FIGURE 7.28
HENRI MATISSE (1869–1954)
*Nude*
Pencil. 12 x 9 1/16 in.
*The Metropolitan Museum of Art, New York.*
*Alfred Stieglitz Collection, 1949.*

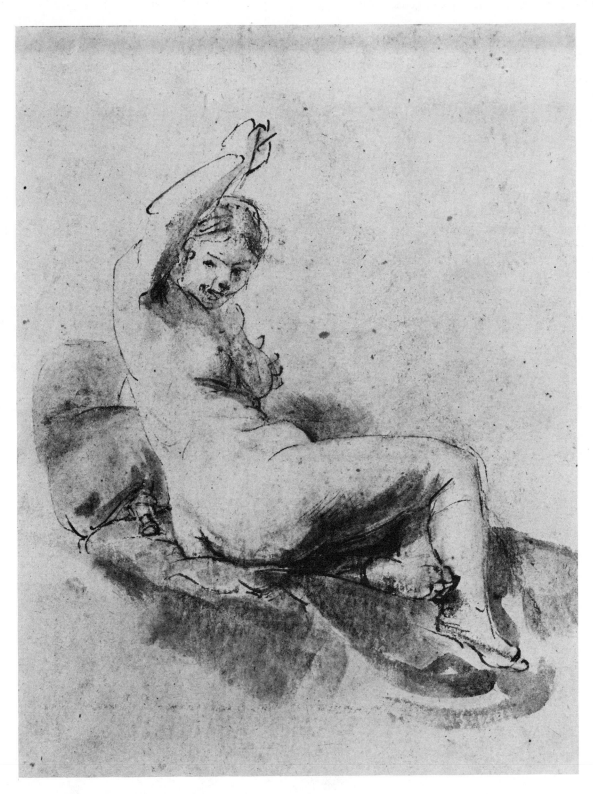

FIGURE 7.29
REMBRANDT VAN RIJN (1606–1669)
*Study of a Female Nude Reclining on a Couch*
Pen and wash. 9 1/8 x 7 1/8 in.
*Courtesy the Art Institute of Chicago.*
*Tiffany and Margaret Blake Collection.*

311

Here, facts and inferences about structure and anatomy tell us a great deal about both, and the drawing's design and expression are alive with energies and meanings at both the abstract and figurative levels. Note, for example, in the upraised arm, that the single line which establishes the broad plane of the lower arm simultaneously performs the following additional functions: It defines the contour of the lower arm from the olecranon process to the lower ending of the ulna, explaining the bony nature of each, and also defining the base of the plane of the back of the hand; it relates, either by its position, length, or hooked endings, to numerous other lines throughout the drawing; and, by its energetic thrust and rugged character, it reveals its own emotive force as well as the physical effort of the arm's gesture. In this drawing virtually every mark "earns its keep" by equally advocating all four factors. Joseph Conrad's comment on the art of writing is just as applicable to drawing: "A work that aspires, however humbly, to the condition of art should carry its justification in every line."*

In these three drawings of the female figure, each artist, determined to convey his aesthetic and humanistic intent, is led to a necessarily different formulation of the factors, and thus to an original graphic invention. Were these three artists to have exchanged models, each would have responded to a

* From the preface to *The Nigger of the Narcissus*.

different hierarchy of perceived actualities and implications, and the result in each case would be uniquely personal. In fact, were every artist shown in this book to have drawn these three poses, we would have had that many different creative expressions. What yours would be, or can become, depends on your perceptual skills, on your temperamental interests and on the insights they provide, on the intent these conditions set, and on your recognition of the interacting nature of the four factors.

If a figure drawing is to be seriously approached as art, it cannot be regarded as an imitative or even a simplifying process. It is the felt ordering of form relationships that simultaneously refer to the figure and to a system of expressive order that reinforces, and is in turn reinforced by, the representational aspects of the drawing.

If we understand the term *representation* to mean the depiction of a subject's essential outer and inner self—its fundamental physical and spiritual character—then unselective realism and unselective subjectivity, in failing to assert these essentials, share a basic disinterest in the profound perceptual, dynamic, and transcendental qualities that nature and life suggest. Moreover, these necessary qualities do not come from either infatuation or mere observation of reality; they yield only to analysis, knowledge, order, and empathy.

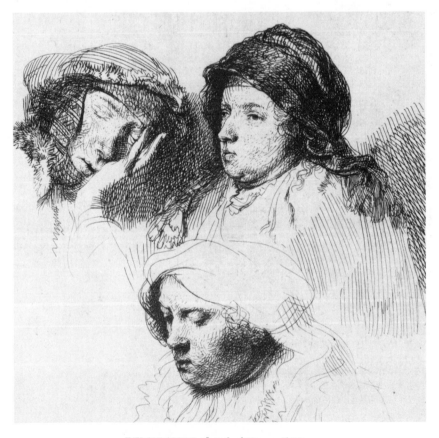

REMBRANDT, detail of Figure 7.22

# BIBLIOGRAPHY

## GENERAL TEXTS

**Anderson, Donald M.** *Elements of Design.* New York: Holt, Rinehart and Winston, Inc., 1961.

**Arnheim, Rudolf.** *Art and Visual Perception.* Berkeley and Los Angeles: University of California Press, 1969.

**Arnheim, Rudolf.** *Toward a Psychology of Art.* Berkeley and Los Angeles: University of California Press, 1972.

**Bertram, Anthony.** *1000 Years of Drawing.* London: Studio Vista Ltd., 1966.

**Blake, Vernon.** *The Art and Craft of Drawing.* London: Oxford University Press, Inc., 1927.

**Bro, Lu.** *A Studio Guide.* New York: W. W. Norton & Company, 1978.

**Chaet, Bernard.** *The Art of Drawing.* New York: Holt, Rinehart and Winston, Inc., 1970.

**Clark, Kenneth.** *The Nude.* New York: Pantheon Books, 1956.

**Collier, Graham.** *Form, Space and Vision,* 3rd ed. Englewood Cliffs, N.J.: Prentice-Hall, Inc., 1972.

**De Tolnay, Charles.** *History and Technique of Old Master Drawings.* New York: H. Bittner & Co., 1943.

**Edwards, Betty.** *Drawing on the Right Side of the Brain.* Los Angeles: J. P. Tarcher, Inc., 1979.

**Eisler, Colin.** *The Seeing Hand.* New York: Harper & Row, Publishers, 1975.

**Goldstein, Nathan.** *The Art of Responsive Drawing.* Englewood Cliffs, N.J.: Prentice-Hall, Inc., 1973.

**Hale, Robert Beverly.** *Drawing Lessons from the Great Masters.* New York: Watson-Guptill Publications, 1964.

**Hayes, Colin.** *Grammar of Drawing for Artists and Designers.* London: Studio Vista Ltd., 1969.

**Hill, Edward.** *The Language of Drawing.* Englewood Cliffs, N.J.: Prentice-Hall, Inc., 1966.

**Vanderpoel, John H.** *The Human Figure.* New York: Dover Publications, 1958.


## ON ANATOMY

**Barclay, Jeno.** *Anatomy for the Artist.* London: Spring Books, 1960.

**Berry, William A.** *Drawing the Human Form.* New York: Van Nostrand Reinhold Company, 1977.

**Hatton, Richard G.** *Figure Drawing.* New York: Dover Publications, Inc., 1965.

**Kramer, Jack.** *Human Anatomy and Figure Drawing.* New York: Van Nostrand and Reinhold Company.

**Oliver, Charles.** *Anatomy and Perspective.* New York: The Viking Press, 1972.

**Peck, Rogers S.** *Atlas of Human Anatomy for the Artist.* New York: Oxford University Press, 1951.

Perard, Victor. *Anatomy and Drawing,* 4th ed. New York: Pitman Publishing Corporation, 1955.

Richer, Paul. *Artistic Anatomy,* trans. Robert Beverly Hale. New York: Watson-Guptill Publications, 1971.

Royce, Joseph. *Surface Anatomy.* Philadelphia: F.A. Davis Co., 1965.

Schider, Fritz. *An Atlas of Anatomy for Artists.* New York: Dover Publications, Inc., 1957.

Thomson, Arthur. *A Handbook of Anatomy for Art Students.* New York: Dover Publications, Inc., 1964.

Vanderpoel, John H. *The Human Figure.* New York: Dover Publications, Inc., 1958.

## FOR ANATOMICAL MATERIALS

Kilgore International
172 W. Chicago Street
Coldwater, Michigan 49036

Medical Plastic Laboratory
Gatesville, Texas 76528

Ward's Natural Science Est. Ltd.
Box 1712
Rochester, N.Y. 14603

## ON PERSPECTIVE

Ballinger, Louis. *Perspective, Space and Design.* New York: Van Nostrand Reinhold Company, 1969.

Burnett, Calvin. *Objective Drawing Techniques.* New York: Van Nostrand Reinhold Company, 1966.

Watson, Ernest W. *How to Use Creative Perspective.* New York: Reinhold Publishing Co., 1960.

## ON MEDIA AND MATERIALS

Dolloff, Francis W., and Roy L. Perkinson. *How to Care for Works of Art on Paper.* Boston: Museum of Fine Arts, Boston, 1971.

Watrous, James. *The Craft of Old Master Drawings.* Madison, Wisc.: University of Wisconsin Press, 1957.

# INDEX

# E

# F

CATHOLIC THEOLOGICAL UNION
NC765.G641981          C001
FIGURE DRAWING  2ND ED.  ENGLEWOOD CLIFF

3 0311 00072 1923

WITHDRAWN

NC 765 .G64 1981

Goldstein, Nathan.

Figure drawing

DEMCO